Righting Wrongs

Three Decades on the Front Lines
Battling Abusive Governments

Kenneth Roth

Alfred A. Knopf
New York
2025

Library of Congress Cataloging-in-Publication Data
Names: Roth, Kenneth, author.
Title: Righting wrongs : three decades on the front lines battling abusive governments / Kenneth Roth, former Executive Director of Human Rights Watch.
Description: First edition. | New York : Alfred A. Knopf, 2025.
| Includes bibliographical references and index.
Identifiers: LCCN 2024023085 (print) | LCCN 2024023086 (ebook) |
ISBN 9780593801321 (hardcover) | ISBN 9780593801338 (ebook)
Subjects: LCSH: Human rights advocacy—Handbooks, manuals, etc. | Roth, Kenneth. | Human rights workers—United States—Biography. | Human Rights Watch (Organization).
Classification: LCC JC571 .R759 2025 (print) |
LCC JC571 (ebook) | DDC 323.092 [B]—dc23/eng/20241028
LC record available at https://lccn.loc.gov/2024023085
LC ebook record available at https://lccn.loc.gov/2024023086

To Annie

Contents

Preface

In countries with the rule of law, most people look to the courts to enforce human rights. But in many countries, judges have been corrupted, compromised, or killed, and are therefore unable to stop the government from violating rights.

Human Rights Watch, which I directed for three decades, figured out how to deploy the public's sense of right and wrong to pressure the political branches of governments to respect rights. The process is not ideal—a strong, independent judiciary is often better—but it can be remarkably effective. This book pulls back the curtain to show the strategies that we used, both what worked and what did not.

People, of course, want human rights, at least for themselves, but governments that are intent on retaining power by suppressing political opposition often resist. The result is a struggle, one in which the never-ending duty of the human-rights movement—of people who care about rights—is to increase the price of oppression, to shift a government's cost-benefit calculation so that abuse no longer seems as desirable. Much can be done, but the process is rarely linear.

The Reverend Dr. Martin Luther King Jr. famously said, "The arc of the moral universe is long but it bends toward justice," yet there is no guarantee of respect for rights. Indeed, in a less remembered part of the same speech, Dr. King admitted as much: "[H]uman progress never rolls in on the wheels of inevitability. It comes through the tireless efforts and the persistent work of dedicated individuals."

As I show, it is entirely possible for a relatively small group of people—Human Rights Watch and our allies—to succeed in curbing or mitigating abuse. But even when the pressure falls short, it is still often felt, helping to prevent further deterioration. Almost always, a price can be imposed for misconduct in order to discourage officials from behaving badly, though the route may not at first be obvious. My colleagues and I constantly had to analyze where our points of leverage might be. We found that the combination of creativity and perseverance regularly yielded productive paths to right the wrong.

There are plenty of human-rights challenges today: the autocratic threat to democracy, pervasive war crimes in many armed conflicts, the rise of some governments that attack human-rights fundamentals, as well as climate change, poverty, inequality, and the risks of artificial intelligence. But this is no time for despair. These challenges underscore the urgency of the tasks before us. Tellingly, governments went to great lengths to avoid the pressure we brought to bear, which speaks to its power.

I am writing this book because I have found that when people understand the tactics we used to push back against abusive governments, they are encouraged to join the effort. Some people support human rights in the abstract but doubt that much can be done to guarantee them. They think of human-rights activists as well intentioned but ineffectual. I was determined to build an organization that would not settle for gestures but sought concrete results. Demystifying this work—illustrating what we did to change government policy, not simply by standing for rights but by exerting pressure to uphold them—helps people to move from perfunctory support to active engagement. Knowing that real change is possible, that the perennial skeptics are wrong, encourages people to help make that change happen.

The strategies I describe are hardly the only ways to defend human rights. As an international human-rights organization, Human Rights Watch had options and priorities that might differ from those of a local or national rights group. But these strategies worked for us.

The pressure techniques I outline, while used to defend human rights, can be deployed in other fields as well. As I show, the key to changing the conduct of governments is pushing them to live up to widely shared moral standards. That strategy can work wherever the conduct of individuals or institutions falls short of public expectations—in academia, health care, business, anyplace where norms of behavior exist or can be promoted.

Many progressives develop expertise and propose good ideas but put too little effort into pushing the target government or institution to make the change they seek. Good ideas alone are rarely enough to overcome the comfort of inertia; generating pressure on a target is usually needed to tilt the balance in their favor. That requires understanding how to exert pressure and figuring out where it can be applied most effectively.

As I describe the many battles that my colleagues and I fought, drawing on my own recollections and notes as well as those of my colleagues, this book can be seen as a handbook for action. In outlining our experience addressing many of the world's most difficult countries and pressing issues, my point is less to prescribe particular strategies than to stimulate thought and discussion about ones that might be pursued. There are rarely simple answers, and regular reassessment is required. The examples I cite show approaches that can work, but there is ample room for disagreement, as there was within Human Rights Watch. Debate is healthy. It produces a stronger movement.

Governments might seem large and immutable, but only a few people are needed to expose their misconduct and to generate pressure for reform. Information, carefully collected and strategically deployed, can be powerful. As Margaret Mead reportedly said, "Never doubt that a small group of thoughtful, committed citizens can change the world; indeed, it's the only thing that ever has." Using the strategies that I detail, Human Rights Watch demonstrated the truth of her observation. I am proud of and eager to share the tools and techniques that we developed to make the world a better place.

Righting Wrongs

1

Idlib, Syria

I think it's important to start by saying that even in the most dire situations, it is possible to make a difference. And when the stakes are life and death, even a small difference can be tremendously important. One of the biggest challenges we faced during my time at Human Rights Watch was trying to stop the slaughter of civilians in Syria. The enormity of the problem required initiative and persistence to build enough pressure to have an impact.

After brutal repression of peaceful anti-government protests in early 2011 yielded an armed conflict, Syria became synonymous with mass atrocities. The carnage was so awful that it was a central focus of Human Rights Watch and a personal preoccupation for me. Despite the magnitude of the challenge, we helped to curtail this unspeakable cruelty.

Throughout the fighting, the Syrian government ripped up the rule book—international humanitarian law—that is designed to spare civilians the hazards of war. Instead, it targeted civilians. It dropped barrel bombs on them (oil drums filled with explosives and shrapnel to maximize damage), deployed chemical weapons against them, starved them, and forcibly disappeared, tortured, and executed them. It was an appalling, deliberate effort to defeat an insurgency by using war crimes and atrocities.

To better understand the horrors unfolding, I periodically visited Gaziantep, the Turkish city known as a sister of Syria's Aleppo. During my visits, Gaziantep was the hub for humanitarian operations in rebel-held northwestern Syria. I spoke with refugee families, orphans, humanitarian workers, and especially doctors, who were impressively trying to provide health care in very dangerous circumstances. I became deeply concerned about their plight and the fate of the people they were trying to serve.

The doctors vividly described the dreadful conditions of life under the Syrian government. One anesthesiologist who had been serving in the military told me of having been forced to sedate sixty-three people in detention when the United Nations–Arab League special envoy, Lakhdar Brahimi, visited Idlib in 2012. The purpose was to silence them and make it easier to hide from Brahimi their shackles and wounds from torture and medical neglect. He found the experience so unbearable that he fled to opposition territory. An internist with whom I stayed in Gaziantep described working late at night after his regular job in Aleppo to see patients in secret clinics, who feared arrest if they appeared at a government-run facility. He also fled. Three of his students were arrested and killed for having worked with him. I couldn't help but be appalled by these stories and determined to do my part to try to ease this suffering.

Even though international humanitarian law protected the hospitals in opposition areas where these doctors worked, they were a favorite target of Syrian forces and their Russian allies. One vascular surgeon described desperately trying to stop the bleeding of patients after their hospital had been bombed. The doctors moved some hospitals underground to hide and protect them, but those, too, were attacked. When the UN Office for the Coordination of Humanitarian Affairs (OCHA) persuaded reluctant doctors and humanitarian organizations to provide the coordinates of their hidden hospitals, naively hoping that it might deter the attacks, the Syrian and Russian militaries targeted them more precisely. Nearly one thousand medical workers—doctors, nurses, ambulance drivers—were killed.

Despite the support of troops sent by Iran and its allied Lebanese militia, Hezbollah, the government of Syrian president Bashar al-Assad had lost large swaths of the country to rebel forces and was stuck in a military stalemate. That changed in September 2015, when President Vladimir Putin sent the Russian military. Government forces gradually retook much of the country, including the rebel-held enclaves of eastern Aleppo in 2016 and Eastern Ghouta in 2018. Alas, the Russian military only intensified Assad's war-crime strategy.

Syria's Idlib province, in the northwestern part of the country, and a few surrounding bits of territory became the last area still controlled by armed forces opposing the government. By 2020, three million civilians lived in Idlib, roughly half having been forcibly displaced from elsewhere in Syria. Many of the displaced had lived in areas under siege by the Syrian army. When these areas fell, they were given the choice of living under Assad's ruthless rule or boarding his notorious green buses to be shipped to Idlib. Many chose Idlib. At least one million civilians were crowded into camps, described as "sites of last resort," along the border with Turkey. As the number of Syrian refugees in Turkey mounted toward 3.5 million, the Turkish government gradually closed its border.

The civilians in Idlib were subject to regular bombardment by Syrian and Russian planes and helicopters. Those bombers deliberately targeted schools, markets, and apartment buildings, as well as hospitals, as Human Rights Watch's investigation and reporting showed. Pursuing the classic, if criminal, counterinsurgency strategy of draining the sea to catch the fish, the attackers' aim was to chase civilians from Idlib to make it easier for Syrian troops to recapture the territory from the rebel forces living among them.

During one of my visits to Gaziantep, a Syrian doctor from a hospital in Idlib told me, referring to the United Nations secretary-general through the end of 2016, "We're tired of always hearing Ban Ki-moon say that he is 'concerned' or 'shocked'" by the bombing of civilians in Syria. I fully understood his frustration, but the fault hardly lay with Ban. Russia's and China's vetoes had paralyzed the UN Security Council, and no nation offered much beyond occasional expressions of outrage.

Human Rights Watch began as we always did—we investigated, documented, and reported on these war crimes. The first point of such reporting is to shame the perpetrators. Because most governments claim to uphold human rights, we can tarnish their reputations—and generate pressure for change—by spotlighting their abusive conduct.

The difficulty in the case of Syria was that Assad, already willing to do whatever it took to cling to power in what he saw as a life-and-death struggle, had little reputation left to lose. He sometimes tried to cover up his atrocities, but they were often meticulously recorded and publicized—by opposition Syrian videographers who posted their work on YouTube, a commission of inquiry established by the UN Human Rights Council (the world's top multilateral body on human rights), as well as Human Rights Watch and allied organizations. Showing that he was bombing civilians in Idlib, as he had bombed civilians in many other parts of Syria, was not going to be enough to end his war crimes.

Putin was another story. Now that Putin has committed similar atrocities in Ukraine to avoid risking a defeat that would jeopardize his rule, he has moved closer to Assad's realm of shamelessness. But at the time, Putin tried to maintain an aura of respectability. He did not want to be seen as a war criminal. That gave us leverage, as I outlined in July 2018 in an article in the *New York Review of Books*. Knowing that the Syrian military needed Russian support and that the Russian government was susceptible to pressure, we decided to focus on Putin.

We knew that shameful publicity alone would not be enough. We would need to combine it, as we so often did, with pressure from sympathetic governments. We focused on Germany and France, as the two most important members of the European Union, and Turkey, because of its significant interest in northern Syria and its respectful relations with Russia. I also spoke with an official from Iran, a key political and military ally of Assad. Behind each of these efforts were years of outreach and relationship building.

Turkey was a difficult interlocutor because Human Rights Watch regularly reported on and criticized the increasingly autocratic rule of President Recep Tayyip Erdogan. We had also reported for years on the violent abuses of his predecessors. Yet some officials maintained a degree of independence and were receptive to speaking with Human Rights Watch and hearing us out on Syria.

We had numerous sober, businesslike meetings over the years with senior Turkish officials. Sometimes the meetings paralleled my visits to Gaziantep, which reinforced for me the enormous stakes. I was often accompanied by Emma Sinclair-Webb, Human Rights Watch's researcher for Turkey—a Brit who spoke beautiful Turkish and knew the country extraordinarily well. One deputy prime minister took copious notes as we spoke in Ankara in January 2016, as if he did not want to forget a single word. The same month, I met with Turkey's then prime minister, Ahmet Davutoğlu, after a late-night dinner at the World Economic Forum in Davos, Switzerland. In September 2018, Emma and I saw the deputy foreign minister in Ankara. In October 2019, I held a long and remarkably candid conversation with a senior Turkish security official at a Munich Security Conference meeting in Doha, Qatar.

After the flight of more than one million refugees to Europe in 2015, most crossing by raft or small boat from Turkey to nearby Greek islands, the European Union paid the Turkish government 6 billion euros to stop further refugees from leaving. Turkish officials told me that if the loss of civilian life in Syria became too high, it would again allow Syrians to flee, but that was not the same as stopping the slaughter.

In Ankara in September 2018, I met with a large group of Western ambassadors over dinner at the Norwegian ambassador's residence, urging them to convey to their contacts in the Turkish government my concerns about the need to protect civilians in Idlib. I was encouraged by their interest but appalled at their lack of any apparent strategy. I outlined how pressure on Putin could make a difference.

I pursued talks with the Iranian government because it was a key military backer of Assad. It also used Syrian territory to resupply Hezbollah, its ally against Israel in southern Lebanon. Both Hezbollah troops and Shia militia organized by the Iranian government provided important on-the-ground support to Syrian government troops throughout the armed conflict. I worried that they might contribute to a bloodbath in Idlib.

At the time, I met periodically with Iran's then foreign minister, Javad Zarif. He had studied in the United States, spoke perfect colloquial English, and was open to meeting with human-rights groups. I routinely joined representatives from several colleague organizations such as Amnesty International, the International Crisis Group, and Crisis Action to speak with him on the sidelines of various international gatherings—the Munich Security Conference, the World Economic Forum, and the United Nations General Assembly. He was always an honest interlocutor with me. I was surprised in Davos in January 2014 when he turned to me and said, "I teach human rights. And I tell my students that it's a mistake to think that Human Rights Watch reports only on Iran. It also reports on Guantánamo and Israel." In February 2019 at the Munich Security Conference, we discussed Idlib. He assured me that, because of the threat to civilian life, Iranian forces would not take part in any offensive there. He also said that he had just visited Lebanon to meet with the leader of Hezbollah, and it would not take part either.

As I said, a key part of our strategy was to enlist European Union leaders to pressure Putin. German chancellor Angela Merkel and French president Emmanuel Macron were the two most influential, and I met periodically with both. Human Rights Watch maintained offices in Berlin and Paris, where the primary job of our "advocacy" staff was to influence German and French foreign policy on human rights. (We maintained offices in other key capitals as well.) Most of their work was done with other officials, but on occasion I was called in to meet the chancellor or the president. When possible, I was joined by Wenzel Michalski, then our Berlin-based Germany director, or Bénédicte Jeannerod, our Paris-based France director.

Merkel and Macron were the sort of leaders with whom I enjoyed meeting. They both led powerful countries whose intervention on human rights mattered. Both expressed sympathy, although I knew their other national interests would often take priority over human rights. Both had the self-confidence to engage in a frank and open conversation—not a set-piece talking-point exchange that accomplishes little.

In an early October 2018 meeting at Merkel's office in the modern German Chancellery in Berlin, I asked her to intervene personally with Putin. I spoke of the horrible humanitarian toll of the Syrian and Russian attacks on civilians in Idlib and explained the potential for another refugee crisis in Europe should the killing become so severe that Turkey would be forced to reopen its borders with Syria. I stressed that she and Macron had leverage over Putin because he valued his relations with them.

In September 2018, Bénédicte and I made similar points with a senior French Foreign Ministry official, and Bénédicte repeated them later that month in a meeting with Macron and then foreign minister Jean-Yves Le Drian. The German and French governments obviously knew what was happening in Idlib; our job was to move the problem higher on their agenda for action. We continued to press the point in direct meetings with government officials and in the media.

Slowly, the pressure on Putin increased, although as so often happens, the process was not linear. In September 2018, Erdogan warned in a meeting with Putin and Iran's then president, Hassan Rouhani, that an all-out assault on Idlib would result in a "bloodbath," yet Putin refused to agree to a ceasefire. However, a few days later, in a meeting with Erdogan, Putin did agree at least to create a demilitarized buffer zone between opposing forces in Idlib.

In October 2018, several weeks after my meeting with Merkel, she, Macron, and Erdogan met with Putin. Macron, supported by Merkel and Erdogan, pressed the Russian government to exercise "very clear pressure" on Damascus for a "stable and lasting ceasefire in Idlib." But even the buffer-zone agreement was never fully implemented, and by May 2019, Syrian and Russian forces were bombing civilians intensively.

On February 20, 2020, while at a European Union summit in Brussels, Merkel and Macron called Putin to press him to stop bombing civilians and civilian structures in Idlib. A few days later, what was said to be a Syrian airstrike killed at least thirty-six Turkish soldiers in northwestern Syria. The Turkish military quickly targeted Syrian troops in retaliation. That reminded Putin and Assad that Turkey was a potent military force willing to act if things got out of hand.

The combined pressure finally worked. On March 5, 2020, after six hours of negotiations in Moscow, Erdogan and Putin agreed to a ceasefire. That largely stopped major attacks on civilians in Idlib. Only in 2023 did that begin somewhat to break down, especially after an October drone attack on a Syrian military graduation ceremony by unknown assailants killed at least eighty. The attacks came to a definitive end with the sudden fall of the Assad regime in December 2024. For at least three years before then, if not longer, millions of people in Idlib were able to carry on their lives without constant fear of sudden death from the skies.

As Idlib illustrates, most human-rights work is incremental, progress sporadic. Violations of human rights wax and wane. Persistent pressure is often needed to sustain progress. Moreover, when progress occurs, Human Rights Watch can rarely take credit alone. Local human-rights defenders, sympathetic journalists, well-intentioned officials, and engaged members of the public are valued allies. The defense of human rights is a team effort.

That defense also requires humility. It is not an endeavor of easy or permanent victories. But modesty is not the same as resignation or indifference. Mitigating human-rights violations may not sound as dramatic as ending them definitively, but it can make an enormous difference for the people affected. That is what kept me going during my three decades leading Human Rights Watch.

Formative Years

I grew up in Deerfield, Illinois, a comfortable middle-class suburb of Chicago. My father had fled Nazi Germany as a twelve-year-old boy. He did not dwell on the past, but when my three siblings and I asked questions, he talked about it.

At first the stories were funny—about the fast, mischievous horse that delivered meat for my grandfather's butcher shop in Frankfurt. As we children became older, the stories became more serious—about life as a young Jewish boy living under the Nazis—and they made us aware of the evil that governments can do. My father was forced from his neighborhood school to a Jewish one. He worried about being punished on some pretext such as riding his bicycle on the sidewalk, but more seriously about my grandfather being arrested.

The Nazis insisted that Jews turn in any weapons they possessed. My grandfather had served in the German army in the frontline trenches during World War I, and as apparently was the tradition, he took his rifle home with him when he finished his service. This presented a dilemma: he feared arrest if he kept the rifle and it was discovered, but he also feared it could be used as a reason to arrest him if he turned it in. So my grandfather broke the rifle down into its parts and put them into his jacket pocket. He took my father and his brother to a nearby park, and as the boys skipped stones into a pond, my grandfather pretended to join them but skipped rifle pieces, disposing of his dilemma.

My grandfather, who grew up in a tiny village outside of Frankfurt, had only a sixth-grade education but was plenty intelligent. He knew upon Hitler's seizing power in 1933 that he would need to get the family out of Germany. The government was still letting Jews leave; the problem was finding a government that would accept them. The biggest obstacle was financial. The U.S. government reluctantly allowed some Jews to enter, but they needed to show that they would not become wards of the state. That was not easy for my family, because they were living hand to mouth. They were thus forced to move to New York in stages: first, a great uncle, who was able to enter because he had lived there briefly before; then, my grandfather and aunt; and a long nine months later, after my grandfather had been able to assemble the needed funds, my father and his brother, my grandmother, and her mother. The last group left Germany in July 1938, four months before Kristallnacht. It had taken my grandfather five years to get all immediate family members to safety. His travails made me forever appreciate how difficult it can be for people fleeing persecution to find safe haven.

I was born in 1955. My mother was outspoken in her progressive views. It was not beyond her to fire off well-crafted letters to government or business officials when their actions displeased her. My parents were hardly far left—during college I had long debates with my very capitalist father about the merits of socialism—but they had a strong sense of right and wrong.

The news was not a big topic of conversation at the dinner table, but we were regular subscribers to the *Chicago Tribune* (which I delivered for pocket money for several years as a young boy). We often watched the nightly news on television. I was very aware of the Vietnam War and the protests against it. I also vividly remember watching on TV the police repression of protesters during the 1968 Democratic Convention in Chicago. My first memory of witnessing a human-rights violation was of an execution during the Biafran war in Nigeria that, disturbing as I found it, somehow made it onto an evening broadcast.

My father gave us our first taste of politics. With four children in the Deerfield public school system, he ran for and won a seat on the local school board, ultimately serving as its chair. My siblings and I were his campaigners, walking a good part of the town distributing leaflets door to door.

When the village held a referendum on whether to consolidate the two school districts in the town, my father and most of the people in our school district opposed it; they felt the proposed combined tax rate would be too low to sustain the quality of the schools. Again, he deployed his child-labor campaign team to distribute literature. We were with him in the center of town as he was putting up a poster in the local dry cleaners. Someone from the other school district walked in, and they had a shouting match—something that was *very* out of character for my usually calm, rational, mild-mannered father. I took from him many of the traits that I would display at Human Rights Watch.

Both my parents were the product of New York City public schools. My father did not think he would go to college—no one from his family ever had—until a high school teacher told him about scholarships. He ended up attending City College in upper Manhattan, which was free, and majored in mechanical engineering. Of his one hundred classmates, he was one of only two to secure a job upon graduation.

My mother, who was born in the Bronx but whose parents had come to the United States to flee the antisemitism in Poland and Belarus, attended Hunter College, also a free city school, and majored in mathematics. My parents met at a dance and seemed to know by the end of the evening that they would marry.

Despite their modest beginnings, my parents were intellectuals of sorts. Both secured master's degrees at Northwestern University, my father in business, my mother in education. My mother became a high school math teacher, and my father entered the business world, mostly for a company that sold industrial packaging, where he slowly worked his way up the corporate ladder. He had always wanted to be a lawyer but felt in the 1940s that the profession did not welcome Jews. After he retired in his sixties, he attended Northwestern University School of Law for a year. For decades, my parents were members of one or more book groups.

I attended Brown University after falling in love with the beautiful campus and the colonial-era buildings surrounding it. Modest-sized Providence, Rhode Island, where Brown is located, was about as big a city as I could feel comfortable in after my suburban upbringing.

When it came to choosing a profession, I knew I needed something with a public purpose. I can't pinpoint a particular reason—it was my reaction to my upbringing and the political era in which I grew up—but it was a deeply engrained part of who I was. I did not think I would be happy with a traditional business career. I decided to become a lawyer because it seemed the most likely path to public service.

By the time I graduated from Yale Law School in 1980, international human-rights work had emerged as a new frontier. Jimmy Carter, the U.S. president at the time, seeking to distance himself from U.S. atrocities in Vietnam and U.S. support for the 1973 coup of General Augusto Pinochet in Chile, had made human rights the "soul" of his foreign policy. U.S. support for friendly autocrats was still the rule of the day—it was the Cold War, after all—but Carter raised the bar for how foreign policy would be judged.

I had become interested in international work due to my modest travel abroad. When I was sixteen, my parents for the first time took the entire family to Europe. We landed in Amsterdam, rented a Volkswagen bus (even though my father called Volkswagen Beetles "Hitler mobiles"), and gradually drove through the Netherlands, Belgium, and France until—the real point of the trip—we arrived in Germany. We visited Frankfurt, saw my father's old apartment building (which, unlike my grandfather's butcher shop, had survived the Allied bombing), and visited the local Jewish cemetery, where several of my relatives were buried, and the Jewish school where the Nazis had sent my father.

We traveled to the tiny village where my grandfather had grown up, Nieder-Ohmen, about seventy kilometers northeast of Frankfurt. We met an older woman who remembered not only my grandfather but also the day that my great-grandmother had announced his engagement to my grandmother. That woman contacted the mayor, who showed us the small Jewish cemetery on the outskirts of town. He said the Nazis had knocked over the tombstones but not destroyed them. Everyone in the cemetery was named Roth or Stern, and it contained the graves of my relatives dating back several generations.

Sadly, my father never taught my siblings and me German. When we were growing up, he was not keen on things German.

In high school, I took French courses but had no aptitude for the language and little interest in learning it. That changed entirely by chance. While in college, one of my high school friends spent a semester in Quebec City. During a visit, I communicated with the locals in what might best be described as pidgin French, as I searched my memory for fragments from high school. It was the first time the language had come alive for me. It was fun, I found, to communicate in another language. I resolved to go to France the next summer to learn French.

The company that my father worked for had a small subsidiary in France, where I was able to arrange a modestly paid internship. I returned to France after I graduated from college and worked as a waiter in a restaurant in Paris.

Today, the people applying for jobs at Human Rights Watch typically have experience working around the world. I had nothing like that, but it was enough to whet my appetite.

—

My human-rights career did not begin auspiciously. I signed up for the one human-rights course on offer at Yale Law School, but it was canceled. To this day, I have never taken an academic course on human rights. I graduated from law school and entered a world where human-rights jobs were scarce. In New York, Helsinki Watch, the precursor of Human Rights Watch, had all of two employees. Amnesty International had 150 employees in London—still tiny by today's standards.

I decided, of necessity, to do human-rights work as a volunteer. Initially, during my brief tenure in private practice and continuing while I was a federal prosecutor, I offered my services on nights and weekends on and off for six years. It speaks to the amateurish nature of the human-rights movement at the time that, when in December 1981, under Soviet pressure, the Polish government declared martial law to quash the independent Solidarity trade-union movement, I, an inexperienced, non-Polish speaker, was assigned to cover Poland.

I was utterly unqualified, but the work hooked me. I monitored events from afar, traveled to Warsaw to meet with the handful of dissidents who were able to operate, and wrote a couple of embarrassingly simplistic reports for publication. I found the dissidents inspiring. Their insistence on working despite government repression and the periodic jail terms meted out deeply impressed me. It reconfirmed for me that, in whatever way I could, I wanted to join their cause.

More prosaically, my work also made me known within the small circle of human-rights activists in New York. In 1987, when Human Rights Watch (still known as Helsinki Watch, Americas Watch, and Asia Watch) had grown to the vast size of some twenty employees, the board of directors, I was told, felt that Aryeh Neier, who was functioning as CEO though without the formal title, should have a deputy. I was contacted and jumped at the opportunity, despite my trepidation at taking a job that I was unsure my would-be boss wanted to exist. After what seemed like a cursory interview process, including a conversation with what then served as the informal board, I was offered the job.

I was just finishing the traditional four-year stint at the U.S. Attorney's Office for the Southern District of New York—the federal prosecutor's office in Manhattan. Most of my colleagues were heading off to become partners in major law firms. I was joining a tiny organization that none of them had heard of. They thought I was out of my mind. So did my parents. But I was elated. It was the best professional move I ever made.

I was offered the job in February but was told not to show up until November because Human Rights Watch (still not using that name) had to raise the money to hire me. I could have stayed at the U.S. Attorney's Office, where I had become chief appellate attorney for the criminal division, but the interlude provided a chance to do something different. The investigation of the Iran-Contra scandal was just starting, so I moved to Washington, DC, to join the independent counsel—the prosecutor in charge of the criminal investigation. When the funding became available for the job at Human Rights Watch, I moved back to New York.

I spent the next five years under Aryeh's mentorship. He had directed the American Civil Liberties Union (ACLU) before moving to Human Rights Watch and was the intellectual architect of the methodology that the organization uses. I was fortunate to have him as my guide and instructor. One essential thing that Aryeh illustrated for me was the possibility of being an activist with intellectual sophistication. It is not my nature to spend lots of time rallying in the streets or picketing government buildings. Luckily, that was not the job. Aryeh showed me that one could advance human rights by engaging in public-policy debate at the highest levels and maintaining rigorous standards of analysis. That played to my interests and what I thought to be my strengths.

My wife, Annie Sparrow, has analyzed my professional life through the lens of Malcolm Gladwell's book *Outliers*. She points out that the year of my birth gave me a fortuitous advantage in launching a human-rights career. That is not crazy numerology. As Gladwell notes, many of the generation who first made it big in technology were, like me, born in or around 1955 (Bill Gates, Steve Jobs, Eric Schmidt). They came of age just as many of the big technological advances were occurring, so they were well placed to seize these opportunities.

I am hardly a tech billionaire, but the human-rights movement also came of age with modern communications technology. The development of the movement can be understood in terms of the history of that technology: the faster information could travel, the better we could address abuses in a timely manner. I joined Human Rights Watch shortly before email took off. Indeed, just after becoming executive director in 1993, I received a one-time windfall grant and decided to invest it in the basic infrastructure we needed to begin using email.

From the web to smartphones to social media, communication with and about distant places has become quicker and easier. Human Rights Watch benefited enormously from these communication advances.

Gladwell also talks about the importance of devoting oneself passionately to a task to excel. He writes of the need to spend at least ten thousand hours perfecting a skill to become a top performer. I am sure that I put in many more than ten thousand hours as I worked with the Human Rights Watch staff to develop and apply our strategies. The defense of human rights was never just work; it was exactly what I wanted to be doing. I was happy to devote long hours to it for decades, which enabled me not only to improve the skills that I needed for the job but also to immerse myself sufficiently in the field to feel comfortable innovating.

I feel incredibly fortunate to have held a job that I found so fulfilling. In the terms used by today's human resource professionals, I set a poor example of work-life balance. The defense of human rights became my life. My closest colleagues as well thought nothing of sending each other messages during weekends or evenings, as events dictated. We built our personal lives around the demands of the job.

That is not to say that I was neglectful of personal matters. Unless I was traveling, I made a point of being home for our family dinner at 7:00 p.m. When my two daughters from my first marriage were young, I would bathe them and read them bedtime stories. I explained my work by saying that there were a lot of mean presidents in the world, and my job was to make them be nice. In my daughters' early years, I restricted trips to a week or ten days at a time and avoided deviations. The work of the remarkable activists who welcomed me into their lives, their culture, and their struggle for basic rights was far more important than glimpsing another tourist attraction.

It could be jarring to jump from a tranquil domestic life to the horrors of the world. I never made a conscious decision to keep a certain emotional distance from this evil, but it helped me to maintain an analytic rigor—and probably enabled me to sustain the work for so many years. I'm not sure that it is a better way to live, but it is who I am.

My personal orientation shaped the approach of Human Rights Watch. Rather than seeking empathetic statements of solidarity with victims, we generated pressure on abusive governments to change. If that seems callous, I can only say I was seeking the best way of eliminating what caused their victimhood. My personal motivation stemmed in large part from outrage that governments could act so cruelly, and I developed an instinct for figuring out a government's point of vulnerability so we could push back.

Annie, a pediatric intensive-care physician who turned to addressing global public-health issues, repeatedly traveled with our son, and at times me, to the Syrian border at the height of the conflict and to a remote island in the eastern Democratic Republic of Congo. She was far more emotionally involved with the people affected by violence and abuse than I allowed myself to be. It was not unusual for her to be moved to tears by a person's plight. She took it as a personal crusade to break down my clinical detachment by introducing me to people directly affected by atrocities whom I might not have spent much time with. Those experiences left a deep impression on me and are among the most vivid memories I have, but did not fundamentally change my more analytic orientation. I had to maintain that to do my work.

For vacations, I enjoyed traveling with my family. I attended my share of my children's school events, soccer matches, and playground activities. And for a good two decades and running, I took part in a book group. Given the enormous amount of reading about the real world that I did for Human Rights Watch, I was happy that the group read only fiction.

—

As Human Rights Watch became a more global institution, my travel schedule became more demanding. By the end, leaving aside the COVID-19 pandemic years, I was spending roughly half my time on the road. It was not always easy to head off yet again to the airport, leaving my family behind, sometimes with anxiety about a challenging destination. But once I landed, I was inevitably drawn into the rush of events and taken by the urgency of the cause.

To maintain this hectic pace, I tried to stay in decent physical shape. For decades I was a runner, usually in New York's Riverside Park or Central Park. In recent years, I turned to biking. When I traveled, I sought out hotels with a gym. I always made the time for exercise. I often thought through the details of my next article while running or biking because I found I could think more creatively then. It also made me calmer, more focused during the rest of the day, and gave me the endurance to stay energized.

My mother died at age eighty-nine in 2019, my father at age ninety-five in 2021. By the end of his life, he saw how his experience as a young boy had inspired me to do what I could so that others would not have to flee their homes the way he had.

3

Pressure for Change

I joined Human Rights Watch with the glorified title of deputy director, but at first I was mainly a researcher, which is what the organization called its investigators. These early opportunities to be in the field—to work with local activists and conduct investigations—were invaluable and continued to guide me as my responsibilities expanded. They instilled in me an enormous respect for the difficult work of researchers and the importance of deferring to their expertise. They showed me how an investigation could be translated into significant pressure for change. The importance of objective fact-finding, untainted by personal preferences or political views, became part of me. Witnessing firsthand the plight of people subjected to repression and abuse—getting to know them as people rather than as abstractions—also reaffirmed my desire to do human-rights work.

After I had been offered the job at Human Rights Watch, but before I'd started working, I was sent to Czechoslovakia in March 1987 to attend the trial of the "Jazz Section," a club sanctioned by the Communist Party. Because the club seemed tame enough, it was allowed to publish a newsletter without prior censorship. Rather than the stale agitprop of a Communist organ, it reported on a surprisingly vibrant underground cultural scene, moving well beyond jazz. Its publications became "the most widely read uncensored source of cultural information in the country," according to *The New York Times*, with an estimated seventy thousand readers.

The government tried to shut down the Jazz Section, but its leaders took the unprecedented step of appealing, and without asking permission, continued to operate pending judicial review. As Karel Srp, its fiery chairman, put it: "We could hardly believe in the 1980s there could be anyone who would want to ban jazz music." The government responded by prosecuting Srp and four other Jazz Section members in what was the country's first major political trial of the decade.

We two hundred or so independent observers were not permitted into the Prague courtroom where the trial took place; we had to stand in the courthouse corridor. Among those standing with me was Vaclav Havel, the dissident playwright. He, too, was known for pushing the limits of permissible expression. He had been a lead drafter of the Charter 77 declaration calling for respect for human rights, for which he had spent more than four years in prison. As a young and inexperienced human-rights defender, I was thrilled to be standing side by side with someone of his enormous reputation in pursuit of greater freedom for his country. Havel summed up the stakes by saying, "The Jazz Section represents a model of behavior that is dangerous for a centralized power. If everyone acted as they did it would be the end of the totalitarian system." After the fall of communism in the "Velvet Revolution," Havel became president of his country.

The trial illustrated the efforts of people in Czechoslovakia to test the limits of permissible public discourse at a time when the Soviet leader, Mikhail Gorbachev, had introduced the idea of *glasnost,* or openness. Not permitted to watch or hear the legal proceedings, we observers could only cheer as the defendants were brought in and ensure that the world knew of the Communist authorities' effort to stop the crumbling of their repressive order. The blind obedience that such governments try to inculcate is antithetical to the creativity and spontaneity of endeavors such as art. I wrote about the trial in my first published article for a magazine about religion, politics, and culture called *Commonweal.* I felt like a footnote to tectonic events, but it was an important step for me. The experience gave me an early indication of the power of independent expression to subvert autocratic governments.

The five defendants were sentenced to short or suspended prison terms. The judge conceded that their cultural work was "commendable" but insisted that such activities must be "regulated." It became clear two years later, though, with the fall of the Berlin Wall and the collapse of the Communist governments of Eastern Europe, that the free spirit of the Jazz Section leaders represented the future, their repressors a failing effort to sustain the past. I didn't have the foresight to see where the country and region were heading, but the experience was electrifying.

—

My first contact with that new Eastern Europe came in March 1991, when I visited Albania as part of the first nongovernmental human-rights delegation ever received in the country. My colleagues were activists from throughout Europe under the banner of the Vienna-based International Helsinki Federation for Human Rights. Helsinki Watch, a member, had helped to found the federation with the aim of fostering rights groups across Europe so that criticism of Soviet repression would be less U.S.-centered.

Infatuated with Stalin, Enver Hoxha, the longtime Communist dictator of Albania who had died in 1985, had kept the country an isolated enclave of repression. His paranoia was reflected in the small concrete bunkers that dotted the countryside as a laughable defense against the feared invasion that never came. I was told that couples had begun to use the bunkers for private liaisons. But the brutality of his regime became clear to me as I spoke to some of the victims. During one moving evening sitting on the steps of the main mosque in the central square of Tirana, I spent hours talking with gaunt men who had just been released after serving prison terms of more than twenty years. They described beatings during interrogation, trials without lawyers, regular mistreatment, and arduous work conditions, typically in mines. Many of them had been convicted of "agitation and propaganda" for speaking against the Hoxha dictatorship. Others had been convicted for complaining about economic conditions or writing poetry with, as one put it, "too free a hand."

The new president, Ramiz Alia, presented himself as a reformer. During our two-hour meeting, he listed his government's accomplishments in education, health, employment, and life expectancy. Asked whether his party would relinquish power if it lost an imminent election, he said that the party had "always been first violin—sole violin—but if it must, it will get used to being second violin." But referring to Albanians' increasingly open displays of discontent, he spoke resentfully of their "collective psychosis," which he described as people standing "with crossed arms and open mouths waiting for others to feed them." At least we were able to press him successfully for the release of the remaining political prisoners.

Albania *was* opening up. In May 1990, the government had rescinded several criminal laws that it had used to silence dissent, and in December, it had proposed a new constitution, which included many rights guarantees. An opposition party, the Democratic Party of Albania, was campaigning vigorously in the country's first parliamentary elections since the 1920s, which were held just after my visit.

Despite the progress, outrages were still taking place. I visited the port of Durres, where doctors at the local hospital reported two dead and eight wounded after troops stormed a ship filled with people trying to flee to Italy. The would-be emigrants refused to disembark, leading troops to storm the ship.

Our delegation held a news conference in a Tirana hotel to push for reforms, particularly regarding media freedom. Such a news conference would have been unthinkable just a short time earlier. Within a year, Sali Berisha, a charismatic cardiologist, would be elected president, foretelling a more democratic future.

———

I witnessed a very different transition when I visited Kuwait in May and June 1991, shortly after the U.S. military had repulsed Iraqi troops following Saddam Hussein's August 1990 invasion. The country was slowly returning to normal—streets had a haunting feel, with many shops still closed, and little pedestrian traffic—but at least Iraqi troops were no longer preying on the locals. I investigated Iraqi abuses and soon realized that Kuwaiti forces, the U.S. government's allies, were also responsible for serious crimes. President George H. W. Bush's administration enjoyed the plaudits for having liberated Kuwait from Saddam's ruthless forces but did not appreciate the spotlight on the vengeful Kuwaiti government it had reinstalled.

I sat in a Kuwaiti courtroom as people were prosecuted for alleged collaboration with the occupiers. The suspects repeatedly com-

plained of severe beatings during interrogations, at times displaying scars and damaged limbs. After spending months in appalling
conditions of detention and watching fourteen fellow prisoners be
beaten to death, they all confessed.

Twenty-four people were charged with producing *al-Nida*, a pro-
Iraqi occupation newspaper. Most admitted having worked for the
journal but insisted that Iraqi forces had compelled them. The main
"evidence" against them was the supposed testimony of a "secret
source" as conveyed by a Kuwaiti intelligence officer who refused to
provide any details. It was hardly a fair trial. These outrages gave me
ample motivation to reveal the atrocities of the reinstated Kuwaiti
government.

Yasser Arafat, the leader of the Palestine Liberation Organization,
had supported Saddam's seizure of Kuwait, evidently seeing him as
a strong leader willing to stand up to Israel. Palestinians in Kuwait
were blamed for his actions, assumed to share his pro-Iraq sympathies, and targeted as a result.

I received a tip from members of the Palestinian community about
a possible mass grave at al-Riqqa cemetery, on the southern outskirts
of Kuwait City. As is routine for Human Rights Watch researchers,
I was in close touch with many of the Western journalists who had
come to Kuwait in the aftermath of liberation. We quickly befriended
each other, and the CNN correspondent, overwhelmed by his own
assignments, lent me a cameraman as I looked for the mass grave.
In a corner of al-Riqqa cemetery, I found a section marked "collective graves," which contained victims of Iraq's secret police and many
who had died at Kuwaiti hands after liberation. Gravediggers whis-
pered to me that many of the bodies showed signs of torture. One
unidentified male buried after liberation was recorded as having been
received not from a hospital but from a police station. I gathered my
nerve and went to the police station, CNN cameraman in tow, to ask
about him. As a citizen of the country that had just liberated them,
joined by a reputable news network, I assumed a degree of protection
to make inquiries. At the police station, I was told variously that the
man had been a drug addict and a car accident victim, but there was
no plausible explanation for why his body hadn't been brought to a
hospital morgue.

Three Palestinians and one Iraqi told me they had been brought to the same police station and were put through a routine so orchestrated that the officers had names for the torture chambers—the party room, the barbecue room, and the drinking-juice room. In those rooms, uniformed troops beat prisoners with sticks and poles, subjected them to electric shocks and burns with cigarettes and heated rods, and forced them to drink what smelled like sewage water. The unidentified male may have succumbed to such treatment.

My sympathies had been with the Kuwaitis for having suffered through Saddam's occupation, but that was no excuse for Kuwaiti forces' contemptible behavior afterward. I published an op-ed piece on these atrocities in *The New York Times* to press Kuwaiti authorities to end them, and my colleagues later produced a major report on postliberation Kuwait abuses: "A Victory Turned Sour." The experience reminded me of the importance of not prejudging a situation, and examining all sides in any conflict—basic principles that still guide Human Rights Watch investigations.

—

I had to deliver a similarly difficult message of principle in Haiti. My first visit to the country was in November 1987, nearly two years after the fall of President Jean-Claude Duvalier. I was supposed to observe Haiti's first free election, except that a few hours into the voting the army decided to stop it. It murdered fourteen people at a polling station in Port-au-Prince, while gunmen drove around the city shooting at random.

As the events were unfolding, I was working in the Holiday Inn hotel in Port-au-Prince, headquarters for the journalists and human-rights defenders who were monitoring the election. The size of our group and its international character made us an unlikely target, but that was not the case for the few observers in the hotel where I spent the night a short distance away. We planned an escape route should an attack occur, but with the hotel perched on a cliff, a quick exit would have been difficult. That evening was when I felt most scared during my many years at Human Rights Watch. With commercial flights halted, the U.S. government chartered a plane so observers could leave.

I continued to follow Haiti closely. On another trip, my colleagues and I visited the Casernes Dessalines, a vast old army barracks in

Port-au-Prince that doubled as a prison where detainees were tortured. The commander was Colonel Jean-Claude Paul, who had a reputation for brutality and murder. We went to see him in the hope that we might deter these abuses by exposing them. As we entered the Casernes, we saw prisoners being ushered out the back, presumably so we could not speak with them. Colonel Paul invited us into his office, which he kept in shadowy darkness, with incense burning and an Uzi submachine gun on his desk. The meeting, in which I did not want to get my interlocutor unduly exercised, was not productive. Paul died in his home soon thereafter from what was said to have been poisoning.

One of the most important public figures working for a democratic transition in Haiti was Jean-Bertrand Aristide, a priest at a small parish in Port-au-Prince. A thin, diminutive man, Aristide was a powerful speaker, using wordplay and allusion to rally a crowd. He was impressive, embodying the hopes of the Haitian people to escape decades of ruthless dictatorship.

He was attacked by plainclothes gunmen twice while army troops looked on. The second attack, in September 1988, occurred while he was celebrating mass at his church of St. Jean Bosco. It left thirteen parishioners dead, seventy wounded, and the church burned to the ground. He escaped and went into hiding. When he reemerged and I met with him, there was a worrisome cool reserve. He spoke deliberately, with barely controlled rage. I understood his fury, but feared where it might lead.

A few months later, his decision to run for president excited the Haitian people. In December 1990, under the banner *Lavalas,* the Flood, he swept Haiti's first free and fair election with 67 percent of the vote.

As president, Aristide moved quickly to assert civilian authority over the army, firing generals and replacing them with people who he hoped would be reformist. Many army members were resentful, so violence against Aristide and his followers was an ever-present threat. Without a loyal security force, popular violence flourished, often taking the form of "necklacing," the placing of a gasoline-filled automobile tire around a victim before setting it aflame. It was also known as *Père Lebrun,* after a tire salesman whose television ads showed him popping his head through his product. Aristide applauded students when they threatened to use *Père Lebrun* to force a court to impose life sentences on accused coup leaders, praising it as a defensive tool.

Aristide's desperation was understandable, but for a president to encourage popular violence was not only a clear violation of the right to life but also a spark for a potential cycle of violence that was unlikely to end well for the Haitian people. Difficult as it was to do, Human Rights Watch, after long having condemned the conduct of the Haitian security forces, published a report criticizing Aristide. I published a critical article in *The New York Review of Books* and met with Aristide to press him on the issue, to no avail. In September 1991, he was overthrown in a military coup. He later returned to the presidency but was ousted again. Aristide was not in the same league as the military officers he was trying to replace, but it was important not to allow my sympathies for his goals to color my application of human-rights standards.

—

On my first visit to Cuba, in 1988, I learned the importance of persistence. The Cuban authorities had agreed to the visit to show that their human-rights conditions were not as bad as some Cuban exiles in Miami were claiming. The Cuban leadership was also trying to put on a good face since the UN Commission on Human Rights was considering whether to send an investigative team to Cuba. That gave us leverage.

My colleagues and I were allowed into Havana's main prison, Combinado del Este, where most long-term political prisoners were held, and given permission to speak with them in a main prison wing. I, however, wanted to see the punishment cells, known as the "Rectangle of Death," which Cuban human-rights defenders had described to me as horrible. The prison authorities refused. So my colleagues and I sat down in the prison yard and politely refused to leave. Trying to defuse the situation, the authorities claimed not to know anything about any punishment cells, but said we were free to look for them.

Fortunately, Cuban activists had given me a hand-drawn map of its location in a nondescript building that could have passed for a warehouse. Inside, the men were held in tiny, barely lit cells. During the summer, the building was called the "pizzeria" because of the sweltering conditions. The inmates were fed just enough to keep them alive. By speaking to the occupants, we were able to publicize the conditions and contribute pressure to close it.

Two years later, in 1990, I was again allowed into Cuba, using the pretext of a UN conference on criminal justice. I was joined by José Miguel Vivanco, a Chilean lawyer, longtime director of Human Rights Watch's program on Latin America, and an enormously effective advocate for human rights throughout the region. We spent as little time as possible at the conference and instead sought to speak to dissidents. For much of the time, we were followed by surveillance officers in three cars who made little effort to conceal their presence.

We visited with a woman who had recently been released from prison and begun mouthing a pro-government line. We wanted to establish whether coercion was behind her conversion. As we left her apartment, we noticed a young couple passionately kissing, but as we started walking away, they immediately followed. That would not be a bad job to have, we joked.

—

As my responsibilities expanded along with Human Rights Watch, I rarely had time to conduct investigations. My visits to countries were usually confined to the capital and involved a strategy session with local activists, meetings with government officials, and a briefing for journalists. I loved the investigative work because it put me in close touch with the victims of abuse who brought the issues to life, but the local activists who were fighting on their behalf were the most inspiring. As I spent less time in the field, alas, I lost that immediate connection to the people most affected by my work. But I came to recognize that my personal value added—my special skill—was the ability to develop and pursue strategies for pressuring governments. I confess to liking my clashes with abusive leaders because of the goals we were pursuing.

Human Rights Watch had no police force to deploy in defense of human rights, nor could we issue judicial orders for governments to uphold human rights or dangle economic incentives as enticements for better behavior. Rather, shaming was central to the pressure that we exerted on governments to force them to respect rights. That required rigorously investigating misconduct, reporting on it as quickly and accurately as possible, and shining a spotlight on it through traditional and social media. Where possible, we combined shaming with diplomatic or economic pressure exerted by governments that were sympathetic to the defense of human rights, which required encouraging them to act—as we did for Idlib—and generating media attention when they did not. When we could, we met with officials from abusive governments to drive home the need to reform.

Each step in this process required its own strategies, which we refined over time. The development of these strategies also tracked our evolution as a global institution with significant clout in most corners of the world. These campaigns were of course a team effort, but as head of the organization beginning in 1993, I often played a role in devising and executing them.

Shaming

The capacity to shame begins with the claim made by most governments that they uphold human rights. That has become a pillar of a government's standing. Obviously, many governments fall short. That discrepancy can be stigmatizing, embarrassing a government before the international community and, most important, its public at home. Shaming is not name-calling; the point is not to stigmatize with epithets but with facts, by portraying a government's misconduct. *Shame is different from guilt.* Human-rights abusers may feel no personal remorse whatsoever, but they would prefer to avoid the opprobrium of others. Our job was to force them to behave better regardless of their character.

This is not a matter of "lecturing" governments, as French president Macron, Chinese president Xi Jinping, and Yale law professor Samuel Moyn have disparagingly suggested. Rather, the capacity to shame government leaders is premised on their desire not to be seen as serving only themselves. That even brutal dictators usually care about their reputation is perhaps surprising. They must at least pretend to serve the public, and most members of the public want their rights respected. Even dictators need a large degree of public acquiescence in their rule. The enormous resources that some dictatorships invest in censorship and propaganda to bolster their human-rights reputations show the importance they attach to it. Rule by brutality and fear can work for some time but is risky, because a disgruntled public is always on the lookout for a way to oust the tyrant.

Abusive governments also care about their reputations because being seen to respect human rights is often the key to unlocking international benefits, such as military or financial aid or favorable terms for trade. An abusive official always wants something from the international community, even if it is just being invited to a major summit so they can be photographed with respected leaders. If we can persuade other governments to withhold desired benefits until human-rights abuses end, we create a powerful incentive for reform.

As I said, Human Rights Watch highlighted the discrepancy between pretense and practice by carefully investigating and reporting on government abuse. That generally required traveling to the scene of the abuse, interviewing victims and witnesses, and compiling as accurate and objective an account as possible of violations.

To prevent the delegitimization that attended exposure of their human-rights shortcomings, governments often resorted to a predictable pattern: First, they tried to cover up, as for example the Chinese government did in trying to hide its mass detention and persecution of Uyghur and other Turkic Muslims in Xinjiang. But in an increasingly connected world, where smartphones are ubiquitous, access to social media is widespread, virtual private networks (VPNs) can circumvent internet censorship, and satellites can peer into remote parts of a country, cover-up is difficult.

Even after we published details about human-rights violations, governments devoted much energy to avoiding bad press. Often, they started by denying our findings and lying about their conduct, as the Russian government did regarding reports of its war crimes in Ukraine. Governments accused us of misunderstanding, of bias, or of being misled, as the Israeli government frequently did regarding reports of its repression and abuse of Palestinians.

These retorts were not terribly effective because we were extraordinarily careful about our fact-finding. From day one, researchers were told that their top priority is accuracy. I would rather have had a researcher come home empty-handed than to return with inaccurate information. We aspired for the sober rather than the sensational, for exactitude rather than exaggeration. Because we were so careful, we welcomed battles over the facts. A government's obfuscation and spin went only so far in the face of a detailed recitation of evidence.

———

Libya under the longtime dictator Muammar Gaddafi illustrated our ability to use a government's concern with its image to make human-rights progress. I visited Libya in January 2006, when Gaddafi was trying to redeem his horrible reputation to attract Western invest-ment. He had stopped supporting terrorism, abandoned his nuclear program, and paid compensation to the victims of the bombing of a passenger airline over Lockerbie, Scotland. His biggest remain-ing problem was his human-rights record. With that in mind, we approached the government and sought permission to send an inves-tigative team to Libya. Gaddafi agreed.

The sponsor of the trip was, of all people, Gaddafi's son, Saif al-Islam Gaddafi, whom I had met previously and who at the time was eager to portray himself as a reformer and human-rights defender. Five years later, in 2011, the International Criminal Court would charge Saif with crimes against humanity for his conduct in the waning days of his father's rule, after he had threatened "a river of blood" in Benghazi if protests against his father continued. But in 2005 and 2006, he was helpful to our efforts to secure the release of political prisoners as well as compensation for the families of a noto-rious prison massacre. Others around his father were less interested in human rights.

For three weeks in April and May 2005, Human Rights Watch was allowed an investigative team in Libya. It was led by Fred Abra-hams, an experienced American researcher. Despite some govern-ment obstruction, the team secured one-on-one private meetings with prisoners who said there had been certain improvement in prison conditions, and some political prisoners had been released, but serious problems remained.

As a condition of conducting the investigation, we had promised the Libyan government to present our findings in advance of the planned publication of our report. That brought me to Tripoli. Work-ing with Saif Gaddafi's organization, we had identified 131 political prisoners. Most had spent seven or more years in detention after unfair trials for nonviolent activity. Our aim was to secure their release, but when we shared our critical findings with midlevel officials, our hosts exploded (or, more likely, pretended to explode). We had to endure a charade of anger and hurt feelings. We were accused, among other things, of not understanding Libya. They kept suggesting that publication of the report should be delayed and seemed to think that they could bludgeon us into not publishing it at all.

I let their tirade go on for a while, then said that we were going to hold a news conference a few days later in Cairo, where journalists would undoubtedly ask us about our meetings in Tripoli. We could say: "All they did was yell at us." Or we could say: "The conversations were productive, and they promised various reforms." Which would it be? I asked. The Libyans, visibly taken aback, said they would have to consult their superiors.

The next morning, we sat in our hotel lobby wondering if the whole trip had been for naught. That afternoon, however, we received word that we would be seen again. This time, the officials spoke apologetically of a "misunderstanding." The deputy interior minister offered to let us look at files stacked on his desk about political prisoners we had identified. We discussed several of them. Five weeks later, I was gratified to learn that the 131 political prisoners we had spotlighted had been released.

Investigations

At Human Rights Watch, as I've said, researchers' ability to affect government policy lies in the power of the information they collect and the expertise they develop about a country or issue. One often ignored element of our influence is that we could pay people who were, or became, experts—that is, we hired people who often knew more about a topic than virtually anyone else. When I raised enough money to hire a new researcher, I was buying the capacity to develop and maintain expertise. Properly deployed, it could move governments. That was a huge incentive for me to keep fundraising.

Researchers came from various backgrounds—lawyers, journalists, academics, activists. The best ones had in common persistence—the ability to keep pushing to obtain the facts, even in the face of formidable obstacles—attention to detail, and a quest for objectivity. Their job was to find the facts as they were, regardless of their political views or advocacy goals.

Ideally, we wanted people who spoke the language of the country where they worked, people who were able to operate culturally and logistically in their country of focus and often had the most nuanced understanding of it. Translators could be used, but that made conversations more halting and cumbersome. We also wanted people who were self-starters, who didn't wait for instructions.

At first, our researchers were mainly based in our New York headquarters. Eventually, Brad Adams, an American attorney and the superb longtime director of the organization's Asia program, pioneered the placement of researchers in their countries, or at least regions, of focus. His having been based in Cambodia while working for the UN human-rights office, he said, had enabled him to develop and maintain a deeper understanding of the country's human-rights issues, and we sought to replicate that advantage.

Amnesty International used to have a rule against researchers covering their countries of origin—a precaution against bias. We pursued a different approach, ensuring objectivity through careful supervision by researchers' regional or thematic directors as well as skilled veterans in the central office, who reviewed all reports before publication. When I left Human Rights Watch, we had more than eighty nationalities on staff, able to speak roughly the same number of languages.

We created security issues as we implemented Brad's system throughout the organization—governments were more apt to retaliate against one of their own nationals—but the advantages were considerable. Our researchers were trained to cut through bias, to (politely) cross-examine and corroborate witnesses, and to combine witness testimony with available physical or photographic evidence. Given the usual government rebuttals, getting the facts right was essential for shaming.

The investigative process is necessarily painstaking. Imagine researchers in a war zone trying to reconstruct wartime events. If they encounter a dead body on the ground, what is its significance?

It could be a soldier killed in combat, or a civilian killed by an otherwise lawful attack on a nearby military target, or it could be the result of an illegal summary execution, a war crime. Each situation needs to be analyzed by interviewing survivors and witnesses, examining debris, considering available satellite imagery as well as videos or photographs posted on social media, and seeking the response of those implicated in the abuse. Only when we were certain about how an event had played out did we publish. We knew that our findings would be scrutinized, that governments would challenge them, so we made sure that our reporting was solid.

In most countries, we worked closely with local human-rights activists, who typically brought to the table an intimate understanding of their country. They helped us to identify the most important issues, to determine the ones for which we had the most significant leverage and value added, to develop effective strategies for change, and to locate witnesses and others with relevant information. We added our reputation for accurate fact-finding and the ability to project our findings to a global audience of journalists and policymakers.

—

When Human Rights Watch began as Helsinki Watch in 1978, there was little factual dispute about the dissidents whom Soviet-backed governments were locking up with little regard for their rights. Our job was to spotlight their fate, to generate pressure for their release, and to enable their infectious quest for freedom to take hold in the population at large. These dissidents appeared to be isolated, embattled individuals standing up to an entrenched, monstrous system. But in fact, their bravery—their insistence on stating the truth and envisioning a more just society—showed the fragility of a system that could not tolerate such individuality and free expression.

Jeri Laber led this effort as the original director of Helsinki Watch and then the head of what became the Europe and Central Asia division of Human Rights Watch. She traveled to most Soviet bloc countries, quietly meeting with dissidents and writing about them, often in *The New York Times* or *The New York Review of Books*. She also wrote a compelling book about her experiences, *The Courage of Strangers,* candidly describing how she conducted human-rights investigations when few people had undertaken them.

When Americas Watch, the companion to Helsinki Watch, was launched in 1981, the facts in the Central American conflicts of El Salvador, Nicaragua, and Guatemala—its principal initial focus—were deeply contested. The U.S. government was backing the Salvadoran and Guatemalan governments against leftist rebel groups and the Contras against the leftist Sandinista government in Nicaragua. We thus adopted a different modus operandi, publishing deeply researched reports. As became our tradition, Americas Watch reported on abuses by both sides in those armed conflicts. When we found that forces backed by the U.S. government were committing abuses, contradicting the image that Washington tried to portray of freedom fighters opposing abusive communists, we were immediately attacked by officials of President Ronald Reagan's administration, such as Elliott Abrams, assistant secretary of state for human rights and then for inter-American affairs. Their allies in Congress and the right-wing media joined in. When journalists covering these conflicts conducted their own investigations, they found that the Americas Watch reports were accurate. "That helped to give the organization credibility with the press and its reputation was much enhanced," as Aryeh Neier explained. "It seems possible that Human Rights Watch would not have achieved the prestige it enjoys today were it not for the attacks it faced during its formative years."

Much of Americas Watch's research in Central America was carried out by Jemera Rone, a tall, redheaded American working from a temporary office established in El Salvador in 1985. As I witnessed firsthand when I spent time with her in El Salvador and Guatemala in 1989, she had the grace, calm, and good humor to talk her way past checkpoints and to navigate tense situations. In a meeting with the Salvadoran defense minister, I was impressed by her ability to secure his respect while she was reporting on war crimes committed under his command. A former corporate lawyer, she brought the required persistence and comprehensiveness in uncovering the facts and a deep-seated objectivity and impartiality. Her reports contained extensive, detailed testimony, which made it difficult to refute her findings. Sadly, she was seriously injured in a 2006 car accident at Washington's Dulles Airport, never fully recovered, was forced to retire, and died in 2015 at the age of seventy-one.

Communications Technology

Shaming governments by reporting on their misconduct was most effective if we could learn about the misdeed in a timely manner. The evolution of communications technology was a godsend in that regard, and closely parallels the development of the human-rights movement.

In the earliest days of human-rights activism, information moved by sailing ship or steamer. That meant that only large, long-lasting problems could be addressed, such as slavery or women's suffrage. It was difficult to generate outrage over more fleeting problems. The creation of the telegraph allowed war correspondents to cut through the self-glorifying tendencies of military commanders in a timely manner. War correspondents' accounts of the Civil War led Abraham Lincoln in 1863 to commission what became known as the Lieber Code, setting forth the first modern standard of conduct for soldiers in combat.

When Amnesty International was created in 1961, its researchers periodically traveled from its London headquarters to the sites of abuse abroad, but between trips, they had to rely on snail mail to learn about, say, the status of a political prisoner. International phone calls were too expensive for regular use. Researching a report therefore took a long time, meaning that longer-lasting patterns of repression remained the primary focus. Amnesty began issuing "urgent actions" in 1973, but the aim was still to get members to send letters of protest by mail.

With the widespread use of fax machines in the mid-1980s, an entire page of information could be sent for the cost of a short international phone call. We could collect information from sources in repressive countries and convey our reaction to journalists quickly and cheaply. The emergence of email accelerated the process, and made even simpler communication and coordination among activists, journalists, and governments. Suddenly, we could describe atrocities today with the aim of ending them tomorrow.

These trends only intensified with the emergence of smartphones and social media. Today, governments find it increasingly difficult to hide their abuses. It has become almost unthinkable that a government could cover up mass atrocities, as the Khmer Rouge did in

Cambodia in the 1970s. The Chinese government is the only one so far that has devoted the considerable resources needed to censor particular social media posts, but even Beijing is often playing whack-a-mole as the Chinese people concoct creative ways to circumvent the censors. If governments want to censor social media, they usually must block an entire platform, which can be unpopular. Even as the war in Ukraine raged, the Kremlin allowed Telegram and YouTube to function, providing an avenue for Russians who sought information beyond their government's propaganda.

Collecting and disseminating information about human-rights abuses is now easier than it has ever been. Shaming can take place entirely on social media, and sometimes that suffices, but jumping from social to traditional media is often a prerequisite to the most effective shaming—if only because policymakers tend to be more aware of traditional media.

Information conveyed by others on social media is useful for collecting evidentiary leads, but it is no substitute for an investigation. Human Rights Watch developed a (deserved) reputation for carefully examining the flow of information to parse reality from rumor, the verifiable from the concocted. That remained the central role of researchers even when leads emerged from social media.

The dissemination of real-time reporting made possible by the evolution in communications technology can be double edged. On the one hand, it permits the world to access information about atrocities almost immediately. I recall being transfixed by a 2011 BBC interview with Sidney Kwiram, who had joined our team of researchers in Libya during the final days of Gaddafi's government, as she walked among the bodies of recent execution victims while talking on her cell phone. The horror in her voice was palpable, though she refused to draw conclusions about what she was witnessing until she was able to interview survivors. Nonetheless, it was tremendously compelling.

On the other hand, there is no vetting such reporting. Twitter (now "X") and similar networks did not lend themselves to vetting either. My colleagues and I encouraged the Human Rights Watch staff to publicize their work on Twitter, but the effectiveness of the medium diminishes as the currency of the tweet recedes. Real-time tweeting works best. I had to trust the staff to post on social media with the organization's principles in mind, as I did when they gave media interviews. A more conservative approach would abandon a medium that today plays a central role in advancing the public discussion of human rights.

In general, though, Human Rights Watch was known for the layers of review that took place before we published anything. James Ross, an American lawyer and the organization's longtime legal and policy director, oversaw that process. His knowledge of human-rights law and principles, and his ability to reshape initiatives to keep them within those principles, was unparalleled. My profound trust in him enabled me to focus on Human Rights Watch's external work, confident that he would keep our publications principled and defensible.

While social media gives people a public voice even if they lack ready access to traditional media, it has also become a tool for the enemies of human rights, who can disseminate their perspectives—including false denials, concocted justifications for repression, and outright lies—unfiltered by the editors and journalists of traditional media. Autocratic leaders have become adept at using social media to foment hatred and discrimination and to promote divisive views. They profit from social media algorithms that reward vitriolic and hate-filled messages that generate "engagement." In my view, the net effect of social media for the human-rights cause is positive, given the importance of the free flow of information for the defense of those rights, but it is a close call. Human Rights Watch came to rely heavily on social media to disseminate its findings and analyses. When I left, the organization had a total of twelve million followers on Twitter, Facebook, and Instagram. My personal account on Twitter had more than half a million.

X has become the medium where virtually every journalist and official has a presence. Elon Musk's purchase of Twitter put this role at risk, but I don't see an imminent replacement. Obviously, more formal publications and interviews still matter a great deal, but they are downright lumbering compared to the speed of X. As a result, a significant part of today's conversation takes place in 280-character sound bites.

I have become a fan of X, despite my reservations. I appreciate the immediacy. X allows a real-time response to new developments, which can shape media coverage. Drafting a press release and getting it through the layers of review at Human Rights Watch could take hours. Composing a tweet takes minutes, and posting on Twitter allowed me to signal to journalists that I was commenting on an issue, which encouraged them to contact me or to quote my tweets.

Public officials were surprisingly sensitive to my tweets. For example, shortly after UN rights chief Volker Türk took office in October 2022, his aide called me to complain. I had been criticizing Türk for his lack of public protest against the Chinese government's persecution in Xinjiang. I said I would be happy to stop my tweets as soon as Türk started condemning China. It was valuable to know that he felt the pressure.

Although one would think that social media is impersonal—the user speaks to an audience, not an individual—it retains an oddly personal dimension. For example, prior to my June 2022 meeting with Ugandan president Yoweri Museveni, his private secretary boasted to a Human Rights Watch researcher that he knew me. I had not previously met him, but he followed me on Twitter. I regularly ran into people who felt that we were acquainted because of Twitter, which made it easier to collaborate.

I also came to see the advantage of the enforced brevity of Twitter. One can always link tweets together in a thread, but that makes it harder to keep people's attention. It is thus important to reduce what one wants to say to the essence, a useful discipline that makes me both a more careful reader and a sharper communicator.

I am regularly attacked on social media by trolls—people who see their role as going after anyone who criticizes their favorite government. Supporters of the Israeli government are by far the worst. I almost never respond because trolls are not interested in reasoned discussion, and they would love for me to draw attention to their message. Still, human-rights activists must engage with social media because our absence would leave the field wide open to lies. We must fight the battle where it is waged.

—

The evolution of communications technology obviously changed the nature of human-rights reporting. Some of the original founders of Human Rights Watch came from the publishing industry, including the first chair of the board of directors, Robert Bernstein, who was CEO of Random House. Our initial reports tended to be book length; it was important to recite the many facts behind our conclusions to establish our credibility. Although timeliness suffered, and with it the ability to address fast-moving events, our early reports were novel enough that they attracted significant media attention. My first report, issued in 1983 on Poland after martial law was imposed, was embarrassingly amateurish, entirely dependent on secondary sources, yet managed to generate a *New York Times* article.

When I became executive director, I tried to introduce more of an impact orientation, since books took so much time and effort to produce. Establishing a historical record was important, but we were activists, not historians. I wanted us to produce reports that led to changes in policy and practice, as Aryeh had done. We were already a proven observer, so a shorter report or even a news release usually sufficed.

That change in emphasis, combined with the communications breakthrough, gave us greater capacity to shape media accounts and policy responses. We began to issue publications that were detailed enough to sustain their conclusions—to stigmatize with facts—but short enough to be published quickly. Our rapid-response bulletins became far more common than our major reports.

An illustration of the power of that new type of reporting came in August 2008 during the five-day Russia-Georgia war. Russia-backed Ossetian militia had attacked five ethnic Georgian villages as Russian troops looked on. Two Human Rights Watch researchers, Tanya Lokshina and Anna Neistat, entered South Ossetia, where the fighting was taking place—the only independent observers on the ground—and their reporting allowed us to issue a press release and, as Tanya put it, "raise hell" with Russian authorities. Russian forces immediately reacted by blocking the main road to prevent Ossetian forces from entering the area and maintained that position for five days, enabling the International Committee of the Red Cross to locate—with our help—and evacuate the remaining Georgian civilians.

I established a team of emergency researchers, investigators without a particular country portfolio who specialized in working in war zones or throwing themselves into other crises. Later named the Crisis and Conflict team, their task was to maximize the possibility of real-time deterrence. They also provided added capacity for the thinly stretched research staff, because there was rarely more than one or two researchers assigned to a country. (Often, one researcher was responsible for multiple countries.) Emergency researchers provided backup when human-rights problems in a country exploded, such as during the armed conflicts in Syria and Ukraine.

The team attracted many of Human Rights Watch's most talented researchers, including Tirana Hassan, an Australian lawyer I selected in 2020 as our first chief programs officer—in essence, my chief deputy—with the aim of positioning her to take over the organization when I left. After a global search, the board of directors named her Human Rights Watch's third executive director in March 2023.

—

When it was impossible for a researcher to gain access to the site of abuse to interview survivors and witnesses—the government may have barred us, or access may have been too dangerous—we fell back on alternative investigative techniques. We communicated with people by phone, email, or WhatsApp, or met with refugees outside the country. Often local human-rights activists, with whom we were in touch, could reach the scene of serious abuse even if we could not. In 2017, Human Rights Watch entered a partnership with Planet, a San Francisco–based satellite company that launched dozens of small satellites to take reasonably high-resolution pictures of the entire globe every day. We could ask for images of a particular area over specified dates to see how events (at least of a certain size and visibility) unfolded. Our analysts were trained to read satellite imagery. Specialized researchers also used open-source analysis. When people witness something unusual or significant, many take a photograph or video on their mobile phone and post it on social media. Other useful information could be found, surprisingly, on government websites and databases.

The Syrian conflict was the first war in which this information was widely available. Teams of opposition videographers, as noted, routinely documented Syrian and Russian war crimes and posted their findings on YouTube. In Syria, as well as in the war in Ukraine and other conflicts, the open-source researchers scraped social media sites to collect evidence about abuses they were investigating. Of course, just because something is posted on social media does not make it accurate; repressive governments would post fake information all the time. The open-source researchers sought to verify and corroborate, or dismiss, anything found on social media.

Prose remained the essence of our reporting, but the visual became such a powerful supplement to the written word that we began using it regularly. For example, during the Myanmar military's 2017 ethnic cleansing of Rohingya, our researchers spoke to those being expelled as they entered Bangladesh. Some gave accounts of murder, rape, and arson, but because Rohingya were so despised in Myanmar, because so many people in the country discounted anything they said, it was useful to supplement their accounts with satellite imagery. The imagery clearly showed the burned villages that the Rohingya were describing, and later showed the Myanmar military bulldozing the sites.

The introduction of initially photographs and then videos to our work was led by Carroll Bogert, an American journalist, former foreign correspondent in the Soviet Union and China, and my longtime partner and invaluable costrategist as associate director of Human Rights Watch. She was aided by Maja Hoffmann, a generous donor known foremost as a patron of the visual arts, who believed deeply in the power of the image. Ready-made videos enabled television broadcasters to better cover our reports. As we disseminated our findings through not only traditional but also social media, far more people viewed video renditions than read the reports themselves. The multimedia department was soon overwhelmed by demand for its products.

Security

Because my responsibilities as executive director largely precluded me from undertaking time-intensive field research, I rarely faced significant dangers. At times I was vulnerable, but I was not about to start walking around with a bodyguard, and I doubt one would have made much difference anyway. I did worry, however, about Human Rights Watch researchers operating in repressive environments and researchers in war zones who could face random violence. To be honest, we were not always as careful with our researchers' security as we should have been. Early on, we mainly left risk management to each researcher's judgment, and some researchers were less careful than others, especially members of our emergency team. Their efforts to gather the facts were impressive, as a dramatic Netflix documentary, *E-Team,* demonstrated. Our reputation owes a lot to their perseverance in even the most difficult situations, but I now realize we were lucky they all returned home safely and never faced lengthy detention.

In my last decade as executive director, we bolstered our efforts in this area by hiring a full-time security officer to work with researchers on managing risks in the field. We also invested in a digital security officer, given governments' interest in gaining access to our internal communications and data. Even so, we deferred significantly to the judgment of each researcher and their supervisor. We also stressed that senior management would back any researcher who felt security risks were too great to undertake a particular investigation.

Standards

Once an investigation was completed, we had to assess our findings. Most assessments of a government's human-rights practices are factual—did the government commit the acts in question? But the evaluation of some conduct depends less on what happened than on whether the behavior should be deemed a human-rights violation. The technical answer as to what qualifies can be found in widely ratified international treaties, which outline in considerable detail how governments are supposed to treat people—the freedoms that governments are supposed to allow and the responsibilities that they have a duty to fulfill. Those standards were important for our legitimacy—if a government questioned why we were holding it to those standards, we could often point out that it had ratified the treaty that codifies them. Yet for our purposes, the precise wording of the treaty mattered less than what the public believed was right or wrong—or, more important, what human-rights groups, through our investigations and reporting, could persuade the public was right or wrong. Virtually every law or treaty needs interpretation. When does ill-treatment become torture? What limits can a government appropriately place on free speech? What are the elements of a fair trial? As I said, in many places where we worked, the courts lacked the capacity or inclination to make those determinations, so we had to advocate in the court of public opinion.

Part of the challenge is that human rights by their nature are meant to restrain government conduct even if a majority of citizens favors that conduct. Particularly in such circumstances, we must persuade the public that violating human rights is wrong, otherwise our exposure of the conduct will not prove shameful. Public morality is not fixed. It changes with circumstances and over time. An underappreciated but fundamentally important part of the work of human-rights groups is the effort to shape that morality, and that is where compelling facts come into play.

I learned early in my legal career about the power of facts, when I served as a clerk for Edward Weinfeld, a U.S. District Court judge in Manhattan, who at the time was widely considered the most distinguished federal trial judge in the country. He had skipped college and gone directly to law school—an unusual route for American lawyers—which left him uninterested in legal theory. He believed that only the facts mattered, that if he understood the facts, he would know how to decide a case. He rejected realism, the dominant legal view when I was in law school, which holds that a judge's inclinations and prejudices tend to determine the court's ruling.

His "old-fashioned" view was instrumental in forging my approach to defending human rights. My brief experience as a civil litigator and somewhat longer experience as a prosecutor taught me as well that most people are persuaded by facts, not law. The law influences people's view of propriety, and people's predispositions certainly affect how they assess a given situation, but the facts play the central role in persuading the public whether a government or individual acted properly.

Our reporting, therefore, did not spend much time on human-rights law. We used it as a framework—otherwise, we would be just another group with an opinion—but we looked to people's moral judgment to assess the facts we presented, and we tried to present the facts as compellingly as possible, spotlighting the plight of individual victims to shape that moral judgment. If the public did not disapprove of the government behavior we described, citing a treaty was unlikely to change their mind.

Our reports needed to reflect the objectivity and seriousness that we brought to our investigations, but they were meant to be gripping reads, appealing to not only people's minds but also their emotions. We wanted people to understand viscerally the wrongfulness of the conduct described.

Fortunately, the moral judgments of most people largely correspond to human-rights standards. That is certainly true when it comes to how they want to be treated themselves. I have never encountered someone who wants to be summarily executed, tortured, censored, jailed without due process, discriminated against, or denied housing, education, and health care. However, what people want for themselves is not necessarily what they want for others. People may want to deprive others of these rights for reasons of selfishness, animosity, or political advancement.

One key challenge for the human-rights movement is to persuade people that others should be treated the same way that they want to be treated themselves. In part, that is a matter of persuading them to see themselves as part of a larger community in which everyone deserves respect for their rights. In part, we must make clear to them that the likelihood of a government violating their rights increases if they countenance the government violating the rights of others. That was the insight of Pastor Martin Niemöller in his famous verse that begins, "First they came for the communists, and I did not speak out, because I was not a communist."

When governments succeed in making human-rights violations popular, it is harder to shame them. If we were to point out, for example, that Hungarian prime minister Viktor Orbán was closing the door to asylum seekers, it would have no effect, because such abuse was popular with his core constituency. Shaming is difficult whenever a leader succeeds in demonizing a segment of the population, such as immigrants or lesbian, gay, bisexual, and transgender (LGBT) people. The same is true when a leader claims to be defending "traditional" or national values from the "interference" of international actors.

Fortunately, even when abuses are popular with one audience— say, a far-right leader's base—those same acts may remain shameful with others. City dwellers are often more rights-oriented than rural residents, for example. Shaming can also work if the abusive government depends on aid or assistance from countries where the populist agenda remains shameful. That gave rise to the strategy we used to address autocratic policies in Poland and Hungary (more on that later).

A similar strategy can be pursued when a government uses censorship to prevent its citizens from knowing that its reputation is taking a beating; such a government still cares about its international reputation. It wants the international community to see its officials as legitimate leaders and to extend them the benefits that such status confers. Human Rights Watch thus could speak to that community to influence the conduct of the target government, as we did in the case of China. We also targeted the Chinese diaspora, particularly students, many of whom stayed in touch with friends and family in China and would later return there.

We felt that challenging the persecution of LGBT people, when popular, required a different approach. As interpreted by various UN treaty bodies, discrimination on the basis of "sex" is understood to prohibit discrimination on the basis of not only gender but also sexual orientation and gender identity, because the only distinction between, for example, a straight and gay man is the gender of the people with whom he has "sex." But that legal analysis matters less than persuading the public that it is wrong to penalize LGBT people because of such a fundamental aspect of who they are. Here, a certain pragmatism was required. We tried to fight the worst abuses of LGBT rights. That is how, in 2008, even the Vatican, which considers same-sex relations to be "sinful," was persuaded to oppose violence and discrimination against LGBT people as well as the criminalization of same-sex relations.

In 2010 we convinced UN secretary-general Ban Ki-moon to attend an annual Human Rights Day (December 10) event on LGBT rights that we helped to organize at the United Nations. He used the occasion to speak for the first time about the importance of decriminalizing same-sex relations between consenting adults and ending violence and discrimination based on sexual orientation and gender identity. This was a remarkable step for Ban, a South Korean, given how conservative his country is on LGBT issues. In 2014, we adopted that approach to help secure a landmark UN Human Rights Council resolution on the same issue.

We tried to rack up easier wins where we could, with the aim of building momentum for more global recognition of LGBT rights. That meant a greater focus on, say, Latin America and Southeast Asia, where significant progress was made, in comparison with Africa. In 2007, Argentina, Brazil, and Uruguay took the lead in introducing the Yogyakarta Principles, which detailed the application of international human-rights law to sexual orientation and gender identity. Brazil, Chile, Colombia, and Uruguay led the UN Human Rights Council resolution. We also fought hard against any backsliding on what should have been favorable terrain, such as in 2019, when parts of Poland, a member of the European Union, started to declare "LGBT-free zones."

A number of governments claimed that LGBT rights were Western impositions antithetical to their culture, as if no one in their country would want such rights independently. Ironically, as we pointed out, the "sodomy" laws used to prosecute LGBT people were often written by colonial powers, particularly Britain. Similar charges of Western influence were made with respect to women's rights and religious freedom. Autocratic leaders such as Uganda's president Museveni often revved up such demonization of unpopular minorities to redeem their popularity at a time when the public was tiring of their leader's oppressive rule.

Responding to such claims required speaking through the voice of local people instead of our own. Graeme Reid, the thoughtful and insightful South African who was the longtime director of Human Rights Watch's LGBT rights program, expertly navigated these tactical choices. We pursued a particularly effective example of this approach in the Middle East and North Africa by compiling a video and accompanying report of LGBT activists in the region describing their own lives and their efforts to fight discrimination.

We did something similar for women's rights. In Saudi Arabia, we sometimes spotlighted Saudi women who sought the right to drive, or the right to travel or work without the need to secure the consent of a male guardian. Promoting local actors showed that it was local authorities imposing their views, not Western governments.

In Egypt under President Hosni Mubarak, police posing as

gay men arranged meetings through online chat rooms and then detained and tortured the victims. When I consulted with members of our leading partner at the time, the Egyptian Organization for Human Rights, they implored me not to take on the issue for fear it would discredit their attempts to address Mubarak's political repression. We understood their concern but did not want it to stop us. So we decided to focus on the problem of torture, not only against gay men but also against a range of other victims, such as dissidents and Islamists. This paralleled our larger strategy, later often articulated by Graeme, of trying to build broader concern for the rights of LGBT people by presenting them as the canary in a coal mine, a warning of wider attacks on rights to come.

In the context of this broader effort, I traveled to Egypt for a 2004 news conference to release our report on the entrapment and torture of gay men. The Egyptian Organization for Human Rights did not join us, but five other Egyptian organizations did, including the Egyptian Initiative for Personal Rights, led by a young activist named Hossam Bahgat. He was to emerge as one of Egypt's leading human-rights voices, though persecuted by the government of President Abdel Fattah El-Sisi. After the news conference, we arranged for forty-four members of the U.S. Congress to write to Mubarak condemning the arrests. It was heartening to see the number of arrests drop dramatically, although over the years police occasionally resurrected the practice.

I made a significant mistake on LGBT rights in 2012 in dealing with a wealthy Saudi donor who insisted on a written statement that Human Rights Watch would not use his gift to defend LGBT rights in the Middle East. I accepted the restriction because I knew we had plenty of other money to support our work on LGBT rights in the Middle East, so the condition for this one contribution would make no real difference. In 2019, someone sent us a letter bringing to light the arrangement. That I had agreed to the condition caused consternation among Human Rights Watch staff, so we decided to return the gift. I apologized for not sufficiently appreciating that some people would take my acceptance of the donor's terms as legitimizing differential treatment for LGBT people, though that was not my intent.

Media Attention

Once we assembled our evidence and published a report, our aim was to maximize media attention regarding governmental abuse. When I left Human Rights Watch, there were one thousand media mentions of our efforts on a typical day. Due to such attention, abusive governments took a reputational beating, which frequently led to their attacking us. We won those battles because our reports were so carefully investigated, written, and reviewed. Moreover, if a first report failed to secure significant reform, we kept reporting the government's misconduct. Ultimately, governments recognized that the only way to end the bad press was to stop the bad conduct.

Governments have always lied, sometimes organizing their own propaganda (remember *Pravda*?). To disseminate lies through the mainstream media, governments had to contend with journalists and editors, many of whom conscientiously sought to convey the truth. Social media has changed that. Governments and their allies now enlist trolls who convincingly twist reality, making it more difficult for the public to recognize the propaganda. And there is almost always some media entity willing to republish what they say. The dissemination of "fake news" made our efforts at public shaming more difficult. The distortion on social media, the cacophony of claim and counterclaim, made it harder to discern the truth.

The Russian and Chinese governments in particular have become more sophisticated with their broadcast efforts. Russia's RT, formerly Russia Today, and China's CGTN mimic in appearance, pace, and tone a Western news channel such as CNN or BBC. Many people recognize that these are government propaganda outlets, but many do not.

Our reputation for objective reporting helped us to counteract these efforts. Most journalists understood that when Human Rights Watch issued a report, it was fair and accurate. Their coverage of it magnified the reach of our voice and made it easier for conscientious consumers of the media to arrive at the truth.

For as long as I led Human Rights Watch, some people bemoaned the demise of "naming and shaming" as an effective tool. They imagined halcyon days in which governments supposedly jumped at the command of human-rights groups rather than face media opprobrium. In 1999, for example, David Rieff wrote in *The New York Times* that the human-rights movement was "in trouble" because our investigations and reports "no longer have the impact they once did." In fact, it was never as simple as the critics suggested. Shaming is a process that rarely yields quick results. Developing the political will among sympathetic governments to apply diplomatic and economic pressure against an abusive one also almost always requires a shift in public opinion about the target over time. Yet the enormous efforts that governments make to counter criticism of their rights abuses show that *they* continue to care about shaming. That is true even for the most powerful governments, such as China, making it likely that shaming shifts the cost-benefit calculations that lead to human-rights violations.

Some have offered alternatives to shaming, but they are unsatisfactory. The idea that trading with a country over time will lead to a stronger economy and hence a middle class that insists on its rights has now been profoundly discredited; witness the cases of China and Russia. The idea that providing educational opportunities so officials can become more enlightened about the best way to respect human rights—often referred to as "technical assistance"—is laughable in most repressive countries. Those officials would like nothing more than to substitute quiet seminars for public condemnation. The idea that building a human-rights "movement" will suffice ignores how rarely popular mobilization occurs, how difficult it is to sustain, how few issues a public will mobilize to address, and how the publicizing of government misconduct—the essence of shaming—is necessary for popular mobilization.

Shaming, alas, does not always work. Some leaders, particularly those who believe that staying in power is the key to staying alive, have become so repressive that they have little reputation left to tarnish, such as Syria's Bashar al-Assad or North Korea's Kim Jong Un. But most leaders want to maintain a reputation for serving their people, to ease domestic discontent and to avoid becoming international pariahs. Shaming and the pressure it helps to spawn are not panaceas, but I believe they are the best option we have. The alternative is fatalistic acquiescence, an option I reject.

—

Communicating effectively with journalists is a skill I had to develop. As I would regularly point out, it is essential to keep things simple, even though the world is complex. Journalists look to Human Rights Watch to guide them to the essence. All of us at Human Rights Watch had to distill the vast quantity of information in our heads into the key points to communicate.

Broadcast media today typically have only a few minutes of airtime, and they often contacted us with certain preconceptions about how an on-air conversation would go. I always entered a broadcast interview with two or three key points that I wanted to make—people rarely remember more than three points—and then figured out a way to get them across. My answers began by responding to the questions asked, but I then pivoted to make the points I felt were most important. I knew it was essential to keep all comments crisp and to the point. Broadcast journalists are intolerant of long answers, favoring quick, incisive interventions to keep their audience engaged. That requires clarity of thought. The old adage that I would have written something shorter but I ran out of time is doubly true for broadcast media.

Sharp, focused commentary is less important when briefing a print journalist, but I found it was a must if I wanted to be quoted, the ideal way to get my points across. Length restrictions are imposed on print journalists, so a wordy comment is less likely to be used than a pithy one. Many broadcast and print journalists like to use repeated questions to push sources past their comfort zone in the hope of enticing them to make a provocative comment. I found the key to avoiding that pitfall was not to be afraid to repeat myself—"As I said . . ."

Another way to convey a message is to write an opinion piece or a policy analysis. Most major newspapers have a page reserved for such pieces, and some important journals specialize in them. I wrote hundreds of these articles during my time at Human Rights Watch. Editors at these publications had a plethora of submissions to choose from, so breaking through required many of the same attributes as a successful media interview. Points had to be stated clearly, logically presented, and conveyed with powerful, engaging language.

In my earlier days, we depended on people buying a physical copy of a publication to notice the article. Social media changed that; we used it to promote any URL, although a prestigious locale certainly helped to get an article noticed.

One method to attract media attention was to spotlight a particular victim. We tried to make government abuses come to life with compelling individual examples rather than statistics about patterns. In one of my two appearances on *The Colbert Report*—by far the most challenging of my television appearances, because I had to struggle to keep up with Colbert's fast-paced deadpan jokes—I was asked to name a next-generation Nelson Mandela. I chose Liu Xiaobo of China and Nabeel Rajab of Bahrain, each of whom exemplified a determination to achieve rights-respecting democracy in their country. Each at the time faced long imprisonment for their work. Aleksei Navalny, a charismatic opposition figure, played that role in Russia until his death in a remote Arctic prison. Jamal Khashoggi, the opposition journalist who was murdered by the Saudi government in Istanbul, played that role for Saudi Arabia. Narges Mohammadi served that function for women's rights in Iran.

Because publicity was key to our ability to shame abusive governments, my colleagues and I made ourselves as available as possible to the media. Most journalists were sympathetic, but I also made a point of appearing on hostile media to reach a broader audience. Before Bill O'Reilly was taken off the air because of a sexual misconduct scandal, I appeared regularly on his show on Fox News. He liked the give and take, calling me a "stand-up guy" for joining him. Right-wing broadcasters like Tucker Carlson and Sean Hannity thought they could use me to make points that their conservative audiences would like, but I figured out how to make my points. I recognized that they were well prepared on only the narrow point on which they wanted to grill me; if I could shift the conversation slightly to a related topic, their hesitation on a fast-paced show allowed me to exert sufficient control over the dialogue to deliver my message.

I even appeared a few times on Russia's RT. Knowing it was a propaganda station, I insisted beforehand that they run the entire interview without edits. I figured I would be able to control the conversation enough to insert my views into whatever they wanted to discuss. Twice they honored our arrangement, but the third time, in

November 2015, RT added a running line of obviously fake Twitter commentary. That was the last time I appeared on RT.

Not only hostile media asked tough questions. BBC presenters have a deserved reputation for challenging their guests. The most intense ones host *HARDTalk,* a half-hour endurance test of being pelted with difficult questions. I subjected myself to the nerve-racking ordeal three times. I never took offense at tough questions and tried to answer them as calmly and objectively as I could, which was not always easy.

Despite the gravity of our work, our dealings with the media were not uniformly grim. In February 2019, as we were drawing attention to Beijing's persecution in Xinjiang, Sophie Richardson, our China director, asked me to lead a news conference in Geneva. As Chinese authorities were forcibly indoctrinating detained Uyghurs, they compelled them to sing for visitors a rendition of the children's song "If You're Happy and You Know It, Clap Your Hands." To highlight this callousness, Sophie dared me, as I described it, to sing a verse at the news conference, which of course I did, ending with the clap, clap of my hands.

My most difficult media appearance was in Brazil—and not for the reason one might imagine. I was appearing on the popular show *Roda Viva.* A group of journalists sat in an elevated circle firing questions at me, seated below, for nearly an hour and a half. I did not have great difficulty answering the questions, but as the show proceeded, it became more and more difficult to keep my (evidently tainted) lunch down. I could have asked for a break, but the show was filmed as if live and I was afraid that my request for a pause would be interpreted as a reaction to being pelted with questions, so I struggled to quell my stomach. My answers became shorter and shorter as the show proceeded, but I got through it.

My most rewarding news conference was in Kabul in March 2012, when we released a report on the imprisonment of women and girls in Afghanistan for "moral crimes," written by Heather Barr, an American lawyer and an enormously effective researcher who at the time was covering Afghanistan for Human Rights Watch from her base in Kabul. These supposed crimes were either poorly defined or not defined at all by any Afghan penal code. As I walked into the large hotel hall in Kabul for the conference, I saw scores of television cameras, most from tiny broadcast facilities. The sheer number spoke to the vibrant civil society that was developing in Afghanistan after the Taliban were toppled in 2001. Sadly, the Taliban's resurgence in 2021 reversed that progress.

Meeting with Abusive Governments

Beyond generating pressure on abusive governments from afar, we tried to speak with their officials directly. That enabled us to drive home for them our awareness of their government's abuses and our ability to reveal them. An in-person meeting, if it went well, could be a way to discuss solutions. Of course, these could be difficult meetings—no official likes to be criticized or to have their misdeeds exposed—so the challenge was to keep the conversation constructive.

My preparation for head-of-state meetings always included substantial consultation with our researcher for the country. Typically, they prepared a background memo and drafted talking points. We then met and kicked around strategies. I wanted to know as much as possible about an official's temperament so I could try to regulate the tone of the meeting. Most important, I wanted to know how the leader was likely to respond to the points I would make so I could be prepared with a rebuttal. The last thing I wanted was for officials to leave a meeting feeling they had an effective defense to our criticisms. The same logic applied to our reports. The best reports anticipated and rebutted a government's defense. If a report presented only our findings, and the abusive government responded upon publication, journalists would be left to describe two sides to a dispute, leaving the reader in a poor position to choose. But if the report anticipated the abusive government's likely defense and rebutted it, that would influence what journalists wrote.

After the preparatory discussions, I drafted notes for the meeting, which helped me to organize my thoughts and master the most important facts. I tried to keep my notes to a single page—enough to remind me of the order in which I wanted to raise points but without too much detail—because during the meeting my attention had to remain focused on my interlocutor. My effectiveness would have diminished if I had to comb through lengthy notes.

Once the meeting began, as often as not I left my notes in my jacket pocket. The ability to speak from memory rather than notes made a stronger impression. I wanted to make clear that I was expressing my personal convictions rather than repeating something that the staff had told me.

I almost always brought the most expert staff member with me to government meetings, and I told them to intervene if they thought their more nuanced understanding would help to steer the conversation productively. That was not typical protocol—an official's aides rarely interjected—but I wanted to ensure that we made the most persuasive arguments.

I often felt a heavy responsibility entering the room for such meetings. Reading the room during the first few minutes was important. Subtle hints of body language or tone of voice, the formality of the handshake, or the facial expression could signal whether the meeting had the potential to be constructive or should be steered toward a tough, "lay down the law" approach. My style, which reflects my temperament, was never to raise my voice, regardless of my outrage at what the government was doing. I could not allow myself to be overwhelmed by emotion. These were high-stakes meetings, and I had to stay calm and analytically focused on the task at hand. I spoke firmly but politely, yet I was not "diplomatic" as the term is typically understood, meaning that I did not use euphemisms or pull my punches.

I tried to control not only the tone of a meeting but also its pace. There was always more to cover than time, and government officials tended to speak at length on uncontroversial topics to avoid more difficult ones. Managing the agenda meant watching the clock to know when to move on. If the agenda was crowded, I saved one or two "last-minute" topics to mention as the meeting was closing. A brief discussion of the topics was almost never precluded despite the supposed absence of time.

Government officials also tried to control the agenda. For example, in a 2012 lunch meeting that Corinne Dufka, our West Africa director, and I had with President Alpha Condé of Guinea, he opened the meeting with a seemingly endless monologue, a classic ploy used by officials who want to avoid discussing their human-rights problems. We were able to interject our concerns only when I politely suggested that he begin his lunch before it got cold. As he settled into his repast, we took him to task for failing to prosecute the military officers who were responsible for committing a notorious massacre with mass rapes at a stadium in Conakry in 2009. (Many of the perpetrators were finally convicted after trial in July 2024.)

Meeting with senior officials is sometimes disparaged as elite rather than popular advocacy, but it is the best way to ensure that the ultimate decision-maker fully appreciates the consequences of their behavior. Moreover, to dismiss it as elite ignores that its power comes from a very non-elite source—the ability to shame the government for its conduct by reflecting the public's sense of right and wrong.

It was necessary to treat even heads of state as peers, something that was difficult for me at first (I was as intimidated as the next person) but became easier as I gained experience. Leaders may like groveling but do not respect it. I represented an effort to hold the government to international standards—an appropriate concern for a head of state—and tried to carry myself that way.

With the collapse of the Soviet Union in 1991, Uzbekistan, a Soviet republic, suddenly became an independent state, the most populous by far in Central Asia. The leader of its Communist Party, Islam Karimov, became president of the new country and repurposed the repressive Soviet machinery to serve his harsh personal rule. He targeted pious Muslims who practiced their religion outside of state institutions, subjecting them to arrest, incommunicado detention, and prison sentences of up to twenty years for violations of strict laws on religion and alleged "anti-constitutional activity." Torture was rampant, and some prisoners died in custody.

In 2000, my colleagues and I met in Tashkent with the justice minister, the foreign minister, the first deputy prime minister, the deputy general prosecutor, and the deputy chair of the Supreme Court, all of whom described the rules against torture, the procedures for fighting torture, and the officials assigned to investigate torture. It sounded impressive—except that Uzbeks kept telling us that they had been tortured, and no one was ever disciplined or prosecuted for it.

It was clear that the officials with whom we met had little interest, and in some cases little ability, to stop the torture. At least we let them know that we saw through their nonsense. At a meeting in the Interior Ministry, knowing that people were being tortured in the basement, I said as much, explaining that the laws and procedures were meaningless if the results were so negligible.

I had another tough meeting in June 2011 with the Egyptian military council that took power after the fall of Hosni Mubarak. Heba Morayef, a Cairo-based Egyptian who was our researcher at the time, also attended. Twice, the lead general exploded in rage when we objected to, first, the trial of civilian protesters before military courts, and, second, the military's threats to journalists who criticized it. If he was trying to intimidate us, he failed. At one point he defended the intrusive and demeaning "virginity tests" to which the military subjected certain women protesters, claiming the practice was necessary to ensure that the women were not raped in detention. I asked whether that meant that women who had previously had sex were fair game for rape. His excuse played so poorly that, by the end of our meeting, he promised to end virginity tests. To lock in his commitment, we announced it the next day at a Cairo news conference.

My meetings with the late Ethiopian prime minister Meles Zenawi illustrated how we tried to open channels of communication with senior officials in repressive governments. My first meeting with him took place in 2009. I was joined by Leslie Lefkow, an American lawyer who oversaw Human Rights Watch work on the country. Meles, seen as a towering figure in Africa because of his intellect, presided over a government that brooked no dissent. Although it was an improvement over its ruthless predecessor, independent political activity was largely prohibited. Critics faced harassment, arrest, and even torture. The government was committed to economic development, but it steered international development assistance toward loyalists. It made it extremely difficult for human-rights groups to operate in the country, subjecting activists to criminal prosecution. Indeed, just before I saw Meles, his government expelled our researcher Ben Rawlence, who had entered the country as a tourist because the government would not allow an open investigation.

Meeting in Meles's somber, paneled office in Addis Ababa, we talked for two hours as he defended his government's behavior. Toward the end of the meeting, which remained constructive in tone even if there was little agreement, I asked Meles why it was possible for me to meet with him in the capital while his security forces had just expelled our researcher. He said (passing the buck) that the Ethiopian government was a collective leadership, so he could not resolve such matters on his own. He suggested instead that we continue to sneak in our researchers!

In 2010, I had just taken the main stage to speak on a late-afternoon panel at the Munich Security Conference when I noticed Meles seated in the second row. We nodded to each other. When my panel concluded, an aide approached and said that the prime minister would like to see me in his hotel room. I canceled my dinner plans and, with just the two of us present, held another two-hour conversation. I did not persuade him to ease his repression, but I took his openness to discussing his rule as modestly encouraging. Alas, he died in 2012 at age fifty-seven.

I held a more typical meeting in June 2022 with Ugandan president Museveni. The locale was his wife's rural estate in southwestern Uganda, which my colleagues and I reached by military helicopter from Kampala. It was an all-day affair, as Museveni annoyingly forced us to sit around while he and his wife held an interminable meeting with a small group of political supporters, all dressed in Museveni's trademark yellow. Because of the pandemic, we met outside at a considerable social distance. I deliberately started with things to which it would be easier for him to agree, such as prosecuting a security official who had been running a detention, torture, and extortion racket, and accepting the principle that journalists should be allowed to monitor police conduct at protests without getting shot. Once he assented to these points, including a pledge of "zero tolerance" for torture and other abuse by the armed forces, I moved on to topics that I knew for him would be more fraught, such as removing his ban on Facebook and easing his restrictions on foreign funding of civic groups. The meeting stayed congenial.

After the meeting, his communications staff informed journalists that Museveni had told me, "No one can teach me about the subject of human rights because that is what I fought for," alluding to his overthrow of the tyrant Idi Amin. That was a low bar, but it was still high enough from my perspective, because it reflected his acceptance of the need to respect human rights. I made a point of telling the

Ugandan media the next day about the commitments he had made so the journalists could maintain pressure on him to keep them.

When a government is more democratic than autocratic, the biggest challenge can be cutting through a leader's false belief that the country's forces are respecting human rights. In November 2011, at the manicured onetime presidential office and residence in Mexico City known as Los Pinos, I met for two hours with then president Felipe Calderón. Our purpose was to discuss a new Human Rights Watch report on torture, executions, and "disappearances" by his military as part of its deployment against drug cartels. I was joined by our Americas director, José Miguel Vivanco, and Nik Steinberg, our Mexico researcher at the time, who was the principal author of the report. (Nik went on to join the U.S. government and became chief speechwriter for Secretary of State Antony Blinken.)

Because the drug cartels had corrupted so many local Mexican police forces, and the new national police force was still small, Calderón deployed military forces against the cartels, launching, in 2007, a "war on drugs." However, the military had no experience in traditional police investigative techniques—using informants, wiretaps, and tips from the public—so it was prone to torture and other abusive methods. Yet Calderón for years adamantly denied that the military had committed a single abuse, when in fact abuses were surging. We had detailed that extensively, so in the meeting I instinctively did something that I had never done before or since: I suggested that we read our report together.

We went paragraph by paragraph, case by case, starting with one of a young father whom Mexican Marines had forcibly disappeared in November 2010 after a routine traffic stop. Calderón soon saw that our report was detailed, which allowed me to discuss what the president could do to halt the abuses we described, the purpose of the meeting. Gratifyingly, within weeks he publicly acknowledged for the first time the military malfeasance and adopted some of our key recommendations for preventing future abuses, such as ending the interrogation of suspects on military bases, creating a national database of the "disappeared," and approving a new protocol for the use of lethal force.

It was possible to engage in constructive conversations with a surprising range of officials. In September 2017, I met with the emir of

Qatar at a townhouse on Manhattan's Upper East Side during the annual opening of the UN General Assembly. Qatar was becoming more prominent as its hosting of the 2022 World Cup approached. I had recently visited the country, mainly to discuss conditions for migrant workers who were laboring on World Cup facilities, and had met with various senior officials, but not the emir, who had been traveling. During the meeting in New York, he and I sat in the customary adjacent chairs at the end of a room, with a line of his aides along the wall. Because the meeting had been set up hastily, I was unaccompanied. After each suggestion that I made about better rights practices, he turned to his aides and said, in essence, "We can do that, can't we?" Of course, they agreed. The government was clearly eager to please. The biggest problem was that the meeting was going so well that I forgot a basic rule—never smile during official photographs. The Saudi government, which at the time had a deeply adversarial relationship with Qatar, used one of the resulting photos to suggest that whenever I criticized Saudi conduct, I was being paid by the Qatari government to do so. Postings on Twitter embellished the photo with a crude drawing of the Emir handing me cash under the table.

—

Some governments that violate human-rights abuses are just neglectful or unaware rather than calculating. Such governments are best approached in a spirit of collaboration. An example of that was my 2016 trip to Jakarta.

Under the leadership of Shantha Rau Barriga, our program working on the rights of people with disabilities mounted a major campaign to address the problem of shackling, the act of chaining or confining in animal sheds or small rooms people with psychosocial disabilities such as depression, schizophrenia, or bipolar condition. Their families typically felt they had no choice due to the lack of mental-health services and support in local communities. Shantha and her team documented the practice in more than sixty countries and made significant progress in curtailing it. I joined her to address the problem in Indonesia, where more than fifty-seven thousand people had been shackled at least once in their lives.

Affected people there needed access to locally available counseling and medicines to live independently and free of shackles. These services tended to be dispensed by provincial governments. Since each province in that enormous country can be vast, some people in need of help had to make a three-day trek to the provincial capital. The obvious solution was to train community health workers to provide counseling and access to medication.

We thought the health minister would be sympathetic to our view, so we entered a meeting with her with the aim of keeping it collaborative. One of our local partners had told us that we would be meeting the minister on her birthday, so we brought along a cake. She appreciated the gesture, and the meeting proceeded positively. She agreed to explore our suggestion for providing basic mental-health services locally and committed to making medication available across the country's nearly ten thousand primary health centers. (During the meeting, she also repudiated the public claim of one of her deputies that homosexuality is an illness in need of a cure—while the deputy sat at the same table opposite us, eyeing the ground.)

Within a year, the Indonesian Health Ministry had trained twenty-five thousand experts who would train staff in every primary health center across the country. The ministry also rolled out a community outreach program in which health workers went house to house to collect data, raise awareness, and provide services relating to twelve measures of family health, including mental health. As of September 2020, the program had reached roughly 70 percent of Indonesian households—forty-eight million of them—effectively turning the tide on shackling.

Enlisting Influential Governments

We routinely met with senior officials of influential governments, usually democracies, to encourage them to exert pressure for change on abusive governments. Many democratic governments treat the promotion of human rights as part of their foreign policy, but they often must be encouraged to play an active role. That encouragement can come through the media, by its spotlighting their responsibility to defend human rights or even their complicity in bad conduct. Ideally, though, we sat down with officials from these governments to make the case for constructive action.

Such third-party advocacy seems an obvious tool, but not everyone agrees. Amnesty International for many years was reluctant to engage in it for fear of reinforcing global power imbalances. Instead, it focused on mobilizing its members to pressure governments. In his book *The Endtimes of Human Rights*, Stephen Hopgood of the School of Oriental and African Studies, University of London, praised the moral purity of early Amnesty supporters who stood "as spiritual guardians outside the prevailing global regime of politics and money" while maintaining a "detachment from power politics." The more recent move to "decolonize" the human-rights movement—to promote local rather than international actors—is born of a similar instinct.

The human-rights record of Western governments is hardly beyond reproach. That is certainly true of the U.S. government, which has both the largest overseas security-force presence and a disturbing record of at times using those forces abusively. It also supports many abusive governments. Some believe that such dirty hands should preclude human-rights advocacy. Others, often waving the banner of anti-imperialism, would rather focus on remedying Western ills than addressing repression by non-Western governments.

I understand these objections but have never found them sufficient to reject influential democratic governments as potential defenders of human rights. Yes, one should work to redress global power imbalances, but how can I say to a political prisoner languishing in custody or a villager facing violent attack that they must put up with their plight because I do not want to enlist an influential government that could have helped because their power is arguably unfair? Yes, we should insist that all governments live up to global standards, but how can I tell a family expelled from their home or a child deprived of an education that they must grin and bear it because the influential governments that might help them have checkered human-rights records themselves? Yes, we should seek to remedy the continuing harms of Western imperialism, but can we really insist that the plight of people suffering at the hands of non-Western governments is less important? Accordingly, we devoted significant attention to the public-policy work needed to enlist influential governments, making it a trademark of the organization.

An initial goal was to have a seat at the table with the most senior officials setting foreign policy for those governments. Policymakers tend to see activist organizations as only a thorn in their side. I wanted us to be seen as a respected contributor to policy discussions. That required entering these meetings with at least the same sophistication as our interlocutors.

Aryeh Neier had already set the organization in that direction. As I mentioned, he epitomized professional advocacy. My aim was to continue to embellish that tradition. We succeeded in part because our research gave us a deeper understanding of the relevant facts than most government officials possessed. Governments have embassies around the world but are constrained by security fears (we traveled where they did not) and competing concerns (economic, political, cultural, consular), while we could focus exclusively on human rights. I attended many government meetings in which the Human Rights Watch researcher had the most detailed understanding of the problems being discussed.

In addition, we tended to be more creative in devising ways to advance human rights. Even well-intentioned governments often had not thought through the options in as much detail as we had. We were frequently the ones who came to the meeting with suggestions about bilateral or multilateral pressure that could be exerted on an abusive government.

———

Governments that violated human rights at home but whose help we sought on foreign policy were sophisticated enough to recognize the principled basis of our interventions and were willing to discuss common foreign-policy concerns even as we criticized them for their domestic rights practices. We never pulled our punches on domestic wrongdoing to secure cooperation on foreign policy.

"Do the right thing" is not an argument that tends to work with policymakers. Rather, we considered the range of national interests that a government was pursuing and explained where human rights fit among them. We took on those who asserted that other foreign-policy interests were more important, describing why better respect for human rights would advance the national interest. We might explain that a democratic government's support for a friendly autocrat was breeding resentment among the people of the autocrat's country, or that closing one's eyes to an abusive wartime practice would create a precedent of lawlessness that would endanger friendly militaries.

We researched the realistic policy options for the official with whom we were meeting, which required talking to people in their government. We put ourselves in the shoes of our interlocutor and sought to make refined, feasible recommendations, believing these were more likely to be taken seriously than more generic ones. A Dutch justice minister, Ernst Hirsch Ballin, once told me that what attracted him to Human Rights Watch was that we understood the political possibilities before him as a minister.

Our policy sophistication led journalists to seek us out not only to describe human-rights violations but also to assess the response by the world's major powers. The media in an influential country might not be terribly interested in distant repression, but spotlighting their government's response created a story that was seen to be more appealing to local readers, increasing our ability to shame the target government. Our heightened media profile enhanced our clout with the influential government.

I am not a rabble-rouser. I have no special skills for speaking at rallies or mobilizing a crowd. But I could speak in compelling terms about the reasons to defend human rights and the policy steps to be taken. Because I was often the most visible representative of Human Rights Watch—in the media, at policy forums, or in government meetings—the organization's profile inevitably paralleled my personality. That approach tended to play better with government officials than a more incendiary style.

Professionalizing our advocacy, over time, made more governments willing to receive us at senior levels. They came to accept us as regular participants in their policy debates, and we came to expect such meetings—and asked for them. *The Washington Post*, in describing our campaign to create the International Criminal Court, wrote that Human Rights Watch (along with Amnesty International) "might as well be major countries, measured by the clout they have in laying the intellectual and political groundwork for the kind of permanent court they want."

Globalizing Advocacy

In the 1980s, we focused mainly on Washington. The U.S. government's support for the highly abusive right-wing governments in El Salvador and Guatemala and the Contra rebels in Nicaragua made it a useful surrogate for those forces. People in the United States may not otherwise have been preoccupied by atrocities in small Central American countries, but they were troubled by their government's support for them. A similar public concern helped us to attack the U.S. government when it supported abusive governments elsewhere and to enlist its influence on behalf of human rights.

As power became more dispersed, our advocacy, of necessity, became more global, with offices established for this purpose in key capitals around the world. Globalizing this presence (to match our global research footprint) was one of my big priorities. Because the media is so important for influencing governments, a global communications presence was a natural corollary.

The first step I took toward building advocacy capacity beyond Washington was to open an office in Brussels, the effective capital of the European Union. The EU had an obvious interest in promoting human rights globally and an economic clout that rivaled that of the United States.

For the role of first director of our Brussels office, and the only one during my tenure, I hired Lotte Leicht, a Danish lawyer who had previously worked at the Vienna-based International Helsinki Federation for Human Rights. Lotte developed an extensive set of contacts among European foreign-policy officials; she regularly texted ambassadors in Brussels and foreign ministers in their capitals, many of whom she knew personally. She could be relentless in badgering officials to address current abuses and to bring past perpetrators to justice.

Working with the European Union could be difficult because, under EU rules, external policy decisions must be agreed upon unanimously. With any member state able to veto action, that tends to produce lowest-common-denominator decisions. Lotte excelled at finding workarounds. She repeatedly emphasized that the unanimity rule should provide the floor, not the ceiling—that EU member states could act on their own or in subgroups even if action by the full EU was stymied.

Lotte worked closely with the EU high representative (effectively the EU foreign minister) and the high representative's European External Action Service (the EU foreign ministry) to secure strong human-rights statements. Although the high representative as a political matter could not deviate too far from the position of EU governments, and key decisions such as the imposition of sanctions still needed member-state unanimity, high representatives were empowered to issue statements in their own name. From the perspective of the target government, a high representative statement could almost substitute for a common EU position.

Over time, we added advocacy and media offices in other European capitals, including Paris, Berlin, London, and Stockholm. While the European Union as a whole continued to be an important target of our advocacy, many of our foreign-policy initiatives focused on particularly powerful EU members, especially Germany, France, and, when it was still a member, Britain. Their national positions mattered.

In the mid-2000s, I realized that complementing our advocacy in Washington with advocacy in various European capitals was still not enough. Often, the most powerful actor in an abusive country was not a Western power but a regional one—Japan in East Asia, India in South Asia, South Africa in much of Africa, or various Latin American democracies in their region. I thus began the gradual process of opening more advocacy and communications offices. George Soros made an extraordinary contribution to these efforts.

George had been an early supporter. When we were only Helsinki Watch and Americas Watch, we used to meet every Wednesday morning, typically in the board room of Random House, the U.S. publisher, of which, as I mentioned, Robert Bernstein, the chair of our board of directors, was the CEO. When Bernstein was ousted from Random House in 1989, the meetings moved to the Human Rights Watch office, at the time opposite the New York

Public Library. These meetings were strikingly ad hoc. One week a researcher reported on a trip to the Soviet bloc. The next week another researcher described a trip to Latin America. Anyone who showed up could contribute to strategizing about what we should do to address the human-rights problems identified. George periodically attended and became a financial contributor—among his first acts of philanthropy. Over time, his contribution grew considerably. In 1993, when Aryeh Neier stepped down as executive director of Human Rights Watch, he left to head George's foundation, called Open Society.

In 2010, to enable us to become a genuinely global organization not only in the scope of our research but also in the reach of our advocacy and communications, we planned a major fundraising campaign. Michele Alexander, my longtime partner as Human Rights Watch's development director who was responsible for much of our spectacular growth, made a donor pyramid, indicating how many people would have to contribute at various levels to meet our financial goals. Our aim was to secure five-year commitments—long enough to hire staff. We were worried about a financial cliff at the end of the five years but hoped that most donors would stick with us. In any event, five years would give us time if needed to find replacement contributors.

At the top of Michele's pyramid was a slot for someone who would give $10 million a year for five years. It was an ambitious goal. No one had ever come close to a gift of that size to Human Rights Watch. With Aryeh's blessing, I arranged to meet George at his office atop a high-rise in Midtown Manhattan. Aryeh joined us, and so did Bob Kissane, who was a member of our board, the founder of a fundraising firm, and an important adviser for many years.

As was my usual practice for meetings with prospective major donors, I did not send any paper in advance. I preferred to follow up with written materials once I understood with more nuance how a donor's interests might intersect with our ambitions. That allowed donors to play a greater role in defining the part of our work they might finance and enabled me to fine-tune a proposal to meet their requirements.

I described my vision for Human Rights Watch's future, how we needed to build a genuinely global organization to match the global reach of our research. George listened carefully and told me he agreed we needed not only to globalize our advocacy and communications efforts—we discussed offices that I hoped to open in Brazil, South Africa, India, and elsewhere—but also our fundraising, including outside Europe and North America. We batted around ideas, and then I came to the "ask." I explained that of all the people in Human Rights Watch's universe, George was the only one with both the means and the possible inclination to support us at the top level. Would he consider a gift of $10 million a year for five years?

George thought for a moment and then said he would do it for *ten* years. I was dumbfounded. Within two weeks, Michele and I had worked out the details—including benchmarks for diversifying our fundraising. The gift was major news, including articles in *The New York Times* and *The Guardian,* and a remarkable vote of confidence in our organization. It was the largest gift that George had made to a civic group and the largest by a big margin that Human Rights Watch had received. It transformed the organization into a truly global institution.

The gift, though, sparked questions. Would such a large gift make us beholden to George and his views? His gift at the time represented about 25 percent of our revenue. I said that George knew the organization well, understood the principles we applied, and would never make such a large gift to an organization that would deviate from those principles at the whim of a donor. Throughout my three decades leading Human Rights Watch, George never sought to impose his views on our work.

Globalizing Human Rights Watch's advocacy made sense, but some of the particulars turned out to be more complicated than I had anticipated. Some of the newer offices proved fruitful. The one in Japan played a key role in 2013 in persuading the UN Human Rights Council to create a commission of inquiry (a high-profile investigative and reporting body) for North Korea. The Australia office was an important voice for Southeast Asia as well as China. We began treating more countries as potential advocacy allies. We hoped to enlist Brazil, India, and South Africa. Each seemed to be a strong democracy with the potential to promote rights more broadly, at least in its region.

India at times had been a positive force for rights in Nepal, Bangladesh, Sri Lanka, Myanmar, and Tibet. In 2012, the Indian government, holding a rotating seat on the UN Security Council, voted favorably for resolutions addressing human-rights abuses in Syria. In 2012 and 2013, the Indian government supported resolutions at the UN Human Rights Council pressing Sri Lanka to investigate its military's large-scale war crimes. I had raised both issues in meetings with officials and at think tanks in Delhi and Mumbai. South Africa was influential in Zimbabwe, the South African Development Community (SADC), and the African Union. Brazil had been pressing for global standards to rein in mass electronic surveillance.

Even when one of these governments was less helpful than we had hoped, we generated pressure for more support. For example, during the 2012 session of the World Economic Forum in Davos, I held a contentious televised debate with Brazil's foreign minister about his country's abstention from a 2011 UN Security Council resolution condemning government atrocities in Syria. Over the next couple of days, the Brazilian press picked up the exchange and found the minister's position as troublesome as I had. That was exactly the kind of scrutiny that we needed to bring Brazil's foreign policy more in line with human-rights values. Having an office in Brazil meant we could attract such coverage regularly, helping to provide an alternative to the government's perspective on global issues.

This willingness to play a positive rights role diminished significantly with the arrival of Prime Minister Narendra Modi in India, President Jacob Zuma of South Africa, and President Jair Bolsonaro of Brazil. We had to drop plans to open an office in India because of severe restrictions enforced by the Modi government on access to charitable funds from abroad. In South Africa, the government's foreign policy focused on little beyond regional SADC issues. And in Brazil, our office in São Paulo became preoccupied with defending Brazil's democratic institutions and their ability to address serious abuses under a government that, for the first time since the military dictatorship, challenged basic democratic norms.

Severe repression also forced closure of our office in Cairo and limited the scope of our office in Bangkok. But other offices thrived, with Nairobi becoming a major hub for work in eastern Africa and

Beirut for work in the Middle East. We came to understand that we should deploy our regional offices flexibly, enlisting influential governments anywhere in the region, not focusing on only the government of the country where the office happened to be located.

Businesses

As a technical matter, human-rights law speaks to governments, not to private entities such as corporations. Yet we did extensive and quite successful work on corporations, which demonstrated the importance of presenting facts that people see as "wrong"—of appealing to people's moral judgments rather than legal chapter and verse.

In broad terms, we insisted that companies avoid complicity in the human-rights violations of governments. Were companies taking sufficient steps, we asked, to avoid contributing to those violations—or profiting from them—as spelled out in 2011 in the UN's nonbinding Guiding Principles on Business and Human Rights? We applied those principles, for example, when we pressed companies to avoid doing business in Israel's illegal settlements.

When I first began talking to business leaders about their human-rights practices, they tended to consider me delusional. Taking a chapter from Milton Friedman, their sole concern, they said, was to make a decent return for their shareholders. Human rights, in their view, should be left to activists.

Media attention, aided by our investigations and those of our allies, altered that benighted attitude. An exposé about a company's complicity in human-rights violations—in its workplace, its supply chain, or its effect on others—could be a reputational disaster, with significant financial consequences. It could affect the company's standing among its consumers and its shareholders, and its ability to attract and retain talent.

Our 1996 investigation of assembly plants (*maquiladoras*) in Mexico along the U.S. border revealed that the companies were dismissing pregnant women because they did not want to pay for their legally mandated maternity benefits. When confronted about this blatant discrimination, many of the companies effectively said that maternity benefits were expensive. After we published our report and mounted a public campaign, General Motors, a large *maquiladora* employer, suffered a reputational black eye and had no choice but to change this discriminatory practice.

The evolving view of companies could be seen in the more proactive position taken by the Canadian company Barrick Gold when, in 2010, we discussed with it a draft report on its Porgera Mine in Papua New Guinea. We found that the mine's security forces had carried out numerous gang rapes of local women. After the company's own investigation confirmed our findings, Barrick chose to coordinate its response with the release of our report. It condemned the rape, announced a "zero tolerance approach to human-rights abuses," and laid out the results of its investigation and the disciplinary measures it had taken. The company took a less severe media hit as a result.

For our work to be successful, businesses have to care about their reputations. Most major corporations do, but some enterprises do not have brand names or high profiles, draw very little media scrutiny, and therefore worry less about reputational damage. One ironic effect of this obscurity is that it helped to move larger, brand-name companies away from their instinctive opposition to government regulation of human-rights practices. When major businesses came to understand the benefits of respect for human rights—happier, more productive workers; less reputational risk—they also understood that respect for human rights would require investment. Fearing that while they made these investments, no-name companies would secure a competitive advantage by ignoring the issue, the larger companies pushed for government regulation requiring every business to abide by the same standards. Most often brand-name companies did not push for *strong* regulations, just enough to enable them to say they did what was required to avoid complicity in rights abuse. But still, this corporate openness to at least some government regulation of human-rights practices was an important improvement.

4

_____

Leading and Building
an Organization

W hen I took over as executive director of Human Rights Watch, I had no formal training and little experience running an organization. Aryeh was a giant in the field. I benefited enormously from having him as a mentor for five years, but I did not pretend to carry his weight. I was thirty-seven and had much to learn. I had to figure out what my management style would be, what internal culture I would promote, where I would direct our work, where I would focus my personal efforts, how I would handle fundraising, and where I would situate Human Rights Watch within the broader rights movement. It all felt quite daunting.

I was surrounded by colleagues with whom I consulted, asked advice, and made collective decisions. But I was the boss, never entirely a peer, which introduced a certain distance that seemed difficult ever to truly close. I befriended a handful of other nonprofit CEOs, since we faced similar issues and could be more open with each other. Certain donors and board members played that role for me as well. But most of the time running the organization day-to-day, I felt very much on my own. That only made my steep learning curve more difficult.

A key initial task for me as a young and inexperienced leader was to set a tone for the organization. What did I expect of staff? What principles should guide their work? What priorities should they set? I had to figure this out while trying to establish some authority with the staff, which I found awkward at first because a short time earlier I had been their peer.

Much of what I stressed built on the culture established by Aryeh. I insisted that we be guided by human-rights principles rather than political or partisan preferences. I wanted our investigations and reporting to be accurate, fair, and scrupulously objective, without sensationalism or bias, without ever interpreting the facts to fit our position, but by looking at the facts to determine our position. I wanted the staff to be creative and probing, never complacent, and focused pragmatically on impact. Our mission was not simply to publish strong reports or to advocate for good policies but to make a difference in the world.

I had time for direct involvement in hiring only for the organization's most senior positions, but I regularly indicated the kind of people whom I felt we should seek. I wanted staff who were smart, sophisticated thinkers who could write and speak compellingly about the problems we addressed. I wanted staff with the linguistic and cultural skills to operate in the countries where we worked. But most important, I wanted staff to wake up each morning and think about how they could concretely advance our cause. I sought staff who were self-starters, who had the drive to get things done.

Having hired such intelligent, driven staff, I sought to give them responsibility commensurate with their ability. Because so much of Human Rights Watch's effectiveness derives from our expertise, I wanted as many decisions as possible made by staff experts—mainly, the researchers and advocates. That, I felt, would produce a more dynamic and effective organization than one in which staff waited for direction from above.

Some of the organization's priorities were set centrally by senior management, but most were determined in a bottom-up process. Researchers, for example, after consulting with local activists, would propose an annual plan—one that inevitably was modified as events intervened but that would presumptively guide the work. This plan was reviewed by the researcher's regional or thematic director and ultimately by central program staff, but with deference.

Giving the staff ownership over their work enabled us to thrive. Their expertise led us. A big part of the reason for the organization's considerable media profile, for instance, is that we did not put forward central spokespeople but the experts themselves. They often knew more, in a nuanced and interesting way, than the journalists with whom they spoke, which made them good sources and eminently quotable. Journalists had an incentive to keep coming back.

On occasion, a researcher or advocate asked me to issue a statement or to write an article for them, to demonstrate that the weight of the organization was behind them, but I tried to avoid that. The organization's backing was implicit in their title, especially given that Human Rights Watch was known carefully to vet and control the messages we sent. Much more was to be gained by the researchers and advocates developing their own media profiles.

I have seen the heads of other civic groups dominate the limelight at the expense of their staff, taking the most high-profile media opportunities themselves. That struck me as unfair and shortsighted. I came to realize that my legacy would be determined far more by what we accomplished together under my leadership than what I could be cited to have done personally. The best way for Human Rights Watch to succeed was to have our staff members building their profiles and contacts, and the ability to advance their own projects. Giving them ownership of their work maximized their energy and creativity. That was especially important given the many projects that we pursued simultaneously. A decentralized organization was the only way to manage these parallel efforts effectively.

I would often ask questions about a project, probe a colleague's strategy, make suggestions, but I rarely vetoed their plans. I deferred to their expertise. My job was not to perfect their work but to ensure that it met a certain standard. At first that was difficult—I tend toward perfectionism and edit my own material relentlessly—but I came around.

As for my own role, I focused on issues for which there was no assigned researcher or advocate, such as speaking about patterns or policies among multiple countries. Each year, I wrote the introduction to the organization's World Report, which summarized our work over the prior year in some one hundred countries. That required identifying a global trend of sufficient importance and originality so the media would want to write about it, which was not easy. I had to finish the introduction by early December for publication in mid-

January, so I had to spend six weeks fearing I would be blown out of the water by some intervening event that contradicted my thesis. Fortunately, that never happened. Writing the World Report introduction was by far the hardest thing I did each year, in part because, by tradition, I circulated a draft for comment to the entire staff, and the staff was not shy about responding.

On publication day, I would present the World Report at a news conference. We tried to choose a city that had some relevance to the thesis of my introduction, and where there were many journalists.* By the time of the news conference, I felt comfortable defending my introduction, but the presentations were challenging because the journalists could ask me about any development in the world. To prepare, I asked the staff to give me a short page on each of their areas of responsibility, outlining the three key points they wanted me to make as well as any hostile or challenging questions that I might expect. I coped with the questioning because the need to respond on a wide range of topics was not that different from many of my other dealings with the media. It was part of my job to keep sufficiently abreast of the most important global human-rights issues.

The public speaking that the job demanded did not come naturally for me. I don't have a demonstrative personality, so my ability to engage an audience evolved over time. At first, I made too many abstract points, was too stiff in my delivery, and spoke too fast, as if I had to cram in every detail. Partly after helpful suggestions from board members, partly through trial and error, I learned to slow down and to tell stories explaining how we got things done. It took me a while to appreciate that audiences reacted best when I spoke to them as if we were having a conversation, looking them in the eye, with no text and no formality.

Within Human Rights Watch, I tried to maintain an atmosphere of intellectual vibrancy and creative probing, which I believe was important for our effectiveness and made the organization a compelling place to work. Staff members were often surprised that I

---

* When in January 2020 the Chinese government blocked my entrance to Hong Kong, it was to prevent me from presenting the World Report, which that year spotlighted the Chinese government's threat to the global human-rights system. The expulsion helped to prove my point.

encouraged them to disagree with me and each other, but in my view, free debate is the way to arrive at the best strategy. I did not believe that internal debate should go on endlessly; extended consultation and deliberation could become an elaborate form of procrastination. When I felt that the staff was avoiding taking a position on an issue because it was too complicated or fraught, I sometimes drafted a proposed op-ed that reflected a given point of view, one to be reviewed by interested staff members as a priority. The perspective that I expressed in my initial draft did not necessarily prevail—I was happy to defer to a smarter argument or a better approach—but it resolved the issue. Once we settled on a public message, everyone—including me—was expected to adhere to the organization's line.

Having a long-term vision for the organization was important, as was building a consensus around it among the staff and board and figuring out how to implement it. But I had little patience for the extended discussions that often accompanied strategic planning, which tended to be a time-consuming way of getting to the intuitive. By the time a plan was produced, it risked being outdated.

I could not avoid an occasional strategic-planning process—every organization is expected periodically to undertake one—but once it was completed, I did not rush to begin a new one. I always had a strategic direction in mind, which I discussed with others, but I did not seek an entire new plan to undertake a new initiative or to reallocate resources. A quicker deliberative process—more on the fly and instinctive—worked fine.

I had a similar attitude about formal processes for monitoring and evaluation. It was easy to know whether a human-rights project had succeeded in generating pressure on the target government—we saw the media coverage and we knew if allied governments took steps to pressure a recalcitrant one. So we hardly ever spent time formally evaluating our work—Did we pursue the most effective strategy or could we have implemented it better? Did we do anything that was counterproductive? Were there lessons to be learned? In part this was a matter of priorities. Evaluating past work, even with the aim of improving future work, most often did not seem worth the time and effort for many on staff when there were so many pressing issues to address. It was also difficult to define a successful campaign. Preventing abuses from getting worse, rather than diminishing abuses, could be seen as a success or a failure.

This is an area where the academic community could be helpful. Today, too much of what passes for contributions by human-rights academics is written by armchair critics, professors who rarely travel and whose criticisms often ignore the facts. Others, as a substitute for field investigation, find correlations among databases that only roughly approximate actual human-rights practices. I would be thrilled if more academics took the time to travel to abusive countries to interview primary actors with the aim of understanding the value, or not, of human-rights interventions. Some do—Professor Kathryn Sikkink of the Harvard Kennedy School is a prime example—but too few.

—

By today's standards, my management style might have been considered too laissez-faire. In my regular meetings with my direct reports, we discussed the substance of their work, strategizing about the best way forward, but did not spend much time discussing their workload, their work-life balance, their management problems—the kinds of things that are increasingly considered de rigueur. All of that takes time, and it was not my inclination to devote much of my overpacked agenda to it. I loved working with colleagues on programmatic issues. I even liked the fundraising because I enjoyed the relationships I forged and the ability to build the organization. But I never felt much excitement about management and preferred to leave it to others. I tried to set a tone for how I wanted our work conducted but largely left it to senior managers to bring issues to my attention when they thought it worthwhile. Only if I felt that a manager was underperforming would I get more involved, trying to improve performance or, if necessary, encourage a departure.

In my later years at Human Rights Watch, I had to address the internal issues that now preoccupy many progressive organizations. We wanted to be a welcoming workplace for people from a broad array of backgrounds, we wanted to encourage input on organizational decisions from our enormously diverse staff living in many different parts of the world, and we wanted to treat people respectfully, recognize their talents, and meet their ambitions for growth. The challenge was to prevent these internal issues from overwhelming the organization and diverting it from its primary mandate to defend human rights.

Perhaps surprisingly, the times when I was most disheartened were not when I was fighting an uphill battle for human rights against some implacable tyrant, but when I was fighting with the staff or board about internal issues that were distracting us from our external work. I understood that workplace concerns were important. We were an employer, responsible for the staff's salaries, job satisfaction, and career progression. But I sometimes longed for the days when passion for the work was generally enough to keep us going.

I understand the argument that getting an organization's internal house in order makes it better able to address the world. Fortunately, at Human Rights Watch, that never dominated our core work. I found that the more senior staff, whose positions gave them greater capacity to influence events, were more inclined to keep an external focus. Junior staff were more likely to direct their activism inward to address workplace issues, although there were many exceptions. The more senior staff would quietly gripe among themselves when internal concerns took up too much time but were reluctant to speak out for fear of seeming indifferent.

Getting this balance right was difficult. I sympathized with the internal concerns and wanted to see them addressed, but I also tried to keep the organization focused on our primary mission. Global challenges are too great to await resolution of all internal issues. Maintaining an external focus was also essential for staff motivation, because the main reason that people came to work at Human Rights Watch was, obviously, to defend human rights.

My hiring preferences undoubtedly contributed to internal challenges. Hiring staff with drive brings in some difficult people with sharp elbows. As sensibilities changed in recent years, with more emphasis on how staff were treated, questions were raised about whether they impeded the teamwork we needed to be most effective. The line between a director who held staff to high standards and one who was creating a work environment that was too challenging or even hostile was not always clear and could be deeply contested. The focused drive of these difficult colleagues played an important role in establishing Human Rights Watch's reputation for innovative, results-oriented work. I worried that a different management style would discourage that impactful intensity.

—

When I left Human Rights Watch, I received notes from staff saying how much they appreciated various aspects of my leadership. Many cited my ability to strategize or my communication skills. I was surprised that I was complimented because I made myself available to all staff, tried to downplay hierarchy, and put a premium on good ideas wherever they originated. That could be time-consuming, especially since it became known that I would respond to any staff member who emailed me, but I thought it was worth the time to stay in touch with a broad array of staff. The bonds that we built made it easier to work together. I especially tried to maintain relationships with each researcher and advocate so that I understood the basics of their work and could check in with them naturally as needed. In many cases, I traveled and worked closely with them.

I was surprised to be praised for treating people kindly. Why wouldn't I?

Two staff members told me they became determined to join Human Rights Watch after watching me respond to criticism on television. The staff seemed to appreciate knowing that if they did their job well, they had my backing, even if a deluge of attacks followed. That, in my view, is what heading a human-rights organization requires. I never liked being attacked—who does?—but I found the defense natural, because I believe deeply in the principles, and because I had confidence that the staff, guided by the organization's culture, would apply those principles conscientiously. As I saw that defense succeed again and again, it reinforced my confidence. I also liked the battles, enjoying the opportunity to challenge those who tried to excuse or cover up serious abuses. When the criticism came, I took the critics on.

I insisted on flying coach, which also earned me surprising praise. I have long legs, and not great circulation in them, but I compensated by trying to get an aisle seat so I could get up and walk around. I did not think it was right for me to spend scarce funds on expensive business-class tickets when there were so many more important needs. It also reflected my determination not to act like a prima donna. I instinctively recoiled when people treated me as anything other than an ordinary person. I did not need or like "special" treatment. That is just who I am.

I avoided building a large executive staff because I felt it would distance me from the core of the organization's work. I had constructed Human Rights Watch so that it had every kind of expertise we needed—research, advocacy, legal, communications, development, administrative. I never saw the point of replicating that expertise on an executive staff rather than working directly with existing staff experts. That also empowered the experts.

An executive staff could have written drafts of articles that I published, but I vastly preferred writing my own—one of my favorite parts of the job. It could have written speeches, but I hated working from texts and preferred speaking from brief outlines, which I assembled myself because it forced me to think through a speech. It could have acted as an intermediary with staff to limit intrusions on my time, but I wanted the greater proximity to the work. An executive staff might have helped me to figure out which countries I should visit, what speaking engagements I should accept, where I should focus my fundraising. But I benefited for many years from a superb executive assistant, Kiran D'Amico, who managed this all quite well by consulting with the broader staff. I realize my hands-on preferences were idiosyncratic, but it worked for me.

—

Directing Human Rights Watch required playing a leadership role not only for the organization's staff but also for the broader international human-rights movement, since we were one of the two big global human-rights groups. Getting that relationship right could be complicated, especially toward the end of my tenure, when so much emphasis was placed on decolonization.

We long felt a special responsibility to try to protect local human-rights activists and their organizations. They were on the front line of our struggle and far more vulnerable to retaliation—harassment, arrests, and physical attacks—by the abusive governments we addressed. Because our international status and connections made it more costly for governments to target us, we tried to use that relative privilege to protect our local colleagues by generating pressure if any of them faced persecution.

Local activists, as I said, were also close partners, a necessity for understanding the terrain, setting priorities, determining strategies, locating victims and witnesses, and generating local pressure. The first port of call when I or my colleagues visited a country was almost always the local human-rights organizations. When it was safe and useful for them, local partners joined us to publicize our reports, whether by jointly holding a news conference or by featuring them on videos and social media posts. In some cases, we published reports together.

Some critics in my later years at the organization wanted us to hand off even more responsibility to local partners. Mark Malloch-Brown, a former president of the Open Society Foundations, and Jack Snyder, a Columbia University professor, encouraged groups like Human Rights Watch to focus more on promoting the work of local groups rather than shaming abusive governments.

Many institutional foundations were similarly disinclined to fund large organizations. They preferred giving grants to smaller, less prominent groups. That had a certain logic. Human Rights Watch had developed sources of revenue that extended well beyond the institutional foundations. In addition, local activists had more capacity than we did to build a domestic constituency for rights, which was important for sustained pro-rights pressure. Governments worried about their reputations abroad, but they were particularly sensitive to protests and pressure at home.

But these preferences for local groups overlooked the fact that shaming at the global level was often a prerequisite to creating the political space for local activists to emerge. If we were to wait until Uyghurs in Xinjiang could defend themselves from Beijing's persecution, we might wait a very long time. While there are strong Uyghur rights activists in exile, my contacts with them suggested that they welcomed our backing and that of other international allies. International pressure could also be an important complement for local activists, as our work on the Amazon illustrated.

Given the importance of generating international pressure through the media and the interventions of influential governments, it was not clear who would pursue these parallel efforts if Human

Rights Watch and our international colleagues were to focus mainly on training or supporting local partners. Some of them did have the stature and means to undertake international advocacy, but most did not. In my view, our proper role was to defer to and highlight local groups when we could—giving them a seat at the table as often as possible—but recognize that we continued to play an essential global role. I believe our roles were complementary.

Many donors and supporters also prioritized building a "movement" over investing in professional organizations such as ours. This enthusiasm peaked after particularly successful popular protests, such as Black Lives Matter or Occupy Wall Street. The emergence of social media made movement building even more attractive.

The public-assembly role of social media first became highly visible during the 2011 Tahrir Square uprising in Egypt against then president Mubarak—the heyday of the Arab Spring. Thousands of people showed up based on messages passed from friend to friend, acquaintance to acquaintance. (That was also when I actively began to use Twitter.) Until government surveillance, propaganda, and disinformation caught up, social media seemed to have tilted the balance from autocrats to the people.

The emergence of such movements can indeed be inspiring, but they are difficult to sustain. People may take to the streets in response to a particularly egregious act, such as the police murder of George Floyd, but it is difficult to keep people turning up day after day, as energy and commitment wane. To sustain pressure, more formal organizations—and leaders—are needed. They are more likely to stick with an issue even as protesters return to their daily lives. The Brazilian human-rights activist Lucia Nader speaks of the "solidity" of organizations in contrast to the "liquidity" of individual activism.

A movement can generate pressure for change, but determining the exact change needed often requires some level of expertise—to collect and analyze relevant facts, to determine feasible policy options, and to make informed recommendations. Social media can produce a crowd, but it cannot build expertise. Nor does it create leadership. That can be an advantage when an autocratic government aims to decapitate a movement, because there is no single person or small group to arrest. But leaders can develop the expertise needed to serve as the most effective interlocutors with governments or other powerful forces. Theoretically, leaders can be volunteers, but ordinarily organizations are necessary to provide the employment that most people require to develop expertise.

Public mobilization is difficult and rare. Only certain injustices are sufficiently outrageous to spark a broad public response. Many important rights issues never generate such concern. They may be more technical in nature or affect fewer people. Relying on movement building as a primary rights strategy would leave these lesser but important issues unaddressed.

These considerations do not require abandoning movement building, but we should leave considerable room for professional activism to supplement mass mobilization. For some donors, supporting professional activists may not be as rewarding as building a movement, but it is an essential part of what is usually needed to get things done.

—

Among institutional foundations, the Ford Foundation deserves special mention. It gave the initial grant to create Helsinki Watch. It later gave additional grants to start Americas Watch and Asia Watch and to support other programs, and it remains a significant supporter of Human Rights Watch and many other rights groups.

Our early experiences with Ford, alas, were a bit fraught. The first problem arose when we wanted to create a program devoted to women's rights. The idea behind this and other thematic programs—we later created them for children's rights, LGBT rights, the rights of refugees, and the rights of people with disabilities, and had one in the works for older people—is that these populations tended to be neglected by country researchers. More traditional rights issues—political imprisonment, censorship, wartime abuses—very often monopolized their time. Specialized staff were needed if the plight of these groups was to be addressed adequately, as well as to partner with the growing network of organizations devoted to their rights. The creation of thematic programs made Human Rights Watch's work better by ensuring that we addressed the full range of people whose rights might be in jeopardy. By publicly incorporating these issues within our work, we made clear that they were core human-rights concerns. Enabling thematic researchers to work within Human Rights Watch ensured that they could benefit from the expertise of country researchers in devising their strategies.

Yet in 1989, when we decided to create a "Women's Rights Project," Ford balked. The Ford staff believed that our addressing women's rights issues would "dilute the stigma of a human-rights violation," as they put it. Today it is unthinkable that anyone in the human-rights movement would hold such a view, but at the time, the movement was understood more narrowly. Amnesty International then focused mainly on executions, torture, and political imprisonment. Hillary Clinton would not give her famous "women's rights are human rights" speech at the UN Conference on Women in Beijing until 1995. And some regarded the abuse of women as a largely private affair, even though my colleagues and I pointed out that systematic government neglect of violence against women made the issue one of government discrimination and hence an appropriate human-rights concern. Our first women's rights report, on Brazil in 1991, made this point. Ford went so far as to threaten to reduce our grant if we went forward with a women's rights program. In 1990, we did it anyway, and they reduced their grant. (Ford later came around, built an active women's rights program, and, at one stage, hired our women's rights director.)

Another point of disagreement with Ford had to do with the politically charged armed conflicts in Central America in the 1980s. We had to report on both sides if we were to maintain our credibility. International human-rights law sets standards only for governments, but international humanitarian law imposes them on rebel groups as well. In addition, human-rights law does not explain what the "right to life" means in the context of war, when the killing of combatants is permitted. Humanitarian law provides more precise rules about the steps that must be taken to avoid harming civilians.

Ford worried that our reporting on rebel abuses would put pressure on local human-rights groups to do the same, when some local rights groups protected themselves from rebel retaliation by refraining from such reporting. Ford thought it would be impossible for local groups to protect themselves by portraying themselves as neutral, akin to the approach taken by the International Committee of the Red Cross to protect its staff in the field.

In 1992, Ford commissioned a major study, seemingly to prove that our approach was wrong. Ford was seconded by a New York–based group, the Lawyers Committee for Human Rights, now Human Rights First. The study was assigned to the respected Chilean human-rights lawyer José "Pepe" Zalaquett, who was aided by Sebastian Brett. Without drawing firm conclusions, their draft largely accepted our approach, and Ford ultimately acknowledged the value of using international humanitarian law, which is now a central tool in wartime for the entire human-rights movement.

My final disagreement with Ford was more personal. In 1993, shortly after I had been named executive director of Human Rights Watch, one of Ford's senior staff members paid a visit. He asked about my plans. Among them, I said I hoped to double the organization in size over the next five years. Our budget at the time was $7 million. "You can't do that," he said. "You have already tapped out all the sources of funding." I ignored him. We doubled in size over five years, then did it again, and then did it again. When I left Human Rights Watch three decades later, the annual budget was $100 million.

That growth was not easy. When I became executive director, I had never raised a cent in my life. The public statement announcing my appointment to the staff and supporters observed understatedly that in this regard I would "need the help of all of us."

Like most people who take on fundraising for the first time, I found the process daunting. I was conscious of how much money we needed to raise to meet our budget and utterly unsure of how we would do it.

By far the best thing I did in those early years was to hire Michele Alexander as the organization's development director. We had an extraordinarily close and trusting relationship for some twenty-five years. She was an essential partner in making Human Rights Watch what it is today. I would still do much of the upfront work for the biggest donors, but Michele put it all together behind the scenes. She was a deep believer in the importance of building relationships, that fundraising should not be about quick asks and should never be transactional. People should not be made to feel like ATMs. It should be about bringing people into the organization, making them friends and partners in our work, and trusting that the funds would come. It was still sometimes necessary to ask for a gift, but often it was not. That focus on relationships helped to build a community, which in turn attracted more donors as they saw the depth of people's commitment to each other and to the work of the organization.

Over time, Michele constructed a network of support committees in twenty-three cities around the world. In each, we identified two or three respected individuals and asked them to bring in other potential supporters. They were aided by a local staff person whom the organization hired. We then had researchers and advocates speak periodically with the committee to keep them abreast of our work.

Typically once a year, each committee held a fundraising dinner. We made sure to present compelling speakers and videos to give the audience a quick and powerful understanding of the organization's work. Donors often bought tables, enabling them to invite friends and introduce them to the work. The dinners represented only a modest percentage of our overall income, but they were key to building a sense of community among committee members. Over time, each of these city committees became the hub of an expanding network.

Michele also had the ability to identify and hire atypical talent. Many of her staff members had little if any prior fundraising experience, but they had the passion, drive, and presence to serve as highly effective representatives of the organization, and that turned out to be far more important.

Of necessity, I got over my fear of fundraising and came to enjoy it. I saw what we could do by adding another researcher or advocate, so I worked to make that possible. I especially liked meeting people and engaging them in our work.

Fundraising kept us on our toes. The need to continue selling the organization to donors required us to ensure that we had something to sell, that our impact was sufficient to justify the investment. We needed, as well, to be visible enough in the media so people could see some of the pressure we were exerting.

Highlighting one's impact could be frowned on in activist circles. A premium was placed on mentioning the many actors who contribute to any human-rights progress. I always felt that if credit sharing were taken too far, if Human Rights Watch were to fade into the background as a public actor because we were so eager to acknowledge others, it would be harder to build and sustain the organization and therefore would harm the broader movement of which we were an important part. That was not a politically correct position, but I think it was the right one.

A growing organization was also important for liberating the staff's imagination. An organization that is stagnant limits its staff's vision of the possible. An organization that is growing encourages staff to think about what it could do if it just had some additional funds. I wanted to make sure that we were always growing.

We had an unusual donor base in that a large percentage of our funds came from major donors. These donors tended to be smart, accomplished people—a pleasure to sit down and converse with.

I learned that the key to securing significant gifts was to tell stories about what Human Rights Watch had accomplished. Many people believe in human rights and are willing to make a modest contribution as a statement of their values. But to secure more substantial investments, I needed to show that donors could help change the world. I needed to show impact. So I told impact stories, which had the added advantage of illustrating for people how we got things done.

The major-donor orientation of our fundraising forced me to play an unexpected bridging role. These donors inhabited a privileged world. My job was to connect them to the beneficiaries of our work, people who were far less well off. Sometimes we arranged for them to meet. Usually, it was left to me and my colleagues to show how wealthy people could help those harmed by human-rights violations. That meant that I had to live comfortably between the world of repression and human-rights abuse, and the world of wealth and privilege. At first the contrast seemed jarring, but I became accustomed to it, as did many of my colleagues, who regularly were called on to speak in people's palatial homes or at glittering fundraising dinners before returning to their more modest lives.

One conception of human-rights fundraising is to describe the terrible things that governments do, hoping that the shock elicits a willingness to help end the horror. I found that was more likely to turn the listener off. I only touched on the despicable conduct to establish there was a problem. My job was to show how we as a collective—Human Rights Watch and our supporters—could fight back, how we could increase the cost of abuse, which is the first step toward curtailing it. I focused on the solutions.

That is also how I managed my own mental health. I spent much of my working day dealing with people's hardships, but I directed my attention to how we could alleviate them. That became my instinctive response to the abuses we documented. It also aligned with my nature. I sometimes wondered whether I was being naively optimistic, but I did not become immersed in misery. I tended to assume that things could improve and tried to figure out how to make that happen. That is undoubtedly how I was able to handle the job for so long.

Many of my colleagues seemed to adopt a similar perspective. We talked about what we could do to address the horrors. We were all unavoidably affected by the cruelty at the center of our work—in later years, the organization made therapists available to the staff—but the emotional burden was mitigated by our purpose in collecting these accounts. I sometimes analogized our work to that of a doctor who dealt all day with people's illnesses but stayed sane by focusing on trying to cure them. Framing the world from this purposeful perspective was also an unwritten though essential part of my job description as I worked to keep staff and supporters motivated.

Human Rights Watch, like Amnesty International, did not seek or accept any government funding. Because we criticized governments, we had to be independent of them. We could not feel obliged to pull our punches for fear that a government funder might dislike our criticism. We also did not want to be seen as pursuing the agenda of any government. Nor did we accept funds from the United Nations or similar multilateral institutions, because they were important targets of our advocacy.

This approach proved invaluable. When officials whom we criticized would search for reasons to reject our findings, some would try to pass us off as government pawns, particularly of the United States, given our base in New York and U.S. origins. It helped to silence this diversionary tactic by noting that we did not take a cent from Washington or any other government.

At one point, a few board members suggested that we might accept funding from more neutral-seeming governments. Canada, the Netherlands, and various Scandinavian governments were mentioned as possibilities. I opposed the suggestion, which was never adopted, because I preferred saying that we did not accept funds from *any* government. I also did not trust governments that seemed committed to human rights to continue on that path. The Canadian government had been known for its commitment to human rights—it had been a key partner in securing the treaties banning antipersonnel land mines and establishing the International Criminal Court—but it took a significant turn to the right under Prime Minister Stephen Harper, the Conservative leader who served from 2006 to 2015. His government cut funding for groups that criticized Israel.

Rejecting government funding required us to develop the capacity to raise funds from private sources. Our meteoric growth would not have been possible had we remained focused on the relatively static sums available from governments.

Even among our private supporters, we maintained a strict conflict-of-interest policy. Corporations accounted for a minuscule part of our revenue because they tended to see their charitable contributions as part of their marketing budget, which led to a preference for such issues as education or health care rather than the edgier work of Human Rights Watch. We would not accept funds from senior corporate officials—directors and officers—if their corporation was involved in human-rights abuse or other activity that we deemed harmful, such as selling tobacco products. Similarly, we would not take funds from an individual if their company was the subject of an investigation or report by us. We also did not accept funds from senior officials of a company that was a direct competitor of a company that we were investigating or reporting on, even if they were not known to be doing anything wrong. We did not want the target of our work to be able to say that we were pursuing them only because one of their competitors had given us money.

The person assigned to enforce this policy was Arvind Ganesan, the longtime director of our program on business and human rights (since renamed the program on economic justice and rights). Arvind's experience investigating the conduct of businesses made him well suited to analyze potential conflicts of interest. He also has a careful, dispassionate temperament that made him ideal for assuming this enforcement role.

Because of our focus on major donors, some two-thirds of our funding came from people or foundations that gave one hundred thousand dollars or more each year. When I left the organization, there were roughly 140 such donors. They provided stability, because major donors developed personal relationships with the organization that kept them giving during economic downturns. There were also tens of thousands of smaller donors who contributed through the mail, online, or at events.

I am skeptical about the argument that a broader base of smaller donors would have provided greater legitimacy. It sounds good for an organization to say that it represents many members, particularly if its influence derives from its ability to mobilize those members, as Amnesty's does. Indeed, traditionally, civil society was composed mainly of membership organizations whose purpose was to represent its members. But that is not how we operated. Our influence derived not from our membership but from our fact-finding, our policy analysis, our ability to attract media attention, and our capacity to enlist powerful government allies.

Moreover, insisting on a broad membership as a key to legitimacy reduces civil society to another majoritarian institution. Civil society is supposed to be more varied than that. Some civic groups may indeed represent the mainstream, but some represent minority points of view; that is their right, an essential part of democracy. Human-rights organizations, in particular, must maintain their independence from majoritarian institutions if they are to monitor and, if necessary, criticize them.

In the end, I believe advocacy organizations such as Human Rights Watch achieve influence not by virtue of their membership but because of the persuasiveness of their message. Did our donor base make us too conservative? We focused on improvements that were feasible within a reasonable time. That was a product of our impact orientation, not our donor base.

Developing New Programs

Despite my usual effort not to micromanage staff, I played a more active role when we were creating a new program. Staff new to the organization often assumed that our voice alone was enough to secure change. They did not understand how much of our influence depended on our ability to investigate facts and introduce them publicly in order to build pressure for change. Apropos, when we created a program on human rights and the environment, I spent considerable time working with colleagues to fashion a meaningful plan of action. An early director was fixated on getting governments to make official statements that treated the need to address climate change as a human right. I couldn't imagine anyone suddenly being moved to act simply because someone said climate change was a "human-rights" problem. I pressed for a more impactful approach.

I started from the premise that Human Rights Watch should not replicate the work of environmental groups. Rather, I looked to our methodology of exposing probative facts and applying human-rights standards to generate pressure. The most obvious approach was to demonstrate how climate change was harming people today. We looked, for example, at the effects of climate change on First Nations people in Canada and pregnant women in Florida. By putting a human face on the current effects of climate change, we could push governments to live up to their human-rights duty to help these victims. Such work is obviously important for the people whose lives are upended by climate change, but I found it insufficient because it was too fatalistic. I wanted not just to address how the world must adjust to climate change, but also how the world can act to stop climate change. To some extent putting a human face on climate change could generate some modest additional global pressure to stop it, but I felt our organization could make a more significant difference if we sought to end human-rights violations that contribute to climate change.

In conversations with colleagues, including Daniel Wilkinson, the interim director of Human Rights Watch's environmental program, we settled on two broad areas of work that were later agreed to by Richard Pearshouse, who became the director. One was to examine the health effects of coal mining and coal-fired power plants. Environmental groups already exert pressure to curb such carbon emissions because of their effect on global warming. But the mining and use of coal also pollute local communities, harming the health of their inhabitants. By documenting that damage, we could treat the issue as one involving the right to health. That would add pressure to address the problem locally, which would augment pressure to address the global problem of climate change. Human Rights Watch has pursued this approach in South Africa, Bosnia and Herzegovina, and the United States.

A second area of work addressed deforestation. Keeping forests healthy and vibrant is an important way to fight climate change because, as is widely known, forests serve as carbon sinks—they take carbon from the atmosphere. We felt we could make a significant contribution to curbing deforestation by addressing the human-rights dimensions of the problem. Our experience showed that forests are best protected by people who live in them sustainably. That was the approach described to me by Emmanuel de Merode, a Belgian prince who directs Virunga National Park, known for its mountain gorillas, in eastern Democratic Republic of Congo, when I met with him there in 2015. He sought to enable local people to live with and even profit from the park, giving them a personal incentive to protect its natural beauty. That is also the approach taken in Mozambique's Gorongosa National Park by Greg Carr, the founder of the Harvard Kennedy School's Carr Center for Human Rights Policy.

Nefarious actors often use violence and intimidation against people who sustainably coexist with a protected area to chase them away. Then the attackers clear-cut or burn the forest for timber or agriculture. If we could generate pressure to stop such human-rights violations against sustainable forest inhabitants—pressure that was distinct from the traditional focus of environmental groups on the deforestation itself—we might make a serious contribution to the fight against climate change.

That was the strategy we pursued in the Brazilian Amazon. Brazil's president at the time, Jair Bolsonaro, pretended that Amazon deforestation was carried out by small farmers trying to eke out a living. Our investigation showed that criminal networks were attacking forest defenders—Indigenous communities, environmental activists, even the state's environmental officials—and destroying the forest. Satellite imagery of the Amazon showed major roadways built to bring in heavy equipment and to remove valuable timber. These were hardly small-scale operations. The imagery also showed certain stark lines, with healthy forest on one side and cleared forest on the other. The lines often corresponded with the official demarcation of Indigenous land, illustrating the important role that forest inhabitants can play in protecting their environment.

We collected extensive evidence of attacks on local forest defenders and the systematic failure of the authorities to hold the attackers to account. We showed how Bolsonaro was effectively greenlighting these crimes by publicly criticizing Brazilian environmentalists while his administration dismantled the country's environmental agencies.

Our findings received substantial coverage in the Brazilian media. In one case, I joined my colleagues in São Paulo to hold a news conference that was carried widely, including on the country's dominant channel, TV Globo. I also met with senior officials in Brasilia, including a contentious meeting with the foreign minister who defended Bolsonaro's approach. But none of it was working. We needed international pressure on the Brazilian government—another area where we could provide value added to the traditional work of environmental groups.

Bolsonaro favored the destruction of the Amazon because he thought it would contribute to Brazil's economic growth. His administration also wanted a free-trade agreement between Mercosur, the South American trade bloc of which Brazil is the dominant member, and the European Union. That gave us leverage. The draft agreement stipulated that trade would not occur at the expense of the environment. Human Rights Watch and our allies persuaded EU governments not to ratify the accord until the Brazilian government better protected the Amazon. Daniel Wilkinson took the lead, meeting repeatedly with European officials. I brought it up in one of my meetings with President Macron of France.

Another source of leverage was Brazil's bid to become a member of the Organisation for Economic Co-operation and Development, which was an even bigger priority for the Bolsonaro administration than the EU-Mercosur trade deal. When his administration tried to secure an invitation to participate in the OECD's environmental committee, we torpedoed the effort by sending a fourteen-page letter to all OECD member states detailing the destructive consequences of Bolsonaro's policies in the Amazon. We also persuaded fifteen U.S. senators to publicly call on President Joe Biden to condition

U.S. support for Brazil's OECD bid on progress in reducing deforestation and ending impunity for attacks on forest defenders. And we helped convince the OECD to announce that such progress (or lack of it) would be a factor in evaluating Brazil's membership bid.

Many of our interventions regarding the EU trade deal and the OECD made headline news in Brazil and contributed to public awareness that Bolsonaro's Amazon policies were isolating the country and depriving it of important economic opportunities. That is partly why Human Rights Watch became one of the few organizations with which the Brazilian Ministry of the Environment met. Bolsonaro and his ministers often ignored criticism from local environmental and human-rights activists, but they could not afford to be oblivious to the international consequences of their policies. That is likely why they toned down their public statements that had endorsed deforestation.

These concerns would ultimately be a factor in Bolsonaro's October 2022 reelection loss to Luiz Inácio Lula da Silva, who had a history of better protecting the Amazon when he last served as Brazil's president, from 2003 to 2010. During Lula's first year in office in 2023, deforestation of the Amazon dropped 36 percent.

In short, the key to making a new right meaningful is not simply to state it as a right but to investigate and publish facts that transform an abstract right into a matter of right and wrong that a significant community, whether local or international, cares about, and to use that concern to exert pressure on the relevant government to change.

When I left Human Rights Watch, it was considering how best to address public health. One adviser talked about the need to stop the "white supremacist, colonial approach" that characterizes global public health, to create a "people-centered approach" to address disparities in the global health order. He vowed to "expose and undo structural racism, patriarchy, and classism embedded in the design of Western public-health systems."

I have little tolerance for such rhetoric, which is increasingly heard in progressive circles. Yes, it can be stirring for those who already see the world that way, but I doubt it changes anyone's mind. It is also aimed at the wrong people. Progressives may champion it, but they rarely have enough clout on their own to move public policy. Our primary audience, as I repeatedly told the staff, should be the movable middle, the people who can tip the balance of public opinion toward the action advocated. Politically correct rhetoric of this sort is likely to turn off the segments of society that we most need to secure change.

—

To an audience in the United States, most civil and political rights seem familiar, including the right not to be arbitrarily arrested; the right not to be tortured; the right to freedom of speech, association, and assembly; the right to a fair trial; and the right not to face discrimination on various invidious grounds. International human-rights law also treats as coequal a series of economic, social, and cultural rights. Among them are rights of access to health care, housing, and education.

Aryeh had avoided addressing economic and social rights, but I felt that if our formal legitimacy rested on our application of international human-rights law, we should avoid picking and choosing among the rights enshrined in that law. Yet many issues related to economic and social rights are too political for an international human-rights group to address effectively. For example, should a government invest limited resources in schools or clinics, or in infrastructure such as roads or ports to enable the economy to grow, making more funds ultimately available to meet social needs—or some combination? Assuming that a government was conscientiously making these decisions, Human Rights Watch had no standing to intervene.

It is axiomatic that for Human Rights Watch's methodology to work, some particular government or institution must feel shamed. If we simply condemn poverty somewhere but fail to demonstrate the responsibility of particular actors, to show that they are not acting conscientiously to remedy the situation, no one is shamed. I summed up the prerequisites for effective shaming as requiring a violation of human rights, a violator, and a remedy.

I saw the possibility for the convergence of these prerequisites in the requirement of the International Covenant on Economic, Social and Cultural Rights, the relevant treaty, that a government "to the maximum of its available resources" allocate those resources "with a view to achieving progressively the full realization of the rights." Behind that legalese, as I understood it, was a requirement to use available resources in good faith to address the most urgent economic and social needs. That was a standard with sufficient teeth that I felt Human Rights Watch could apply.

If we could demonstrate that a government was deploying available resources to less weighty matters—vanity projects, pointless military expenditures, corruption, or simply the retention of power—our shaming methodology could be employed. We could treat this lack of proper allocation of available resources as a violation, the government in question as the violator, and an end to this misallocation as the remedy. A similar analysis could be used for government policies that, on ideological grounds, needlessly impede people's economic and social rights.

When I first proposed this approach in 2003, I was lambasted. I had been appalled by how many people seemed to treat any deprivation as a violation and to use economic and social rights as an excuse to push for more government expenditures on their pet projects without an analysis of what money was available and what the competing needs were.

I wrote an article critiquing this approach, in which I acknowledged that while local civic groups have every right to press their own government to spend funds one way or the other, an international group needs to be more principled. If we are not to usurp the rights of local voters, we should focus on government expenditures that clearly fall short of the requirements of economic and social rights. That is, we should focus on expenditures that fail to reflect a conscientious government effort to respect those rights, rather than expenditures that we just happen not to like.

For years, academics used my article to argue that I was refusing to uphold economic rights. That is not what the article says, and a perusal of Human Rights Watch's website would show that we did not operate that way in the three decades that I ran the organization. Our approach forced governments to allocate available funds to those most in need. For that reason, it was not terribly popular among governments of the Global South. They would rather persuade richer governments to provide development aid. They point to the section of the treaty on economic and social rights that asks governments to help realize those rights "through international assistance and co-operation." They also invoke similar language on the "right to development," which is not in the treaty but is codified in a UN General Assembly declaration. Their idea was to shift the burden for upholding economic and social rights from the national governments themselves to international donors. Indeed, the right to development effectively asks donors to provide aid without the scrutiny of the recipient government that economic and social rights require. As if in illustration, the Cuban government, whose repression contributes to the country's dire poverty, typically took the lead at the UN General Assembly in promoting an annual resolution on the right to development.

The declaration is also not terribly effective at mobilizing international assistance. It is not a legally binding treaty, and its provisions are vague, with no specification of the amount to be given or who the donors should be. That makes it difficult to generate pressure for rich governments to act. There have been nonlegal efforts to fill in the gaps—most notably the eight Millennium Development Goals and then the seventeen Sustainable Development Goals—but these do not allocate responsibility for achieving these goals.

Philip Alston, a New York University law professor and former UN special rapporteur on extreme poverty and human rights, believes it is a mistake to equate economic rights with poverty alleviation or economic development, which are not the same as the legal entitlement of rights. He urges the human-rights community to spend more time persuading governments to codify economic rights in law, and to establish institutions to monitor progress toward honoring those rights, and to hold governments accountable for any failure. He has a point.

Indeed, I pursued a variation of it when I gave a plenary address to the International AIDS Conference held in 2000 in Durban, South Africa. I argued that progressively realizing the right to health required, at minimum, that each government adopt a plan to achieve that right, a timetable for implementation, and a reporting scheme on progress. That would establish accountability for shortcomings that would make shaming possible.

Samuel Moyn, in his book *Not Enough,* suggested that when Human Rights Watch addressed economic rights, we focused insufficiently on inequality. The two are related; great inequality, if improperly taxed, can limit the government resources available to fulfill economic rights. Inequality may also speak better to people who are not impoverished but feel they are stagnating—the "left behinds," who seem more inclined to endorse the far right's efforts to upend the democratic system. Yet Moyn failed to suggest how, given our methodology, Human Rights Watch might have addressed inequality. Theoretically, we could have published a comparative chart by country of Gini coefficients, a measure of inequality. But we had no capacity to conduct that specialized investigation; we would have had to publish someone else's numbers. We could have delved into the issue of comparative tax rates for the wealthy, but again, we have no special expertise or value added in this area. As I said earlier, our ability to move public-policy debates is due far less to the positions we take than to our ability to present new facts that we make a dedicated effort to collect. Otherwise, we would be intervening for show rather than for policy change. That is a recipe, if repeated over time, for diminishing Human Rights Watch's influence while making no practical difference. It would be unhelpful to be known as an organization that spouts politically correct positions unconnected to a serious strategy to influence policy.

Many wealthy governments have development programs that give bilateral grants directly to lower-income countries, but such work mainly falls to international agencies such as the World Bank, to which rich countries contribute. Through much of its history, the World Bank treated economic development as divorced from human rights, but that began to change under the 1995–2005 presidency of James Wolfensohn, with whom I met to urge this change. At first, the conservative bureaucracy saw their primary duty as dishing out funds to credible development projects, and they feared that a consideration of human-rights practices would get in the way. But with our encouragement, the bank began to recognize that at least certain human rights were relevant to the success of development projects. Those include the rights that are required for transparency, which are needed to fight corruption, and for public participation in formulating development priorities, which can help to ensure that the most urgent public needs are met.

An approach to economic and social rights that stresses the duty to progressively realize them using available resources does have some limitations, which can be frustrating. UN experts have devised the concept of "core" rights—essentially, basic necessities—which they assert must be met absolutely, not progressively. That is well and good for wealthier governments with adequate resources, but it begs the question of what governments in low-income countries should do when they lack the necessary resources. There is nothing wrong with being aspirational, with trying to fulfill all economic and social rights, but if the human-rights movement demands complete fulfillment in the absence of available resources, we lose credibility. Over time, the stigma of our denunciation would diminish.

One approach to economic and social rights where Human Rights Watch did not make much progress was in using them as an entrée to encourage broader public embrace of human rights. For example, some populist politicians in Europe have attacked human rights as providing protection only for minorities, asylum seekers, or even terrorists, but not for most of a country's residents. Sadly, that persuaded some people that human rights had nothing to offer them. For example, the British Conservative Party sought to undermine human-rights protections in the United Kingdom by pursuing legislation that would limit enforcement of the European Convention on Human Rights in Britain.

Alston, the NYU law professor, felt that the mainstream majority could be persuaded of the importance of human rights by focusing on rights that benefited them, such as economic and social rights. Deploying this insight, some of my colleagues decided to focus on certain social benefits for low-income people in Britain. Improving access to those benefits can, indeed, be described as an effort to uphold economic and social rights, but the beneficiaries did not discernibly move from that defense of the social-service programs they needed to a broader embrace of human rights. They seemed willing to accept the benefits for themselves while denying human rights to others, such as the right of immigrants not to be deported to countries where they faced likely persecution.

When people benefit from some human rights, that is not enough to persuade them that all human rights are important. People need to be convinced not to pick and choose among rights, to favor only those that benefit them while ignoring those that benefit others. That requires building a concept of rights as a totality rather than as a buffet of entitlements from which some can be selected. People must see their government's ability to ignore some people's human rights as weakening protection for everyone else; that if the government takes away others' human rights today, it might eliminate theirs tomorrow. That requires a more sophisticated argument than simply labeling a particular desirable benefit a human right. It requires building a Kantian view of human rights—recognition that we should treat everyone the way we want to be treated. Some people may reject such a view because they believe they will always be on the side of the powerful or the majority, never the persecuted minority. Some may refuse to identify with people who differ from them by such attributes as race, ethnicity, religion, or economic circumstances. To counteract these narrow conceptions of rights bearers, we must build a broader sense of community—a belief that every member of that community, even if different, deserves similar treatment. Or more to the point, we must show that we all benefit from living in such a system, even if some people by virtue of their privilege believe they can get along without it.

Such community building is not easy. It is a less visible and underdeveloped but fundamentally important task of the human-rights endeavor. It requires demonstrating a commonality of interests across a nation—not in particular political outcomes (people always differ there) but in a system that imposes certain limits and duties on government.

China

There is no greater threat to the global human-rights system today than the Chinese government under Xi Jinping. No government surpasses Beijing in the combination of its repression at home and its determination to silence many critics abroad. And no other government makes so concerted an effort to undermine the international human-rights standards and institutions that might and do hold it to account, dedicating to the task significant proceeds from the world's second largest economy. Beijing's actions if unchecked portend a dystopian future in which no one is beyond the reach of Chinese censors, and the international human-rights system is so weakened that it no longer serves as a check on government repression. Because of the stakes, because of the power and influence of the adversary, I immersed myself in our China work, making it a major personal priority.

Despite putting on airs of confidence—the pageantry of self-approbation that typifies Chinese Communist Party gatherings—the government is afraid to subject its rule to popular scrutiny. With nothing approaching a free and fair election allowed, the Chinese government relishes external manifestation of its legitimacy. It wants the international community to see it as serving the people of China rather than maintaining power by the barrel of a gun. That way it can argue to people in China (though never explicitly), You may not have elected us, but everyone else accepts us, so you should too.

The government puts enormous effort into countering and suppressing condemnation of its human-rights record because such censure undermines its efforts to portray itself as widely respected. China's sensitivity to criticism gives us leverage, but the human-rights movement faces a formidable opponent. The way we met the challenge illustrates the organization's methodology as well as the need for patience. A government as powerful as China's does not change overnight. In doing our work, we had to look not only for immediate changes in government conduct but also for indications that the government was feeling the heat.

Officials from the Chinese Communist Party, which controls the government, make the case for their rule by arguing, in essence, that they have expanded the economy, making the people of China materially better off, so they are the right leaders to govern. They also say that the dictatorship of the Chinese Communist Party ensures stability, avoiding the chaos of China's past (even if a good part of that chaos, such as the Great Leap Forward and the Cultural Revolution, was caused by the party).

Hundreds of millions of Chinese have indeed become middle class, with greater freedom than in the earlier days of Communist rule to own property and start businesses. But large parts of the population in rural areas are still impoverished, with little education, no meaningful prospect for social mobility, and severe restrictions on their ability to live where they want (the *hukou* system).

As for the party's claim of wise economic stewardship, China's growth is often measured against the low bar of the Cultural Revolution. Much of the economic growth since then is due less to the guidance of the party—state-run enterprises are notoriously inefficient—than to the energy and hard work of the Chinese once the government allowed private enterprise to flourish. The party's wisdom has also been called into question by Xi Jinping's policies on COVID-19 and his decision to prioritize fending off any perceived threat to his power over building the economy, whether quashing elements of the tech sector or distrusting consumers to spend wisely despite the diminishing returns of government-led infrastructure investment. And perhaps the biggest obstacle to China's continued growth is its aging, shrinking population, a demographic echo of the many years of the party's one-child policy.

The Chinese government became more vulnerable to these frailties as Xi Jinping transformed party rule from a collective enterprise into an increasingly one-man show. Although the Chinese Communist Party makes a point of saying that it is democratic because it consults with the people, Xi's refusal to countenance open discussion of policy challenges and his tendency to surround himself with sycophants inevitably lead to little meaningful consultation and poor decisions. As observers put it in *The Wall Street Journal,* it is difficult, in a country as vast and complex as China, to be "Chairman of Everything."

Unaccountable governments tend to place their own interests above their people's. The frequent result is neglect, stagnation, and poverty, if not hyperinflation, public-health calamities, and economic crises. Using a variation of the political philosopher John Rawls's "veil of ignorance," if one had to pick a country to live in knowing only the nature of the government, it would be risky to bet on an autocrat.

Because most people in China have no possibility of publicly disagreeing with the dictatorship-for-growth imposition—dissent in China is a sure route to prison—the Communist Party can pretend that its rule has public support. To ensure that deception, it has built a vast apparatus for propaganda as well as domestic censorship. Hong Kong represented the exception. By coming to the streets in the hundreds of thousands in 2019–20 to stand for democracy, the people of Hong Kong showed they had no interest in accepting Communist Party dictatorship. That embarrassing, highly visible contradiction of the party's claim of public support pushed Beijing to crush Hong Kong's freedoms. The people of Taiwan, the other part of what is said to be "China" where freedom of expression prevails, are no more interested in Communist Party rule than their Hong Kong counterparts.

Taiwan and Hong Kong also pose an economic threat to the party's argument for legitimacy. Although per-capita gross national income has grown significantly in mainland China, it has grown even faster—and to a considerably higher level—in Taiwan and Hong Kong.

Xi Jinping's government would reduce its human-rights obligations to its ability to expand the economy, ensure security, and promote vague, easily manipulated concepts such as "happiness." At times it promotes the concept of collective rights, but the purpose of rights is to protect the individual from the collective. It rejects universal standards and would have each country define its own path. This view accords the internationally endorsed concept of individual rights no place.

Core civil and political rights such as unfettered debate, let alone free and fair elections, are out of the question in Xi's China because they would jeopardize the party's dictatorship. Yet Xi also rejects scrutiny of his economic and social rights policies. Although China has acceded to the treaty upholding those rights, Beijing does not want to be asked whether it is conscientiously allocating available resources to meet the basic needs of all segments of society, as the treaty requires. That would invite awkward questions about the fate of Uyghurs, Tibetans, Mongolians, and even Han Chinese in poor rural areas. It would also raise questions about the government's enormous expenditures on surveillance and repression when so many people in China are struggling to make ends meet.

The exiled Chinese dissident artist Ai Weiwei, with whom I have shared the stage in public conversation several times, famously documented how shoddy construction of schools had left thousands of students dead after a 2008 earthquake in Sichuan. Beijing had covered it up. Beijing also censors information about poverty, widening income inequality, discriminatory access to public benefits, selective corruption prosecutions, and the one in five children left behind in rural areas as their parents seek work in other parts of the country. In addition, Beijing hides forced demolition of homes and displacements, injuries and deaths that accompany some of the country's massive infrastructure projects, and the permanent disabilities resulting from unsafe and unregulated food and drugs. Beijing does not want people asking why China's social safety net is so porous or why social benefits such as schooling, health care, and pensions are allocated according to where a person was born rather than their income or needs. By reducing human rights to economic growth, Xi eviscerates what human rights are all about.

—

One challenge of addressing human rights in China was the difficulty of conducting investigations. Even in the best of days, during the somewhat reformist era of Deng Xiaoping, the ability of our researchers to wander around China was limited. The late Robin Munro was the organization's first China researcher. Raised in Scotland, he had learned beautiful Mandarin and, in his mild-mannered way, excelled at exposing secrets that the Chinese government preferred to keep hidden.

One of his exposés involved Chinese orphanages, which were mainly filled with baby girls whom Chinese couples had abandoned under the one-child policy, aiming to try again for a boy in the hope that he would better provide for them in their old age. Using the testimony of orphanage staff and inmates, official documents, and photographs of dead and dying children, Robin documented how babies and children in the orphanages were subject to appalling neglect. The embarrassed Chinese government as a result made domestic adoption somewhat easier and allowed a bit more transparency about how orphanages were run.

Robin spent much time in Tiananmen Square during the electrifying pro-democracy protests of 1989. He stayed in the square on June 4, 1989, as the Chinese army violently shut the protests down, the last foreign observer present that dreadful night.

To test Beijing's claim that people were better off under Communist Party rule, our researchers traveled in the period when they still could to various parts of China. One investigation in 2009 and 2010 looked at lead poisoning of children due to pollution. With no right to freedom of speech or association, the Chinese have limited means to influence local officials. Many local governments thus ignored environmental problems as they profited from land sales and industrial development. We also investigated and reported on the abusive treatment of migrant construction workers (2008), the mistreatment of sex workers (2013), barriers to education for people with disabilities (2013), and conversion therapy for LGBT people (2017).

In an example of the creative approaches to investigations that were increasingly needed as travel was restricted, Maya Wang, one of our researchers on China, secured a mobile app that Chinese police used to enter data about each Uyghur in Xinjiang. Through reverse engineering of the app, she was able to re-create twenty-six screens, or pages, of data, including on such matters as whether they had traveled abroad or had relatives or contacts there, and whether they were religious or wore manifestations of Islamic belief. Revealing the range of data that Chinese security forces seemed to deem potentially incriminating—and possibly the basis, beginning in 2017, for detention in a forced reeducation camp—demonstrated the extent of Beijing's efforts to wipe out the Uyghurs' religion, culture, and language.

It also illustrated the highly intrusive surveillance state that Beijing was building, with Xinjiang a possible testing ground for a nationwide system. Checkpoints there were equipped with special machines called "data doors" that, unbeknown to the people passing through them, vacuumed up identifying information from their mobile phones and other electronic devices. In addition, the "social credit system" could be used by local governments to control people's access to desirable social benefits, such as the right to live in an attractive city, send one's children to a particular school, or travel by plane or high-speed train, based on whether they complied with government dictates on how they should behave.

As the Chinese government blocked most independent investigation inside China—whether by journalists, scholars, public-health officials, or human-rights researchers—we had to rely increasingly on remote investigation, such as speaking to people from China who were outside the country. We also used open-source investigation. Finding nuggets of information on social media or in government databases is slow-going work, but it can pay off.

Despite the Chinese government's censorship, any bureaucracy makes mistakes, especially one that values obedience over individual initiative. For example, Baidu, the enormous Chinese social media platform, maintains a Chinese equivalent of Google Maps. At a time when the Chinese government was denying the existence of mass detention centers for Uyghur and other Turkic Muslims in Xinjiang, the bureaucracy evidently worried that people could use Baidu maps to find the detention centers. Someone had the brilliant idea of blanking out the detention centers on the maps. The blanked-out spots became easy ways to locate the centers.

A 2015 Human Rights Watch report on torture in China also relied on government records, which a bureaucracy as vast as China's government needs to maintain to monitor performance. We searched the roughly 158,000 verdicts published on the Supreme People's

Court website over a four-month period in 2014. Allegations of torture were referenced in 432 verdicts, but the verdicts showed that few judges investigated the charges, and judges excluded confessions in only twenty-three of the cases. Over time, the Chinese government tried to limit information posted online or available to the public to stymie open-source investigations.

My own experience illustrates the difficulty of access to China. Apart from my periodic visits to Hong Kong, I was, to my regret, allowed into China only once, in November and December 2005. My pretext was a UN-sponsored conference on corporate social responsibility in Shanghai, which the Chinese government felt obliged to let me attend and speak at. It did so by giving me a four-day visa. The woman at the check-in counter at Beijing's airport who examined my visa on the way out to ensure that I had not overstayed my allotted time burst out laughing. She had never seen such a short visa.

I spent two days in Shanghai and two in Beijing. My time in Beijing coincided with the visit of Manfred Nowak, then the UN special rapporteur on torture, whose news conference I attended. He had been allowed to visit detention centers in Beijing as well as Tibet and Xinjiang and had found that torture, though declining in urban areas, remained "widespread." That was a relatively open period for China. Nothing like such access is allowed anymore.

China has a long history of people traveling to Beijing to petition the emperor to rectify a grievance, not as a matter of law but as an act of discretion, and this tradition continued under Communist Party rule. Indeed, the party had established offices where petitions could be filed in various provincial cities as well as Beijing. The petitioners who made it to Beijing—thousands at any given time—were seen as particularly desperate. Most had given up everything they owned to make the trip. They survived in petitioner enclaves in the usually naïve hope that someone might take their plea for help seriously.

The people who did take these petitioners seriously were local officials against whom complaints were being filed. They were generally uninterested in rectifying grievances but did not want their superiors in Beijing to learn about them. So they sent "retrievers" to Beijing who used violence and intimidation to force petitioners to return home, often detaining them in unlawful detention centers known as "black jails." I saw a petitioner outside Nowak's news conference who was surrounded by hostile plainclothes individuals. A few days later in Hong Kong, I released a report we had prepared earlier on the hardships that petitioners suffered.

Speaking with Chinese officials became more difficult over time. In my early days at Human Rights Watch, some dialogue was possible, so long as it did not happen inside China, a step the Communist Party evidently felt would confer too much legitimacy on us. In November 2008, the Chinese government even sent a delegation to our headquarters in New York. The thirteen Chinese delegates represented the China Foundation for Human Rights Development. They told us that the foundation was engaged in public aid, research, education, and international exchanges, of which our meeting was a part. The delegation was headed by Huang Mengfu, who was chairman of the foundation as well as vice chairman of the Chinese People's Political Consultative Conference. Huang said that the Chinese government prioritized "stability," and that respect for human rights would follow from that. He said that the country's human-rights problems—he was evidently referring to dissidents—involved a tiny percentage of people, and his government was working on a new "National Action Plan on Human Rights," focusing in particular on women's and children's rights.

I pressed for an end to retaliation against human-rights defenders, lawyers, journalists, and civil-society representatives who exposed human-rights abuses and local corruption. I noted that allowing criticism of local officials was key to rooting out corruption and promoting the stability that Beijing sought. Huang acknowledged that "there is much truth in what you have said," but added that the government was already fighting local corruption, which was an inevitable side effect of the transition from a centrally planned to a market economy. He said that any "retaliation" against rights activists was the exception, not the rule.

Nothing further came of the meeting. However, Beijing's willingness to discuss human rights, and occasionally to make modest concessions such as the release of some political prisoners, was not uncommon under Xi Jinping's predecessors, Jiang Zemin and Hu Jintao.

Beginning in 2009, an impressive group of officials and academic experts, half from China, half from the United States, periodically assembled to discuss the rule of law. Beijing appeared interested in establishing a more reliable legal system and was open to suggestions. These conversations were supposed to alternate between the United States and China. In 2013, I joined one session at a conference center on Long Island, but two years later, when we were scheduled to meet in China, Beijing refused to allow me to attend.

I did have occasional encounters with Chinese ambassadors abroad. Fu Ying, a rare senior woman in the Chinese foreign policy establishment, met with me and Brad Adams, Human Rights Watch's Asia director, in London in May 2008 while she was China's ambassador to the United Kingdom. We discussed a range of issues, and she offered to help us meet senior officials in Beijing, but nothing came of it. Fu was a regular participant in the Munich Security Conference, where I occasionally had perfunctory exchanges with her during a session or in the corridor. When I inquired why Chinese officials still refused to meet with us, she said candidly that we were too critical. Human Rights Watch would never temper our criticism to secure access, but it was good to know that our criticisms were hitting their target.

My other encounter with a Chinese ambassador, although involuntary on his part, occurred at the White House in January 2011. President Barack Obama's November 2009 summit in China had been unsuccessful. In the lead-up to that visit, Obama had made the mistake of trying to placate Beijing. He refused to meet the Dalai Lama, and his secretary of state, Hillary Clinton, insisted that human rights "cannot interfere" with other concerns in China. The administration hoped this soft approach would win points that could be cashed in at the summit, but instead the U.S. government looked weak and unprincipled. Needless to say, Human Rights Watch was highly critical.

This time, Obama seemed determined to do better. Before the Chinese leader, Hu Jintao, visited Washington, Clinton gave a strong speech defending civil society and internet freedom in China. During the summit, Obama stood at Hu's side and stressed the "universal rights of all people." Mentioning freedoms of speech, press, association, and religion, he anticipated the false claim that these rights are foreign impositions by noting they are all "recognized in the Chinese constitution." In response, Hu conceded that "a lot still needs to be done in China in terms of human rights"—a statement that would be inconceivable under the more aggressive "wolf warrior" diplomacy that Xi Jinping later encouraged.

The administration underscored the point that human rights should be a regular part of the conversation with China by inviting me to the state dinner for Hu at the White House, a lavish affair. Joined by Annie, I made sure that I was noticed by stopping to say a few words to the assembly of photographers at the entrance. I approached Hu in the receiving line, where he was standing with Obama and their wives. I explained that I represented Human Rights Watch and hoped that groups like mine could discuss abuses with Beijing in the same way that we do with other governments. He returned a blank smile. The pace of the receiving line kept me from pursuing the conversation.

When it came time for dinner, I was pleasantly surprised to find that I had been assigned to the main State Dining Room, at a table with the principal White House adviser for Asia, Jeffrey Bader; the U.S. ambassador to China, Jon Huntsman Jr.; and China's ambassador to Washington, Zhang Yesui. I was seated to allow a long conversation with Zhang. The Obama administration was sending a message.

As ambassador to the United States and previously to the United Nations, Zhang had declined to meet with Human Rights Watch. Now he launched into a spirited defense of China's imprisonment of the 2010 Nobel Peace Prize winner, Liu Xiaobo, who was one of the principal drafters of the pro-democracy Charter 08 and was then serving an eleven-year prison term. In 2017, Liu died of liver cancer while in custody after Beijing refused to allow him proper treatment until seventeen days before his death.

I said I found it puzzling that the Chinese government would prosecute a writer for merely expressing his peaceful views on reforming China. Zhang tried to convince me that Liu was dangerous, citing various positions that Liu had taken, none of which amounted to advocating, let alone inciting, violence. If the Chinese government did not like Liu's views, I suggested, it should rebut them, not make them criminal. Zhang insisted that these ideas, and Liu's promotion of them, endangered China's stability. Unsurprisingly, neither of us convinced the other, but I came away knowing that our conversation would be written up and circulated within the Chinese Foreign Ministry. That was not ground-shaking, but it was something.

The ambassador and I then turned to a broader discussion of human-rights conditions in China: the progress that China had made and the great distance that it still had to go. I accepted Zhang's point that critical observers must be conscious of China's context—he didn't elaborate—but I said that it would help if the Chinese government accepted more regular exchanges with human-rights organizations. Zhang did not dismiss this idea out of hand, but it was clearly a matter that would require assent from people above his pay scale, which never came.

After dinner, as I waited in the East Room for a superb jazz concert led by Herbie Hancock, I had a chance to chat further with Obama. I thanked him for inviting me to the dinner, for being more outspoken on human rights in China, and for finding a way to discuss the issue that was genuine and heartfelt. This was a step forward, but U.S. officials have only rarely taken other ones.

A postscript: Sophie Richardson, then our China director, was invited to attend the September 2015 state dinner for Xi Jinping. When she met Obama, he asked how I was. She said, "permanently prosecutorial." He burst out laughing.

———

For many years, Western policymakers professed that trade with China would lead gradually to its liberalization, that it would expand China's economy and create a middle class that over time would insist on respect for its human rights. Trade would also require an improved legal regime that would gradually extend to noncommercial issues. These propositions suggested that there was no need to exert pressure on Beijing to improve its human-rights practices.

During Bill Clinton's 1992 presidential campaign, he criticized President George H. W. Bush for allowing China to benefit from Most Favored Nation (MFN) trading status despite its repression. Its name aside, MFN meant normal trading status, that goods imported from China would face the same tariffs as those applied to goods from most other countries. The annual debate about whether to renew MFN status was an important moment of human-rights leverage over Beijing. In 1993, Clinton as president announced that it would "depend upon whether China makes significant progress in improving its human-rights record." That began an intense discussion about whether Beijing was making enough progress. Human Rights Watch argued that it was not, citing the continued existence of political prisoners, their inhumane treatment, the persecution of Tibetans, and the lack of any accountability for the crushing of the Tiananmen Square pro-democracy movement.

However, the debate had changed considerably from Human Rights Watch's early battles with the administration of President Ronald Reagan over abusive U.S. allies in Central America. The fundamental issue was less about the nature of Chinese government repression than about how the U.S. government should respond, and whether trade without pressure could ameliorate things or was merely a convenient rationalization for the lucrative status quo. Although the business interests aligned against us were considerable, the issue was debated vigorously in the U.S. media. But instead of making the most of this leverage to advance human rights in China, the Clinton administration in May 1994 delinked China's MFN status from its human-rights conduct.

The next day, Clinton's secretary of state, Warren Christopher, spoke at the Asia Society in New York. I had been invited and made a point of attending. Christopher, a patrician lawyer, calmly made the case for "engagement." "We're not backing away in any way from pursuing human-rights problems," he said, asserting that Washington's human-rights dialogue with Beijing would intensify, as if dialogue without consequences for ignoring the substance of the dialogue would make any difference. He also noted that preferential tariffs would be denied to a handful of products from industries owned by China's military.

When I was called on to ask one of the first questions, a murmur went through the crowded auditorium. Everyone knew of Human Rights Watch's strong opposition to the decision. I made clear that the tariffs on Chinese military goods were token, and that dialogue without pressure would make no difference in changing the Chinese government's conduct.

Human Rights Watch's position is now widely understood to have been correct, including by a wide range of U.S. government officials. We did not oppose trade per se with China, so long as it was not complicit in human-rights abuses, such as trade that benefits from Uyghur forced labor or contributes to Beijing's intrusive surveillance system. However, we vigorously opposed the idea that trade *is* a human-rights policy, that it is a substitute for pressure to improve human rights.

To the contrary, much as trade with Russia and the wealth it engendered gave Vladimir Putin more resources to pursue his aggressive autocratic rule and ultimately to invade Ukraine, so trade with China has enabled Xi Jinping to strengthen his dictatorship by giving him the financial means to reenforce his rule with the legions of security officials that the government employs for its censorship and surveillance regime.

In 2012, Xi Jinping, then vice president and designated next Chinese leader, was about to visit the United States. Because he had not yet assumed the top post, Vice President Biden, rather than President Obama, was his official host. I was invited to the White House to brief Biden about China. We met in the Situation Room, and Biden began talking, and talking, and talking. Finally, after some twenty minutes, I interrupted him. After all, I was there to brief him.

In his public remarks alongside Xi at a State Department luncheon that I attended, Biden mainly addressed tensions over trade but did mention briefly his concern about how "conditions in China have deteriorated and about the plight of several very prominent individuals." Ironically, it was Xi who spoke at greater length on human rights and with a candor that would be unthinkable today:

> We also had a candid exchange of views on human rights and other issues. I stressed that China has made tremendous and well-recognized achievements in the field of human rights over the past 30 plus years since reform and opening up. Of course, there is always room for improvement when it comes to human rights. Given China's huge population, considerable regional diversity, and uneven development, we're still faced with many challenges in improving people's livelihood and advancing human rights.

If only *that* Xi Jinping would return.

—

A trip I took to Hong Kong in January 2020 for what I hoped to be a news conference releasing our annual World Report turned out to be a harbinger of the crushing of the territory's freedom. My colleagues and I had selected Hong Kong as the venue for the release because my introduction to that year's report focused on the threat that the Chinese government posed to the global human-rights system. Releasing the report in Beijing was impossible. After I arrived at immigration control in Hong Kong, I was detained for about four hours before being ushered to a flight back to New York. It was déjà vu.

I had traveled to Cairo in August 2014 to release a report on a major massacre of Muslim Brotherhood protesters during a sit-in in Cairo's Rabaa Square. Forces operating under then defense minister (now president) Sisi and interior minister Mohamed Ibrahim had cordoned off and systematically killed at least 817 protesters over twelve hours. It was one of the largest massacres in recent history. Ibrahim then announced that "the dispersal plan succeeded 100 percent" and gave bonuses to participants.

After a detailed investigation, we prepared a report that I was going to present at a news conference in Cairo. We had given the government an advance copy and were hoping to meet with officials to discuss it.

I flew into Cairo airport with Sarah Leah Whitson, an American lawyer and the longtime director of our program for the Middle East and North Africa, whose drive for excellence and impatience with the region's stultifying repression played an enormous role in making that program one of the organization's most creative and relentless in applying pressure for change. Omar Shakir, the Human Rights Watch researcher who was the principal author of the report, had already entered the country, but Sarah Leah and I were rejected "for security reasons." We spent the night in the airport.

We knew that the denial of our entry would make news but could not go public until Omar was able to leave the country safely. He is Iraqi American, and we feared the Egyptian authorities might detain rather than expel him.

By early next morning, both Sarah Leah and Omar were on their way home, and I was being held in the tiny office of an Egyptian security official. I said, as assertively as I could, that I wanted to go to a lounge. The official, somewhat taken aback, walked me to a departure lounge and handed my passport to the attendant behind the counter, a young woman in a headscarf, with instructions that she should hold on to it until it was time for my flight.

A short time later, she came up to me and asked, "So, what did you do?" I showed her a copy of our report on the Rabaa Square massacre that I had hoped to release. She smiled and returned with an iPad displaying a photograph of herself in Rabaa Square during the sit-in.

I did not let the inability to enter Egypt stop me from holding the news conference, which took place two days later—by video, with journalists in Cairo. The blockage of my entry generated massive media coverage. The government's refusal to allow what until then would have been a routine news conference in Cairo—I had released our annual World Report in Cairo earlier that year—signaled the utter intolerance of any public criticism that would come to characterize the Sisi government. My treatment served as an advertisement for the report. Indeed, I opened my video news conference by thanking the Egyptian government for its help in publicizing the report.

Now, in Hong Kong, the immigration authorities handled me politely but refused to admit that the denial of my entry was a political decision made in Beijing. They insisted that it was a routine local immigration matter, without explaining what I had done wrong.

In planning the trip, we had not been oblivious to this possibility. At the time, Hong Kong was in the middle of months of pro-democracy protests. The month before, the Chinese government had said that it would "sanction" Human Rights Watch and a few other U.S.-based groups in retaliation for new U.S. legislation in support of the Hong Kong protesters. Beijing never explained what that sanction meant. If I was prevented from entering, our communications staff said I should produce a selfie video that I could post on Twitter. That would give an immediacy to my treatment.

While I was in quasi custody, I did not think I could get away with making such a video, but at the gate, as I was about to board the plane, I turned to my "guards" and said, as firmly as I could, "I need a moment to myself." They backed off. I used the minute to do the selfie video—no preparation, no practice, one take. I pressed the button to send it to my colleagues.

For security purposes, I had left my regular mobile phone in New York and had brought only a burner phone. But that phone never seemed to link up effectively to Hong Kong's phone service, only to the wi-fi in the airport. And as I walked down the jetway to the plane, I was losing the signal. So I started walking very slowly. The guards tried to hustle me along, saying they were holding the plane for me, but I dragged my feet until I was pretty sure the video had been sent. It was posted on my Twitter feed and went viral, with twelve thousand retweets. My somewhat disheveled look added to its authenticity. I spent much of the flight back to New York exchanging emails with journalists about what had just happened.

That I was barred from entering Hong Kong made major news worldwide, in part because it illustrated Beijing's gradual crushing of the territory's freedoms. It also served as a teaser for our World Report. Days later, I held the news conference at the United Nations in New York that I would have liked to conduct in Hong Kong. Because of Beijing's assistance with advance publicity, the room was packed. A Chinese diplomat joined us. He made clear that I had been barred entry purely because I had been so critical of Beijing.

—

As China's economy grew, and as more companies and countries believed that their economic welfare depended on their access to the huge Chinese market, Beijing realized that it had a powerful weapon to silence human-rights criticism: it could deny access to any critic. It did that when it essentially stopped purchasing Norwegian salmon because the Nobel Peace Prize had been awarded to Liu Xiaobo. Never mind that the Nobel committee is a private organization based in Oslo that has nothing to do with the Norwegian government, let alone Norwegian salmon companies. When upon an extradition request from Washington the Canadian government detained Meng Wanzhou, the chief financial officer of technology giant Huawei, Beijing blocked the import of Canadian canola and pork products. (It also detained two Canadians in China as hostages.)

After the COVID-19 outbreak in Wuhan, China, in late 2019, Beijing imposed heightened tariffs on key Australian exports when the Australian government pressed in April 2020 for an independent investigation into the origins of the pandemic. Beijing did not want people focusing on Wuhan, where Beijing's cover-up of human-to-human transmission during the first three weeks of January 2020 while millions of people fled or traveled through Wuhan enabled the pandemic to go global. That accounts for its preposterous theory that COVID-19 might have been imported in frozen food. And it certainly did not want anyone exploring whether the virus might have leaked from the Wuhan Institute of Virology, which was collecting and manipulating wild coronaviruses, or been the product of the government's failure to enforce laws against trade in wildlife at the Wuhan market where the virus was spreading early in the outbreak.

Companies have been highly vulnerable to Beijing's retaliation. Most famously, China's media platforms suspended broadcasts of National Basketball Association games after Daryl Morey, then the general manager of the Houston Rockets, tweeted his support for pro-democracy protesters in Hong Kong. He had shared an image that read "Fight for Freedom. Stand with Hong Kong." NBA broadcasts in China were worth hundreds of millions of dollars a year. When the clothing retailer H&M said it did not source products from Xinjiang or tolerate forced labor in its supply chain, China's Communist Youth League attacked it, and references to the company were removed from the Chinese internet.

Desperate to avoid such retaliation, companies appease Beijing. Hong Kong–based airline Cathay Pacific threatened to fire employees who supported or participated in the 2019 pro-democracy protests in the city. Volkswagen's chief executive, Herbert Diess, told the BBC in 2019 that he was "not aware" of reports about detention camps holding thousands of Muslims in Xinjiang, even though Volkswagen had had a plant there since 2012, and we and others had been reporting on the camps since they opened in 2017. Marriott fired a social media manager for "liking" a tweet praising the company for calling Tibet a country and vowed "to ensure errors like this don't happen again." Hollywood increasingly censored its films to placate Beijing's sensibilities, such as the initial digital removal of a Taiwan flag from Tom Cruise's bomber jacket in the trailer for the 2022 sequel to the 1986 movie *Top Gun*.

Chinese censorship has become a global threat. Companies abiding by censorship restrictions when operating inside China now impose that censorship on their employees and customers around the world. Beijing also conducts surveillance of Chinese people overseas and pressures them to avoid criticizing the government, sometimes threatening relatives still in the country. Hong Kong authorities have gone so far as to issue arrest warrants with bounties for the capture of dissidents who had fled to Australia, Britain, and the United States. Meta, the parent company of Facebook and Instagram, said the Hong Kong government was responsible for fifty instances between July 2020 and June 2022 in which Meta removed content globally.

Because the Chinese government was so willing to retaliate economically against critics, few governments dared to criticize Beijing. Given that fear, we persuaded governments that if they banded together in a joint statement, Beijing could not retaliate against them all.

Our focus was Beijing's persecution of Uyghur and other Turkic Muslims in Xinjiang. Every six months or so, alternating between the UN Human Rights Council in Geneva and the UN General Assembly in New York, we worked with various governments—Germany, France, Britain, Canada, Australia, the Netherlands, and the United States—to build support for a joint statement on Xinjiang. At first, governments were fearful, but they proceeded when we suggested that a joint written statement would have no discernible lead author.

In July 2019, we attracted twenty-five supporters of a joint statement issued during a session of the Human Rights Council. A tradition at the council when joint statements are issued on the sidelines is that one of the signatories reads the statement out loud before the council, but the signatories were still scared of retaliation, so only a written statement was submitted. In October 2019, the British government read aloud another joint statement adopted in the context of the UN General Assembly. The sky did not fall on London. Fifty governments were willing to sign a statement in October 2022.

Beijing responded to each group condemnation with a counter-statement signed by the tyrants and autocrats of the world, including Russia, Syria, North Korea, Myanmar, Belarus, Venezuela, and Saudi Arabia. The human-rights records of these signatories undermined the effort. Sadly, even though Muslims bore the brunt of the Chinese government's repression in Xinjiang, the governments of only a few Muslim-majority countries—Turkey, Albania, and Bosnia-Herzegovina—were willing to criticize Beijing. But about half of the members of the Organisation of Islamic Cooperation refused to sign the pro-China counterstatements.

I joined Human Rights Watch's Geneva representative, John Fisher, to speak with the ambassadors of various seemingly moderate Muslim-majority countries. Nothing came of it. Working with Human Rights Watch's UN representative in New York, Lou Charbonneau, I spoke with the Turkish ambassadors to the UN in New York and Geneva about playing a catalytic role with other Muslim-majority countries. That initiative also went nowhere.

A good illustration of the pressure that Muslim-majority governments faced to support Beijing despite its repression of Muslims in Xinjiang took place in 2019 in New York. During the annual opening of the UN General Assembly, I sat down with Imran Khan, the former cricket star who was then the Pakistani prime minister. He had come to New York to press governments to pay more attention to extensive Indian government persecution in Kashmir, the Muslim-majority part of India. I asked him, should he not also be speaking out for the Muslims of Xinjiang? He candidly admitted that the Chinese government, by virtue of its massive aid and investment in Pakistan, virtually owned the country. He could not possibly speak out about Xinjiang without risking enormous economic repercussions. I asked whether he could at least rein in his ambassador to the UN in Geneva, who, remarkably, had publicly *praised* Beijing's treatment of the Uyghurs. He agreed to do that, although he himself later picked up her refrain.

Beijing's effort to buy support from other governments included Xi Jinping's $1 trillion Belt and Road Initiative, an infrastructure development program that touted its loans as having "no strings attached." Their lack of transparency made them seem designed to encourage corruption, which was useful to cement autocratic alliances with the officials who benefited.

The secrecy also allowed no popular oversight to ensure financial viability, which was part of why many loans proved to be debt traps. Some BRI projects are notorious: Sri Lanka's Hambantota port, which China repossessed with a ninety-nine-year lease when Sri Lanka's overall debt became overwhelming; or Kenya's Mombasa-Nairobi railroad, where the government tried to repay its loan by forcing cargo transporters to use it despite cheaper alternatives. BRI projects also tended to ignore local needs, as I saw during a June 2022 trip to Nairobi and Kampala, where new Chinese-built highways were sparsely used because they were toll roads (to pay for them), leaving most Kenyans and Ugandans, who were unable to afford the tolls, relegated to the traffic jams of the old parallel roads. But there was one big string attached to the Chinese government's loans: Beijing insisted on political loyalty as a tacit condition, especially for votes at the United Nations.

Not all signatories of the joint condemnations of Beijing's repression in Xinjiang were members of the UN Human Rights Council, but the growing number of governments willing to speak out created the tantalizing possibility of the council's first critical resolution ever addressing repression in China. That would be a major blow to Beijing's prestige, and so a significant source of pressure for the government to ease its repression in Xinjiang. Fearing possible condemnation, the Chinese government had long made considerable efforts to undermine the council's work. It prevented domestic critics from traveling abroad, denied key international experts access to the country, organized its allies to sing its praises, and presented blatant disinformation.

One casualty of these efforts was Cao Shunli, a Chinese lawyer who police at Beijing's airport detained in September 2013 as she was about to board a flight to Geneva, where she planned to participate in a training session on human rights ahead of a UN Human Rights Council review of China. She died in custody six months later at age fifty-two.

Beijing routinely voted against efforts to monitor or condemn other governments out of concern that it would create a precedent that would then be employed against China. The Chinese government at various times turned its back on the Syrian civilians facing indiscriminate airstrikes by Russian and Syrian planes; the Rohingya Muslims ethnically cleansed from their homes by the Myanmar army's murder, rape, and arson; Yemeni civilians under bombardment and blockade by the Saudi-led coalition; and the Venezuelan people suffering economic devastation due to the corrupt and repressive mismanagement of Nicolás Maduro.

The Chinese government had not always been as inalterably opposed to the defense of human rights. On the UN Security Council, it for many years allowed human-rights resolutions to proceed so long as the situation did not too closely parallel Beijing's own domestic practices (or involve governments that had recognized Taiwan). For example, as Gaddafi sought to crush a 2011 uprising against his rule, China supported a resolution establishing an arms embargo on Libya, imposing targeted sanctions on certain Libyan officials, and referring the country to the International Criminal Court. But under Xi Jinping, most efforts to defend human rights were deemed threatening because they strengthened a UN human-rights system that might turn its attention to China.

In Beijing's view, the Human Rights Council should only be a forum for polite, general conversation among governments—"constructive dialogue" without "finger-pointing"—with due deference to each sovereign nation's interpretation of human rights. It urged "win-win cooperation," later renamed "mutually beneficial cooperation," in an effort to frame rights as a question of voluntary cooperation rather than legal obligation. It wanted governments to "refrain from imposing their own values . . . on others," assuming that Beijing's repression reflects a cultural characteristic rather than Chinese leaders' unadulterated despotism.

Beijing failed to undermine most work of the council, which continued to order investigations and issue condemnations for many countries, including Syria, Myanmar, Venezuela, and Ethiopia. But by using its economic clout, the Chinese government succeeded in fending off any investigation or condemnation of its own repression.

We sought to change that. A key prelude to our effort, we felt, was a report on Xinjiang by the UN high commissioner for human rights, at the time the former Chilean president Michelle Bachelet, which we had encouraged her to produce. Bachelet had rightly insisted on "unfettered access" for an investigation in Xinjiang, which the Chinese government refused, countering that she could come for a "friendly visit." Bachelet seemed to be using the standoff to delay publication of her report.

I discussed that during a meeting with her in October 2021 in her office in the grand Palais Wilson overlooking the lake in Geneva. We always had a cordial relationship, even if at times I had to nudge her to take a more proactive stance. When I brought up the report, knowing that she had a draft sitting on her desk, she told me she worried that she did not have enough cases to make it persuasive. I urged her to use remote monitoring to fill in the gaps, the way we were often forced to do. She added considerably more testimonies, and in December 2021, her spokesperson hinted that the report would be published imminently.

The UN secretary-general, António Guterres, sabotaged that plan. Having served as Portuguese prime minister and then head of the UN Refugee Agency, he was extremely sophisticated about global politics. My meetings with him covered a lot of ground, as he offered spirited defenses of his positions. Alas, he turned out to be a human-rights disappointment, reluctant to use his public voice in an effective way. He didn't want to put at risk his ability to secure phone calls with important leaders. That was indeed part of his job, but he was so concerned that leaders might react badly to his targeted human-rights advocacy that he did very little of it.

When he spoke about human rights, it was usually in broad, generic terms. He might say that it is important to respect women's rights, but because he did not name a particular abuser, no one felt the heat to change. People respond to particular instances of injustice, not generic statements. When Guterres named names, it was typically when the government was already a pariah, such as the Myanmar junta, or the Russian government after its invasion of Ukraine, or the Israeli government for its bombing and besieging of Gaza following Hamas's October 2023 atrocities against Israeli civilians. In those cases, he took little political risk.

My greatest frustration with Guterres, though, involved Xinjiang. His timidity came to a head in February 2022 when he was determined to attend the Beijing Winter Olympics, even though many people (including me) had said it was inappropriate to take part in an event designed to "sportswash" the Chinese government's reputation as it was committing crimes against humanity in Xinjiang. In Beijing, he announced that he had secured an invitation from the Chinese government for the high commissioner to conduct a "credible visit" to Xinjiang. Bachelet then had no choice but to delay her report and accept the "visit"—Beijing's preferred term—that her boss had arranged, not the unfettered access that she had held out for previously.

Her visit was, predictably, a show tour. She had no opportunity to speak privately and safely with Uyghurs who had been in detention, let alone those who were still there. She refused to criticize the Chinese government's persecution; instead, apparently thinking naively that she might enhance her influence, she parroted Beijing's nonsensical justifications.

Bachelet's report was then further delayed for months as she contended with Beijing's efforts to weaken and delay it. She finally did issue a strong report, describing persecution that "may constitute . . . crimes against humanity," but did so literally thirteen minutes before the end of her term on August 31, 2022. That meant she had no capacity to press the UN Human Rights Council to address Beijing's persecution in Xinjiang. That task fell to her successor, Volker Türk, a longtime aide of Guterres.

Türk had never used his public voice to defend human rights. Yet public pressure is the only effective tool for officials like the high commissioner, who have no other source of pressure at their disposal. The high commissioner has no aid package to present, no trade benefits to offer, only the ability to investigate, expose, and condemn. When Zeid Ra'ad Al Hussein, the Jordanian diplomat, had assumed the post of high commissioner in September 2014, I said as much to him. My advice was to "come out swinging," which he did. He was consistently outspoken and is widely regarded as among the strongest UN rights chiefs.

In Türk's initial two years in office, he used his public voice on other countries, but with regard to China, he said simply that he stood by Bachelet's report on Xinjiang, the least he could do. He never explicitly embraced its charge of possible crimes against humanity; he merely noted that "my Office [meaning his predecessor] has documented grave concerns," citing "large-scale arbitrary detentions and ongoing family separations." Rather than contribute to the public pressure on Beijing, he vowed "to engage with the Chinese authorities" through "dialogue"—music to the ears of Xi, who was more than happy to engage and engage and engage and talk and talk and talk to avoid the delegitimization that public condemnation brings. On the most challenging issue he faced, Türk utterly failed.

Guterres was even worse. Through a spokesperson, he distanced himself from the report, stressing Bachelet's "independence," said it was "important for everyone to see the Chinese response" to the report, in which Beijing had denied all wrongdoing, urged only that the Chinese government "take on board" the report's recommendations, and stressed that China "is a very valuable partner" and "we very much hope that that cooperation will continue"—hardly a statement of profound concern about possible crimes against humanity targeting the Uyghurs of Xinjiang.

Given Bachelet's publish-and-run report and Türk's and Guterres's refusal to criticize China on Xinjiang, the human-rights community was forced to address Xinjiang at the UN Human Rights Council without the active support of the UN high commissioner for human rights or the UN secretary-general, potentially potent allies. Nonetheless, we took a gamble and, in October 2022, pressed for the first time for the council to place Xinjiang on its agenda by discussing Bachelet's report. We lost the vote—19 to 17, with 11 abstentions—but the outcome suggested that momentum was in our favor and the tables may be turning on Beijing's efforts to block scrutiny of its persecution in Xinjiang. Significantly, yes votes included the Global South countries of Somalia, Honduras, and Paraguay, and cosponsors included Muslim-majority Turkey and Albania. But those that voted against the people of Xinjiang included Muslim-majority Indonesia, Qatar, and the United Arab Emirates, and among those that abstained were major democracies: Argentina, Brazil, India, Malaysia, Mexico, and Ukraine. To illustrate how much the vote mattered to Beijing, Xi Jinping is reported to have personally telephoned several (unidentified) heads of state to urge a pro-China vote.

—

The repression became so severe in Xinjiang, and the rationalization that trade would improve human rights so empty, that the possibility reemerged of using economic pressure. Sophie Richardson, our China director, joined with other rights groups to push through the U.S. Congress a powerful piece of legislation, the Uyghur Forced Labor Prevention Act, signed by President Biden in December 2021. It presumptively bars all imports from Xinjiang unless the importing company can demonstrate that forced labor was not used. Given the opacity of supply chains in Xinjiang, that is difficult if not impossible to show. The industries affected include importers of products made with cotton (about 20 percent of the world's cotton comes from

Xinjiang), polysilicon (45 percent, used in solar panels), tomatoes (25 percent of tomato paste), and aluminum (10 percent). If firmly implemented, with attention to Beijing's efforts to launder Xinjiang products through third countries, the law could add significant pressure on Beijing to curb the use of Uyghur forced labor. That pressure would be more intense if other major economies, especially the European Union, followed Washington's lead, not just by banning the products of forced labor when found but by presumptively banning all imports from Xinjiang. While exports from Xinjiang to the United States plummeted, exports to the European Union in 2022 increased by a third.

Another important potential source of economic pressure on China was a proposed investment deal with the European Union. We wanted to ensure that it did not proceed without guarantees that EU investors in China would avoid complicity in Uyghur forced labor. We had been spotlighting the problem since September 2019 as it became more pervasive and apparent. German chancellor Angela Merkel was our key interlocutor because the investment deal was being finalized during the second half of 2020 while Germany held the rotating EU presidency.

When in October 2020 I met with Merkel by video (because of the COVD-19 pandemic), she was cautious. She was always influenced by the German business community, which had a strong interest in trade with China. Germany's economy depended on exports, and China was one of its largest customers. With her term as chancellor ending—she had already announced she would not seek reelection—her main concern seemed to be getting the deal done before her EU presidency concluded.

Merkel settled on a weak compromise. She conditioned the deal not on the Chinese government ending its use of forced labor or even ratifying the leading international treaties against forced labor, but on Beijing pledging to make "efforts" to ratify them, a meaningless commitment. Although Beijing later did ratify the treaties, it gave no sign that it would comply with them. Shortly after Olaf Scholz took over from Merkel as chancellor, he spoke at the Munich Security Conference, where I asked him publicly about the weak terms of the investment deal. His defense ignored the difference between subscribing to a treaty and complying with it.

In 2021, the investment deal was stymied. The European Union, together with the United States, the United Kingdom, and Canada, had responded to Beijing's grave abuses in Xinjiang by imposing targeted sanctions on various Chinese officials and entities. Beijing, in turn, sanctioned various European politicians, diplomats, and scholars including, most significantly, several European parliamentarians. That led the European Parliament to reject the forced-labor subterfuge on which the investment deal had been premised.

In March 2023, Beijing signaled its desire to revive the investment deal. It seemed to hope that if it lifted its sanctions against European officials, the deal could proceed. But with the Chinese government refusing to end the use of Uyghur forced labor, European Commission president Ursula von der Leyen suggested during her April 2023 visit to China that the investment deal was dead.

—

Looking back, there was nothing inevitable about the success of the Chinese government's assault on the global human-rights system, and nothing quixotic about opposing it. Despite the government's economic clout and its willingness to blackmail others that dare to spotlight its repression, Beijing was vulnerable to international censure.

There were some indications that this pressure was making a difference. As the spotlight intensified on the mass detention centers in Xinjiang, Beijing went from denying their existence to portraying them as benevolent "vocational training centers." In 2019, Beijing claimed that trainees had "graduated." Some were released, but others were given criminal penalties and moved to an expanded prison system. Others were placed in forced labor, sometimes outside of Xinjiang. These shifts suggested an effort by the Chinese government to disguise its efforts to coerce Uyghurs to stop being Uyghurs, indicating, once more, that Beijing was feeling the heat. That implied that further pressure could make a positive difference.

As governments end their infatuation with the Chinese market and find safety in numbers from Beijing's retaliation, the prospect of a formal UN condemnation of the Chinese government's repression—Beijing's nightmare—may force the Chinese government to decide whether to continue the repression that it calculates it needs to stay in power or to try to recapture the international acceptance that it hopes to use to promote its legitimacy at home. That Beijing continues to care about its international reputation is perhaps the most important source of leverage we have to mitigate its repression, because broad international acceptance will not come without a substantial shift in Beijing's human-rights conduct.

Moreover, China's autocratic model is looking less attractive. The Chinese Communist Party claims to deliver better than democracies, which it portrays as slow and contentious. But Beijing faces the uneasy task of managing a huge and complex economy without the public input and debate that political freedom allows. Because of its policies, it faces an aging and shrinking population with a resulting shortage of workers, a bloated real estate sector mired in debt, an investment-led economy with decreasing dividends, inadequate investment in health care and other social services that makes consumers reluctant to spend, and a dependence on state-run industries that are an inefficient core of the economy.

The "zero-COVID" lockdowns seemed to have awakened the Chinese middle class to the nature of the Communist Party. When the people oppressed were distant ethnic groups or an occasional dissident, most people in China since the reforms of Deng Xiaoping went about their daily lives with little fear of persecution. But the lockdowns, beyond being disruptive, showed the party's capacity to subordinate the individual to its dictates. Ordinary people found themselves struggling to find food or obtain medical care, causing needless deaths. In December 2022, facing the largest nationwide protests since the Tiananmen Square pro-democracy protests of 1989, Xi abruptly reversed course. Many of the protesters had denounced not only the lockdowns but also rule by Xi and the Communist Party.

Because he had seen his zero-COVID approach as infallible despite the emergence of highly transmissible variants, he never invested adequately in vaccination of older people or intensive-care units. Nor did he allow import of the most effective mRNA vaccines, seeing these Western vaccines as a blow to China's prestige. Beijing tried to cover up the consequences of these disastrous policies by undercounting COVID deaths and suppressing reports when hospitals and morgues became overwhelmed. When one province mistakenly posted data on cremations, extrapolations suggested that the real nationwide death toll from the post-zero-COVID wave was not the officially proclaimed 83,150 but 1 to 1.5 million.

Xi's attacks on parts of the tech industry, because he feared they were becoming too powerful, hobbled one of the most vibrant sectors of the economy. While seeking foreign investment, Chinese authorities questioned and detained workers with foreign companies for doing standard due-diligence investigations. Most economists view enhanced consumer spending as necessary to reinvigorate China's sagging economy, but Xi preferred investments that the state controlled despite its shrinking utility. With the economy struggling, jobs becoming scarce, and the population plummeting, the Chinese government wanted women to leave the labor market and stay home to have babies.

Given these problems, Xi will find it increasingly difficult to portray his dictatorial rule as superior to more accountable political systems, making him more vulnerable to efforts to stigmatize his repression. In a country as vast and powerful as China, domestic pressure for reform will always be key, but given Beijing's sensitivity to international stigmatization, that external pressure can help open space for domestic activism.

The enormity of the problem posed by China requires a long-term perspective. But Human Rights Watch made a difference by continuing to spotlight the worst abuses regardless of the difficulty of investigative access, by cutting through the facile justifications offered by some governments for responding inadequately to that repression, and by organizing as much international pressure for positive change as possible.

Russia and Syria

Russian president Vladimir Putin has an even harder time than the Chinese government in presenting a positive vision for his rule. He cannot offer even the false utopia of Soviet communist ideology. His disastrous decision, in COVID-induced isolation talking only to yes-men, to invade Ukraine, thinking it would be a cakewalk, is a powerful example of the dangers of unaccountable, authoritarian government. Initially facing widespread protests, his postinvasion reign became increasingly closed and repressive.

Just as the Chinese Communist Party tries to measure its progress from the devastation of the Cultural Revolution, Putin has the advantage of having taken power after the chaos and privations under Boris Yeltsin, Russia's first post-Soviet leader. Putin presided over a rise in global oil and gas prices that helped to fund the Russian state budget and significantly raised living standards in Russia. But Putin always seemed most concerned with enriching a handful of cronies—and himself. He never made much effort to improve conditions for private enterprise or to diversify the economy, which was stagnating even before his invasion of Ukraine.

Offering no positive vision for the future, the best that Putin can do is to lionize the past, trumpeting his support for supposedly traditional values. He extols the family and religion and attacks the cosmopolitanism of Western elites. His nostalgic veneration of Russia of old recalls the supposed halcyon days when Moscow was regarded as a world power. Never mind that those were also the days of economic hardship and the gulag. Putin has resurrected Stalin as the model of a strong leader, while shutting down Memorial, the human-rights group dedicated to recording Stalin's atrocities that was awarded the 2022 Nobel Peace Prize.

Putin's retrograde message may be attractive to his base, centered in the Russian hinterland where, unlike Moscow and Saint Petersburg, fewer have benefited from the Western connections that he undermines. But his reverence for a supposedly idyllic past is insufficient to attract broad popular support. Although he has no respect for human rights, as illustrated by his repression at home, his atrocities in Ukraine, and his rejection of contemporary norms such as the rights of LGBT people, he doesn't explicitly reject human rights. Instead, the Kremlin's strategies to defend its repressive rule include enormous efforts to highlight anything that might make life in the West look bad. Russian propaganda outfits such as RT as well as state-run domestic television are filled with coverage of disasters and misconduct in the West. It is as if no bad news in the West is too obscure to highlight. The Kremlin suggests that while the Russian government has its faults, so does everyone else.

The Kremlin's social media trolls also promote divisiveness in the West. The Kremlin seeks both to stymie Western government action by fueling controversy and to portray democracy as paralyzed. The boisterous cacophony of democracy is contrasted unfavorably with the orderly march of authoritarian rule.

In addition, Putin attacks fact-based discourse, an early devotee of "alternative facts." Russian propaganda blithely asserts absurd falsehoods, calculating that while some of its concoctions will be called out, no one can address them all, and some people will believe them. This propaganda goes beyond denying reports of the Kremlin's own human-rights violations—many governments do that; it makes endless false claims, no matter how outlandish, to shift the blame or to obfuscate reality. The Kremlin needs only to confuse, not persuade. Russian propagandists promote a distrust of all facts. If facts are unreliable, then shaming is more difficult, because shaming depends on acceptance of reality.

Such cynicism is not easy to counter, but our meticulous fact-finding helped. We served as a trusted source to which people could turn, making it harder to claim that the facts were unknowable.

In Ukraine, the Kremlin spread the lie—without proof—that for atrocities such as the massacre in Bucha or the bombing of the Mariupol theater, the killings were either fake or done by Ukrainians. Human Rights Watch and others collected eyewitness testimony, physical evidence, photographs, and further proof that these were in fact Russian war crimes. Within Russia, the closed information environment left many people believing the Kremlin's lies. Those who sought the truth could find it through channels that remained open—Telegram and YouTube—or by using VPNs, but the average passive consumer of the news did not bother. Yet, given the significant number of antiwar protests and other acts of defiance in Russia early on despite the censorship and propaganda, and despite the threat of prison for publicly challenging the Kremlin, facts remained powerful. Indeed, the Kremlin would not be making such an effort to keep facts away from its nationals if those facts were not influential. Shaming remained possible.

—

At the United Nations, some governments were sympathetic to Russia because they had benefited from Russian arms or military support, remembered Soviet support for their anticolonial struggles, or embraced the Kremlin's view that human rights were Western impositions. When it came to Ukraine, however, Putin's cynical strategy ran aground on public horror at Russian atrocities.

Putin tried to build support by trumpeting his invasion of Ukraine as a defense against a supposed threat from NATO and a stand against the West. That rhetoric had some resonance—some significant governments, including India and South Africa, tried to avoid taking sides—but it couldn't camouflage what was an unprovoked effort to exert colonial-style dominance over Ukraine.

Russia's veto prevented the UN Security Council from addressing Ukraine. But overwhelming majorities in the UN General Assembly, where there is no veto, condemned both Russia's invasion of Ukraine and its later declared annexation of four Ukrainian regions, and called for Russian forces to withdraw and to respect international humanitarian law. The General Assembly also suspended Russia from the UN Human Rights Council, something that had happened only once before, for Gaddafi's Libya, and rebuffed Russia's later effort to rejoin the council.

The Human Rights Council, in turn, established monitoring mechanisms not only for war crimes in Ukraine but also for domestic repression in Russia—a first for one of the five permanent Security Council members. Forty-three states referred the situation in Ukraine to the International Criminal Court. The ICC was empowered to address the war crimes, even though the Russian government never joined the court, because the Ukrainian government had conferred jurisdiction for crimes on its territory. Within days of Russia's invasion, the ICC's chief prosecutor, Karim Khan, opened an investigation. In March 2023, he filed initial charges against Putin and his children's rights commissioner for the war crimes of forcible transfer and deportation of Ukrainian children to Russia. In March and June 2024, he charged four Russian military commanders for missile attacks on Ukraine's electrical infrastructure. Putin remained vulnerable to additional charges under the doctrine of command responsibility. In addition, Ukrainian prosecutors opened tens of thousands of war-crime cases. Several European governments, foremost Germany, opened criminal investigations under the concept known as universal jurisdiction. That principle, established initially to combat piracy, allows certain of the most serious crimes—torture, war crimes, crimes against humanity, genocide—to be prosecuted in any national court that its government empowers to pursue such cases. The strong international response to Russian war crimes reaffirmed that the protection of civilians remains a central tenet of the modern rules for warfare.

For Putin to ignore the ICC charges indefinitely will require remaining president for life, a feat that is difficult to pull off. Once a president loses power, the successor government can face significant pressure to surrender him for trial. Just as the Serbian government, eager to resume normal relations with Europe and the United States, surrendered its former president Slobodan Milosevic for trial in The Hague in 2001, so a future Russian government, desperate to lift sanctions imposed because of Putin's invasion of Ukraine, might have a considerable incentive to surrender Putin.

Putin's world is already shrinking. The August 2023 summit in South Africa for BRICS, the group of governments that initially included Brazil, Russia, India, China, and South Africa, proved too risky for him to attend. When Omar al-Bashir, then Sudan's president, was facing ICC charges and joined an African Union summit in South Africa in 2015, he had to flee quickly after a South African court ordered his arrest. Putin did not want to risk similar embarrassment.

As in any major armed conflict, we deployed teams of investigators to Ukraine, traveling as close to the front lines as was reasonably safe. Our researchers visited localities after Russian forces had left to collect testimony from eyewitnesses of abuse, gather physical evidence, and take photographs. As a matter of principle, we reported on abuses by both sides, though the vast majority of abuses were by Russian forces.

Where our researchers did not have physical access, we deployed our open-source investigators to collect and verify hundreds of videos posted on social media and to analyze satellite imagery. Other researchers interviewed people who had fled the site of atrocities. For the Ukrainian city of Mariupol, this remote investigation allowed us, among other things, to assess the number and types of buildings that the often indiscriminate Russian bombardment had damaged or destroyed. Indiscriminate bombing is a war crime. To make these findings more compelling, our open-source researchers, working with a specialist group, created a digital before-and-after reconstruction to show the extraordinary damage. The organization also used such visualization to illustrate the effect of Russian forces' use of indiscriminate cluster munitions at a crowded railway station in Kramatorsk. Cluster munitions open above ground and typically disperse scores of lethal bomblets over a wide area.

My colleagues and I were able to deploy some of our Ukraine research during a dramatic April 2022 Security Council event at the United Nations. The purpose was to highlight the need to punish the people responsible for the war crimes in Ukraine. I joined the main panel along with Michelle Bachelet, then the UN human-rights high commissioner, and Karim Khan, the ICC prosecutor. At the time, Ida Sawyer, the director of our Crisis and Conflict program, was in Kyiv. I introduced her, and she gave a powerful video presentation of her team's findings to the assembled diplomats, bringing a concrete dimension to the diplomatic discussion in New York.

There are obstacles to prosecuting Putin and his entourage for the crime of aggression in Ukraine. The ICC's Assembly of States Parties gave the court jurisdiction beginning in July 2018, but only when the accused's government has explicitly accepted it or the UN Security Council has conferred it. The Russian government has not accepted the ICC and would veto a Security Council resolution. At best, the UN General Assembly or a combination of states might create a special tribunal. An international tribunal could be empowered not to recognize immunity for a head of state, but the U.S., British, and French governments favored a hybrid tribunal, with international elements added to Ukraine's national court system, even though the Ukrainian justice system recognizes head-of-state immunity. (The Ukrainian courts might try to create an exception for Putin, but that would be vulnerable to legal challenge.) These Western governments preferred a hybrid tribunal because they worry that an international tribunal might set a precedent that could be used to prosecute one of their own officials for a future war. It would be a shame if Western fears for their own officials allowed Putin to escape prosecution for his crime.

———

A key moment for the human-rights movement in the Soviet Union was the 1975 Helsinki Accords, signed by thirty-three European nations as well as the United States and Canada. Leonid Brezhnev's government embraced the accords because it saw them as ratifying the division of Europe that Churchill, Roosevelt, and Stalin had agreed to at Yalta as World War II was ending. The Soviet government therefore went along with the "third basket," which affirmed respect for "human rights and fundamental freedoms, including the freedom of thought, conscience, religion or belief, for all without distinction as to race, sex, language or religion." It also confirmed "the right of the individual to know and act upon his rights and duties in this field," which was understood to include the right to monitor the human-rights practices of one's government. The accords marked the first Soviet acceptance that human rights are a legitimate subject of international concern. The Soviet government was so proud of its achievement in securing Western recognition of its sphere of influence in Europe that *Pravda* showed Brezhnev signing the accords on its front page and reprinted them in their entirety.

Soon afterward, in 1976, eleven people in Moscow formed the Moscow Helsinki Group to monitor Soviet compliance. Many of them were promptly imprisoned. Their call to the West to create monitoring groups to try to protect them gave rise, in late 1978, to Helsinki Watch, the first of five regional Watch groups that were to become Human Rights Watch.

In 1992, a year after the Soviet Union collapsed, we opened an office in Moscow, initially under the leadership of Rachel Denber, a deeply committed Russian-speaking American who has overseen our work in most of the former Soviet Union ever since. The Kremlin put up with the office. Our Moscow-based researchers were able to travel most of the country to monitor and report on conditions.

I saw that relative openness in November 1999, when I first visited Moscow to release a major report, "Confessions at Any Cost," on torture by police in Russia. A young Russian woman, Tanya Lokshina, who served as my interpreter, displayed impressive knowledge about human rights in the country. She would later become director of our Russia work.

We were received by a broad group of senior Russian officials—essentially everyone we wanted to see short of Putin, who had recently become prime minister—including the prosecutor general and the minister of internal affairs. The meetings were serious, respectful, constructive, and gave us modest cause for hope. The officials did not deny that torture was being employed, although they disputed the scope. A main message of our report was that the authorities were not investigating allegations of torture. They promised to look into it. Over the next decade, the authorities collaborated with rights groups in combating torture, with prosecutions in some high-profile cases.

At the time, things were far from hopeful in Chechnya, a republic of the Russian Federation in the northern Caucasus where an insurgency sought independence. During the most atrocity-filled early parts of the Second Chechen War in 1999 and 2000, our researchers were stationed on the Chechen administrative border in the neighboring North Caucasus republic of Ingushetia. Speaking with Chechens as they fled the conflict, and making occasional forays into Chechnya, they issued more than sixty bulletins, press releases, and letters detailing Russian forces' assaults on Chechen civilians. Grozny, the Chechen capital, was bombed so intensively that the UN called it "the most destroyed city on the earth."

We used the information we collected to build international pressure to curb abuses. Based largely on our evidence, the UN Human Rights Commission condemned Russian conduct in Chechnya—its first condemnation of one of the permanent members of the UN Security Council. The Council of Europe's Parliamentary Assembly suspended Russia's voting rights and urged member states to bring Russia before the European Court of Human Rights. The court, in turn, issued repeated judgments against Russia based in part on our findings, although the Russian government, while paying the damages ordered, tended not to change the practices condemned. In Ingushetia, our researchers successfully pressured the Russian government to stop the forcible return to Chechnya of some three hundred thousand displaced people while abuses continued. In Moscow, senior officials met with us and vowed to curtail abuses and prosecute offenders, suggesting they were feeling the heat. The atrocities gave an early illustration of the depths to which Putin would go.

By 2003, Putin, who had become president, had taken control of the three major television broadcasters, the primary source of information at the time for most Russians. But the rest of the Russian-language media still cited our work some 150 to 200 times per month. Things remained open enough in June 2005 that the Human Rights Watch board of directors held a meeting in Moscow to mark the tenth anniversary of our office. We hosted a large reception at the Museum of Contemporary Russian History that a broad range of activists felt comfortable attending. On the day of the reception, the museum, located on a major Moscow boulevard, draped a large Human Rights Watch banner across its façade.

There were other signs of openness. In May 2005, an armed protest had broken out in Andijan, in eastern Uzbekistan, against the dictatorship of Islam Karimov. Gunmen attacked several government buildings, broke into the city prison to release twenty-three popular local businessmen who faced charges of religious extremism, and mobilized people to attend a protest on the city's main square later that day. The vast majority of the thousands of people who gathered there were unarmed. Without warning, Uzbek security forces surrounded the square and killed hundreds as they fled.

The Uzbek government promptly closed off the city, trying to prevent details of the massacre from leaking out. Some survivors escaped to neighboring Kyrgyzstan, some fifty kilometers away, but Anna Neistat, a Russian lawyer who directed our Moscow office after Rachel Denber before becoming a researcher with our emergency team, was determined to collect additional testimony from survivors in Andijan. Using her Russian passport, she entered Uzbekistan dressed as an unthreatening local woman. She was able to pass through six government checkpoints and reach the city. She documented not only the massacre but also the cover-up: the government tampering with the crime scene and intimidating witnesses. No one else had been able to collect such detailed information. Within a month, she had issued a detailed report, which I released, with the Human Rights Watch board in the room, at a jam-packed news conference in Moscow. The report helped persuade the European Union to issue visa bans against the Uzbek officials believed responsible. More than four hundred witnesses who had fled Andijan for neighboring Kyrgyzstan were resettled in various countries as refugees for their safety.

It was not long before things in Russia took a violent turn for the worse. In Chechnya, we worked closely with the Russian human-rights group Memorial's most visible researcher, Natalia Estemirova, who was based in its office in Grozny.* In July 2009, Tanya Lokshina spent a week in Grozny conducting an investigation with Natalia. Natalia gave an interview about one appalling case in which Russian forces had executed a villager in front of his residence for allegedly giving a sheep to the rebels. Unidentified security personnel soon murdered Natalia.

The unchecked atrocities that Putin unleashed in Chechnya gradually spread to the rest of Russia. In 2006, Anna Neistat wrote:

The first TV reports to be subjected to full-scale censorship were from the Chechen war zone, in 2000. The first groups

---

* Human Rights Watch honored her in 2007 for her impressive work documenting atrocities during the Second Chechen War.

targeted by Russia's anti-NGO policies were the human rights organizations that criticized the war in Chechnya and publicized the abuses there. Thousands of Russian policemen who have served in Chechnya are now applying the brutal practices they learned there across the country.

One victim of such practices was the journalist Anna Politkovskaya. For nearly seven years, starting in 1999, she traveled to Chechnya for the independent newspaper *Novaya Gazeta*. Anna took "tremendous personal risks to tell stories of indiscriminate bombing and shelling, atrocious mop-up operations by federal forces, brutal killings, disappearances and torture of civilians," Tanya wrote. In 2006, she was killed in the lobby of her Moscow apartment block, one of six *Novaya Gazeta* journalists and contributors to have been murdered between 2000 and 2009.

The violence in Chechnya began spreading across the neighboring republics of the northern Caucasus including Dagestan, where in 2012 Tanya was planning one of several investigative trips. Someone in the Russian government wanted to prevent that. She began receiving text messages on her mobile phone from someone claiming to represent a local fundamentalist Muslim group. The person knew where Tanya lived and what she was doing, making explicit reference to Tanya's pregnancy at the time and threatening to harm her and her unborn child. The texts included details that could have been obtained only by someone having monitored her phone.

Given the deadly attacks on other leading rights activists, we had already taken basic precautions to secure our Moscow office and Tanya's home. But these targeted threats led us to pull Tanya out of the country for a while.

Before she left, we held a news conference in Moscow to denounce the threats and filed official complaints with Russian authorities. Russia's visa system made it impossible for me to attend the news conference as I wanted to do, so I sent a video from New York. I said that threats of this sort would not stop our work on Russia but would reinforce our determination to proceed. Tanya and another member of the Human Rights Watch staff received two more threatening messages just before our planned news conference. We went ahead with it anyway.

Tanya once met with Dmitry Medvedev during his 2008–12 interlude as Russian president, as he kept the seat warm for Putin, who temporarily became prime minister again due to constitutional term limits. Putin would never meet with us. In December 2014, I was able to speak in Moscow with Mikhail Fedotov, at the time Putin's top human-rights adviser, but I encountered Putin only once, in February 2007, at a distance.

When direct access is limited, sometimes the best we can do is to make use of a public event. I used this technique with the former Iranian president Mahmoud Ahmadinejad, who would not meet alone with Human Rights Watch. However, I was invited to meet with him as part of a group organized by the Council on Foreign Relations during his September 2006 visit to the UN General Assembly in New York.

Ahmadinejad seemed cocky and confident about his ability to make a good impression. Extended conversation was impossible, but I did ask him why his government was imprisoning journalists, closing newspapers, and sponsoring elections that were not free and fair. In response, Ahmadinejad claimed that Iran was freer than the United States.

My encounter with Putin came during the Munich Security Conference, where participants in the main events are crammed into the modest-sized ballroom of a storied old hotel. Putin talked as if he were reviving the Cold War, denouncing the "unipolar world," meaning one led by the United States. George W. Bush's disastrous 2003 invasion of Iraq had clearly struck a nerve because of the unchecked assertion of U.S. military power. Putin also was upset with NATO's expansion into many of the countries that had been under Soviet domination.

After his speech, I asked him publicly about the "unipolar government" that he was building in Russia, where dissent and criticism were not allowed. Putin's answer was long, meandering, and largely unresponsive.

———

A major focus of Human Rights Watch's work on Russia during the 2010s involved Syria. Russia's September 2015 military intervention there reflected in part Putin's dislike of the precedent of a popular uprising overthrowing a dictator. He also undoubtedly wanted to distinguish himself from Obama, who had not intervened to prevent the 2011 Tahrir Square uprising from toppling Egyptian president Mubarak. Putin wanted to show that he stuck with his allies, however brutal.

Putin pretended to be defending the right of the Syrian people to determine their own future—a reference to the external military support for the Syrian rebels. The reality was that the Assad government, through its ruthlessness, was determining the future on its own. When the Syrian people spoke out through protests, the common response was arbitrary detention, torture, and execution, and forced disappearance.

I could not help but be appalled by the repression. It also became a passion of Annie's. Now a professor teaching global public health at a major medical school in New York City, she has been addressing the effect of repression and wartime atrocities on health for two decades. Because of the deliberate attacks on health care, the effect in Syria was dramatic. With so many doctors having been killed or having fled the country, those who remained often lacked training on how to treat the physical and mental trauma of people living in a war zone. Medical students, dentists, or pharmacists were stepping in to do what was needed. Annie was one of a group of doctors who regularly traveled to Gaziantep to train contingents of Syrian doctors. She invited me to accompany her to gain my own appreciation of the atrocities being committed across the border.

Beyond introducing me to the doctors, she encouraged me to share a cramped apartment with a Syrian refugee family from Aleppo who had become aid workers, visit an orphanage for Syrian children who bombarded me with questions about how the world saw the war, and meet with many of the humanitarian workers based in Gaziantep. The plight of Syrians became such a personal issue for both of us that I would sometimes ask jokingly at the dinner table whether we could talk about anything other than Syria. The answer was often no. This immersion gave me a very personal sense of the viciousness of the war, reinforcing my determination to do what I could to stop these atrocities. It became a central focus of my work.

Putin deployed the same war-crime strategy in Syria that he had used in Chechnya and would later pursue in Ukraine. The world's failure to respond firmly enough to Russian atrocities in Chechnya and Syria laid the foundation for their repetition in Ukraine. In 2015 and 2016, Russian and Syrian bombing largely devastated opposition-held parts of eastern Aleppo, once Syria's largest city. With the residents suffering under a punishing siege as well as indiscriminate attacks with cluster munitions, barrel bombs, incendiary weapons, and high-explosive bombs, opposition forces ultimately surrendered. Journalists at the time compared eastern Aleppo to the devastation of Grozny during the Second Chechen War.

With equally devastating results, Russian forces repeated these tactics in Eastern Ghouta, a suburban and rural area east of Damascus, and Idlib province. As I said, they deliberately bombed hospitals, markets, schools, and apartment buildings, in some cases repeatedly. The apparent aim was to create such difficult conditions for civilians that they would leave, making it easier for Syrian ground troops to move in and overcome the remaining rebel forces.

My colleagues and I at Human Rights Watch tried to move Russian public opinion about the war crimes in Syria—part of our plan to persuade the Kremlin to exert pressure on Damascus to stop bombing civilians. On my way to Moscow in December 2014, I took a detour to Kyiv. In February of that year, following the Maidan Square popular uprising that ousted Ukrainian president Viktor Yanukovych, a Putin ally, Russia-backed forces had seized Crimea from Ukraine. In April, similar forces had invaded large parts of the Donbas region of eastern Ukraine. Human Rights Watch researchers onsite had investigated the war crimes committed, but I wanted a firsthand understanding of them so I could address them in Moscow.

My reception in Moscow in December was very different from my prior two trips. A crackdown on Russian human-rights groups had been under way since Putin resumed the presidency in May 2012. The only government meeting I was granted was an exasperating and pointless one with two midlevel Foreign Ministry officials. However, I was able to speak about Syria and other global issues to a packed auditorium of students and faculty at the elite Higher School of Economics in Moscow. The faculty seemed to be aware of what I was discussing, but for many of the students, as Tanya put it, it was an "eye-opener." They seemed to have little idea that the Syrian government was "fighting" the rebels in large part by bombing civilians in rebel-held territory. I spent a lot of time talking about the indiscriminate barrel bombs that the Syrian air force was dropping on opposition-held cities—eighty-two thousand attacks over the course of the war. What was common knowledge in much of the world was largely unknown within Russia.

The Russian government had recognized in a February 2014 UN Security Council resolution that the Syrian government was doing the things I described. But the Kremlin was facilitating Assad's civilian-killing machine by providing military assistance, including servicing Assad's helicopters, which often dropped the bombs.

As the Russian government became more isolated abroad because of its seizure of Ukrainian territory, the Kremlin doubled down on its efforts to silence critical voices at home. During my December 2014 visit, I held a news conference at Interfax, the high-tech, polished media center in Moscow that Human Rights Watch usually used. I was able to address Syria, Ukraine, and repression inside Russia. But within several years, Interfax stopped hosting organizations that criticized the government. I said at the time that Russia was suffering the worst crackdown on dissent in the country since Soviet times—something that, sadly, I could have said truthfully again and again as time went on.

The Russian government used a variety of techniques to stifle civil society, all of which we reported on. Perhaps the most notorious was the "foreign agents" law, adopted in July 2012, shortly after Putin began his third presidential term amid widespread protests over alleged electoral fraud. The term "foreign agent" in Russian carries connotations of being a spy, and its application guaranteed being ostracized by all government officials, subject to onerous official inspections and reporting requirements, and having to post a long, demeaning disclaimer on every public utterance. The charge was applied to media organizations, human-rights groups, politicians, journalists, and activists.

In June 2015, a new law on "undesirable" foreign organizations authorized the extrajudicial banning of foreign or international groups that allegedly undermined Russia's security, defense, or constitutional order. Russians who maintained ties with "undesirables" faced penalties ranging from fines to six years in prison. The law allowed the Kremlin to criminalize working for a group whose criticism it disliked, such as any organization associated with the late opposition leader and anti-corruption campaigner Aleksei Navalny. The law was also used to disqualify independent candidates for office.

Leading opposition figures were poisoned or killed. In February 2015, Boris Nemtsov was murdered just outside the Kremlin, days before he was to lead a protest against Putin's 2014 invasion of Ukraine. "In the months running up to the killing, Nemtsov was being followed across Russia by a government agent linked to a secret assassination squad," according to a BBC investigation. The European Court of Human Rights later chastised Russian authorities for their perfunctory investigation into who ordered the killing. Before he died in prison in February 2024, Navalny was almost killed in an August 2020 attack by the Russian Federal Security Service, or FSB, using the Novichok nerve agent. The FSB also poisoned Vladimir Kara-Murza, an independent journalist, in 2015 and 2017.

Despite all this, we could still make a difference—mainly where the Kremlin did not feel its power was under threat. For example, our 2013 report on migrant workers at sites for the 2014 Winter Olympics in Sochi contributed to what a senior Russian official said was the payment of $8.3 million in unpaid wages. When we issued our 2014 report on abuses against Russian children with disabilities who were placed in state orphanages, the ministry in charge said it distributed the report to all state agencies concerned with child welfare, instructing them to find ways to implement our recommendations. Our reporting in 2017 on the detention and killing of gay men in Chechnya under its president, Ramzan Kadyrov, contributed to the public revelation that he and Putin had discussed it during a meeting in Moscow, and the abuses largely stopped.

Things declined dramatically with Putin's full-scale invasion of Ukraine in February 2022. As the war went far worse than Putin expected, accounts of Russian war crimes emerged, and Russian popular discontent with the "special military operation" mounted, the Kremlin launched draconian wartime censorship of independent media and human-rights groups. In January 2023, it would shut down the Moscow Helsinki Group.

The previous year's Nobel Peace Prize laureate, Dmitry Muratov, the chief editor of *Novaya Gazeta,* the leading Russian independent newspaper, had to suspend the paper's publication because censorship laws made the staff vulnerable to criminal prosecution. Hundreds of journalists for independent Russian media left the country in the spring of 2022 to continue their work from abroad. In April 2022, the Russian government closed our office of thirty years in Moscow as part of a broader Kremlin attack on international organizations in Russia. Amnesty International and thirteen other groups were shut down too. Our staff continued to monitor conditions from abroad, but that was far from ideal.

In May 2022, the Kremlin "sanctioned" a long list of people, including me. The move had no immediate impact on my life, though it presumably bars me from traveling again to Russia. I wear it as a badge of honor.

—

Due to the difficulty of mobilizing Russian society to oppose the war crimes in Syria, we focused on opportunities in international forums to condemn, and ideally prosecute, the crimes. Because the Syrian government never joined the International Criminal Court, it had no automatic jurisdiction over the mass atrocities there. In May 2014, a resolution was introduced in the UN Security Council to refer Syria to the ICC—an alternative route to jurisdiction—but Russia, joined by China, vetoed it. We were forced to look to the UN General Assembly, though not as a path to the ICC, because it didn't have that power. However, unlike the 15-member Security Council and the 47-member Human Rights Council, the General Assembly is composed of all 193 UN member states, which makes advocacy time-consuming. But the atrocities of the Syrian conflict were appalling enough to warrant trying to encourage them to address the impunity.

I had proposed the idea of using the General Assembly in various forums, and I wrote about it in a December 2016 article in *The New York Review of Books*. Slowly, it gained acceptance. One option was to ask the General Assembly to create a Syria Tribunal, but many were understandably reluctant to take that step for fear of undermining the International Criminal Court. The ICC, with potentially global reach, was created after a series of country-specific tribunals (for Yugoslavia, Rwanda, Sierra Leone, and Cambodia) as a substitute for such narrowly focused tribunals. Instead, we sought to create, in essence, a prosecutor without a court. Though lacking the power to issue indictments or arrest warrants, the prosecutor would collect, analyze, and preserve evidence and build cases for prosecution in whatever tribunal became available. After months of advocacy in European capitals, the idea took off.

A key ally in the effort was tiny Liechtenstein. While most countries rotate diplomats among posts every three to four years, Liechtenstein tends to keep its mere handful of diplomats in place. As a result, its ambassador to the United Nations in New York, Christian Wenaweser, was the dean of the ambassadorial core. He had been in his position since 2002, knew everyone, and was widely respected. He also believed deeply in justice for those who committed mass atrocities. Liechtenstein was joined by Qatar, which offered important Middle East endorsement, and Germany, the Netherlands, and Canada, which had far larger diplomatic missions in New York capable of doing the legwork needed to visit the other missions to rally support.

The result was an overwhelming win. By a vote of 105 to 15 (with 52 abstentions), the General Assembly established what became known as the International, Impartial, and Independent Mechanism (or IIIM) to conduct investigations and assist national judiciaries to prosecute the most serious crimes in Syria. The IIIM in its first seven years was headed by Catherine Marchi-Uhel, a no-nonsense former French judge with years of experience with international tribunals. Working from her Geneva office, where I met with her to discuss the sharing of evidence and to compare analyses, she quietly and methodically built cases for prosecution. One important venue for prosecution was national courts in Europe under the doctrine of universal jurisdiction. As of December 2023, the IIIM had received 325 requests for assistance from 16 jurisdictions and had assisted 162 distinct national investigations. In March 2024, Catherine was replaced by Robert Petit, a Canadian prosecutor who had coheaded the effort in Cambodia to prosecute the Khmer Rouge.

The threat of prosecution, while important, was a long-term prospect. We thus had to generate more immediate external pressure as well. The UN Human Rights Council in Geneva was already deeply engaged in the Syrian conflict. With our backing in August 2011, it established a commission of inquiry led by Paulo Sérgio Pinheiro, a

Brazilian jurist, professor, and long-standing human-rights defender. The commission did yeoman's work, doggedly documenting and reporting atrocities in Syria, but Assad was one of the few leaders who was largely beyond shaming. He was seemingly willing to commit any atrocity to stay in power, and the people of Syria were already doing everything they could to oust him.

To shame where we could, we refined our usual strategy, focusing on the handful of atrocities that were deemed especially heinous, such as the Syrian government's network of detention centers used for torture and execution. One courageous photographer for the Syrian military, who used the pseudonym Caesar, had the unenviable task of taking pictures of the bodies that emerged from Assad's detention centers. He smuggled out of the country 53,275 of those digital photographs showing at least 6,786 bodies. After that, there was no denying the extent of Assad's atrocities.

Nadim Houry, a Canadian-Lebanese lawyer fluent in Arabic, French, and English, who was our deputy Middle East director at the time, was based in Beirut. With calm dispassion and meticulous care, he was able to verify the identity of twenty-seven of the victims by locating and speaking to their family members. The families spent months or years seeking news about the fate of their loved ones, often paying huge sums to people with alleged ties to government agencies. Only two ever received death certificates, which unhelpfully noted heart or respiratory failure, the euphemisms that the Assad government often used for people who had been tortured to death. None received the bodies of their family members for burial.

These were horrible stories, but given that our primary strategy was to target Assad indirectly through Putin, we needed to focus on areas where the Russian government was particularly sensitive. Russia's military support for the Syrian government made the Kremlin indirectly responsible for all Syrian government conduct, but there was no evidence that Russian troops played a significant role in Assad's detention centers.

Russia's main contribution to the conflict was from the air, which explains why Putin took a special interest in fending off reports about any unlawful bombardment, including by the Syrian planes it was assisting. Over time, targeting civilians with any weapon became an issue of public concern, as during our campaign to stop all bombing of civilians in Idlib. During earlier periods of the war, however, the debate centered mainly on the use of chemical weapons. Syrian forces were estimated to have launched at least 336 such attacks through 2019, using chlorine and sarin. When inhaled in large amounts, chlorine mixes with water droplets in the respiratory passage to become hydrochloric acid, which destroys the cells in the lungs, causing victims to drown as their lungs fill with fluid. Sarin, an odorless nerve agent that is far more lethal, interferes with an enzyme that stops muscles from contracting, often leading to an inability to breathe.

Chemical weapons played a particularly insidious role in Syria because their chemicals are heavier than air and sink, which meant that Syrians who took shelter in their basements during bombardments were *more* vulnerable to chemical attacks. Children, given their smaller stature, were especially vulnerable.

The Syrian government's first confirmed use of sarin was in August 2013 to attack Eastern Ghouta, the opposition-controlled area near Damascus. Some fourteen hundred civilians were killed and thousands more affected. Beyond global outrage at so many people being slaughtered, questions immediately arose about the international response. A year before, in August 2012, President Obama had declared that the Syrian government's use of chemical weapons would cross a "red line" and bring "enormous consequences." Most people assumed he meant some form of military intervention.

At first, the Syrian government, backed by Moscow, blamed the rebels. Putin published an op-ed in *The New York Times* claiming that opposition forces had used the chemical attack "to provoke intervention by their powerful foreign patrons." Anna Neistat responded in *The Guardian* by noting Putin's hypocrisy in opposing an International Criminal Court investigation of atrocities in Syria.

By September 2013, we had demonstrated that the Syrian government was responsible. One type of rocket used, reconfigured to deliver sarin, had never been seen before in the Syrian conflict and had been filmed only in government hands. The estimated fifty to sixty liters of sarin in each rocket—ten to twelve were fired—were well beyond the quantity that anyone claimed the rebels might possess. And the trajectory that could be traced for two rockets suggested a launching pad at a government military base adjacent to

Assad's presidential palace. A UN investigation commissioned by Secretary-General Ban Ki-moon largely confirmed our conclusion.

Obama seemed poised to respond with military force, joined by Britain and France. But the British Parliament in late August 2013 voted narrowly against taking action, and Obama, facing pressure from Capitol Hill, quickly announced that he would seek authorization from Congress, which was unlikely to be forthcoming. At the G20 summit in Saint Petersburg a week later, Obama and Putin agreed to work together to address Syria's stockpile of chemical weapons. Days later in London, U.S. Secretary of State John Kerry announced that the Syrian government could avoid military action by surrendering its chemical weapons. He and Russian foreign minister Sergey Lavrov soon worked out the details.

As a result, the Russian government agreed to a September 2013 UN Security Council resolution ordering "the expeditious destruction" of Syria's chemical-weapons program as well as "stringent verification" measures. Until then, whether the issue had been condemning atrocities, imposing sanctions or an arms embargo, or referring Syria to the ICC, Russia's response had always been a stated or threatened *nyet*. The possibility of U.S. military intervention changed the Kremlin's calculations.

Although at various stages during the Syrian conflict our staff debated whether we should call for military action as a matter of humanitarian intervention to stop the slaughter of civilians, we could not reach enough consensus to take a position. I personally favored a limited intervention—for example, targeting the aircraft being used to bomb civilians—but the Middle East staff was worried, among other things, that, without aircraft to fend off attacking forces, the Assad government would be toppled. It feared that the force taking over could be ruthless—something like the Islamic State, which was then seizing swaths of territory. In addition to its videotaped executions, ISIS also used chemical weapons.

Syria, one of the world's last holdouts, promptly joined the Chemical Weapons Convention (CWC). By June 2014, the process for ridding Syria of its chemical weapons was incorrectly said to have been completed. But the Syrian military continued to use chemical weapons, including a devastating April 2017 sarin attack on the town of Khan Sheikhoun that killed at least ninety people. The Kremlin claimed that a Syrian bomb had hit a rebel cache of sarin. It most certainly had not.

As we showed with the help of Syrians on the ground, the use of sarin in Khan Sheikhoun was one of four examples of nerve-agent use over the course of a few months in the vicinity. The massive negative publicity around those attacks compelled Syrian forces to stop their use (although limited chlorine use continued). We do not know whether Assad made this decision on his own or under pressure from Putin, but it showed the continuing relevance of shaming, even in Syria, at least on certain issues.

One related procedural victory involved the Organization for the Prohibition of Chemical Weapons (OPCW), the lead agency for enforcing the CWC. The OPCW does invaluable work monitoring and deterring potential violations of the CWC, but it was empowered to say only whether chemical weapons had been used, not to identify who used them. That facilitated the Russian and Syrian denials about Syrian responsibility. Under Western pressure, the Russian government supported UN Security Council resolutions in 2015 and 2016 creating and extending what was known as a Joint Investigative Mechanism, or JIM, to work with the OPCW to identify perpetrators. After two years, in which the JIM had confirmed Syrian government responsibility for chemical-weapons use in several attacks, the Russian government vetoed renewal of the JIM, ending its mandate in November 2017.

At that point, a French and British government initiative, ultimately supported by twenty-eight other governments, led to a 2018 resolution among the states party to the CWC. Passed by a vote of 82 to 24, it gave the OPCW permission to identify perpetrators. The Russian government fought this effort vigorously but lost. As a result, the OPCW attributed likely responsibility to the Syrian government for a chlorine and two sarin attacks in March 2017 and a chlorine attack in February 2018.

In February and April 2017, the Russian government vetoed efforts at the Security Council to impose sanctions on, and even to condemn, the Syrian government for its chemical-weapons use—a position that I had challenged the Russian representative to avoid during a plenary panel on Syria at the February 2017 Munich Security Conference. In April 2021, in a move that Human Rights Watch encouraged, the states party to the CWC voted 87 to 15 to suspend Syria's voting rights under the convention. It was important, as my colleague Lou Charbonneau put it, because the Syrian government could no longer pretend to be "a responsible government complying with one of the most adhered-to weapons bans in history."

The consequences of the OPCW's new power were apparent in its investigation of an April 2018 chlorine attack that killed forty-three civilians in the besieged Syrian town of Douma, outside of Damascus. The OPCW concluded that a chemical attack had occurred and Syrian forces were responsible. A week after that, the U.S., British, and French governments conducted a limited airstrike against what was said to be three Syrian government chemical-weapons facilities. The Syrian government reportedly was relieved that the military response had been so limited, and then largely stopped using any chemical weapons, with only one additional known case through 2023.

There was something perverse about the world's fixation on the Syrian government's use of chemical weapons, which at the time accounted for fewer than 2 percent of Syria's estimated death toll of 115,000, while leaving unimpeded the major means of slaughter. If pressure could force the Syrian military to stop using chemical weapons, why could similar pressure not have been exerted to stop the indiscriminate slaughter of civilians by other means?

—

Beyond targeting people in opposition-held areas, the Assad government tried to force them into submission by depriving them of basic necessities. International efforts to assist these desperate civilians were entirely dependent on Syrian government cooperation, which was limited. The problem was particularly acute in the medical realm. Annie wrote in 2013 in *The New York Review of Books* about how the Syrian government targeted doctors on the pretext that those treating injured protesters were assisting "terrorism." In 2018, she explained in *Foreign Policy* how the government "deleted" from convoys all lifesaving medical supplies on the same pretext.

There was no avoiding working with the Syrian government to send humanitarian aid to parts of the country that it controlled, but for opposition-held parts of northwestern Syria, humanitarian aid could in theory be provided cross-border directly from Turkey, bypassing government-dominated areas. Because the UN is a club of governments, however, its lawyers decided, controversially, that the UN's Office for the Coordination of Humanitarian Affairs (OCHA) could deliver aid only with the Syrian government's permission, which it had no intention of granting. The only other "legal" route for such cross-border deliveries of humanitarian aid, according to UN lawyers, was by authorization of the UN Security Council, which required contending with the Russian veto.

In January 2013, OCHA announced that it was unable "to reach the vast majority who are in need in the opposition-held areas" and sought permission for cross-border transfers, which we backed. Five days after the UN Security Council resolution ordering the Syrian government to rid itself of chemical weapons, the Russian government, still feeling pressure from the narrowly averted U.S. military intervention, agreed to an October 2013 Security Council "presidential statement" urging Syrian authorities, in the toughest language that the Russians would allow, to permit humanitarian aid "where appropriate, across borders from neighbouring countries in accordance with the UN guiding principles of humanitarian emergency assistance." The Syrian government largely ignored it.

Valerie Amos, who headed OCHA at the time, tended to be circumspect for fear of offending Damascus and obtaining even less cooperation, but there was no doubt that the humanitarian needs were great. At the January 2014 meeting of the World Economic Forum in Davos, for which *The New York Review of Books* rushed Annie's article on the problem to press, Amos spoke obliquely about Syrian government obstruction in her public comments. Separately, she admitted that cross-border aid remains "a red line for the Syrian government."

I spent an enormous amount of time speaking publicly about the problem. In January and February, I did countless media interviews on the subject. I made it a major part of the news conference releasing Human Rights Watch's annual World Report that year in Berlin. In February, at the Munich Security Conference, I was given the main stage for a speech highlighting the urgent need for action on the Syrian humanitarian front. To make Syria a reality for the officials in the room, I began my speech with a brief video produced by our multimedia team showing Syria's deliberate bombing of civilians and civilian institutions. With some two hundred ministers and dignitaries in attendance, there was no better forum to address the people with the power to curtail the dire situation.

Ultimately, to get past the Russian roadblock on humanitarian aid to northern Syria, we developed what we called the Sochi strategy, as I explained to the ministers gathered in Munich. From February 6 to February 23, 2014, the Russian city of Sochi hosted the Winter Olympics, a big public-relations boon for Putin that he hardly wanted spoiled by a lot of unwelcome media attention to how Russia was contributing to the suffering of civilians in northern Syria. That gave us leverage on Putin not to use his veto.

For the Sochi strategy to work, we needed UN Security Council members to introduce a resolution. The one drafted adhered to the legal conceit that the government of the territory receiving aid must consent to that aid, but "demand[ed]" that Syrian authorities provide consent. Australia, Luxembourg, and Jordan took the lead, making it easier for Russia to acquiesce because it was seen as less of a geopolitical issue. France and Britain then joined the effort.

The Obama administration initially opposed the Sochi plan. It was not inclined to exert pressure on Russia because it still viewed the Kremlin as a potential partner for peace in Syria rather than a facilitator of Assad's atrocities. John Kerry, the U.S. secretary of state, was pursuing the Geneva II peace process with the hope of ending the atrocities by ending the war. Even as the Syrian government bombed and besieged civilians in opposition-held areas, Kerry was not inclined to ratchet up pressure on the Kremlin.

The U.S. government was also reluctant—more appropriately, in my view—to treat UN Security Council approval as necessary for cross-border humanitarian operations. It did not want to endorse the view of the conservative UN lawyers that sovereignty should prevail over humanitarian need, especially when the Turkish government and Syrian rebel groups, which controlled the two sides of the relevant border, welcomed the aid operation.

The Russian government tried to stall until the Olympics ended, at which point the public relations need to accept a resolution would disappear. But on February 22, the last possible day given time-zone differences, the Russian government consented to a unanimous UN

Security Council resolution to authorize cross-border humanitarian aid.

The Syrian government ignored the resolution. That led the UN Security Council to adopt a July 2014 resolution "deploring" Syrian authorities for not complying with its earlier demand and authorizing UN humanitarian agencies to use four specified border-crossing points for a period of 180 days. That's when the aid began to flow. It is not entirely clear why the Russian government agreed to this tougher resolution as well, but a key factor was probably its desire to maintain some goodwill despite the global condemnation of Russia's invasion of Crimea, which began shortly after the Sochi Olympics, prompted by the ouster of Ukraine's pro-Russian president as the Olympics were closing. Russia allowed renewal of permission for these border crossings for periods of only twelve and then six months, meaning that Russia's consent was needed over and over, making it a bargaining chip.

Beginning in January 2020, the Russian government insisted on reducing the number of border crossings. By July 2021, there was only one left. Meanwhile, the Russian and Syrian governments kept pressing for all aid to be delivered through Damascus.

The Russian government had been threatening to end all cross-border humanitarian operations by July 2023. The devastating earthquake that struck southern Turkey and northwestern Syria in February 2023 changed the calculus. With the death and destruction so massive, openly obstructing aid would have been too callous even for the Russia-Syria alliance. The Syrian government thus consented to two additional small border crossings, initially for three months and then for another three.

In July 2023, the Russian government said it would accept no more than another six-month extension. Most other members of the Security Council wanted a twelve-month extension, but Russia vetoed that proposal. This time, however, the others apart from China, tired of the repeated short extensions, refused to go along with only six months. That seemed to end the UN's nine-year program for cross-border humanitarian aid. At the last minute, the Syrian government said it would consent to keeping the main border crossing open for humanitarian aid, so long as it was "in full cooperation and coordination" with Damascus. But the whole point of the cross-border operation was to avoid Damascus's diversion and blockage of aid. In the prior two years, while the UN had sent more than 24,000 trucks of humanitarian aid cross-border, the Syrian government had allowed only 152 trucks across front lines from within Syria. Damascus backed off, and in August 2023, the Syrian government agreed to allow the UN to keep operating cross-border, but it was unclear how long that permission would last.

A broad range of international lawyers and scholars disputed the narrow interpretation of the UN Charter regarding UN cross-border humanitarian aid, arguing that providing life-saving aid should take priority over assertions of national sovereignty, but Secretary-General Guterres supported the UN lawyers. The alternative would be for governments to fund cross-border humanitarian operations themselves, bypassing OCHA and its adherence to the views of UN lawyers, as the U.S. military did in June 2023 to provide humanitarian aid arranged by a Washington nonprofit organization to a small group of displaced Syrians in the Rukban camp in southwestern Syria. The issue was resolved with the December 2024 fall of the Assad government. Until then, it illustrated the power of information about people's suffering, properly deployed to pinpoint government responsibility, to play a significant role even in Syria to limit, if not end, that suffering.

—

Putin's invasion of Ukraine has been a disaster not only for the Ukrainian people but also for human rights within Russia. In a reversion to practices of the Soviet era, Russia has morphed from an authoritarian state where some critical voices including ours were grudgingly tolerated, to a dictatorship that allows no room for dissent. Human-rights groups can only operate underground, opposition politicians are given draconian sentences for speaking about Russian atrocities in Ukraine, independent media can no longer function, and foreign correspondents can be thrown behind bars on concocted espionage charges.

This downward trajectory shows the limits of human-rights advocacy. Enormous pressure has been exerted on the Kremlin—widespread condemnation, extensive economic sanctions, criminal prosecution, even arming its adversary in war—but it has not been enough to stop Putin from trying to prevent Ukraine from serving as a major example of democracy on Russia's borders. There was a time when his concern with his reputation, and the linked economic relations, could be used to restrain him, but because his disastrous decision to invade Ukraine imperils his rule, he is desperate. In his struggle to survive, he seems to have no qualms about taking the Russian people down with him. That makes him difficult to influence.

I still look to the Russian people. Given the pervasive propaganda and extensive censorship, many Russians support Putin despite his repression at home and his war crimes in Ukraine. But many other Russians are deeply unhappy about the direction of their country. Few will risk prison to speak out, but many are waiting for the opportunity to choose a more democratic, rights-respecting future for their country. They have lived through a significant period of relative freedom after Soviet rule and are not happy about returning to life under a dictatorship. For that reason, international pressure remains important as a signal of solidarity with the Russian people. Some backers of Ukraine have been inclined to treat all Russians as enemies, hoping that their suffering will push them to stand up to their government. I think a more productive approach is to treat them as potential allies.

The enthusiasm generated by Russian opposition leader Aleksei Navalny as he exposed, ridiculed, and decried the corrupt, self-serving Kremlin and its oligarch allies shows a broad yearning for a government that serves its people rather than itself. Having courageously returned to Russia to face certain detention even after the Russian intelligence agency tried to kill him, Navalny died while kept in cruel conditions in prison, but the desire for rights and freedom lives on among many of his followers. The strong public sentiment that the human-rights movement needs to exert pressure for change remains intact. Even in this dark moment, that is reason to persist.

Saudi Arabia

Saudi Arabia's exceptional wealth makes generating pressure on it difficult. Conditioning financial assistance on respect for human rights is a nonstarter. Moreover, no country is eager to be excluded from the Saudi government's massive purchases of arms and other such "necessities." Yet the need for pressure has increased dramatically since the Saudi crown prince, Mohammed bin Salman, became the country's de facto leader in 2017.

He began showing his colors within months of assuming power, when he detained nearly four hundred of the country's most powerful people in Riyadh's Ritz-Carlton Hotel, where many of them were tortured until they surrendered a good part of their wealth. He detained Lebanon's then prime minister, Saad Hariri, and forced him to resign, until public outrage compelled the crown prince to reverse course. Although he introduced social reforms, he imprisoned activists who pushed for those reforms as well as other critics. The women's rights activists who demanded the right to drive, for example, were locked up, even as their demands were met. He wanted to ensure that any change was understood as a product of monarchial benevolence rather than popular demand.

We looked for opportunities to shame the government and intensify pressure for it to curb its repressive practices. It was not easy, but we had our successes.

Before bin Salman rose to power, there was a time when the Saudi government was more willing to discuss its human-rights practices.

My one trip to Saudi Arabia, in 2006, took place during that period. I headed a delegation that included Sarah Leah Whitson, the director of our program for the Middle East and North Africa. The trip, Human Rights Watch's first in nearly four years because the government had been unwilling to grant access, was facilitated by Prince Turki Al Faisal Al Saud, who regularly attended the World Economic Forum in Davos, was always open to conversation with me, and presented himself as a reasonable interlocutor. Our schedule in Riyadh was filled with appointments to see one minister after another, each occupying a palatial office, often serving us copious amounts of food. But we hoped to take advantage of our rare official presence to meet as well with the country's small dissident and human-rights community. The researchers with us often left our official meetings to visit Saudi activists.

But some of the people with whom we wanted to speak were in prison. After considerable nudging, including a press release, the authorities allowed us to visit al-Ha'ir prison, the country's principal penitentiary, located just outside Riyadh. The government hoped to get away with a show tour. First, there was the usual overview from the warden, a standard time-wasting ploy used by prison authorities the world over to limit the time left for visitors to speak with inmates. My colleagues and I rushed through that meeting as quickly as possible. To see prisoners, we were ushered into a large common room that had been decorated with an elaborate spread of beautiful carpets obviously rolled out just for our visit. A troupe of white-uniformed waiters with big chef's hats stood inside the room staffing a juice bar.

I cannot imagine in the history of the world that such a luxury was ever offered to a group of prisoners. We thanked the officials for their hospitality, said we were not thirsty, and explained that we would rather spend time with the prisoners—in the privacy of their cells. The guards warned us that that would be dangerous. We said we would take our chances. We proceeded to have lengthy conversations with the prisoners about why they had been detained, the pressure exerted on them to confess, the lack of fair trials in the Saudi justice system, and their mistreatment in detention.

We wanted to meet Mohammed bin Nayef, at the time the interior minister, a post he had inherited from his father, who had held it for decades. Bin Nayef had responsibility for many of the country's internal security forces. He was also said to have cooperated constructively with U.S. counterterrorism officials after the September 11, 2001, attacks. (Bin Nayef was crown prince from 2015 to 2017, then ousted and placed under house arrest by Mohammed bin Salman.) On our last evening in the country, during a dinner hosted by the British ambassador, word came that bin Nayaf would see us—at 12:45 a.m.

The Interior Ministry is a vast, modern office building. Bin Nayef was in an upper corner office, seemingly the only office in the entire building still functioning at that hour. He was more than happy to discuss his counterterrorism strategy. He explained that, unlike the punitive approach taken by the Bush administration at Guantánamo, he hoped to rehabilitate terrorist suspects so they could reintegrate into society. As he put it, these suspects had been taught to "love death," hence their willingness to undertake suicide missions. He wanted to teach them to "love life." He described how he tried to get them jobs, wives, and families—reasons to live.

We visited a low-security center where some former Guantánamo detainees were kept, and there were no obvious signs of abuse—a far cry from Guantánamo. Most of the inmates were reluctant to talk, though, and it was impossible to determine why; perhaps it was fear of retaliation, or simply distrust of any Westerner after their horrible experience with the U.S. government.

Bin Nayef could be cagey; he said, implausibly, "I don't involve myself in politics." Still, it was hard to imagine him being an inferior ruler to the callous bin Salman.

—

Convincing Western governments to take a stand on Saudi abuses requires creativity and a lot of work. The UN Human Rights Council has never condemned the Saudi government's domestic repression. The closest we have come was on the sidelines of the council—a March 2019 joint statement sponsored by Iceland, signed by thirty-six governments, that criticized the repression. In addition, in October 2020 and again in October 2024, at Human Rights Watch's active urging, the UN General Assembly rejected Saudi Arabia's candidacy for the UN Human Rights Council. But our most significant success regarded Yemen.

The Saudi-led coalition of nine Middle Eastern and North African governments backing the Yemeni government entered the civil war there in March 2015. Its bombers struck civilians in hospitals, markets, mosques, weddings, funerals, factories, detention centers, even a school bus filled with children. An estimated nine thousand civilians died. The Saudi government rarely admitted error or prosecuted anyone. The attacks contributed to what was said at the time to be the world's worst humanitarian crisis.

Our goal was to deter these attacks by persuading the UN Human Rights Council to create an investigative and reporting mechanism. Our first task was to identify a potential sponsor. The European Union declined, but the Netherlands government agreed. It was later joined by Canada, Belgium, Luxembourg, and Iceland. My colleagues and I worked closely with Dutch diplomats, including the foreign minister at the time, Bert Koenders. Much of this work was done by John Fisher, a New Zealand national who at the time was our highly effective representative at the UN in Geneva. With his unrelenting energy and mile-a-minute speaking style, he spent countless hours corralling diplomats to support the effort.

Elements of the Dutch business community were said to be unhappy that their government was going head-to-head with Saudi Arabia. Explaining the importance of this endeavor to people in the Netherlands became part of my job. I had appeared previously on *Nieuwsuur*, the leading nightly television news program in the Netherlands, and now one of its producers asked me to speak about the Yemen initiative. Dutch diplomats knew that I would highlight the significance of this life-saving effort, but they asked me to remember to praise Prime Minister Mark Rutte, who was taking political heat for his government's sponsoring of the resolution. Naturally, I did.

Given the magnitude of the war crimes being committed in Yemen, my colleagues and I felt that it would be appropriate for the UN Human Rights Council to establish a commission of inquiry. That was a step beyond the usual special rapporteur assigned for situations of serious abuse, a single human-rights professional tasked with investigating and reporting. A commission of inquiry usually contained three professionals, supported by more UN staff, and had more of a criminal justice feel, including a mandate to collect and preserve evidence.

It was a tough battle at the Human Rights Council. The Saudis were determined to avoid an inquiry into their conduct in Yemen. Just three days before the scheduled vote, the Saudi government suddenly announced that it would grant women the long-sought right to drive. We welcomed the move but ignored the diversion. Working closely with Dutch diplomats, John did his usual outstanding job of rounding up supporters. The night before the vote, we calculated that we would prevail by a small margin. Evidently, the Saudis did too. With just hours to go before the vote, they consented to scrutiny of Yemen, but only if the investigating body was not called a commission of inquiry. They agreed to call it a Group of Eminent Experts, but it had the same mandate.

A year later, when it was time to renew the GEE, I traveled to The Hague. By then, Bert Koenders, a center-left politician known as a strong proponent of human rights, had been replaced as foreign minister by Stef Blok, who had more of an economics background. Blok was from the political center-right, but, given the success of the prior year, shared Koenders's enthusiasm. He readily agreed to have the Netherlands government take the lead again. He made a point of being photographed with me so he could document our meeting on Twitter, always a good sign.

For four years, the GEE reported regularly on war crimes in Yemen, by all sides. It confirmed and augmented our findings. This reporting sparked further international reaction. Denmark, Finland, Germany, the Netherlands, and Norway stopped selling arms to Saudi Arabia. The U.S. Congress voted to stop arms sales; President Donald Trump vetoed the legislation, but President Biden suspended the sale of offensive weapons in January 2021 upon taking office. After we condemned Saudi use of cluster munitions in 2017, there were no further confirmed reports of use of these indiscriminate weapons in Yemen.

In September 2021, though, the Saudi government took advantage of the council's virtual meetings during the COVID-19 pandemic to mount a counterattack. Using bribes (e.g., a new embassy for Togo) and threats (telling Indonesia that it might no longer recognize its COVID vaccination certificates for Muslims traveling to Mecca for the hajj), the Saudi government managed to terminate the GEE.

Four countries that had abstained in 2020 voted no in 2021: Indonesia, Bangladesh, Senegal, and Togo. That was enough. It was the first time in the Human Rights Council's fifteen-year history that a proposed resolution had been defeated.

Some people question whether the UN Human Rights Council can make a difference on the ground, whether the "naming and shaming" inherent in such scrutiny matters. Governments fight hard to fend off such scrutiny, but does it change their behavior? Over the next few months, civilian casualties in Yemen nearly doubled. It was only an agreement to a ceasefire several months later, in April 2022, that brought the killing down.

—

A less successful effort to address the Saudi-led bombing in Yemen involved the UN secretary-general. A "list of shame" was first requested by the UN Security Council in 2001 to record governments and nonstate armed groups that were responsible for grave violations of the rights of children in armed conflict. The list produced in 2023 included more than sixty entries.

As explained in 2022 by Jo Becker, our ever-innovative children's rights advocate:

> Listed parties may be subject to UN Security Council sanctions, and according to UN guidelines, are removed from the list only after signing and implementing an action plan to end their violations. The process works: to date 39 parties have signed such plans, with 12 ending their violations.

In 2016, Ban Ki-moon listed but then quickly removed the Saudi-led coalition due to a Saudi threat to end hundreds of millions of dollars of assistance to UN programs. He publicly stated that he had acted under blackmail, noting that it was "unacceptable" for a UN member state to exert such financial pressure. He explained that he had been forced to forsake the children of Yemen because he

> had to consider the very real prospect that millions of other children would suffer grievously if, as was suggested to me,

countries would de-fund many UN programs. Children already at risk in Palestine, South Sudan, Syria, Yemen, and so many other places would fall further into despair.

Secretary-General Guterres returned the Saudi-led coalition to the list in 2017, attributing 683 child casualties and 38 attacks against schools and hospitals to the coalition, but he did it with a characteristic Guterres fudge. He created a new category of parties credited with taking steps "aimed at improving the protection of children" and placed the Saudi-led coalition in it, even though there was little evidence of such efforts. In 2018, he did the same thing, even though a UN expert panel on Yemen had concluded that any step by the Saudi-led coalition to minimize child casualties was "largely ineffective." The secretary-general's own report had found negligible differences in the number of Yemeni children who had been killed or injured—670 children in 2017 compared with 683 in 2016. He also found "a significant decrease" in coalition attacks on schools and hospitals, when a "modest decrease" would have been more accurate.

When Ban removed the Saudi-led coalition from his list, he made Riyadh pay a large reputational price. The Saudi government undoubtedly suffered more critical press from its blatant blackmail than it would have received from simply being placed on the list. Guterres's action softened the stigmatizing blow. Worried about antagonizing a major UN contributor, he undoubtedly would defend himself for having found a way to list the Saudi-led coalition that Riyadh accepted, but at what price?

In March 2019, in advance of the 2019 designation, I had one of my periodic meetings with Guterres on the thirty-eighth floor of the modernist UN Secretariat building in New York. We were seated in the conference room adjacent to his office, each joined by several staff members aligned on opposite sides of the table. I pointed out that in 2018 the number of child casualties caused by the Saudi-led coalition had increased, and that the Saudi mechanism to supposedly mitigate these attacks was a farce. I also said that the Saudi government's investigations lacked any credibility and fell far short of international standards. Guterres ignored what I told him, listing the Saudi-led coalition again with the same exculpatory caveat. In 2020, Guterres removed the Saudi-led coalition from his list altogether despite 222 child casualties and four attacks on schools and hospitals attributed to the coalition in Yemen during the previous year.

—

The notorious October 2018 murder of exiled dissident journalist Jamal Khashoggi at the Saudi consulate in Istanbul compelled us to find a way to intensify pressure on the Saudi crown prince. We quickly figured out a plan. The next month, Mohammed bin Salman would travel to Argentina for the annual G20 summit. In one positive reaction to its 1976–83 military dictatorship, Argentina has a strong law on universal jurisdiction, meaning its courts are empowered to investigate and prosecute the most serious human-rights crimes even when committed outside the country. We had a respectful relationship with the Argentine justice system based on our efforts to defend its independence from attacks by the governments of presidents Nestor and Christina Kirschner, who were trying to stop probes into their corruption. We quickly assembled evidence of the crown prince's responsibility for the torture of dissidents in the kingdom and the bombing of civilians in Yemen, both crimes that are covered by universal jurisdiction. We then filed a formal criminal complaint with an Argentine federal prosecutor who, based on the evidence we assembled, brought it before an investigating judge. The judge approved opening a formal investigation on November 28, 2018, the day that bin Salman arrived in Buenos Aires. The decision made headlines around the world.

We knew that this investigation was unlikely to result in prosecution. The crown prince was representing his country and so was undoubtedly traveling on a diplomatic passport. That would give him immunity from prosecution during his visit. Plus, a judicial investigation takes time, and bin Salman was scheduled to be in Argentina for only a few days. Still, we knew that the mere opening of an investigation would be shameful and send a message about the seriousness of the abuses for which the crown prince was accused. He had clearly hoped that the G20 summit would allow him to reenter the fold of respectability. Instead, his ruthless reign was again under the spotlight.

His entire visit proved to be an embarrassment. The crown prince and his four-hundred-member delegation had booked rooms in the

Four Seasons Hotel in Buenos Aires. He decamped to the Saudi embassy instead. At the summit, he was a pariah. Vladimir Putin gave him an ostentatious handshake, but the official photograph of the assembled leaders showed the crown prince, as Reuters put it, "standing at the far edge of the group portrait and ignored." I quickly published an op-ed about the episode in *The Washington Post,* where Khashoggi had been a columnist.

The signal had been sent. The crown prince's flagrant violation of the most basic human rights had a cost. Few wanted to be associated with him at a moment when the blood on his government's hands was so fresh. Alas, such isolation does not last.

—

When campaigning for the presidency in 2020, Joe Biden had called the crown prince's government a "pariah" and said he would "make them pay the price" for killing Khashoggi. But with the November 2022 midterm elections approaching amid a surge of inflation, Biden wanted to reduce the skyrocketing price of gasoline, so he agreed to meet the crown prince in July 2022 in Riyadh to press him to pump more oil.

Conscious of the trip's sensitivity, Biden's national security adviser, Jake Sullivan, agreed to meet in advance with me and the heads of several other human-rights groups. In the meeting, Sullivan asked me what difference it makes to push the Saudi government to respect human rights. I told him about the sharp spike in civilian casualties in Yemen following the Saudi government's successful effort to end the UN Human Rights Council's Group of Eminent Experts. He was unaware and seemed impressed. I urged him to ensure that Biden would say something publicly about bin Salman's repression. Government officials often think that it is enough for them to make private representations to their counterparts, but that leaves the people of the country in the lurch. They see photos of their leader being treated respectfully but hear no commentary on their leader's repression. I wanted Biden to treat the people of Saudi Arabia as a primary audience.

I remembered Biden's meeting with Putin in 2021. Emerging from a villa along the lake in Geneva for a news conference, Biden allowed that they had discussed "human rights." The comment came across as perfunctory. Anyone who had hoped that Biden would push Putin to curb his worsening repression was left disappointed. I did not want that repeated in Saudi Arabia. I stressed the need for Biden to speak publicly and in some detail about the crown prince's detention of activists, critics, and anyone he perceived as challenging his rule.

Biden's meeting with the crown prince is probably most remembered for the fist bump between the two. Biden apparently wanted to avoid the warm gesture of a handshake, but it backfired, because the fist bump came across as too chummy for so ruthless a leader as the crown prince. Biden never seemed comfortable being too confrontational about human rights in meetings with counterparts, and there was a limit to what Sullivan could do to change Biden's nature, even assuming he tried. After his meeting with the crown prince, Biden said they had discussed "human rights and the need for political reform." He specified only that he had raised "the murder of Khashoggi." He said he had agreed with the crown prince to work to extend the ceasefire in Yemen to avoid more "carnage" but made no mention of the Saudi-led bombing of Yemeni civilians. These bland statements were wholly overshadowed by the fist bump.

Bin Salman told Biden that OPEC Plus—the OPEC countries and ten others, including, most significantly, Russia—would increase production, but it turned out to be by only one hundred thousand barrels of oil a day. That was a tiny percentage of its authorized production of roughly forty million barrels daily and was unlikely to have had any meaningful effect on the price of gas.

Even that pathetic promise did not last long. By October 2022, OPEC Plus announced plans to cut production by two million barrels a day. Within a year, five million barrels a day were being withheld—the equivalent of 5 percent of global supply. That increased prices, with the effect of subsidizing Putin's invasion of Ukraine. Biden threatened "consequences" but did nothing. By June 2023, the Biden administration had reembraced the crown prince, hoping to encourage him to normalize relations with Israel and stop drifting toward China. In August 2024, the administration resumed sales of offensive arms.

Meanwhile, the crown prince's repression of critics intensified. As *The New York Times* reported, "The kingdom's courts are meting out harsher punishments than ever to citizens who criticize the government, with prosecutions built on Twitter posts ending in prison sentences of 15 to 45 years." One retired teacher was sentenced to death (later overturned) for his social media posts. The crown prince also led efforts to rehabilitate Syria's Assad, welcoming him back in May 2023 as a member of the Arab League after his suspension in 2011. I could not help but think that the crown prince had the Saudi-led war crimes in Yemen in the back of his mind as he showed the world that even the mass atrocities of Assad could be forgotten.

—

Although the Saudi military was the main actor in Yemen, it led a coalition. Less attention was paid to its other members, the most important of which was the United Arab Emirates, which tended to receive an undeserved free pass because Dubai, its major commercial city, is seen as relatively liberal. Businesses embrace it, it is a hub for Emirates airline, and foreigners vacation there.

Human Rights Watch reported regularly on the UAE government's abuses. It ran a detention center in Yemen where torture was routine. Indicative of its intolerance of dissent, it imposed a ten-year prison sentence on Ahmed Mansoor, a leading Emirati human-rights defender and a member of our advisory committee for the Middle East and North Africa. At least sixty other rights defenders, activists, and dissidents have been detained since 2012. In July 2024, many were handed additional sentences of from fifteen years to life in prison. In addition, the UAE has provided military assistance to the Rapid Support Forces in Sudan, the paramilitary group that is notorious for its atrocities.

At first blush, Princess Latifa would hardly seem to be the person to illustrate repression in the UAE. She is the daughter of Sheikh Mohammed bin Rashid Al Maktoum, the fabulously wealthy ruler of the Emirate of Dubai and the UAE vice president, prime minister, and minister of defense. But she became a compelling example of the government's intolerance.

Sheikh Mohammed does not put up with independence among the women in his family. In August 2000, Latifa's sister Shamsa, then almost nineteen, had tried to flee a family compound in England. About two months later, she was abducted and forcibly returned to Dubai, where she disappeared. She was believed to be alive but drugged and in a precarious mental state.

Latifa had been an intrepid young woman—she took up sky-diving—but she tired of the constraints on her life. She had not been allowed out of Dubai since the episode with her sister. So, in February 2018, at the age of thirty-two, she secretly arranged with a friend to flee by boat. They managed to cross the Indian Ocean and approach the coast of India when their boat was boarded by commandos, who forcibly returned them to Dubai.

Before her flight, Latifa had made a video to be released by a trusted person in the event she were captured: "If you are watching this video, it's not such a good thing. Either I'm dead or I'm in a very, very, very bad situation." For most of the rest of the year, no one heard anything else from her, and it was unclear whether she was even alive.

On Christmas Day, a handful of photographs suddenly appeared in the media of Latifa having lunch with Mary Robinson, the former president of Ireland and the second UN high commissioner for human rights. When I reached out to Robinson, she told me that Latifa "has serious bipolar problems," "is quite vulnerable from a medical perspective and is now receiving specialist care in a supportive family context." She said similar things to BBC Radio 4. She added that the family did not "want her to endure any more publicity." All of that sounded suspiciously like Sheikh Mohammed's talking points, and seemed out of character with the poised, self-aware young woman in the video. It also was not how her friends described her.

Robinson had been duped, as she later admitted, by her friend Princess Haya bint Hussein, the glamorous Jordanian princess who had married Sheikh Mohammed. At that point, Princess Haya seemed to believe the party line, although she later understood the truth, divorced Sheikh Mohammed, and waged a bitter child-custody battle with him in a British court, which she won. Mohammed's treatment of his daughters became evidence for why he could not be trusted with Haya's two young children.

Because Robinson mentioned our exchange during a BBC interview, my name became associated with Latifa's, so the media sometimes reached out to me for comment. I periodically posted about her case on Twitter to sustain public attention. And I was in regular touch with David Haigh, a British lawyer who became a principal campaigner for Latifa's freedom and helped secretly to arrange for her to have a mobile phone with which she could communicate, including by sending clandestine videos in which she described her conditions of detention.

I sometimes asked myself why I was spending so much time on behalf of a wealthy Emirati princess. Yet, her father was exactly the kind of man who got away with horrible repression of dissidents in Dubai, simply because he had helped to build a glittering city and regional playground. He also trained and raced horses, and had occasionally hung out with Queen Elizabeth of England. One way to demonstrate the true character of the man was by showing how he treated his daughter.

Latifa's experience ended up being a huge stain on Sheikh Mohammed's reputation. Major documentaries were produced on her fate by the BBC's *Panorama* and Australian Broadcasting Corporation's *60 Minutes*. In June 2021, following this publicity, Latifa suddenly seemed to have made a deal with her father. Photographs began to appear on social media of her traveling abroad. But the price of her freedom was evidently that she stop communicating with Haigh and other activists who had been helping her. She passed along messages that she wanted to be left alone. That she remained under coercion was certain, but her friends abroad were in no position to second-guess her evident decision to accept a conditional release from house arrest.

The UAE still retains a better reputation than it should. The president, Mohammed bin Zayed Al Nahyan, is often seen as a respected statesman, despite his crushing of all dissent in the country, his having joined the Saudi-led coalition as it bombed Yemeni civilians, and his arming of the ruthless paramilitary group in Sudan. That his close partner in running the country, Sheikh Mohammed, was shown to be such a ruthless misogynist helped to put their reign in perspective.

—

In Saudi Arabia, Human Rights Watch devoted significant attention to trying to improve the plight of the (currently) roughly 3.5 million migrant domestic workers, mainly women, from countries including Indonesia, Sri Lanka, and the Philippines. Many employers treat these workers well, but onerous migration policies, discriminatory attitudes, and their exclusion from labor laws mean that abuse is rife.

Nisha Varia, then a senior researcher with our women's rights program, investigated the treatment of migrant domestic workers during our 2006 trip. Saudi authorities let her visit a Ministry of Social Affairs shelter for domestic workers in Riyadh that typically held hundreds of women, but in a move akin to their dressing up of al-Ha'ir prison, they removed most of the women from the shelter the day before Nisha's visit, leaving only sixty recent arrivals. Still, Nisha was able to expose the scale and severity of abuses in private homes, which had been largely hidden. Her report challenged the Saudi government's claim that any abuses were caused by a few outlier employers. She showcased how government policies and deeply embedded social practices enabled abuse.

Because domestic workers—housekeepers, nannies, and cooks—typically lived in their employer's home, they were effectively always on duty. Some were not allowed to leave the house, at times literally locked in. A day off would have allowed them to notify their friends or embassy of an abusive situation, but many did not have that option or even access to a phone.

Nisha documented instances of domestic workers who had not been allowed outside the household for years, who were cut off from their families back home, and who in the worst cases were enduring severe physical and sexual abuse. Many workers experienced eighteen-hour workdays, unpaid wages, food deprivation, and psychological abuse. She found dozens of cases of forced labor, trafficking, and slavery or slavery-like conditions.

Saudi Arabia, like other Gulf countries, employed the *kafala* (sponsorship) system, but the Saudi version was the most restrictive. A migrant domestic worker needed her employer's permission to enter the country, change employers, or even leave the country. That meant that an abused worker had little recourse. Even if she could retrieve her passport, which many employers kept locked away, escaping to her home country was riddled with risk, given how easy it was for employers to deny permission or concoct criminal charges such as theft (or even witchcraft), which the courts tended to credit over the worker's denial.

Saudi Arabia said that exclusion from its labor laws and such basic protections as a weekly day off was justified for domestic workers because they were treated as "part of the family." The government also said that it did not want to intrude in the privacy of the home. That left these women legally unprotected.

After Nisha's further research in Saudi Arabia in 2008, she and I issued her report from Indonesia, a country from which many of the women had come, to encourage its government to press the Saudi government for reform. The report garnered extensive regional and global media attention. I traveled with Nisha to a rural village in central Java to speak with women who had returned from Saudi Arabia. Some came home empty-handed, but the successful ones had homes that were substantially larger than those of their neighbors, and they spoke of having financed their children's education and their family's health expenses. Lacking decent employment options at home, migrants' families across Asia and Africa depended on the billions of dollars they earned in Saudi Arabia and other Gulf countries. But without robust protections in place, working abroad came with significant risk of abuse.

At first the Saudi government showed little interest in discussing our findings. During my 2008 trip to Jakarta, after several attempts to see the Saudi ambassador, I simply showed up at the Saudi embassy, explaining that I would wait until the ambassador could make time to see me, which he did. Human Rights Watch has kept migrant domestic workers' rights on the Saudi government's agenda ever since.

Reforms have come incrementally, slowly, and often with major gaps. But there is now specific legislation guaranteeing domestic workers a weekly day off, a (measly) nine hours of rest per day, prompt payment of wages, proper accommodation, and vacation and sick leave. Employers in Saudi Arabia are prohibited from delaying wages and physically abusing domestic workers. The standard contract prohibits withholding passports. Workers who face abuse can, at least in theory if not always in practice, bypass the need for their employer's permission to change employers.

There is regular and evolving public debate about domestic workers' rights and employers' responsibilities. In an important conceptual shift, governments across the Gulf are changing the term *khadama* ("servant") to *amila al-manzaliya* ("domestic worker"). Sustained pressure has been essential, and in later years, Rothna Begum, a senior women's rights researcher, led our domestic worker advocacy.

Setting international standards has also played an important role in outlining human-rights obligations in a largely unregulated and historically devalued sector. We worked with domestic-worker and trade-union allies to secure a landmark International Labour Organization treaty, the Domestic Workers Convention, which extends equal labor rights to domestic workers. It entered into force in September 2013 and, as of 2023, had been ratified by thirty-six nations. The convention has spurred legal reforms, awareness campaigns, and enforcement programs in dozens of countries, even where it has not been ratified. The Gulf Arab states have not signed on, but five of the six have since improved labor-law protections for domestic workers. The convention provides clear standards for measuring their efforts. Ensuing national reforms in other countries also provide practical models on such matters as standard employment contracts, strategies for wage protection, incremental labor reforms, dispute-resolution mechanisms, and services for workers facing abuse. Implementation is a huge challenge, and comprehensive reforms, particularly of the *kafala* system, are still needed. But even in as difficult a country as Saudi Arabia, this effort has shown that pressure can yield improvements.

War Crimes

U ntil the 1980s, the human-rights movement addressed mainly peacetime repression, such as political imprisonment, torture, or censorship, applying international human-rights law. Human Rights Watch was the first major human-rights group to address wartime abuse as well, under a distinct set of standards, the laws of war, or international humanitarian law, largely codified in the Geneva Conventions of 1949 and their 1977 Additional Protocols.

Traditionally, the main organization to address international humanitarian law was the International Committee of the Red Cross. In addition to delivering humanitarian aid and assisting prisoners of war during armed conflict, the ICRC is the official guardian of international humanitarian law. As we built a significant body of wartime work, we became an important complement to the ICRC, but operationally we were its opposite: the ICRC communicates with governments confidentially to maintain access to territory and detention facilities, while we, if necessary, sacrificed access to maintain our public voice.

Amnesty International during its first couple of decades spotlighted individual victims—the "prisoner of conscience," the subject of torture, the person facing the death penalty. That personification of abuse helped to mobilize its membership, particularly to write letters. By contrast, most people affected by violations of international humanitarian law are unknown, and it is harder to campaign around a group of them. However, our greater focus on pressing governments to change systematic practices meant we were already habituated to generating public pressure without relying on particular, identifiable victims.

As I said earlier, the Ford Foundation at first opposed the move because international humanitarian law applies to all sides in an armed conflict, and Ford worried that human-rights groups might be endangered if they criticized rebel groups. But upholding humanitarian law soon became mainstream in the human-rights movement, including Amnesty International.

All law, no matter how carefully drafted, contains ambiguities. International humanitarian law, though quite detailed, is no exception. We pressed for interpretation of those ambiguities in a way that enhanced protection for civilians. For example, what does it mean to say that an attack is unlawfully disproportionate if it can be "expected to cause incidental loss of civilian life, injury to civilians, damage to civilian objects, or a combination thereof, which would be excessive in relation to the concrete and direct military advantage anticipated," which is what one treaty says. These standards provide lots of wiggle room, but clearer cases can be reported on as a way of stopping, deterring, or even punishing misconduct.

Our strategy was to use our fact-finding to demonstrate publicly the harmful result of militaries interpreting these ambiguities permissibly. We thereby helped to build public pressure for a more protective interpretation of the law. We helped to make the standards more stringent in practice by raising public expectations of what militaries must do to comply. That had real consequences, helping to reduce civilian death and injury during war.

The 1991 Gulf War

In Central America, where Human Rights Watch first applied international humanitarian law in the 1980s under the direction of Aryeh Neier, we addressed so-called noninternational armed conflicts, or civil wars. I played a central role in overseeing our first application of humanitarian law to an international conflict—the 1991 Gulf War. The primary target was Western militaries. That should have been noncontroversial, in that all of them claim to uphold humanitarian law, but military lawyers are inclined to interpret ambiguities to broaden the latitude of operational commanders.

The ICRC had already tried to influence military lawyers, but we introduced public pressure through the publication of our investigative reports. Western military lawyers (and legal academics with military backgrounds) had enjoyed a virtual monopoly on interpreting the requirements of international humanitarian law, with little public scrutiny of their work, but suddenly they had to contend with public opinion about how the law should be interpreted.

In 1991, as the U.S.-led military coalition chased Iraqi forces from Kuwait and attacked those forces from the air throughout much of Iraq, we examined its compliance with international humanitarian law. Jemera Rone, given her experience applying that law in Central America, was the natural researcher for the task.

One big advantage that our researchers bring to investigations of wartime conduct is that we seek to visit the site of a military attack. That was not something that the U.S. government could do in Saddam Hussein's Iraq. Jemera was able to find out what really happened as opposed to what U.S. military personnel from their distant observation posts thought had happened.

We published Jemera's findings in a lengthy report entitled "Needless Deaths in the Gulf War." We found that nearly a third of the twenty-five hundred to three thousand civilian deaths caused directly by the U.S.-led air attacks could have been avoided by closer adherence to international humanitarian law.

One U.S. target was bridges, which can be legitimate military targets if their destruction can impair imminent military maneuvers. But attacking forces still have a duty to "take all feasible precautions in the choice of means and methods of attack" to minimize civilian casualties. A midafternoon attack on a bridge in Nasiriyya in southern Iraq killed some one hundred civilians. The bridge could just as easily have been destroyed by bombing it at night, when far fewer civilians would have been present. Similarly, a daytime attack on a bridge in Falluja, west of Baghdad, killed scores of people when the bomb went astray and hit a nearby market. The market would have been largely empty had the attack taken place at night. By exposing these situations, our report discouraged such negligence in future wars.

Some of our analysis examined sloppy use of intelligence. In the most devastating case, a U.S. plane dropped two two-thousand-pound bombs on the Ameriyya section of western Baghdad. U.S. targeters claimed they had hit a military command-and-control facility, but the facility was also a shelter being used by many civilians, which the most basic surveillance would have demonstrated. Between two and three hundred civilians were killed in the attack.

We also examined U.S. attacks in western Iraq. The aim there was to stop Iraqi SCUD missile launches against Israel and Saudi Arabia. Our investigation on the ground found that U.S. targeters repeatedly mistook civilian vehicles and structures for SCUD missiles or their support services. Among the civilian targets hit were buses, cars, oil tankers, and Bedouin tents. Our report encouraged more critical scrutiny of "intelligence" before it was used to justify a military attack.

My colleague Letta Tayler played a similar role in 2013 in Yemen, where the distant targeters of U.S. drone and missile attacks kept insisting that they were hitting terrorist suspects, but her on-the-ground research showed that they were repeatedly hitting civilians. Either the targeters were relying on shoddy intelligence, or they were assuming that a certain pattern of life suggested terrorist activity—so-called signature strikes—when it did not. A Yemeni man may have been holding a rifle, but that was not enough to suggest he was a terrorist accomplice; many ordinary Yemeni men carry rifles. The Pentagon often claimed that there were no civilian casualties after a given strike, when our on-the-ground research showed there were many. Our aim was to force targeters to be more vigilant before launching their deadly strikes. Amnesty International issued a similar report on U.S. drone attacks in Pakistan.

During the Gulf War in Iraq, a particularly controversial aspect of the U.S.-led bombing was the attacks on Iraq's electricity-generating plants, which the Pentagon argued would help to isolate the Iraq government and military. The problem was that in Iraq, as in most countries, there was no separate military electrical system, but a single integrated grid on which civilians relied as well. Iraq had a modern economy that used electricity for refrigeration, sanitation, and medical care, among other things. That all ceased to function for a long time after the attacks. Jemera described the cascading effects and argued that the civilian cost was disproportionate to the military advantage. Obviously, the meaning of "disproportionate" is subjective, but by laying out the civilian costs in considerable detail and examining them not only at the moment of the attack but also as they played out over time, we helped to shift military thinking—from considering static lists of targets to a deeper assessment of function before something was considered a legitimate military target.

Richard Cheney, then the defense secretary, said if he had to fight the war again, he "would do exactly the same thing." But the Pentagon tacitly accepted the validity of our findings in its next major bombing campaign in Serbia. It still attacked the electrical system, but rather than destroying electrical facilities, it dropped a web of aluminum fibers that blanketed them and shorted them out. When the Serbian government learned how to repair these facilities quickly, NATO bombers targeted other parts of the electrical system, but still not difficult-to-repair generators. Illustrating how norms had changed, the International Criminal Court in March and June 2024 charged four Russian commanders for missile strikes against Ukraine's electrical infrastructure.

The 1999 Bombing of Serbia

We investigated the seventy-eight-day U.S.-led NATO bombing of Serbia in 1999, which was a response to Serbian atrocities and ethnic cleansing in Kosovo. The investigation was led by Bill Arkin, a Human Rights Watch consultant, whose military background provided important insights into what could have been done differently to prevent civilians from being killed. Bill uncovered ninety separate incidents involving a total of five hundred civilian deaths during the bombing campaign. I joined him for part of the investigation in Belgrade, the Serbian capital. For each bombing site we examined, we attempted to determine why it was attacked and whether the attacking and defending forces had taken "all feasible precautions" to avoid civilian casualties.

Several of the attacks were not directed at legitimate military targets. The most controversial was the attack on the headquarters of Serb Radio and Television (RTS) in Belgrade, where sixteen media workers were killed and sixteen wounded. Before the attack, the U.S. and French governments reportedly disagreed about whether the headquarters was a legitimate military target. Following our investigation, we concluded that it was not. It was not being used to incite violence, akin to Radio Milles Collines during the Rwandan genocide. While it did spew propaganda, as NATO pointed out, that did not make it a legitimate military target because its destruction did not provide "a definite military advantage," as international humanitarian law requires. Attacking military morale can be a legitimate use of military force, but attacking civilian morale is not. Civilian communications can be attacked with sanctions or jamming but not military force. Indeed, there would be a thin line between attacking communications to undermine civilian morale and attacking civilians for that purpose—a major part of Putin's war-crime strategy in Ukraine. Again, such attacks do not provide the "definite military advantage" that international humanitarian law requires.

At times, NATO suggested that RTS could be used to pass military messages. We never saw proof that it was used this way, but even if it had been true, the duty to "take all feasible precautions" to avoid civilian harm should have led NATO to attack, say, the unstaffed transmitters outside the city rather than the staff-occupied studio in its center.

To limit harm to journalists, NATO did warn them (especially foreign ones) to leave the studio, but those warnings were issued over several days, so people started to ignore them. Even though RTS was eventually hit in the middle of the night—an improvement from the bridge attacks in Iraq that we had criticized—many civilian technicians and workers were still in the building.

The other major controversy stemming from the NATO bombing involved U.S. and British use of cluster munitions on at least seven occasions, killing between 90 and 150 civilians. We had not yet secured a treaty banning cluster munitions, but the military commanders should have known that these weapons were inherently indiscriminate and should not have used them, especially in populated areas. Once the media began reporting on civilian casualties from cluster bombs, the Clinton administration ordered that the attacks cease. Yet the U.S. government still has not accepted the widely ratified treaty outlawing cluster munitions. In July 2023, President Biden, amid much controversy, sent cluster munitions to Ukraine.

The 2003 Iraq War

George W. Bush's invasion of Iraq in 2003 provided another opportunity to tighten the requirements of international humanitarian law. One element of that war involved an effort to "decapitate" the Iraqi leadership by targeting Saddam Hussein and other senior commanders. Once the armed conflict was under way, these people were legitimate military targets. Our focus was the means employed.

I had hired Marc Garlasco as a researcher because of (and despite) his unusual background—he had been a civilian employee at the Pentagon tasked with identifying "high-value" military targets in Iraq in anticipation of President Bush's invasion. He quit before the war started and sought to join Human Rights Watch to monitor the conduct of the war. He was careful to abide by restrictions on the disclosure of classified information, but his knowledge of how targets were selected proved invaluable.

During the conflict, the U.S. military conducted fifty strikes on top Iraqi leaders—the infamous "deck of cards"—failing to kill any of them while killing dozens of civilians. As we reported with Marc's help, the U.S. strategy relied on intercepts of senior Iraqi leaders' satellite phone calls, supposedly backed by corroborating intelligence about their precise location. But given the technology of the time, the U.S. military could locate targets only within a one-hundred-meter radius, inadequate precision in a civilian neighborhood. It was therefore not enough to say that a target was believed to be in a certain location; it was essential to ask *how* the military came to that belief and with what degree of accuracy. Many civilian lives could have been spared if targeters had been asked these questions.

Marc left Human Rights Watch in 2009 when it was revealed that, under a pseudonym, he had been collecting Nazi military medals and other World War II artifacts. He had taken up the hobby because of a German grandfather who had been conscripted into Hitler's army, but some people wanted to discredit him as a Nazi sympathizer, which he was not. The issue came to a head when Marc was assisting the monitoring of Israeli bombing in Gaza in 2008–2009. Ironically, because of his Pentagon background, Marc was deferential when it came to analyzing Israeli military conduct, but that did not stop partisans of the Israeli government from attacking him to discredit our work. At first, we defended Marc. I regret that I ultimately accepted the need for his departure from Human Rights Watch because the partisans were using his background as an excuse to avoid discussing the Israeli military's conduct in Gaza.

"Shooting Fish in a Barrel"

One limitation of international humanitarian law became apparent to me during my visit to Kuwait shortly after U.S.-led forces had liberated the country from Saddam Hussein's army. In February 1991, as Iraqi troops fled Kuwait, bombers pummeled them in their vehicles along the main highway leading north to Iraq. The scene became known as the "Highway of Death." I drove along the highway in its gruesome aftermath, seeing one burned, destroyed vehicle after another. Most had contained Iraqi soldiers. One U.S. pilot described it as "shooting fish in a barrel."

International humanitarian law did not provide much if any protection for these soldiers. It allows fleeing combatants to be shot, on the theory that otherwise they could return to fight another day. The sole exception is in the case of a combatant who signals an intention to surrender, in which case he must be captured and cared for. But how do you surrender from a highway as bombers attack from overhead? All we could do was to highlight the human dimension of the problem in the hope of prompting second thoughts should such a situation recur.

A variation of this problem arose in eastern Ukraine after Putin's full-scale invasion. The Russian military treated young Russian men as cannon fodder, launching human wave attacks with huge casualty rates. International humanitarian law does not speak to that tactic, but there is something instinctively appalling about discarding human life so casually. Using Twitter, I highlighted this callousness to generate opposition, but I could not call it illegal.

Aggression

Another limitation of international humanitarian law is that it looks at how a war is fought, not who is at fault for starting a war. Therefore, Human Rights Watch did not attack the "aggressor" or pronounce whose reason for fighting was more "just." We thought it best to maintain neutrality on these often deeply disputed subjects to avoid raising questions about our objectivity as we sought to protect civilians in the way the war was fought. We did not press for ceasefires either, because the timing of a ceasefire inevitably has a political dimension, depending on which side in an armed conflict feels it has the upper hand. In Ukraine, it became a highly contested issue whether the Ukrainian government should accept a ceasefire while Russian troops controlled parts of its territory, which was seen by some as rewarding Russian aggression. The timing of a ceasefire in Gaza before the Israeli government had proceeded as far as it wanted in undermining Hamas's military capacity after its October 7, 2023, attack was similarly controversial.

Samuel Moyn of Yale Law School criticized our approach, saying that our focus on international humanitarian law sanitized war and thus made war more likely. He argued, in effect, that we would save more lives by trying to stop wars rather than mitigating their harm. He offered no evidence for this assertion, and I consider it dangerous because it seemed to prescribe a return to the concept of "total war"—when targeting civilians was considered fair game—in the hope of making war so horrible that no one would want to start one. The Syrian government with Russian backing fought a "total war" for a decade starting in 2011, and while the world rightly found this strategy revolting, that did not stop the Russian government from taking the same approach in Ukraine starting in 2022.

It is risky to suggest that we should let things get worse to enhance the incentive for change. Just as I never accepted the old Marxist maxim that we should eschew reform to accelerate the revolution, I would be reluctant to forsake the mitigating effects of international humanitarian law on the theory that doing so would hasten the day when war is abandoned.

Obviously, some groups like ours can focus on defending international humanitarian law while others oppose aggression, but Moyn suggested that our approach had so dominated moral views about war that there was little room left in the public domain to fight aggression. David Kennedy, a Harvard Law professor, also wondered whether the human-rights perspective has come to so dominate the field that it precludes the emergence of what he called other "emancipatory strategies."

I do not see why a human-rights approach precludes others. Many people have found the human-rights perspective to be a powerful way to address their governments, but it is only one moral framework among many. People who are concerned about the environment, poverty, inequality, or other issues of social equity often do not use human-rights language. And even when they do invoke the concept of rights, they frequently do it more as a way of saying that their concern is really important, not to preclude other moral frameworks. International humanitarian law has been around for a lot longer than Human Rights Watch. We promoted it but were hardly the cause of its moral power. If many are drawn to uphold it, they must see value in its ability to mitigate harm to civilians beyond parallel efforts to stop wars. I certainly do. And it has hardly precluded other voices from opposing war itself, such as the highly respected International Crisis Group, a conflict-resolution organization.

One aspect of our work that came closest to opposing war involved the definition of when hostilities become an armed conflict. The characterization has enormous legal significance, because under international humanitarian law, each side is entitled to shoot to kill opposing combatants, regardless of whether lesser measures, such as detention, might be possible. By contrast, in nonwar situations, a government must abide by international human-rights standards of the sort that apply to the police. These law-enforcement rules permit the use of lethal force only as a last resort to meet an imminent lethal threat. Otherwise, suspects must be detained.

The issue arose during the civil war in Yemen, to which the U.S. government was not a party. U.S. officials believed that Islamist extremists there were plotting an attack on the United States, so the Obama administration authorized the use of drones to kill suspects. There is something disconcerting about killing people from afar, particularly when the drone operator is killing from the comfort and safety of an office somewhere in the West. But discrepancies of power have long been inherent in warfare and do not of themselves make for a legal violation. Indeed, drones, with their pinpoint accuracy and ability to hover for lengthy periods to verify a target and select the most propitious moment for attack, have the potential to reduce civilian harm.

I argued in *The New York Review of Books* that because the U.S. government was not at war in Yemen, it had no right to apply war rules. Under policing rules, because the Islamists in Yemen posed no imminent threat, the U.S. government could not summarily kill them. Admittedly, detaining suspects in lawless Yemen was difficult, but the U.S. government would not even discuss detaining a suspect rather than killing him. The Obama administration maintained that a threat could be nipped in the bud. However, in the absence of an armed conflict, lethal force can be used in that effort only as a last resort to meet an imminent lethal threat. A government is not allowed to shoot someone just because it thinks they might sometime in the future commit a terrorist act.

This issue was also part of my critique of the George W. Bush administration's "global war on terror." Because of the magnitude of the September 11, 2001, attacks on the World Trade Center and the Pentagon, Bush got away with calling his initial response a "war." The invasion of Afghanistan was a classic armed conflict, but the Bush administration wanted to use the war paradigm for its worldwide efforts to combat terrorism, even though in no other country was there the kind of sustained armed conflict needed to justify the war characterization.

The existence of a war affects not only the power to use lethal force but also allows a party to the conflict to detain opposing combatants until the end of the conflict to prevent them from returning to the battlefield. In nonwar situations, suspects can be detained only if criminally charged and tried. Bush used the "enemy combatant" characterization to justify the endless detention without charge or trial at Guantánamo.

But the war characterization was dangerously elastic, as I argued in a 2004 article in *Foreign Affairs*. After all, if al-Qaeda suspects were "enemy combatants" for the purpose of detention, they were also enemy combatants for the purpose of being killed. That is, if suspects really were combatants wherever they were in the world—as the U.S. government claimed—then a suspect walking down the streets of London or Paris could be killed rather than detained. Once in custody, of course, execution of even a combatant is prohibited under international humanitarian law, but the law does not require taking a combatant into custody as opposed to shooting him.

And why stop with this "war" on terrorism. There is already a rhetorical "war on drugs." What if a government pretended that it was a real "war" and started summarily shooting drug suspects? That is what former Philippines president Rodrigo Duterte did, sparking global condemnation and an International Criminal Court investigation. By never articulating the limits of its "global war on terror," the Bush administration encouraged such logical extensions. It is easy to imagine how, say, the Chinese government might use this logic to target Uyghur "terrorists" abroad. That is why it is generally understood that for war rules to apply, a certain level of armed hostilities must exist. For wars between two countries, *any* fighting will constitute an armed conflict. But for "noninternational armed conflicts"—wars between a country and one or more nonstate groups—the law is less clear. That is part of why the Bush administration was able to get away with its facile characterization of its counterterrorism efforts. But the ICRC's official commentary defining war requires "that the violence needs to have reached a certain intensity and that it must be between at least two organized Parties/armed groups." With rare exception, the Bush administration's "global war on terror" did not qualify under these criteria.

By highlighting the dangers of the Bush administration's convenient characterization of al-Qaeda suspects as enemy combatants, we contributed pressure to end reliance on it. That, in turn, generated pressure to remove as many suspects as possible from the endless detention of Guantánamo. In addition, in October 2022, President Biden imposed new limits on the use of lethal drones outside conventional war zones, allowing it only when "capture is not feasible" and banning "signature strikes" on individuals.

Land Mines and Cluster Munitions

The clearest example of our efforts to secure more protective understanding of international humanitarian law involved the prohibition of "indiscriminate" warfare, attacks that are not directed at a military target in an area that includes civilians. One would have thought that antipersonnel land mines would be a classic indiscriminate weapon; those who lay mines have no idea who they will harm. But for many years, most militaries blithely used land mines despite ratifying treaties that prohibit indiscriminate warfare. A 1980 protocol meant to limit civilian harm by regulating the use of land mines was widely endorsed but largely ineffective.

To press for a ban on land mines, we documented their civilian toll in country after country, often long after an armed conflict had ended. We called land mines "a weapon of mass destruction in slow motion." We cofounded a global coalition of civic groups that became the International Campaign to Ban Landmines. Negotiations began at the UN under the auspices of a catchall treaty known as the Convention on Conventional Weapons, a forum in Geneva to devise new rules for selected arms that had adopted the 1980 protocol. But the forum operated by "consensus," meaning any nation could veto progress. Among those determined to block progress was the U.S. government. Negotiations went nowhere.

The process moved forward only when, with our encouragement, some governments abandoned the consensus straitjacket. The Canadian and Norwegian governments led in establishing the "Ottawa process." Only governments that wanted a treaty banning land mines were invited, leaving the obstructors to waste their time in Geneva. The result was the Mine Ban Treaty, which by 2024 had been ratified by 164 governments (but still not the United States) and has been so successful in stigmatizing the use of land mines that even many nonratifiers have been reluctant to use them. The treaty represented the first time that a weapons system in active use had been banned. In 2022, land mines were used only by the Myanmar military junta and the forces fighting in Ukraine.

Human Rights Watch led a similar campaign to ban cluster munitions. As noted earlier, cluster bombs open above ground and disperse scores of lethal bomblets over a wide area. That makes it difficult to target them with any precision. Moreover, many bomblets do not explode on initial contact with the ground but remain volatile and, like a land mine, can explode whenever someone comes in contact with them.

One would have thought that the prohibition of indiscriminate warfare banned the use of cluster munitions, but it took a dedicated treaty to broadly stigmatize their use. We investigated and reported on their harm in Serbia/Kosovo, Afghanistan, Iraq, and Lebanon. We were the first group to raise the alarm about them and, in 1999, called for a moratorium on their use. As with land mines, we helped to build a global coalition, the Cluster Munition Coalition, which was launched in 2003 and included 250 organizations from more than 70 countries. In 2007, the coalition formally sought a ban.

Once again, the UN's "consensus" approach allowed a handful of powerful governments, including the United States, to block progress. So we moved the negotiations to Dublin to secure a treaty. We pushed for a ban in various places, including the Munich Security Conference, where I was allowed to speak to a plenary forum at its 2008 annual meeting to make our case. By 2023, 112 governments had ratified a treaty banning cluster munitions. There are still important holdouts—including Russia, China, Israel, India, Pakistan, Ukraine, and the United States—but the global use of cluster munitions had diminished radically until both sides used them after Russia's invasion of Ukraine.

For both antipersonnel land mines and cluster munitions, we and partner civic groups brought the issue to the attention of governments and the public, set the international agenda, and became the driving force leading to new international law, eventually working in close cooperation with progressive governments, UN agencies, and the ICRC. This strategy became a model for other efforts, including those that led to the International Criminal Court, the Arms Trade Treaty, and the Treaty on the Prohibition of Nuclear Weapons.

The backdrop to these campaigns illustrates the positive role that institutional foundations can play if they are willing to engage in genuine give-and-take conversations with grantees. In the early 1990s, Peter Goldmark, then president of the Rockefeller Foundation, approached us to offer a substantial grant if we would start a program to address nuclear weapons. The problem was that our methodology, premised on investigating and reporting on the actions of governments, had little to offer the campaign against nuclear weapons given our hope that they would never be used. At that stage, most discussions of nuclear weapons revolved around deterrence theory to which we could add no value. The most we could do was to note that virtually any nuclear attack would have indiscriminate effects and thus likely be a war crime, but that hardly required a major investigative effort.

Instead, we proposed that we establish a program to address weapons that were used, to monitor that use, and to generate pressure against misuse. Goldmark agreed, and Human Rights Watch launched in 1992 what we called our Arms Project, later renamed the Arms Division of Human Rights Watch. With Steve Goose leading the way, it coorganized the International Campaign to Ban Landmines. Jody Williams served as the ICBL's founding coordinator. She and the ICBL were awarded the 1997 Nobel Peace Prize. (Jody and Steve ended up getting married.) Under Steve, it also led our successful efforts to ban cluster munitions and lasers designed to blind soldiers as well as our more recent attempts to ban fully autonomous lethal weapons, colloquially called "killer robots."

9

Israel

No aspect of our work was more closely scrutinized than our reporting on Israel, and no other country was mentioned as often by critics as a source of concern. But ignoring Israeli abuses would have been a profound dereliction of our core principle—to apply the same standards evenhandedly to every government. I learned early on that the best response to people who took issue with our reporting on Israel was not to water it down—the critics would never be placated by anything short of silence—but to ensure that our work was principled and accurate. Because I was so often questioned about this work, I insisted from early in my tenure on personally reviewing every publication we issued on Israel and Palestine; I did that for no other country or situation. Sometimes, I toughened our conclusions.

The Israeli occupation of the West Bank, Gaza, and East Jerusalem and the accompanying repression were part of the work from the start of Middle East Watch—the name originally used by Human Rights Watch in the region—in 1989. No work on the region would be credible otherwise.

My first investigation in Israeli-occupied territory was in 1992 to examine the Israeli security forces' use of torture. I traveled to Gaza with an Israeli American colleague, James Ron, who was leading the inquiry. We managed to get through the highly fortified Erez crossing from Israel to Gaza without incident and met with Palestinian human-rights activists in Gaza City.

I had a tense experience one morning when Jim and I traveled to the southern Gazan city of Khan Yunis. We were supposed to meet a colleague from the respected Palestinian rights group Al-Haq. However, due to a misunderstanding, he arrived an hour after we did. That meant two Jewish guys who spoke no Arabic had to stand on a busy Gaza street for an hour. Predictably, a large group of Palestinian men surrounded us. We acted as nonchalantly as possible, as if hanging out on a Gaza street was the most natural thing in the world for us. Everything stayed friendly enough as we tried, largely unsuccessfully, to communicate. Needless to say, I was relieved when the Al-Haq researcher arrived and verified our bona fides.

My first encounter with a virulent attack for criticizing Israel came during the 2006 war between Israel and Hezbollah. As was typical of Hezbollah, it launched rockets indiscriminately toward Israeli population centers. We documented and denounced these attacks as war crimes. To reach the perpetrators and the public that supported them, we sought to release the report at a news conference in Beirut. Hezbollah threatened demonstrations, the Beirut hotel where we had planned to launch it withdrew permission, and we had to release the report by email without a news conference. Hezbollah went so far as to make the absurd claim that Eric Goldstein, our researcher who cowrote the report, was related to Baruch Goldstein, an Israeli settler who in 1994 opened fire on Palestinians worshipping in a mosque in Hebron, killing twenty-nine and injuring more than one hundred. Eric had to quickly leave Lebanon.

We were also highly critical of Israeli attacks in southern Lebanon, which caused the partisan defenders of the Israeli government to let loose. The issue for a human-rights organization was not Israel's right to defend itself, which the partisans wanted to focus on, but *how* Israeli forces conducted themselves. That Hezbollah ignored international humanitarian law did not give the Israeli military the right to do the same, just as Hezbollah cannot use Israeli abuses to justify its own. International humanitarian law is built not on reciprocity but on an independent obligation of every party to abide by it. No one can justify a war crime by contending that the other side committed war crimes too. Otherwise, given the passions of war and the frequent allegations of misconduct, there would quickly be no international humanitarian law left.

The Israeli military noted that Hezbollah sometimes operated from civilian areas, but that did not relieve Israel of the duty to take all feasible precautions to spare civilians. Consistent with its obligations, the Israeli military warned civilians to leave southern Lebanon but then assumed that anyone who remained must be Hezbollah. Despite Israel's warnings, many civilians did not flee, whether due to old age, disability, poverty, fear, or simply a disinclination to leave their home. Israeli forces still had a legal duty to protect them, but Israel fought the war as if anyone who moved in southern Lebanon could be attacked. We investigated almost two dozen cases of Israeli air and artillery attacks on civilian homes and vehicles, involving 153 civilian deaths including 63 children, in which Hezbollah forces were not present or nearby at the time of attack. (The Israeli military also made extensive use of indiscriminate cluster munitions—a use that helped to advance the treaty banning them.)

Our report on the killing of civilians sparked vitriolic attacks in the pro-Israel Western press. Our supporters, however, with rare exception, read our report, saw that it was well researched with fair analysis, and accepted that Human Rights Watch should not ignore such abuses. They maintained this position even when one pro-Israel group approached some donors to try to persuade them to end their support.

The response of the Israeli government was considerably more measured than the over-the-top hostility of its partisans. These days, the Israeli government mainly avoids meeting with Human Rights Watch, evidently disinclined to have to answer probing questions. But shortly after we released the report on southern Lebanon, I traveled to Tel Aviv to meet with Brigadier General Avichai Mandelblit, who at the time was the chief lawyer—the military advocate-general—of the Israel Defense Forces. Unlike some Israeli officials, Mandelblit demonstrated concern for the rule of law. (In 2019, as Israel's attorney general, he charged Prime Minister Benjamin Netanyahu with corruption.)

Arrayed around a conference table inside Israeli military headquarters, Mandelblit and his staff took copious notes as my colleagues and I recounted our findings. He said that northern Israel was under attack. I said, as he knew, that gave Israel the right to defend itself but not to ignore the requirements of humanitarian law. He stated that

Hezbollah fighters did not always wear uniforms, making it difficult to distinguish them from civilians. I noted that the Israeli military still retained the duty to make that distinction and to refrain from attack if it could not. He claimed to have secret evidence to justify the attacks, which we never saw, while our researchers had collected evidence from southern Lebanon of civilians having been attacked repeatedly without military justification.

In recent years, the Palestinian Authority has been more willing to meet with us than the Israeli government. In July 2019, I led a Human Rights Watch delegation to see the Palestinian prime minister, Mohammad Shtayyeh, in Ramallah, in the West Bank. We had been highly critical of the PA's systematic use of arbitrary detention and torture to silence dissent. Shtayyeh, like many Palestinian officials, wanted to focus instead on Palestinian sovereignty and statehood, issues we did not take a stand on. I pressed him to pay more attention to the rights of Palestinians being violated by both Israeli and Palestinian authorities. He vowed that his government would respect the "right of Palestinian citizens to free speech through constructive criticism" with "no arrests or persecution." He did not keep that promise.

—

Perhaps the most visible challenge to our work on Israel came from the first chair of our board of directors, Robert Bernstein, after he had retired from that position. He was still an emeritus member of the board, which allowed him to attend meetings. He became fixated on our Israel work. A small group of right-wing New Yorkers wanted to stop our criticism of Israel. Overestimating Bernstein's influence, they seemed to think they could accomplish their goal through him.

The board extended Bernstein the courtesy that he deserved. He advanced various proposals for our Middle East work, such as that we should focus on only women's rights or address only countries that did not have vigorous civil societies. His suggestions would have meant ignoring Israeli repression of Palestinians. The board never came close to endorsing his views.

When Bernstein and his allies gave up trying to stop our reporting on Israel, they tried to discredit it. In 2009, he published an op-ed in *The New York Times* attacking our work. It was filled with inaccuracies, such as his claim that we were "ignor[ing]" other repressive governments in the region. He wrote that he'd founded the organization to work on dictatorships, which was true—during his early days with Helsinki Watch, it addressed mainly Soviet repression, before we began addressing atrocities during the Central American conflicts with the creation of Americas Watch. He objected to our work on "open, democratic societies," although he did not suggest any government other than Israel on which we should stop working. Because Israel had its own human-rights organizations and free press that could expose and combat abuses, he wrote, we should devote our attention elsewhere.

It was hardly fair to exempt Israel as a democracy when most of Human Rights Watch's work on Israel concerned its treatment of Palestinians under occupation, who had no say over the government that rules them. The Palestinian groups that sought to protect the rights of people in occupied territory faced constant restrictions and occasional arrests. It was also wrong to suggest that democracies were not worthy of Human Rights Watch's attention. Democracies' safeguards can still be inadequate to halt abuses.

When the media asked me about Bernstein's criticism, I often said that I could answer it in two words: "George Bush." The United States has a vigorous democracy, but no one thought that Human Rights Watch should ignore Bush's program of torture or his endless detention without trial of suspects in Guantánamo, especially because we often had greater ability to reach influential international actors and the global media than local groups. That was certainly true for Israel.

Jane Olson and Jonathan Fanton, then the current and past chairs of the Human Rights Watch board, made these points in a letter published in the *Times*. Nonetheless, partisan defenders of Israel still cite the op-ed in an effort, however outdated and inaccurate, to discredit our criticism of Israeli repression.

Only one donor of significance left Human Rights Watch out of sympathy for Bernstein. But Bernstein lost many of his friends in New York human-rights circles, although he remained a member, and occasionally attended meetings, of Human Rights Watch's advisory committee for the Middle East and North Africa. Shortly before he died in 2019, he attended the annual Human Rights Watch fundraising dinner in New York as a gesture of reconciliation. But his views on our Israel work never changed.

The lack of serious financial consequences from the Hezbollah war and the Bernstein affair helped me to understand that most people who supported Human Rights Watch expected us to do our jobs wherever serious abuses occurred. Even if they were sympathetic to Israel, they accepted our reporting on it so long as it was accurate and fair. I always ensured that it was. When on rare occasion we lost a donor because of our work on Israel, we lived with it.

—

For many years, we were able to operate in Israel and Occupied Palestinian Territory with little interference. Our researchers entered and left the country without major obstacles. The one exception was Gaza, where Israel allowed us in only sporadically from 2007 on, once Hamas assumed power. To ensure ongoing access, we hired a Gaza resident as a research assistant.

The Israeli government increasingly took a shoot-the-messenger approach to human-rights defenders. In November 2019, it deported our Israel and Palestine director, Omar Shakir. The government claimed falsely that he had advocated a boycott of Israel, which its law prohibits. (The government dredged up comments that he had made before joining Human Rights Watch, including as a university student.)

In a major report entitled "Occupation, Inc.," we had urged companies to avoid doing business with the Israeli government's illegal settlements, which can be characterized as war crimes under the Geneva Conventions. The settlements are not Israel, and asking companies to avoid complicity is different from advocating a consumer boycott. The issue was sensitive in Israel because the government saw the "boycott, divestment, sanctions" movement—known as BDS—as a threat due to comparisons with the strategy that contributed to the end of South Africa's apartheid. We never took a position for or against BDS. Two and a half years before deporting Omar, Israeli authorities denied us a permit to hire foreign employees in Israel, claiming that the organization was engaging "in politics in the service of Palestinian propaganda, while falsely raising the banner of 'human rights.'" They reversed course when the effort generated significant bad press for Israel. A year later, the Israeli government admitted that "no information has surfaced" indicating that Omar as our representative promoted boycotts of Israel.

I traveled to Jerusalem to accompany Omar out of the country, but first we held a news conference in Jerusalem that was deluged with journalists and resulted in media attention around the world. At the airport, we were met by more journalists along with activists holding posters saying "You Can't Hide the Occupation." Omar continued to monitor the situation in Israel and Palestine from his new base in Amman, Jordan, working with other staff based on the ground.

In October 2021, Israeli authorities outlawed six prominent Palestinian civil-society groups on the concocted grounds that they were "terrorist organizations." The groups included Al-Haq, the respected Palestinian human-rights defender.

—

Human Rights Watch braced for a new round of attacks when in April 2021 we published our report on the Israeli government's crimes against humanity of persecution and apartheid. As we explained, we meant the finding of apartheid not as an historical analogy to South Africa but as a careful analysis of the facts under the definition contained in international law. We were driven to address the issue by the endlessness of the Israeli occupation.

The traditional answer to those who pointed out oppressive and discriminatory Israeli practices in the occupied territory was to say that these were just temporary, that they would be resolved once the "peace process" concluded. Yet after more than half a century of occupation and three decades of a "peace process" that had gone nowhere, after the continual building and expansion of settlements, that response was no longer credible. There was only a "one-state reality" of entrenched Israeli rule over Palestinians. The sole question was whether Palestinians would be granted equal rights or continue to be subjected to oppressive, discriminatory rule—that is, apartheid.

We had not arrived at our determination easily. It may well have taken us too long—Palestinian groups reached it earlier—but the conclusion that the Israeli government is imposing apartheid has become mainstream, the analysis of every serious human-rights organization that has examined the issue, including the leading

Israeli human-rights group, B'Tselem, and more than two dozen other Israeli groups; Al-Haq and scores of other Palestinian rights groups; and Amnesty International and UN experts.

For many years, leading Israeli politicians, including several former prime ministers—Yitzhak Rabin, Ehud Barak, and Ehud Olmert—had warned that the country was sliding toward apartheid. So had commentators such as the *New York Times* columnist Tom Friedman and such U.S. government officials as Jimmy Carter after his presidency and John Kerry when he was secretary of state. Human Rights Watch and our colleague organizations took the next step.

I was not involved in the research for our report—Omar and his team conducted that—but I was deeply involved in assessing the evidence and working out the strategy. During a Middle East visit, I also consulted extensively with Israeli and Palestinian rights groups. Part of my preparation involved a tour of parts of the West Bank, East Jerusalem, and Israel. With Breaking the Silence, an impressive group of former Israeli soldiers who speak out about the repression that they were once forced to impose, I toured Hebron, a thriving city with a Palestinian population of more than two hundred thousand in the southern West Bank, where a group of Israeli zealots have established a settlement. To protect them, Israeli soldiers have shut down what was once the main commercial thoroughfare. We also traveled to the highest hills in the West Bank to better see how the settlements, outposts, and connecting Israeli-only roads have divided up the area into Palestinian enclaves—B'Tselem counted 165 disconnected "islands"—leaving no prospect of a viable contiguous state.

Some of the most surprising parts of my tour were within Israel. We visited the only Palestinian town along the Mediterranean Sea, Jisr al-Zarqa, which is located next to Caesarea, where Netanyahu maintains a home. Caesarea is filled with luxurious, sprawling estates. It is separated from the Palestinian town by a large man-made berm. Jisr al-Zarqa was crowded, with few services, and not even an entrance to the major Israeli highway that crossed nearby. The contrast was stark and disturbing.

We also toured the Galilee city of Nazareth, the largest Palestinian city within Israel. It exists as a Palestinian enclave only because a Jewish Canadian commander, Ben Dunkelman, refused orders in 1948 to forcibly expel its residents, as was occurring elsewhere in

Israel. Stuck with this major Palestinian population center, Israeli planners set about boxing it in, building various impediments to expansion. One was the suburb known as Nazareth Illit (Upper Nazareth, later renamed Nof HaGalil), where most Israeli administrative services for the area are now based. Its housing was sold mainly to Jewish immigrants from Russia. (Ironically, after two decades or so, these Jews had climbed the economic ladder and were moving out of Nazareth Illit, often selling their homes to Palestinians, hardly the original intent.)

These visits reinforced for me the extensive research done by Omar and his team. Much of the purpose behind Israeli actions was demographic: to keep as many Palestinians as possible outside Israel and Palestine; if not there, then in Gaza, which few in the Israeli government at the time sought to incorporate into Israel; if not there, then in Areas A and B in the West Bank, the hodgepodge of territories left to Palestinian administration; if not there, then in Area C of the West Bank, where the settlements were located along with vast areas for expansion; if not there, then East Jerusalem, the occupied territory that the Israeli government already claims to have annexed; and only as a last resort, in Israel proper, where about 20 percent of the population is Palestinian. The Israeli government imposed various restrictions on movement, immigration, construction, and other aspects of daily Palestinian life to channel the population according to these demographic preferences.

We analyzed these findings according to the international definition of apartheid, as set out in the International Criminal Court treaty (the Rome Statute) and the International Convention on the Suppression and Punishment of the Crime of Apartheid. The two treaties differ slightly, but we interpreted them to require three elements carried out on a widespread or systematic basis:

1. An intent to dominate a racial, ethnic, or national group.
2. Systematic oppression.
3. Specified inhumane acts to carry out that oppression.

We found that these elements came together in the occupied territory.

One "defense" we knew we would face was security. There is no doubt that the Israeli government faces a serious security threat from

Palestinian armed groups that violently attack its citizens; the events of October 7, 2023, made that crystal clear. But security does not account for many aspects of the discrimination that the Israeli government imposes on Palestinians. The land confiscations, the revocation of residency permits, the denial of building permits, and other efforts to alter demographics have nothing to do with security. The building of settlements deep inside the West Bank, next to Palestinians who naturally resent seeing their land seized, arguably makes Israelis *less* secure.

Because we knew that this report would be controversial, we spent much time explaining it to various interested groups and journalists before formal publication. The journalistic coverage was overwhelmingly fair, objective, and, as a result, sympathetic to our findings.

Our development team had voiced concerns about the possible fundraising implications of our report, so we made a point of briefing major donors in advance, though I was determined not to let donor objections deter us. Some supporters left us because of the report, while others increased their gifts.

The Israeli government could find nothing wrong factually or legally with the 213-page report. Some of its partisans resorted to the usual name-calling, saying the report was "a hatchet job" and reflected "animus toward Israel," but we took that as a victory because they had nothing more substantive to say. Some government supporters noted the rights that Palestinian citizens of Israel have. But that "defense" conveniently ignored our report's finding that the three elements of the crime of apartheid came together in the occupied territory.

The growing number of organizations—international, Palestinian, and Israeli—that recognized the Israeli government was committing the crime of apartheid began to change the public narrative. Media references to that apartheid skyrocketed. Even a former head of Israel's Mossad intelligence agency said the Israeli government is imposing apartheid on Palestinians under occupation. Ritual invocations of the "peace process" were increasingly seen as empty, an avoidance of the subject of how the Israeli government treats Palestinians today. As we had urged, the UN Human Rights Council in May 2021 created a commission of inquiry to investigate, among other things, "systematic discrimination and repression based on national, ethnic, racial or religious identity" in Israel and Palestine and to collect evidence of relevant crimes. The International Court of Justice seemed to endorse the apartheid characterization in a July 2024 ruling.

The Israeli government for many years has had no long-term solution to its occupation-without-end of Palestinian territory. Netanyahu in February 2024 reiterated his refusal to countenance a Palestinian state. The more that governments recognize and act on the criminality of the status quo, the greater the chance that the Israeli government's regime of oppressive discrimination and unequal rights will come to an end.

—

Senior Israeli officials have long assumed that they enjoyed impunity for their treatment of Palestinians, but that came to an end in May 2024 when the International Criminal Court chief prosecutor, Karim Khan, sought arrest warrants for Netanyahu as well as Israeli defense minister Yoav Gallant for the starvation strategy that they were pursuing in Gaza—Israel's obstruction of much food and other humanitarian aid to the point of famine. He also sought arrest warrants for three senior Hamas leaders for the atrocities of October 7, 2023, and the mistreatment of Israeli hostages held by Hamas. More charges were expected. In an interview with the *Sunday Times* of London, Khan mentioned in particular Israel's use of huge two-thousand-pound bombs that had decimated neighborhoods.

Attacks on civilians that are indiscriminate or disproportionate, or the deliberate starving of civilians, are broadly understood to be war crimes, but it is less widely known that the settlements are as well, although it is unclear whether Khan will address them. Article 49 of the Fourth Geneva Convention prohibits transferring members of an occupying force's population to occupied territory. Such transfers are termed a "grave breach" of the convention, meaning a war crime. The Rome Statute of the ICC lists "the transfer, directly or indirectly, by the Occupying Power of parts of its own civilian population into the territory it occupies" as a war crime within the court's jurisdiction.

Settlements have been official Israeli government policy for decades, with every prime minister having done their part to advance it. Under Netanyahu's far-right government, which took office in December 2022, settlement expansion accelerated rapidly. The

Israeli government denies that the Palestinian territories are "occupied." It claims they are "disputed." Few governments endorse that view, though President Trump's former secretary of state, Mike Pompeo, an evangelical Christian, said that Israel "is not an occupying nation" based on his "reading of the Bible." The International Court of Justice rejected the Israeli position in its July 2024 decision.

The Israeli government was on notice of the illegality of settlements from the outset of the occupation. In a September 1967 memo marked "Top Secret" sent to Prime Minister Levi Eshkol, the Foreign Ministry legal adviser, Theodor Meron, wrote: "My conclusion is that civilian settlement in the administered territories contravenes the explicit provisions of the Fourth Geneva Convention." A Polish survivor of the Holocaust who fled to Israel after losing most of his family, Meron later moved from Israel to the United States, where, as a professor at New York University School of Law, he served as an informal adviser on international humanitarian law for Human Rights Watch. He was also a judge on the International Criminal Tribunal for the former Yugoslavia.

Toward the end of the Obama administration, in December 2016, the U.S. government abstained on rather than veto a UN Security Council resolution on the illegality of the settlements; all other council members voted for it. The resolution provided that "the establishment by Israel of settlements in the Palestinian territory occupied since 1967, including East Jerusalem, has no legal validity and constitutes a flagrant violation under international law." This was also the long-standing position of the U.S. State Department until Pompeo. U.S. secretary of state Antony Blinken reinstated it.

The ICC's actions regarding Gaza are the product of an investigation opened by the court's prior chief prosecutor, Fatou Bensouda, in March 2021. When she announced that probe along with a parallel one that might have implicated U.S. torturers in Afghanistan, the Trump administration disgracefully imposed sanctions on her and one of her colleagues. The Biden administration removed them.

Still, Biden called Khan's request for arrest warrants for Netanyahu and Gallant "outrageous," claiming it equated Hamas and Israel, though the prosecutor did no such thing; he merely pursued officials on both sides for their own separate alleged war crimes. Given the severity of the offenses, it would have been outrageous had Khan ignored one side's crimes. The dual charges underscore the principle that war crimes by one side never justify war crimes by another.

Antony Blinken said without explanation that the court lacked jurisdiction. That might have been a reference to the old U.S. position (to be discussed later) that the court lacks jurisdiction over nationals of states that have not joined the court even when their alleged crime is on the territory of a court member, but the court's statute explicitly provides for that territorial jurisdiction, and Biden called it "justified" when it was used to charge Putin.

More likely, Blinken was referring to the U.S. view that Palestine is not sufficiently a state for the purpose of joining the court, but an ICC pretrial chamber rejected that argument, based on the UN General Assembly's recognition of Palestine in 2012 as a "non-member observer state." Palestine has used that status not only to join the court but also to ratify a host of other human-rights treaties, which should be welcomed as a statement of commitment, even if actual practice has often fallen short.

Blinken also mentioned the requirement that the ICC defer to good-faith national investigations, but Israel has no history of prosecuting senior officials for war crimes, and there was no known investigation of the starvation strategy at the heart of the ICC case despite warnings from Khan that he was pursuing it. To the contrary, Netanyahu showed only contempt, accusing Khan of "callously pouring gasoline on the fires of antisemitism that are raging across the world" and claiming that "Khan takes his place among the great antisemites in modern times." Rather than investigate serious abuses as they arose, Israeli authorities secretly monitored Bensouda's and Khan's communications so they could open investigations retroactively into incidents of interest to the ICC to try to show that Israel was investigating its own. Israeli intelligence agents even threatened Bensouda in the hope of dissuading her from opening an investigation. This was not a good-faith pursuit of justice.

—

Reporting on Israel is challenging because no other government has such an organized group of supporters that are dedicated to attacking critics, often with little regard for factual accuracy. Indeed, there is a cottage industry of small organizations, typically with deceptively neutral-sounding names, whose purpose is to criticize any group or individual who criticizes Israel. Their frequent charge of bias is meant both to discredit the critic and to change the subject from the government's conduct. Although few informed observers take these one-sided partisans seriously, many people want to believe that the Israeli government does no wrong. These groups also benefit from the tendency of journalists to discuss "both sides" of an issue, a problematic equivalency when the other side to which they give voice consists of propagandists. People often confront me with some inaccurate or misleading statistic or allegation from one of these groups as if it were the gospel truth. It is never hard to refute the statement if the questioner is open to it.

Because of the credibility and reach of Human Rights Watch, we were often the primary target of these groups. Alan Dershowitz, the Harvard Law professor and a leading partisan defender of the Israeli government, claimed that we had "done more to turn the international community and progressives against Israel than any other organization."

The partisans seemed to attack me more than anyone else. One of the leaders of the Israel-right-or-wrong groups called me "the most powerful and obsessive Israel-basher . . . of the 21st century." Apart from my position as Human Rights Watch's director, the vitriol was in part the product of my significant following on Twitter, although it started long before that. I drew ire because, having survived so many of their attacks, I did not hesitate to spotlight Israeli abuses—or the hypocrisy of the Israeli government's defenders. Indeed, I felt a responsibility to do so.

I am sure that part of what drove these partisans crazy is that I am Jewish. The charge of antisemitism is often bandied about to silence critics of Israeli repression, including me—I was also accused of being a "Jew hater." Such absurd accusations only reaffirmed my sense of duty to call out Israeli abuses. It pained me to be ostracized by elements of the community that I grew up with, but I took comfort in knowing that I was far from alone among American Jews who were deeply disturbed by the direction of the Israeli government.

Some of these charges were made at the height of Israel's 2006 war with Hezbollah in southern Lebanon, when Israeli forces were pummeling Lebanese civilians. I wrote: "An eye for an eye—or, more accurately in this case, twenty eyes for an eye—may have been the morality of some more primitive moment. But it is not the morality of international humanitarian law." While defending the disproportionate Israeli military response that I had condemned, Abraham Foxman, then the head of the Anti-Defamation League, accused me of repeating "a classic anti-Semitic stereotype about Jews," although I could never figure out what that stereotype was.

To enhance the antisemitism charge, one partisan disparaged my "thin" Jewish roots and "nominal Jewish background," saying that my "father's history in Nazi Germany" is my "only Jewish identity," even though both my mother and father were proudly Jewish, as am I. To challenge my Judaism, someone edited my Wikipedia entry to note the utterly irrelevant fact (other than to suggest that I am not really Jewish) that I married Annie, an Anglican, in an Anglican church. (It was important to her.) At one point they even claimed that I had converted to Christianity before an editor removed the concoction. My willingness to criticize such underhanded methods only added to my "target" status.

Other Jewish critics of Israeli policy who faced these charges included Peter Beinart, a highly respected journalist who attended an Orthodox synagogue and called out the misuse of antisemitism to silence criticism of Israel, and Richard Goldstone, the revered anti-apartheid South African judge who was lambasted as a "self-hating Jew" and even prevented, due to threats of protests, from attending his grandson's bar mitzvah after he chaired a UN fact-finding mission that was critical of the Israeli military's (as well as Hamas's) conduct during the 2008–09 conflict in Gaza. (He later retracted part of the report that had charged Israeli forces with intentionally killing civilians.)

Journalists also often faced the charge. As one Australian journalist put it, "The aim is to make journalists and editors decide that, even if they have a legitimate story that may criticise Israel, it is simply not worth running it because it will cause 'more trouble than it's worth.'"

Behind the charge of antisemitism is a battle about what the concept means. One working definition, issued by the International

Holocaust Remembrance Alliance (IHRA), states in part that examples of antisemitism include "applying double standards by requiring of [Israel] a behavior not expected or demanded of any other democratic nation." That example lies behind the growing efforts to highlight supposed double standards in how Israel's rights record was assessed.

That argument did not hold up well against us because we treated Israel according to the same standards that we applied to one hundred other governments. As in any conflict situation, we reported on Israeli abuses as well as those by all opposing forces: the Palestinian Authority, Hamas, Islamic Jihad, and Hezbollah. Although we did not address terrorist acts if committed by unsponsored individuals—those are serious crimes but not necessarily human-rights violations—we did address terrorism that seemed to have been sponsored by a government or armed group, such as in our 172-page report "Erased in a Moment" on suicide bombing against Israeli civilians.

Another type of speech that IHRA highlights as potentially antisemitic is "denying the Jewish people their right to self-determination, e.g., by claiming that the existence of a State of Israel is a racist endeavor." Some partisans claimed that it is therefore antisemitic even to point out when the Israeli government is acting in a racist way, such as enforcing apartheid against Palestinians. Some say that because there are few contemporary examples of apartheid—Human Rights Watch also found it in the case of the Myanmar government's treatment of Rohingya Muslims in western Rakhine State—the application of the legal concept to Israel must somehow be antisemitic.

The IHRA working definition of antisemitism also refers to "demonizing" Jews. One prominent partisan equated such demonization with the legitimate criticism of Israel by groups such as Human Rights Watch and Amnesty International and asserted that the purpose of the working definition is to stop such criticism.

An alternative definition of antisemitism, issued by 210 scholars and known as the Jerusalem Declaration on Antisemitism, seeks to avoid such misuse of the concept by including several examples of statements and acts that are not antisemitic, such as "evidence-based criticism of Israel as a state" including "the conduct of Israel in the West Bank and Gaza." It goes on to say:

It is not antisemitic to point out systematic racial discrimination. In general, the same norms of debate that apply to other states and to other conflicts over national self-determination apply in the case of Israel and Palestine. Thus, even if contentious, it is not antisemitic, in and of itself, to compare Israel with other historical cases, including settler-colonialism or apartheid.

Similarly, the Nexus Document addressing the relationship between Israel and antisemitism concludes:

Paying disproportionate attention to Israel and treating Israel differently than other countries is not prima facie proof of antisemitism. (There are numerous reasons for devoting special attention to Israel and treating Israel differently, e.g., some people care about Israel more; others may pay more attention because Israel has a special relationship with the United States and receives $4 billion in American aid.)

I prefer the Jerusalem Declaration and the Nexus Document because, by including examples of what is not antisemitism, they give greater deference to freedom of speech. The IHRA definition, although billed by its authors as only a "working definition," has not been updated to include negative examples, despite its increasing weaponization against legitimate critics of Israeli practices.

Any discussion of the Israeli-Palestinian situation is prone to be heated. It would be a mistake, in my view, to limit such discussion beyond excluding clearly antisemitic expressions. Indeed, Kenneth Stern, the main drafter of the IHRA definition as the American Jewish Committee's antisemitism expert at the time, later warned of this misuse. More than one hundred rights groups including Human Rights Watch stated their opposition to using the IHRA definition.

Gareth Evans, the former Australian foreign minister and past president of the International Crisis Group, summed up the issue well:

Calling out China for its persecution of Uighurs is not to be a Sinophobic racist. Calling out Myanmar for its crimes against

Rohingya people is not to be anti-Buddhist. Calling out Saudi Arabia and Egypt for their murder and suppression of dissidents is not to be Islamophobic or anti-Arab. And calling out Israel for its sabotage of the two-state solution and creation of a de facto apartheid state is not to be anti-Semitic.

Antisemitism is a serious problem. But if people see it as a tool to stifle legitimate criticism of Israel, its meaning will be devalued. The Israeli government may feel temporarily strengthened, but Jews around the world will be left more vulnerable. Jewish leaders therefore are increasingly expressing concern about the misuse of charges of antisemitism to silence legitimate criticism of Israel. In February 2023, "a slate of 169 prominent American Jews, including former leaders of major mainstream Jewish organizations, called on U.S. politicians not to conflate criticism of Israel with antisemitism," as reported by the Jewish Telegraphic Agency. The signatories included former heads of the American Israel Public Affairs Committee (AIPAC), the Conference of Presidents of Major American Jewish Organizations, and the Jewish Federations of North America. In August 2023, a leading Israeli Holocaust historian said that accusing Israel of apartheid is not antisemitic.

One memorable encounter for me with an extreme pro-Israel partisan took place in 2004, when I met with Abraham Foxman, at the time the long-serving national director of the pro-Israel Anti-Defamation League. I went to his headquarters in Midtown Manhattan to see him as part of a reconciliation effort. A few minutes into the meeting in a small conference room, Foxman exploded, carrying on about Human Rights Watch's supposed anti-Israel bias, and stormed out of the room. His colleague continued the meeting as if nothing unusual had taken place. After a while, Foxman returned. He said he thought that Human Rights Watch devoted 20 to 30 percent of its resources to criticizing Israel. When I explained that Israel was only one of, at that point, seventy countries that we covered, that we had only a single researcher assigned to the country (who also covered Palestinian Authority and Hamas abuses), he admitted that he had "learned something." To this day, though, partisans of the Israeli government regularly respond to my tweets on the country as if I criticize only Israel.

One can never suggest to supporters of the Israeli government that spikes in antisemitic incidents or speech sometimes parallel Israel's conduct. To note this correlation is not to blame the victim, as some Israeli partisans charge, but rather a measurable fact, as observed during Israel's military campaign in Gaza beginning in October 2023, which caused high civilian casualties and extensive hunger. Even the Anti-Defamation League noted "a significant spike in antisemitic incidents across the United States" beginning in October 2023 "directly linked to the war in Israel and Gaza." As Jonathan Greenblatt, the ADL CEO, put it, "When conflict erupts in Israel, antisemitic incidents soon follow in the U.S. and globally." Nonetheless, in the minds of some partisans, the idea that a state designed as a haven for Jews could stimulate harm against Jews is inadmissible.

I had one heated exchange on this topic with Jeffrey Goldberg, who became editor in chief of *The Atlantic*. I knew Goldberg casually and had even bumped into him once at Israel's Erez crossing into Gaza. He argued: "Anti-Semitism in Europe did not flare 'in response to Israel's conduct in Gaza,' or anywhere else. . . . This is for the simple reason that Jews do not cause anti-Semitism. It is a universal and immutable rule that the targets of prejudice are not the cause of prejudice."

That strikes me as one-dimensional. Antisemitism is not static. It is not an autonomous force that follows its own internal logic unconnected to the world. Events affect it.

The irony is that while Israeli partisans treat it as taboo to say that the Israeli government's conduct has any effect on antisemitism, they find it totally acceptable to blame human-rights groups for fueling antisemitism through our criticism of the Israeli government's conduct. That is akin to what the Anti-Defamation League, the self-proclaimed leader of the fight against antisemitism, did when Amnesty International issued its report on the Israeli government's apartheid. It said that Amnesty's report "likely will lead to intensified antisemitism." The ADL, the American Jewish Committee, and four other well-known American Jewish groups also said the report "fuels those antisemites around the world who seek to undermine the only Jewish country on earth." Another critic accused me of "stating that Israel's actions were responsible for rising antisemitism rather than

HRW's relentless criticism, including accusations of 'apartheid.'" Evidently antisemitism is suddenly not an autonomous force when it can be used to tar critics of Israeli repression.

The Israeli government's concern with antisemitism is also selective. Some of its supporters are quick to throw the slur at critics, but the government has no trouble sidling up to antisemitic leaders for political advantage. Netanyahu, for example, embraced Hungarian prime minister Viktor Orbán despite Orbán's notorious antisemitic campaigns against George Soros. That Soros was also a critic of Israeli repression undoubtedly contributed to the Israeli government's willingness to close its eyes to Orbán's antisemitism.

Why would Orbán, despite his antisemitism, embrace the Israeli leader? As Peter Beinart pointed out, it is quite possible to be a Zionist, supporting the state of Israel as a nationalist enterprise, while still being antisemitic, disliking liberal Jews in their own societies who tend to prioritize "diversity and equal citizenship" over ethnic "homogeneity" as the basis of a democratic nation.

I suspect that my Jewish background was also annoying to Israeli government supporters because I derived such different conclusions from them about the Holocaust. Like many Jews who have been drawn to the human-rights cause—and who support Human Rights Watch—the lesson that I take from the long history of Jews being persecuted is the need to build a strong set of human-rights norms that raise the stakes for governments or armed groups that attack Jews. However, this should not be a matter of defending only Jews but rather of recognizing that Jews will be safest by working with others to promote a human-rights system in which the persecution of any group faces condemnation. Indeed, the leading American Jewish opponents of antisemitism, such as the ADL and the American Jewish Congress, at first adopted a similar perspective. So did Aharon Barak, the former president of Israel's Supreme Court.

But in recent years the right-wing politicians that dominated the Israeli government seem to have drawn a different lesson from the Holocaust. For them, the Jews were persecuted because they were weak and did not have a state of their own. These politicians are determined not only to defend the State of Israel, as any government would do for its nation, but to be the toughest, most brutal force in the region—the one that no one dares mess with. As Netanyahu described it, "The weak crumble, are slaughtered and are erased from history while the strong, for good or for ill, survive." "Israel had to make clear to the Arabs that they would be hurt far, far more than the pain they could inflict," said Foxman. "In other words, without Israel hitting back (not in an 'eye for an eye a tooth for a tooth' fashion . . .) but in a much stronger way, Israel would have been destroyed long ago."

The lesson I draw from the Holocaust dictates the importance of respecting the rights of Palestinians as part of an effort to build stronger human-rights norms capable of deterring persecution of any group. If Palestinians are treated as exceptions to human-rights protections, so might Jews. But the lesson that the right-wing governments of Israel draw is that Palestinians, as the perceived threat of the moment, should be crushed, and then crushed some more, until they have no choice but to accept their subordination. In other words, the Israeli government sees human rights as an obstacle to its preferred defense, which relies mainly on force, applied as brutally as deemed necessary.

That right-wing lesson obviously does nothing for Jews outside of Israel, but the Israeli government seems to feel that that is their problem, because they have not emigrated to Israel. Indeed, Netanyahu seems long ago to have begun hedging his bets on American Jews as a source of support for Israel, given their tendency to be liberal and believe in rights. Instead, he banks on a combination of AIPAC, which represents highly conservative parts of American Jewry, and Christian evangelicals, many of whom favor a strong Israel not out of any love for Jews but because they see it as a prerequisite to the second coming of Christ, at which point Jews who don't convert to Christianity would presumably go to hell.

The right-wing lesson drawn from the Holocaust is not a wise policy for the Jews of Israel, either, as Hamas's October 2023 slaughter and abduction of Israeli civilians demonstrated. The aim should be to make such flouting of the most basic rights unthinkable. But refusing to recognize one's enemy as deserving rights can only encourage, though never justify, such atrocities.

—

The political pressure not to report critically on Israel was illustrated shortly after I announced that I would be leaving Human Rights Watch. The leadership of the Carr Center for Human Rights Policy, part of the Harvard Kennedy School, wanted me to join them for a year as a senior fellow. I had been involved informally with the Carr Center since its founding. It seemed like a good place to kick around ideas as I wrote this book, so I accepted. All that was needed was the sign-off of the Kennedy School dean, Douglas Elmendorf, which, given that it was a human-rights fellowship, we all assumed would be a formality.

Reflecting that assumption, I contacted the dean to introduce myself in advance of my planned arrival in September 2022. In July, we had a perfectly pleasant half-hour video conversation. The only odd note occurred at the end, when he asked me whether I had "any enemies."

Of course I have enemies, I told him, many of them. That is a hazard of being a human-rights defender. I explained that the Chinese and Russian governments had imposed sanctions on me. I mentioned that a range of governments, including Rwanda's and Saudi Arabia's, hated me. I said that the Israeli government undoubtedly detested me too.

Two weeks later, the Carr Center called to say sheepishly that Elmendorf had vetoed my fellowship. He told Professor Kathryn Sikkink, the highly respected human-rights scholar at the Kennedy School, that the reason was my, and Human Rights Watch's, criticism of Israel.

I was shocked. How can an institution that purports to address foreign policy—that even hosts a human-rights policy center—avoid criticism of Israel? It later emerged that, while Elmendorf did not seem to have strong personal views on the subject, "'some people in the university' who mattered to him did," as he explained to the Carr Center's faculty director, Professor Mathias Risse. By all appearances, these people were either donors or people who were worried how donors would react. The journalist Michael Massing wrote a detailed exposé in *The Nation* outlining the major donors to the Kennedy School who were strong supporters of Israel.

At first, Elmendorf refused to discuss the matter, although the Kennedy School spokesperson elliptically "did not deny [my] specific allegations," as reported by *The Harvard Crimson*. Elmendorf justified his decision by citing my, and Human Rights Watch's, supposed "anti-Israel bias." That was an odd allegation, given that the Kennedy School each year welcomed up to ten midlevel Israeli officials for yearlong fellowships and had even granted a fellowship to a retired Israel Defense Force general. Bias in favor of Israel was plainly not an issue. On rare occasions, the Kennedy School granted a fellowship to a Palestinian, most notably Saeb Erekat, the longtime chief negotiator for the Palestine Liberation Organization. He was undoubtedly critical of Israel, but no one would pretend he was unbiased.

I came to believe that what really must have bothered the people who "mattered" to Elmendorf was Human Rights Watch's *im*partiality. A biased critic can easily be dismissed. But it was precisely the care and objectivity that Human Rights Watch brought to its work on Israel and Palestine (and the rest of the world) that made our criticism difficult to ignore.

I used Twitter to shape media coverage. I distributed the many articles that were written about the dean's veto. I defended the fairness of our work on Israel and Palestine. I asked questions about the university's apparent sensitivity to presumed donor concerns. When I ran Human Rights Watch, as I said, I recognized that certain prospective donors would not contribute to the organization because, as a matter of principle, we would not exempt their favorite country from our critical reporting. But if donors were behind the Kennedy School dean's decision, why was Elmendorf not willing to take the same approach to uphold academic freedom? The principled thing to do would have been to tell donors that they had no right to use their financial influence to compromise intellectual independence. If any university could take such a principled stance, it would be Harvard, the world's richest academic institution.

Elmendorf's decision met an uproar of opposition among Harvard students, faculty, and alumni. It also yielded a lead editorial and two articles, one on the front page, in Harvard's hometown paper, *The Boston Globe*. In addition, I placed an op-ed in the *Globe* as well as *The Guardian*, which also published its own articles on the controversy. I did countless interviews on television, radio, and in print. After two weeks of intense negative publicity and apparently uniform disapproval of his action at an emergency meeting of the Kennedy School faculty, Elmendorf allowed my fellowship to proceed. But as I pointed out to the media, that did not address the broader issue of academic freedom.

Elmendorf never did say who the people who "mattered" to him were. He hid behind the confidentiality of the fellowship process but nonetheless asserted that the people were not donors. That did little to appease concerns that they could turn their attention to others at the Kennedy School who criticized Israel. In September 2023, Elmendorf announced that he would step down as dean at the end of the academic year.

For years, universities and other institutions have penalized scholars and others for their criticism of Israel or advocacy of Palestinian rights. That Elmendorf reversed himself for me, after I was able to mobilize substantial media and public attention, did nothing to protect critics with a less public profile. I asked the Kennedy School, and Harvard University as a whole, to clarify that they uphold academic freedom even for less visible critics of Israel. They never did.

—

As I was completing this book, Hamas's October 2023 murder and abduction of Israeli civilians took place, followed by Israel's bombing and besieging of Gaza, with its enormous toll on Palestinian civilians. Even though I was no longer at Human Rights Watch, I found my commentary was much in demand by the media and on college campuses. The atmosphere was divisive, even toxic, with supporters of Israel and Palestine demonizing and sometimes trying to silence each other. I discovered that my efforts to outline and uphold evenhandedly the requirements of international humanitarian law could speak to a common ground despite the partisan differences. The media kept asking for more, and the academic audiences that I addressed from a broad range of political perspectives were remarkably respectful.

I explained that Hamas's initial attacks were blatant war crimes, but war crimes by one side do not justify war crimes by the other, because, as I said, the duty to abide by international humanitarian law is an independent obligation on each party to a conflict regardless of reciprocity; that humanitarian law requires warring parties to refrain not only from targeting civilians but also from firing indiscriminately into populated areas, as Israeli forces seemed to be doing by flattening certain Gaza neighborhoods; that even a military target must not be attacked if the civilian harm would be disproportionate, such as the Israeli military's repeated use of massive two-thousand-pound bombs in populated areas with predictably devastating consequences for civilians, or its effective closure of many of Gaza's hospitals, greatly aggravating the suffering and risks for civilians under bombardment; that Hamas's wrongful use of human shields and fighting from civilian-populated areas did not relieve Israeli forces of the duty to refrain from such disproportionate attacks; that the Israeli warnings for civilians to flee areas of fighting, an ostensibly humane act, was done in an inhumane way because bombing continued in places where they were told to flee and Israel largely blocked the supply of basic necessities, in violation of the duty to allow access to humanitarian aid for civilians in need.

I noted that Hamas's atrocities and intentions toward Israel were no defense to the charges of genocide that South Africa brought against Israel before the International Court of Justice, and explained why the court found wanting other elements of the Israeli defense, such as its efforts to refute charges of genocidal intent by pointing to the wholly inadequate dribs and drabs of humanitarian aid that it was permitting into Gaza. I addressed the devastation of Gaza, rendering much of it unlivable, in the context of the expressed desire by far-right ministers in Netanyahu's cabinet (on whose votes he depended to stay in power) to expel the population to Egypt. When Israel claimed that a dozen employees of the UN agency serving Palestinian refugees, UNRWA, were alleged to have participated in Hamas's October 2023 attack (UNRWA said it immediately fired those who remained alive and opened an investigation), I criticized the Israeli government's campaign to persuade donors to stop funding UNRWA, noting that it was the sole agency with adequate capacity to distribute food within Gaza and, despite Netanyahu's hopes, its destruction would not force Palestinian refugees to forget they were Palestinian refugees and forsake their right to return, whether to Israel or Palestine. I added that to discuss the context of Hamas's attack—particularly the apartheid and endless occupation—was not to excuse an atrocity for which there is no justification but to point the direction for much-needed efforts to revive the moribund political discussions between Israeli and Palestinian representatives. And I decried the damage to the "rules-based order"—really, to the entire effort to defend human rights—if an exception were made for Israel.

In the cacophony of the moment, it was difficult to know how much difference such messages made. My hope was that, by helping to shape media coverage and the social media conversation, I could generate pressure on the Israeli government both directly and through its Western allies to curtail the enormous civilian toll in Gaza. There is no easy solution to the seemingly intractable Israeli-Palestinian conflict, but sparing the civilians on both sides is essential for the emergence of an atmosphere where constructive political negotiations have any chance of occurring.

My father's immigration card for entering the United States. He fled Nazi Germany in July 1938 for New York.

In August 2006, José Miguel Vivanco, our Americas director, and I meet with Felipe Calderón, right, at his office in Mexico City after he had been elected president. *(Human Rights Watch)*

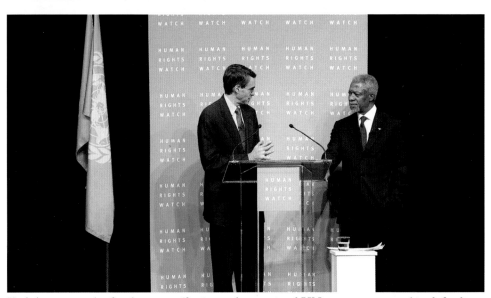

Kofi Annan was by far the most effective and committed UN secretary-general in defending human rights. We developed a very close relationship. New York, December 2006. *(United Nations)*

Presenting our report on the abuse of migrant domestic workers in Saudi Arabia, in Central Java, Indonesia, a major source of those workers, with Andy Yentriyani of Indonesia's National Commission on Violence Against Women, July 2008. *(Nisha Varia)*

President Obama greets my wife, Annie Sparrow, and me at the January 2011 White House state dinner for the Chinese leader, Hu Jintao, who can partially be seen behind Obama. After an earlier disappointing start with China, the Obama administration was making a statement on human rights by inviting me to the dinner and seating me in the main dining room at a table with the Chinese ambassador to the United States. *(White House)*

Meeting UN secretary-general Ban Ki-moon (holding the book), together with his aides and my colleagues, in his New York office in May 2011. Although Ban was sensitive to our criticism, we developed a warm relationship as he became more outspoken in defending human rights. *(United Nations)*

In London with George Soros in October 2011, shortly after he had pledged a remarkable $100 million to enable Human Rights Watch to become a genuinely global organization. *(Human Rights Watch)*

Colombian president Juan Manuel Santos, to my right, and José Miguel Vivanco, to my left, at the presidential palace in Bogotá in October 2011. We discussed the role of justice for past atrocities as part of efforts at the time to wind down the country's civil war. *(Shari Leinwand)*

Speaking later at an informal dinner hosted by President Santos, center, at his residence in Cartagena. We hoped that the goodwill generated by such gatherings could help to move more difficult conversations forward. *(Shari Leinwand)*

At the February 2014 Munich Security Conference, I was given the stage to press for an end to the Syrian government's bombing of civilians and civilian institutions in opposition-held parts of the country and for a UN Security Council resolution authorizing cross-border humanitarian aid to those areas. *(Munich Security Conference)*

Meeting in February 2014 with Thein Sein, the former general turned president of Myanmar, in the glittering presidential palace in Naypyidaw. We discussed the importance of allowing a genuine transition to democracy, which later occurred only in part and not for long. *(Human Rights Watch)*

Ida Sawyer, Human Rights Watch's researcher at the time for the Democratic Republic of Congo, and I pose with President Joseph Kabila in July 2015 at his office in Kinshasa, just after our meeting in which we sought to persuade him to stop delaying the election to select his successor. His parting words were a plea: "As for my future, continue to pray for me." *(Human Rights Watch)*

In Kinshasa, I met with the press the next day. The impromptu nature of the encounter reminded me of the chaos that often impedes the defense of rights in Congo. *(Human Rights Watch)*

During the same trip, in the eastern Congo city of Goma, Ida and I met with youth activists from the group LUCHA, whose protests had been met by arrests and mistreatment. *(Timo Müller)*

The Human Rights Watch staff in Goma gave me this poster to commemorate our work together. It details violence and repression in eastern Congo, the International Criminal Court's prosecution of notorious warlord Bosco Ntaganda, and my vow to continue the struggle until we achieve justice for atrocities and respect for human rights. *(KASH)*

NOS-NTR

Dus ik prijs premier Rutte en minister Koenders voor hun standvastigheid.

Just before the September 2017 vote of the UN Human Rights Council to investigate the Saudi-led coalition's bombing of civilians in Yemen, I appeared on the main Dutch news program, *Nieuwsuur*. Because the Dutch business community was nervous about Saudi retaliation for the Netherlands government sponsoring the effort, I made a point of crediting Prime Minister Mark Rutte and Foreign Minister Bert Koenders for standing up to Saudi pressure.

Meeting with the emir of Qatar in September 2017 at a New York townhouse. The meeting went so well that I made the mistake of smiling during this official photograph. Backers of the Saudi government, which at the time was at odds with Qatar, used this photo to suggest that I was in the pay of Qatar when I criticized Saudi abuses. Some embellished it with crude drawings of the emir handing me cash under the table. *(Government of Qatar)*

I spoke with a group of Syrian orphans outside Gaziantep, Turkey, in July 2018. *(Annie Sparrow)*

At the January 2019 World Economic Forum in Davos discussing open-source analysis as a method of human-rights investigation, before a slide from Forensic Architecture, a group that uses architectural techniques for that purpose. *(World Economic Forum)*

My relationship with UN secretary-general António Guterres was correct but tense because he so often fell short of our expectations in defending human rights, particularly on China. In his New York office, February 2019. *(United Nations)*

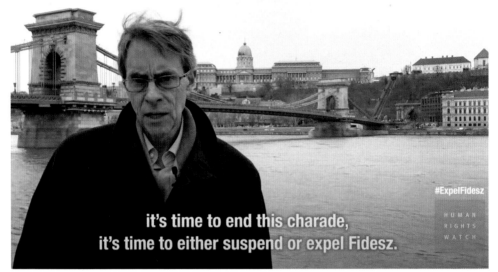

it's time to end this charade,
it's time to either suspend or expel Fidesz.

#ExpelFidesz

HUMAN
RIGHTS
WATCH

Speaking in March 2019 from Budapest on the need to suspend Fidesz, Hungarian prime minister Viktor Orbán's political party, from the European Parliament's center-right alliance because of his attacks on democracy. *(Human Rights Watch)*

In July 2019 in the Silwan neighborhood of East Jerusalem, discussing the forced eviction of Palestinian families. *(Human Rights Watch)*

Yehuda Shaul, founder of the Israeli human-rights group Breaking the Silence, describing the layout of Israel's settlements, outposts, and bypass roads in the occupied West Bank, July 2019. *(Jack Dodson)*

Meeting with Rodrigo Maia, speaker of Brazil's Chamber of Deputies, an important ally in reining in the excesses of President Jair Bolsonaro, October 2019 in Brasilia. Seated next to him is Maria Laura Canineu, our Brazil director. *(Kimberly Marteau Emerson)*

A contentious meeting with Brazil's foreign minister, Ernesto Araújo, opposite me, who defended Bolsonaro's greenlighting of Amazon deforestation, October 2019 in Brasilia. On my side of the table were Bruno Stagno Ugarte, who headed our global advocacy, Maria Laura Canineu, and Daniel Wilkinson, then the interim director of our environmental work. *(Ambassador Robin Renee Sanders, CEO-FEEEDS)*

In November 2019, I accompanied Omar Shakir, center, Human Rights Watch's Israel-Palestine director, as the Israeli government ordered him out of the country. At Israel's Ben Gurion Airport, we were joined by our Israeli lawyer, Michael Sfard, and a group of well-wishers. *(Oren Zev)*

A screenshot from the selfie video I made after Hong Kong authorities blocked my entrance in January 2020, preventing me from holding a press conference to release Human Rights Watch's annual World Report, which that year focused on the Chinese government's threat to the global human-rights system. My disheveled look after the long flight from New York added to the video's authenticity. I posted it on Twitter as I was being ushered onto a plane back to New York. It was retweeted twelve thousand times.

I held the press conference to release the World Report days later to a packed house at the United Nations in New York. The blockage of my entrance to Hong Kong greatly heightened interest in the report. We handed the microphone to a Chinese diplomat, who confirmed, despite the denial of Hong Kong authorities, that I had been barred because of my criticism of Beijing. Joining me at the press conference were Lou Charbonneau, our UN director in New York, and Emma Daly, our communications director. *(Human Rights Watch)*

Critics used this photo to suggest that I was putting an envelope of cash in my pocket after some illicit payoff. The papers were actually my notes for our January 2020 World Report press conference. *(Johannes Eisele/AFP)*

Mausi Segun, right, our Africa director, and Jehanne Henry, left, our Africa associate director, joined me in Khartoum in February 2020 to meet with General Abdel Fattah al-Burhan, at the time the head of the country's transitional sovereign council. At a moment when he was eager for international acceptance, he agreed to our request to cooperate with the International Criminal Court. *(Human Rights Watch)*

In October 2020, during the height of the COVID-19 pandemic, I met by video with German chancellor Angela Merkel to discuss the need for pressure on Hungarian prime minister Viktor Orbán to stop undermining democracy in his country, and on the Chinese government to stop its persecution of Uyghur Muslims in Xinjiang. *(Bundesregierung/Steffen Kugler)*

I spoke with French president Emmanuel Macron during a January 2021 meeting in the Élysée Palace. At my request, he agreed to sponsor a resolution on Egypt at the UN Human Rights Council, only to reverse course later under pressure from his foreign minister, Jean-Yves Le Drian. No other government picked up sponsorship. *(Présidence de la République)*

I questioned German chancellor Olaf Scholz on how he intended to ensure that a proposed European Union investment deal with China would not end up underwriting Beijing's use of Uyghur forced labor, at the February 2022 Munich Security Conference.

I spoke in April 2022 during an informal UN Security Council session in New York on the need to prosecute those responsible for war crimes in Ukraine. Seated next to me was Karim Khan, the International Criminal Court chief prosecutor. *(United Nations Audiovisual Library)*

Speaking afterward to the media. Media coverage of our message was usually essential for policymakers to feel pressure to heed it. *(Human Rights Watch)*

I joined the opening panel in Davos in May 2022 at the newly inaugurated Russian War Crimes House. Supporters of the Ukrainian government had reconfigured the traditional site of Russia House, which the Kremlin had used to promote its interests during the annual World Economic Forum.

With strict social distancing during the COVID-19 pandemic, my colleagues and I met with Ugandan president Yoweri Museveni in June 2022 at a rural compound in southwestern Uganda to discuss his worsening domestic repression. *(Sandor Walusimbi)*

A parting gift from my colleagues in Human Rights Watch's Africa division. *(Maddo)*

A drawing *(Victor Juhasz)* for *The Nation*'s January 2023 cover on the Harvard Kennedy School dean's rejection of my human-rights fellowship because of my criticism of Israel. After two weeks of enormous pressure in the media and protests by Harvard faculty, students, and alumni, the dean reversed himself.

The United Nations

It is easy to deride the United Nations as an empty talk shop, but because shaming plays an important role in the defense of human rights, it is an important forum. No other institution purports to represent all nations, and abusive governments go to great lengths to avoid condemnation from its halls. However, using the UN effectively often requires building broad coalitions of governments, with their varied and sometimes contradictory interests. That can be difficult, but is frequently doable.

Not so long ago, many governments maintained that to comment on their human-rights conduct was to "interfere" in their "internal affairs." The entire point of international human-rights law is to make a government's record a legitimate subject of international concern, but for many years, governments deemed it undiplomatic at the UN to criticize abusive countries by name. With no perpetrators identified, no government felt pressure to reform. That reflected the view that the UN should only "promote" but not "protect" human rights—a perspective that found support in the wording of the UN Charter and was supported by Western governments that worried about reprimand for European colonialism or U.S. racism.

That began to change in the 1960s as governments called out South Africa's apartheid. When Human Rights Watch began working at the UN in the mid-1990s, our work focused on naming names and generating pressure on particular governments. Some governments, typically highly abusive ones such as China, still occasionally objected, resorting to the claim that human rights were an internal matter, but they were an unpersuasive minority.

Aryeh Neier did not think it worth investing time in the UN, which at the height of the Cold War was often paralyzed by East-West rivalries. I took over Human Rights Watch at a time when those tensions were easing. Even in the UN Security Council, which the five permanent members can stymie with their vetoes, cooperative efforts in defense of human rights had become possible, whether establishing international criminal tribunals, deploying peacekeeping forces to protect civilians, or even authorizing military intervention to stop mass slaughter.

Given these changing circumstances, I decided to invest in the UN, starting in 1994. At first, we had the funds for only a single representative, Joanna Weschler, a Polish émigré in the United States who had fled the repression against the Solidarity movement and its backers. She covered both New York, home of the UN Secretariat, Security Council, and General Assembly, and Geneva, where the UN Human Rights Commission (later Council) and high commissioner for human rights were based. In 2001, I hired Loubna Freih, a Swiss woman of Iraqi origin, to open an office in Geneva. Having Joanna work both sides of the Atlantic was bad for her jet lag but good for our ability to mount parallel campaigns in both UN centers, something that was rare at the time. In addition, as Cold War tensions eased, we were unusual among human-rights groups in New York to focus on the Security Council rather than the General Assembly.

Our initial foray at the UN, which I led while still deputy director, highlighted how politicized the organization can be. For a civic group—in UN parlance, a "nongovernmental organization," or NGO—to be able to attend and sometimes speak at UN sessions, the group must be granted "consultative status." The guardian of that status is an obscure body known as the NGO Committee, composed of nineteen states elected to four-year renewable terms. Some highly abusive states flock to this committee to prevent groups that criticize them and their kind from gaining the right to speak at UN sessions. And because at the time the committee preferred to operate by "consensus," meaning unanimity, one abusive state could block consultative status.

That is what happened when we first sought accreditation in 1991. As *The New York Times* put it in an editorial, "A Gang of Six at the U.N." blocked us. The six were the highly abusive governments of Cuba, Iraq, Syria, Libya, Algeria, and Sudan. Human Rights Watch at the time had published critical reports on all of them but Libya. The tired excuse trotted out by the six was that Human Rights Watch, by reporting on their abuses, interfered in their internal affairs. The Cuban delegate accused us of acting as "a kind of international prosecutor" and called our criticism of the 1989 Chinese crackdown on pro-democracy protesters in Tiananmen Square "irreverent." The Sudanese representative said that our report on his government "contains lies." The Iraqi delegate alluded to the fact that the organization's executive director and board chair at the time, Aryeh Neier and Robert Bernstein, were Jewish.

Human Rights Watch was finally granted consultative status in 1993, but only after the pro-rights members of the NGO Committee insisted that it abandon its consensus rule and let a majority vote prevail. We won the vote—with the support even of the Russian government of Boris Yeltsin.

The UN is best understood in two parts, an operational body and a conference room. When it is operational—agencies such as the UN Refugee Agency, the World Health Organization, the Office of the High Commissioner for Human Rights, as well as senior officials such as the secretary-general—it has much latitude to act on its own. In those cases, the character of its leaders, particularly their willingness to stand up to government pressure, determines its effectiveness. When the UN is serving as a conference room, a place for representatives of the governments of the world to assemble, it has no capacity to determine the outcome. It is simply providing a venue for governments to make decisions. Human Rights Watch has focused on both parts. On the operational side, the secretary-general and the high commissioner have the most powerful voices on human rights.

My experience with UN secretaries-general began with Boutros Boutros-Ghali, the former Egyptian diplomat who served from 1992 to 1996. Perhaps reflecting the authoritarian nature of his government, Boutros-Ghali had little interest in human rights, which showed when it came time for him to nominate the first UN high commissioner for human rights, a new post that the General Assembly had created upon the recommendation of the 1993 World Conference on Human Rights. A central reason for having a high commissioner was to have a senior UN official other than the secretary-general who could speak out without the political constraints of an intergovernmental body. As if to sabotage the post from the outset, Boutros-Ghali chose José Ayala-Lasso, who had chaired a UN General Assembly working group that led to the creation of the post but otherwise had no experience promoting human rights. To the contrary, he had served as Ecuador's foreign minister under an abusive military government.

Ayala-Lasso saw his role as opening dialogue with abusive governments, not exerting public pressure on them. He managed to complete his first year in office without publicly criticizing a single government and did so rarely after that. His reliance on personal persuasion made meetings with abusive officials essential, which left him fixated on securing invitations to visit repressive countries. As a result, rather than demanding respect for rights, he pulled his punches. He was so bad that Human Rights Watch and our allies succeeded in hounding him out of office after only three years, when he received a fortuitous invitation to become Ecuador's foreign minister again.

Mary Robinson, the next high commissioner, brought an entirely different stature and approach to the post that reflected in significant part the presence of a new UN secretary-general, Kofi Annan, who nominated her. He served from 1997 to 2006 and, unlike his predecessor, believed strongly in promoting human rights.

Robinson, a lawyer, was concluding her term as president of Ireland when she was appointed high commissioner in 1997. I happened to be in Northern Ireland to release a Human Rights Watch report shortly after the news was announced, so I took a train to Dublin to see her. I was met by a single aide dressed like a court jester who talked me through the protocol for meeting the president. The formality was a bit much, but then Robinson walked in and, in her down-to-earth fashion, belittled the whole thing. We got off to a good start.

She understood far better than Ayala-Lasso the importance of her public voice. She is responsible for establishing the high commissioner's office as we know it today. Aided by Annan, she was the first high commissioner to brief the UN Security Council, an obviously important forum to address the world's most acute human-rights crises. She had no fear of taking on powerful governments. She spoke out against Russian abuses in Chechnya and U.S. abuses at Guantánamo. She visited China, including Tibet, where Beijing often prohibits independent observers to avoid reporting on its repression, and spoke out about imprisoned dissidents and the practice of torture.

Her most controversial effort was preparing for and chairing the 2001 World Conference Against Racism in Durban, South Africa. Both the U.S. and Israeli governments withdrew at an early stage, citing anti-Israel statements in a draft declaration for the conference, which were later removed. The parallel conference for nongovernmental groups was indeed divisive and marred by intolerance, with a final statement that was so over the top on Israel that Human Rights Watch and several of our allied organizations disassociated ourselves from it.

Robinson had nothing to do with the nongovernmental forum, and the concluding document of the government meeting was entirely reasonable. Yet pro-Israel partisans attacked her anyway, holding her responsible, as one critic put it, for failing to "keep the conference on track."

Annan had risen through the UN hierarchy. He was faulted when, as head of UN peacekeeping, under pressure from the U.S. and British governments not to use the peacekeepers in Rwanda in 1994 to try to stop the genocide, he decided not to do so. But by the time he was elected secretary-general in 1997, he was willing to be a leader, taking the revolutionary view within the UN that a nation's sovereignty should not impede efforts to protect people from genocide or crimes against humanity—that there was a "responsibility to protect" them. He was by far the most effective secretary-general from a human-rights perspective. In his soft-spoken manner, he had a gravitas that made people listen and was willing to use his stature to defend rights.

For example, in September 1999, when Indonesian troops were rampaging through East Timor to quash a pro-independence movement, Annan announced that Indonesian leaders could be held criminally responsible for their troops' atrocities—possible crimes against humanity—unless they consented to the deployment of an Australian-led peacekeeping force. Indonesia agreed, the Australians were deployed, and the killing stopped. East Timor went on to become an independent nation.

More than any other secretary-general, Annan tried to mainstream human rights as one of the three pillars of the UN system, along with peace and security, and economic development. He stressed that government abuse leads to armed conflict and that corrupt and unaccountable governments undermine economic development. He dismissed the suggestion that the quest for peace should trump the imperative of justice. Citing Sierra Leone and the Balkans, he said:

> Justice has often bolstered lasting peace, by de-legitimizing and driving underground those individuals who pose the greatest threat to it. That is why there should never be an amnesty for genocide, crimes against humanity and massive violations of human rights. That would only encourage today's mass murderers—and tomorrow's would-be mass murderers—to continue their vicious work.

He forcefully criticized the politicized UN Human Rights Commission and helped build momentum to replace it with the UN Human Rights Council, which he sought to ensure would retain the positive innovations of the commission and improve on them. He was also a big supporter of the International Criminal Court.

He took on the U.S. government for abuses under George W. Bush, although he did so without explicitly mentioning the United States:

> We need an anti-terrorism strategy that does not merely pay lip-service to the defense of human rights but is built on it. That is why secret prisons have no place in our struggle against terrorism, and why all places where terrorism suspects are detained must be accessible to the International Committee of the Red Cross. Leading promoters of human rights undermine their own influence when they fail to live up to these principles.

I became friendly with Annan and saw him periodically in Geneva after his retirement, when he remained an active voice for human rights through the group known as "The Elders." He also chaired an effort that I joined organized by the superb political cartoonist Patrick Chappatte, now known as Freedom Cartoonists, to honor and protect political cartoonists facing retaliation.

In a tender moment, my wife, Annie, and I were dining with Annan and his wife, Nane, at their home just outside Geneva shortly before his untimely death in 2018 at the age of eighty. At one point, Nane asked how Annie and I got to know each other. By my account, Annie periodically visited me in my office to chat, and at times she would wear what in retrospect I jokingly called a "skimpy dress"— actually a reasonable business dress, as she points out, if a bit on the short side. She happened to be wearing the same dress that evening. She stood up and made the mistake of asking Kofi, Would you call this skimpy? The ultimate arbiter, he put his hand to his chin, pondered the question for a moment, and then said, in his deep, slow drawl, "Yes."

Annan's successor, from 2007 to 2016, was Ban Ki-moon, a former South Korean foreign minister, who was earnest and well-meaning but instinctively timid. He was uncharismatic, so even when he said the right thing about human rights, it carried less weight with the media than when Annan had said something similar.

In one of my periodic meetings with Ban, he invited me to leave the conference room on the thirty-eighth floor of the UN Secretariat building in New York, where other staff had joined us, so just the two of us could speak privately in his adjacent office. Human Rights Watch had been criticizing him for being insufficiently outspoken in defense of human rights, and he complained to me that we were making him "lose face." I explained that was not our intent, but we did hope he would be firmer and more public in criticizing serious abusers.

He gradually became so. He turned into an important public champion of LGBT rights—a notable step for him coming from a country with a significant Christian evangelical community that has been quite homophobic. Working closely with the deputy secretary-general, former Swedish foreign minister Jan Eliasson, Ban launched "Human Rights Up Front," an initiative to ensure that UN representatives in a country do not prioritize good relations with the government over the defense of human rights. Ban asked me to serve on his "senior expert group" for the effort.

When security forces in Guinea in September 2009 killed more than 150 people and raped scores of women who had been demonstrating against the government in a stadium in Conakry, Ban created a commission of inquiry. Ban's successor, António Guterres, conveniently denied that he had the power to initiate similar inquiries.

Guterres, the former Portuguese prime minister, became secretary-general in 2017. As I said, he is smart and well informed about a broad range of global problems. I met with him periodically, and we had good, substantive exchanges. But on human rights, he almost always preferred private diplomacy to using his public voice. Again, as I said, he spoke publicly in broad terms about the importance of respecting human rights, but as a rule, he would not criticize a government by name unless it had already become a pariah, such as Russia after its invasion of Ukraine or Israel after its bombing and besieging of Gaza.

———

When the UN serves as a conference room, the most important room houses the Security Council, composed of five permanent members (Britain, China, France, Russia, and the United States) and ten rotating members chosen for two-year terms. The Security Council is the sole UN body with coercive power, although the significance of that distinction is often overstated because the council still depends on governments to enforce its decisions.

The council can act only with the cooperation of the five permanent members, when all of them refrain from using their veto. Britain and France have not used their vetoes since 1989, when, joining with the United States, they blocked a resolution criticizing the U.S. invasion of Panama. The most active veto wielders have been Russia (and its Soviet precursor), which used it to protect itself, as in Ukraine, and its allies, such as Syria; and the United States, which repeatedly used it to protect Israel.

The mere threat of a veto often prevents important matters from being taken up, such as referring North Korea or Myanmar to the

International Criminal Court (China would veto) or addressing the Saudi-led coalition's war crimes in Yemen (the United States would probably veto).

For about a decade after the end of the Cold War, the Security Council often functioned as it should. The Russian government had adopted a relatively cooperative relationship with Western governments on human-rights issues, and the Chinese government used its veto infrequently. In recent years, despite an August 2015 French and Mexican initiative to encourage the permanent members to refrain from using their veto in situations of mass atrocities, the Russian and Chinese governments still regularly used it, or threatened to. It did not help that the Russian government was headed by Vladimir Putin, a man responsible for large-scale war crimes in Ukraine, Syria, and Chechnya, and the Chinese government was headed by Xi Jinping, a man responsible for crimes against humanity in Xinjiang. As I said earlier, both sought to avoid strong global responses to others' mass atrocities as part of their efforts to get away with their own.

As the war in Gaza unfolded following Hamas's October 7, 2023, attack, the U.S. government repeatedly used its veto to protect Israel from critical resolutions. Under an initiative led by Liechtenstein, the UN General Assembly required any UN Security Council permanent member that exercises its veto to defend it before the General Assembly within ten working days. That provided some disincentive to wield the veto but did not stop it.

Given the restraints of the veto, the Security Council was often missing in action. It periodically condemned atrocities in places such as Ethiopia's Tigray region, Sudan's Darfur, Afghanistan, or Myanmar, but in recent years it has significantly curtailed if not stopped the practice of imposing sanctions, blocking arms transfers, deploying peacekeepers, or referring situations to the International Criminal Court—steps that it, among UN bodies, is uniquely empowered to do.

But the Security Council could still be an important forum, even when the veto stands in the way of a formal resolution. Because the veto does not apply to procedural issues, only nine of fifteen votes permit a discussion to proceed. Council members can ask to be briefed on a subject by the UN secretary-general or the UN high commissioner. They can invite testimony about atrocities from victims and witnesses. These actions provide a good opportunity to spotlight an issue that a permanent member would rather ignore.

—

Sometimes when the Security Council was stymied, we worked with the UN General Assembly. We also turned to the General Assembly to address the problem of the old fifty-three-member UN Commission on Human Rights. The commission began productively, drafting the Universal Declaration of Human Rights, which was adopted on December 10 (now Human Rights Day), 1948, and is the foundational document for the human-rights treaties that followed. But once the commission began to investigate and criticize governments for their human-rights violations, it became a victim of its own success. Because of the sting associated with condemnation by the commission, highly abusive governments vied for membership to undermine its work. In a May 2002 op-ed in *The International Herald Tribune*, I said that the commission had become a virtual Who's Who of human-rights violators, where no abuse is too big to be ignored.

In a remarkable April 2005 address to the commission during a session where it had already ignored serious human-rights violations in China, Chechnya, Iran, and Zimbabwe, Kofi Annan sought a new Human Rights Council, whose members would meet higher standards of respect for human rights. In addition to investigating and condemning the worst atrocities, such a council would periodically review the records of all governments to demonstrate the universality of human rights. And he envisioned a council that would be available year-round rather than the commission's six weeks each year.

In 2006, under the presidency of Jan Eliasson, the skillful Swedish diplomat, the UN General Assembly jettisoned the commission and created the UN Human Rights Council. That change introduced several innovations that Annan had urged, including more regular council sessions, the possibility of holding emergency sessions or urgent briefings on a crisis, a review of every country's rights record every four and a half years under the banner of "universal periodic review," and what were assumed to be competitive elections at which the General Assembly would determine the forty-seven states that would sit on the council. The General Assembly mandated that council members "shall uphold the highest standards in the promotion and protection of human rights." The hope was that elections would weed out the most abusive would-be members.

At first, it worked. Each year my colleagues and I targeted a particularly inappropriate candidate for defeat. Several were rejected by a General Assembly vote (Belarus, Azerbaijan, Sri Lanka) or withdrew their candidacy rather than face a humiliating defeat (Syria, Iraq). Even Russia was defeated, in 2016, as its aircraft were bombing Syrian civilians in eastern Aleppo. But after a while, some of the regional groups of governments began to game the system. To circumvent a competitive election, they nominated only the same number of candidates as open positions. Western governments did it as well to avoid the need to lobby the entire General Assembly.

In March 2011, when Muammar Gaddafi's government was ruthlessly suppressing his country's Arab Spring uprising, the General Assembly suspended Libya from the Human Rights Council. And in April 2022, as the Russian military was bombing and executing Ukrainian civilians, the General Assembly suspended Russia—and then rejected its October 2023 attempt to rejoin it. Suspension requires a two-thirds vote. The disciplinary action was highly stigmatizing—and a statement that a certain level of atrocities would preclude council membership. We had actively encouraged both steps.

The Human Rights Council remains an important forum to get things done. Powerful governments such as China, India, and Egypt remain untouchable. But the council established, in December 2021, an investigative mechanism for even a regional powerhouse such as Ethiopia. As I said, the council set up mechanisms to scrutinize Saudi conduct in Yemen (though not inside the kingdom) and the Russian government's conduct in both Ukraine and Russia. The council has also addressed other highly abusive governments, including Syria, Myanmar, Eritrea, North Korea, Yemen, Sudan, Burundi, Sri Lanka, Belarus, Nicaragua, and Venezuela. In a tribute to the stigma attached to this scrutiny, governments make enormous efforts to avoid it, as Saudi Arabia did for its conduct in Yemen.

Some governments cling to the view that the Human Rights Council should never condemn a particular country. They want only generic statements on human rights that do not single out offenders or, at most, offers of technical assistance for respecting human rights. It is not as if a few UN workshops or training sessions would improve the behavior of governments that seriously violate human rights. Their repression is the product of deliberate policy decisions that will be reversed only with sufficient pressure.

Some abusive governments speak of the virtue of "cooperation" or "consensus," which would defuse the pressure needed to defend human rights. "Consensus" tends to mean that the target government must consent to a resolution, which guarantees watered-down blather.

—

We were not empowered to introduce or vote on council resolutions, but we—and other nongovernmental groups—pressed governments to address repressive situations and helped to assemble governmental sponsors and supporters of resolutions. Some offenders avoided scrutiny because of their political or economic clout. One such country that preoccupied me was Egypt, which under President Sisi was suffering by far the most intense period of repression in its modern history. Major Western powers, however, continued to look to Egypt to supply gas, fight terrorism, control migration, and serve as a source of stability in a volatile region. That many of Sisi's policies worked against these goals did not stop the kid-glove treatment.

The French government believed that maintaining the "strategic autonomy" of France's arms industry was important for its national security. Sustaining that industry required major foreign purchasers—like Egypt. Jean-Yves Le Drian, longtime defense minister and then foreign minister, flew regularly to Cairo and maintained warm relations with Sisi. I knew that to change French policy, I needed to focus on President Macron, even though he was hardly immune to subordinating human rights to other concerns. That was illustrated by his July 2022 welcoming of the Saudi crown prince to Paris; his business-promoting, rights-downplaying April 2023 trip to Beijing; and his July 2023 embrace of Indian prime minister Modi, who was silencing critics and promoting Hindu-nationalist attacks on Muslims.

My opening came when Macron reached out in late 2020 to discuss France's role at the UN Human Rights Council, which it had just been elected to join. I had met with Macron twice previously and had been told repeatedly that he enjoyed meeting with me. I engaged him in wide-ranging, give-and-take conversations, challenging him. He had the self-confidence to like such exchanges. He saw himself as a bulwark in the global defense of democracy and was open to my suggestions for how to improve that defense.

The meeting took place in January 2021 in Paris at the height of one of the COVID-19 lockdowns. I arrived in central Paris the evening before and, walking from the Métro to my hotel, crossed an utterly empty Rue de Rivoli, one of Paris's main thoroughfares. It was eerie. The meeting was to take place in an ornate room in the Élysée Palace, the president's home and office, in central Paris. I was accompanied by Bénédicte Jeannerod, our France director, and Bruno Stagno Ugarte, our global advocacy director, who was based in Paris. Bénédicte and I had previously discussed the agenda with Macron's aides, so he was not wholly surprised by the request that I was about to make.

Macron speaks excellent English, and I speak passable French, mainly from my time between university and law school when I was working as a waiter in Paris. But my French is anything but sophisticated, so past meetings had worked best when Macron spoke in French and I spoke in English, allowing each of us the precision of our native tongue. But as I was about to enter the meeting room, an aide asked if I would mind, as a matter of protocol, opening the conversation in French, so I began that way. As I looked around the room, I realized that everyone else was either French or totally fluent in French. Rather than force them all to proceed in English just because of me, I decided to struggle through the meeting in French.

We discussed a range of issues and quickly came to the UN Human Rights Council. I said that it was not enough for Western governments simply to vote favorably on issues that came up, or even to sponsor broad thematic resolutions. Rather, each government, by filling a seat on the council, had a responsibility to take the lead in sponsoring a resolution on a powerful abusive country. These were the most difficult resolutions, most likely to encounter organized opposition, which is why I felt that the governments of Western democracies, with their ample foreign-policy staffs, should take them on.

I asked Macron if France would take the lead on Egypt. I said this knowing of Le Drian's opposition and knowing that, just the month before, in a meeting undoubtedly orchestrated by Le Drian, Macron had welcomed Sisi on a state visit to Paris, literally rolling out the red carpet for him, and given him the *Légion d'honneur,* France's highest honor.

During an August 2019 lunch with Macron, he had agreed with my assessment that Sisi was not a reliable counterterrorism partner because his repression fueled the Islamist threat. Macron went so far as to say that Sisi is "killing himself politically" with his repression. Macron had also shown during that lunch, despite the visible discomfort of Le Drian, who had joined us, a notable willingness to forsake arms sales if that made France complicit in atrocities. In that case, Macron had talked about avoiding French complicity in Saudi war crimes in Yemen. Given this background, I felt I had a fighting chance to extend his concern to Egypt.

We tossed around the idea of French sponsorship of a resolution on Egypt, the chance it had to prevail, the severity of the repression under Sisi, and Sisi's wrongful equation of the Muslim Brotherhood with Islamist extremists. I even said, with a smile, that Macron would have the opportunity to make amends for having honored Sisi in Paris despite his deplorable rights record. Then, to my delight, Macron agreed to sponsor the resolution. I looked across the table at Emmanuel Bonne, Macron's top foreign-policy aide, or "sherpa," as the position is known. His jaw dropped. This was not the result he had expected.

The meeting had gone so well that afterward, as we were chatting, Macron started to *tutoyer* me—that is, to use the informal form of address in French, *tu,* instead of the formal *vous.* It was a friendly gesture, but it left me in an awkward position: ordinarily when someone uses the *tu* form, the other participant in the conversation reciprocates, but I did not feel comfortable doing that with the president of France. At the same time, for me to revert to *vous* while he was using *tu* could have been perceived as a rebuke of his warm overture. French people are good at navigating such situations by avoiding the second-person form of the language altogether. My French is not good enough to pull that off effortlessly, but I managed.

The warmth of the meeting did not last long. What I underestimated was how intensively Le Drian, who had not been present, would oppose Macron's decision. John Fisher, our representative at the Human Rights Council, heard from French diplomats that Le Drian was livid. In the end, France never did sponsor a resolution on Egypt—although it did sponsor one of the joint statements condemning the Chinese government's repression in Xinjiang.

—

The need for the Human Rights Council to focus on Israel's occupation is due in part to the U.S. government's routine veto, or threatened veto, of UN Security Council criticism of Israel. As Eric Alterman points out, between 1946 and 2012, more than half the U.S. vetoes were to defend Israel.

The Israeli government and its supporters have been particularly exercised about Human Rights Council scrutiny. In part, that is because, as I said, these supporters attack anyone who criticizes Israel. But they also object to the council's large number of critical resolutions on Israel and Palestine, and to the fact that the conflict is the only one to have its own permanent place on the council agenda, Item 7. The aim of the critics is not to reduce the number of criticisms of Israel but to eliminate them altogether. That goal underlies a public tussle that I had with Nikki Haley, at the time President Trump's UN ambassador in New York.

We had long argued, as I did in *Foreign Policy*, that if the goal was to stop repeated rather than any criticism of Israel, its governmental supporters should introduce at the council a single overarching resolution on Israel and Palestine. And if they did not like resolutions considered under a special agenda item, they should support a critical resolution under one of the council's regular agenda items. The Trump administration did not like these ideas. Haley also complained that the Human Rights Council included abusive members, a product of uncompetitive slates, but she was unable to persuade even Western governments to discontinue the practice.

The Trump administration was so singularly focused on defending Israel, so one-dimensional in its supposed human-rights policy, that it soon withdrew from the Human Rights Council in protest. No other government had ever voluntarily given up a council seat. Nikki Haley blamed us and other human-rights groups for failing to support her "reform" effort, even though, as I noted in *The Hill,* in the name of stopping criticism of Israel, her approach risked weakening the council. No other government had endorsed it.

The council continued to do important work, remaining far and away the most effective multilateral forum for defending human rights. For the first time, it condemned Venezuela, in large part because the effort was led by Latin American democracies rather than what could have been challenged as an American imperialist endeavor. Iceland, which assumed the U.S. seat, led a successful effort to condemn the mass summary executions of the "drug war" of then Philippines president Duterte. When Joe Biden became president, the United States ran again for a seat on the council and was elected in October 2021, although, apparently fearing rebuke for his support of Israel in Gaza, Biden chose not to seek a second term on the council in October 2024.

Rwanda and the Democratic Republic of Congo

I n recent decades, the part of Africa most plagued by mass slaughter has been the central Great Lakes region. In Rwanda, the genocide of 1994 killed an estimated eight hundred thousand people in just three months. When the rebel Rwandan Patriotic Front (RPF) of Paul Kagame overthrew the genocidal government and chased its backers west into what was then Zaire and is now the Democratic Republic of Congo, along with hundreds of thousands of mostly Hutu Rwandans who were fleeing the RPF advance, countless more died. Kagame later became Rwanda's president.

Because of the appalling extent of the atrocities, I was especially focused on the region. It presented serious challenges: in the case of Rwanda, trying to restrain a president who is admired for having stopped the genocide and rebuilt the country but had become a brutal dictator; in Congo, finding ways to protect rights in a vast country where large regions are beyond the control of the central government and predatory armed groups reign.

I began my involvement with Rwanda shortly before the genocide. Our work was led by Alison Des Forges, diminutive, white-haired, seemingly frail in her bearing—until one got to know her. She had studied in the country for her PhD dissertation; spent many years there; spoke the local language, Kinyarwanda, fluently; and knew many of the country's leading actors. A year before the genocide, in January 1993, she led an international commission of four human-rights groups, including Africa Watch, the regional name at the time of Human Rights Watch, that reported on the killing of Tutsi already under way. She later wrote the definitive account of the genocide, a five-hundred-page report entitled "Leave None to Tell the Story," a virtual guidebook to prosecution. She died tragically at age sixty-six in a 2009 plane crash near her home in Buffalo, New York.

As the genocide unfolded, we needed to put a human face on the vast numbers being killed. Alison spotlighted Monique Mujawa-mariya, a warm, vivacious human-rights activist in Rwanda with whom we worked closely. At the time, we brought a group of human-rights defenders to New York each year to pay tribute to them at a public ceremony and make their stories known. In December 1993, Monique was among them. We arranged for her to join a small group of human-rights defenders from around the world who met Bill Clinton at the White House on December 10, Human Rights Day.

When the genocide began in April 1994, Monique was at home in Kigali, the Rwandan capital, desperately seeking safety. The UN peacekeeping force in the country said it was too busy (or embattled) to rescue her. No one else responded to her pleas. On the phone to Alison, Monique watched as members of the presidential guard proceeded down her street, door by door, pulling people from their houses and shooting them. When they got to her door, she told Alison, "Please take care of my children. I don't want you to hear this." And she hung up. When others tried to call Monique, men answered before disconnecting.

Alison assumed that Monique had been killed. She wrote a note to the staff saying as much. *The Washington Post* published it. We were devastated. As it turned out, Monique had miraculously escaped by running out the back door, concealing herself in the bushes under heavy rain, creeping back into her house, and hiding for three days in the rafters. When young soldiers began camping in her yard, she realized she would have no choice but to negotiate with them. Pretending to be the wife of a military officer, she bought her way out of the country.

Monique's tale was covered extensively by *The New York Times*, *The Washington Post*, and *The New Yorker*, among other publications. Her story brought the horrors of the genocide home in a way that generic accounts and statistics could not.

At the time of the slaughter, Alison made the case for humanitarian military intervention—one of the few times we have called for it to stop mass killing. We had an internal policy allowing us to call for such force in rare situations in which there is genocide or comparable mass murder under way or imminent, there is no reasonable alternative for stopping the killing, and the intervention is likely to do more good than harm. The treaty prohibiting genocide defines it as killing or other enumerated crimes committed "with intent to destroy, in whole or in part, a national, ethnic, racial or religious group, as such." In what might be called Stalin's contribution to the Genocide Convention, it does not define genocide as the mass murder of a political group.

Human Rights Watch has called for such humanitarian intervention in only four circumstances: in 1991, in support of a no-fly zone in northern Iraq to stop a feared revival of the 1988 genocide against the Kurds; in 1992, to break the war-induced deadly famine in Somalia; in 1992–94, to halt the genocide and ethnic cleansing in Bosnia; and in 1994, to stop the genocide in Rwanda. Our policy did not require UN Security Council approval because we did not want to be limited by the vetoes of the permanent members.

It may seem odd to some that a human-rights organization would urge military force, but we are not pacifist. While war is ordinarily an evil to be avoided, if a military intervention can stop a government's mass slaughter, and if that intervention can be accomplished with a lower cost in human lives, then military action may be the more humane option.

The Rwandan genocide was perhaps the clearest case for humanitarian intervention, but the only one of the four in which the military action we sought never occurred. At the time, there were two available military forces in Kigali that could have intervened: the UN peacekeepers, who were already in the country to enforce an agreement to end the armed conflict between the Rwandan government and the RPF, and a French evacuation force, which entered in the early days of the genocide to rescue Westerners. In Alison's view, if those two forces had been given the mandate, they could have stopped the genocide, in light of the weakness of the Rwandan military. Instead, the French evacuation force left with the Westerners, the UN Security Council reduced the number of peacekeepers in Rwanda from 2,500 to 250, and the peacekeepers were never given more proactive orders.

In the initial weeks of the genocide, Alison spent much of her time debunking the view put forth by the Clinton administration and others that the genocide was the product of "age-old" hatred or animosity. That characterization suggested that Tutsi and Hutu had always been killing each other, so there was nothing to be done. Most Americans at the time had never heard of the Tutsi and Hutu, and in the period after the ill-fated 1992–93 U.S. military intervention in Somalia, they were all too willing to accept an excuse for inaction.

In fact, the genocide was the product of a small coterie of Hutu extremists who were intent on combating a military and political threat from the RPF, the largely Tutsi force that had been based in neighboring Uganda, by slaughtering all Tutsi, as well as some moderate Hutu. They whipped up hysteria and hatred toward Tutsi, using the infamous *Radio télévision libre des Milles Collines*. A proper characterization of the origin of the slaughter could have helped to inform better discussions about stopping it.

The Clinton administration was not the least bit helpful. After the October 1993 Black Hawk Down debacle in Somalia in which eighteen U.S. soldiers were killed, Clinton feared the political consequences of losing even a single U.S. soldier. When Alison implored the administration to act, Anthony Lake, the national security adviser, let her write a statement, which he issued, calling for a ceasefire and an end to the violence, but he would not commit U.S. troops to stop the slaughter or allow UN peacekeepers to act. Instead, he urged her to "Make more noise!" as if stopping mass murder depended on opinion polls. The administration would act to stop the slaughter not as a matter of moral leadership, not because it was the right thing to do, but only if we could generate enough pressure to relieve it of the political cost of acting. The slaughter of Tutsi stopped only when the RPF took over the country.

Since the mid-1990s, Human Rights Watch has never again called for humanitarian intervention. As I said, we considered calling for Western governments to destroy the Syrian planes that were dropping barrel bombs and chemical weapons on opposition-held parts of Syria but could not reach sufficient staff consensus to move forward, largely because of fear of unintended consequences.

Our growing disinclination on that score paralleled diminishing enthusiasm for the once-heralded doctrine of the "responsibility to protect" people facing mass atrocities, or R2P. R2P emerged from the laudable view that sovereignty should be understood as contingent on a government's responsibilities toward its people. Driven in part by widespread guilt at the failure to stop the genocide in Rwanda, the R2P doctrine was formally endorsed in 2005 by the UN World Summit—the largest gathering of heads of state in history—at a time when people had more confidence in the potentially beneficial effects of humanitarian intervention. The invasion of Libya in 2012, which, invoking R2P, started off as an effort to prevent the "river of blood" threatened by Muammar Gaddafi's son Saif but ended up as a regime-change effort that left the country in chaos—potentially worse than repression—effectively sounded the death knell for the doctrine. I, too, have lost confidence in the capacity of most military interventions to secure positive change.

The issue of humanitarian intervention had an unexpected effect on my personal life. After President George W. Bush's invasion of Iraq in 2003, I devoted the introduction to our annual World Report to debunking the contention that the invasion was a humanitarian intervention. That claim became important to Bush once Saddam Hussein's much-vaunted weapons of mass destruction were shown not to exist. I argued that while Saddam was indeed a ruthless dictator who had committed genocide against the Kurds in 1988, there was no comparable mass slaughter under way or threatened at the time of Bush's invasion. In my view, the aim of stopping ongoing or imminent mass slaughter was a prerequisite to a humanitarian intervention—punishing or trying to remove a government for past slaughter did not justify the resort to war.

Based on this essay, the Carr Center for Human Rights Policy invited me to the Harvard Kennedy School to debate the issue with Michael Ignatieff, an insightful public intellectual who went on to become the Canadian Liberal Party's unsuccessful candidate for prime minister. He later served as rector of Central European University, as Hungarian prime minister Orbán was forcing this bastion of liberalism to leave Budapest. (It moved to Vienna.)

The moderator of the debate was Samantha Power, the author of a Pulitzer Prize–winning book, *A Problem from Hell: America and the Age of Genocide.* She would go on to serve as President Obama's ambassador to the UN and President Biden's administrator of the U.S. Agency for International Development.

The debate was unfair for Michael. He was known at the time as a "liberal hawk" and a proponent of R2P who was willing to use military force to advance human rights, but Bush's invasion of Iraq was difficult to defend in those terms. Among the three hundred students and faculty in the large Kennedy School auditorium was an Australian doctor who, having practiced for ten years as an intensive-care pediatrician in London and Perth, had come to Harvard to obtain a master's degree in public health. At the end of the debate, she said to her friend, "I could marry that guy." It did not happen for some time—she did not even bother at the time to introduce herself—but I finally did marry Annie in 2010.

In addition to having tried to prevent the genocide and then documenting it, Alison served as a regular adviser and expert witness for the UN Security Council–created International Criminal Tribunal for Rwanda, which prosecuted most of the senior officials behind the genocide, sentencing sixty-one people, including former prime minister Jean Kambanda and Théoneste Bagosora, the army colonel who is regarded as the mastermind of the genocide. Alison served as a witness in eleven of those prosecutions as well as in various national prosecutions, sometimes facing grueling cross-examination by defense attorneys trying to discredit her. It was not easy for her, but I ended up feeling sorry for the defense attorneys. Alison had on her side patience, facts, and a quiet, palpable commitment to the truth.

No prosecutor had her knowledge of the genocide. She was a constant resource, responsible in no small part for so many *génocidaires* being brought to justice. As I said at a memorial service for her, I was technically her boss, but she was my mentor. I learned an enormous amount from her. She also trained an entire generation of researchers who worked on the Great Lakes region. During her early years as a Human Rights Watch researcher, she worked as a volunteer, living off the salary of her husband, a professor. Finally, given the long hours she was putting in, and her extraordinary effectiveness, I insisted on paying her.

You would think that the Rwandan government would lionize

her. In fact, it demonized her. In the last few months of her life, it twice barred her from the country that she loved. She rejected the false claims of a double genocide—one of the accusations that the Kagame government used to try to silence critics—but she found that commanders of the RPF under Kagame should be prosecuted for the execution of an estimated thirty thousand people during and after the genocide. I joined her on one trip to Arusha, Tanzania, the seat of the tribunal, to try to persuade the chief prosecutor, Hassan Jallow of Gambia, to pursue these cases. He refused, instead deferring to a handful of Rwandan domestic prosecutions that were designed to shield senior officials from criminal liability.

Kagame certainly engendered much sympathy for his role in stopping the genocide, but granting him impunity for such large-scale atrocities only encouraged him in the brutality with which he has since ruled Rwanda and dominated eastern parts of Congo. While purporting to cooperate with the investigation of RPF atrocities, the Rwandan government did everything it could to block them, denying Jallow's investigators access to Rwanda and preventing key witnesses from testifying before the tribunal. (The Rwandan government, which at the time had a rotating seat on the UN Security Council, voted against establishing the tribunal in part because it didn't want the prosecutor to focus on anything but the genocide.) The government and its allies also lashed out at Human Rights Watch, and me, for keeping alive the issue of the impunity that Kagame's forces continued to enjoy for these mass executions. Nor did it endear us to them that we reported on Kagame's unrelenting repression as president of Rwanda.

I have encountered Kagame several times at public events such as the World Economic Forum, but I sat down to speak with him only once, joined by Alison, in 1996, shortly after the genocide, when he was technically vice president and minister of defense, though in effect the ruler of the country. To give credit where due, he was austere, soft-spoken, and palpably intelligent. But while he indicated to us concern about discipline among his troops, he denied that they were committing the abuses that we had documented. Such denials would become characteristic of his leadership.

Kagame succeeded in rebuilding Rwanda from the ashes of the genocide into an orderly, prospering nation. But there has been an utter ruthlessness behind that order. Rwandan critics of Kagame were routinely imprisoned and sometimes assassinated. Political opponents were often accused of "genocide denial" or "genocide ideology," which could lead to imprisonment. When I raised this problem during 2009 meetings in Kigali with the prime minister and other senior officials, they cited the risk of renewed ethnic slaughter as a reason to allow no dissent whatsoever. There was no independent media in the country, no independent civic groups, no meaningful opposition political parties. Kagame was also thin-skinned: he blocked me on Twitter (the only leader to have done so).

I had an early taste of the Rwandan government's repression in July 1996, when I joined Alison to investigate a spike in the Rwandan army's killing of civilians. It was my first time in Rwanda, much of which was still devastated. I sensed a ghostly emptiness as I felt the absence of the hundreds of thousands who so recently had been killed—much as I felt in 1990 driving through devastated eastern Cambodia after the U.S. bombing campaign and the murderous reign of the Khmer Rouge. We traveled to Rwanda's northwestern Gisenyi province, where the army had retaliated for the killing of a soldier by massacring forty-seven local residents, including women with infants strapped to their backs. The army tried to cover up the slaughter by falsely claiming that the victims had been caught in crossfire. We found two survivors and interviewed them, but as we finished, Rwandan troops arrived. For all we knew, they were the ones who had committed the massacre. For a tense, scary couple of hours on a remote hilltop and then in a nearby army base, we negotiated our departure. By the time we were allowed to leave, it was dark. Fearing that we were being set up for an ambush, I drove as fast as I dared for two hours along the winding roads back to Kigali. I later wrote about the massacre in *The Washington Post,* hoping to alert people to the dark side of the government that had assumed power in Rwanda.

A 2017 Human Rights Watch report addressed the Rwandan security forces' execution of thirty-seven men for suspected petty offenses. These included stealing a cow, bananas, or a motorcycle, smuggling marijuana, illegally crossing the Congolese border, or using illegal fishing nets. The executions occurred without a hint of due process. When we issued the report, the Rwandan government detained our local research assistant. He was released only after I was able to arrange a meeting at the January 2018 World Economic Forum in Davos with Guinea's president, Alpha Condé, at the time chair of the African Union, to urge him to intervene with Kagame. Our research assistant, once released from custody, was forced to flee Rwanda, his home. He was the fourth member of the Human Rights Watch staff to have been effectively expelled from the country.

Rwandan officials held a news conference in an effort to debunk our report, but it backfired. The government's human-rights commission produced a man purported to be an execution victim whom we had identified. He had the same name as the victim but was thirty years older. The government claimed that another victim had been killed while crossing the Congolese border illegally, but several witnesses testified that they saw soldiers summarily execute him several kilometers from the border for allegedly stealing a cow. The government produced a woman who said that a man who we reported to have been killed was her husband and that he was really working in Belgium, except that the victim never had a passport. One can only imagine the pressure that Rwandan authorities put on these people.

Families of other victims were also subjected to threats and coercion, forcing one family to flee its home. An investigation by the broadcaster France 24, which examined four cases in depth, confirmed our findings and helped to expose the Rwandan government's cover-up. Shortly after the piece aired, Rwandan authorities refused renewal of the work and residency visa for the lead journalist from France 24 in Rwanda. Beginning in January 2018, Human Rights Watch did not deem it safe to base a staff member there.

—

The Rwandan government's brutality and repression have played an important part in fostering the chaos in eastern Congo. The worst period was in the immediate aftermath of the genocide, when Rwandan troops entered what was then Zaire. Since then, the Rwandan military has operated mainly through proxies, enabling it to exploit the region's mineral wealth.

Beginning in April 2012, the Rwandan government sponsored a particularly nasty rebel group, the March 23 Movement, known as the M23. As we reported, families in eastern Congo "feared that the M23 would abduct their children to become soldiers, rape their wives, sisters, and mothers in their fields, or kill their brothers and husbands." In June 2012, the UN high commissioner for human rights, Navi Pillay, called the M23 "among the worst perpetrators of human-rights violations in the DRC, or in the world."

We long maintained a research office in Goma, the largest city in eastern Congo, as well as an office on the other side of the country in Kinshasa. I periodically visited and was greeted warmly by the staff and their families, who seemed to look to me as if I could provide some modicum of safety in their region. I awkwardly assumed the role, fully aware that they were the ones on the front line of this effort.

In September 2012, Human Rights Watch issued a report showing that Rwanda's military was providing weapons, recruits, and supplies to the M23. The government denied it. In November 2012, a group of UN experts largely confirmed our findings. We issued a second report in February 2013 with more evidence, and the government denied it again. A third report in July 2013 yielded the same response.

Given the magnitude of the M23's atrocities, we were determined to persist despite the stonewalling. Before our reporting, most major Western governments supported Kagame. They felt guilty at having done so little (really nothing) to end the genocide, and they were heartened by his deployment of development funds for the benefit of the Rwandan people rather than his personal bank account. Despite the enormous global need for such assistance, it is difficult to find governments that will not squander aid to corruption, so Rwanda became known as a "development darling." As for Kagame's domestic repression, these governments tended to look the other way.

But as our evidence of Rwandan military support for the M23 became undeniable, and as Kagame continued to deny it, he lost credibility. Several Western governments denounced the Rwandan government's support for the M23. Key donors suspended some $240 million in aid in 2012 and 2013. The top U.S. war-crimes official warned Kagame that he could face prosecution before the International Criminal Court for "aiding and abetting" the M23's crimes against humanity.

In March 2013, shortly after a reported split within the M23, its notorious leader, Bosco Ntaganda, known as "the Terminator," who was wanted by the International Criminal Court for war crimes (conscripting child soldiers, murder, ethnic persecution, sexual slavery, and rape), surrendered to the U.S. embassy in Kigali. He asked to be sent to The Hague, where he was convicted and sentenced to thirty years in prison. He apparently thought that prison was safer than the risk of assassination he faced in eastern Congo.

In July 2013, just after our third report on Rwandan support of the M23, U.S. secretary of state John Kerry chaired a high-level session of the UN Security Council devoted to the region. He called on all parties to stop supporting rebel groups like the M23. He did not explicitly name Rwanda, but the State Department spokeswoman already had, citing our reporting. The U.S. and various European governments suspended military aid. Then in October 2013, when a new round of fighting broke out in eastern Congo, Kerry and British foreign secretary William Hague called Kagame directly about his support for the M23. Given Rwanda's dependence on international donors for some 40 percent of government expenditures, Kagame had to stop. The M23 collapsed within days. For nearly a decade, eastern Congo, while still enduring a range of other rebel groups, was no longer plagued by the M23.

To our chagrin, the M23 reemerged in November 2021, again with Rwandan government backing. Kagame's motive seemed to have been fear that Ugandan commercial interests and troops in eastern Congo, whom Congolese president Félix Tshisekedi had invited in to enhance trade and to counter an Islamist armed group known as the Allied Democratic Forces, might corner the market in Congolese minerals.

Giving little credit to Kagame's new denials of M23 sponsorship, the U.S. government and the European Union pressed him publicly to stop, with Washington cutting off military aid and the EU and the U.S. imposing targeted sanctions against certain Rwandan military officials. Now, given Kagame's destroyed credibility, his main strategy was to try to make himself indispensable, whether as a provider of peacekeeping troops in Africa (in Mozambique and the Central African Republic), by offering to receive asylum seekers whom the

British government wanted to off-load, or as a source of minerals. The Congolese government in May 2023 asked the International Criminal Court to investigate Rwandan officials for again sponsoring the M23. The chief prosecutor opened a preliminary examination the next month and a formal investigation in October 2024. Criminal charges would be a powerful supplement to the economic and diplomatic pressure already being put on Kagame.

—

Beyond the enormous problems in eastern Congo, the Congolese government has been notoriously corrupt, since Mobutu Sese Seko was president of what was then called Zaire. That corruption continued as Zaire became the Democratic Republic of Congo. Joseph Kabila, president from 2001 to 2019, was a notorious perpetrator. His father, Laurent-Désiré Kabila, became president in 1997 at the head of an insurgency backed by Rwanda, Uganda, Burundi, and Angola that crossed most of the country and ousted Mobutu, but the elder Kabila was assassinated in 2001. The son, seen initially as a weak figure who would not interrupt power dynamics in Kinshasa, was named president at the age of twenty-nine.

Joseph Kabila was one of my oddest interlocutors. Despite his corruption and other abuses, he cared about his human-rights image and was eager to please. For example, he surrendered more suspects to the ICC than any other national leader. I first met him in 2009 in Goma. We had just published a report on rape by Congolese security forces in eastern Congo, and I wanted to discuss how he could stop it. I was joined by two Human Rights Watch researchers for Congo, Anneke Van Woudenberg and Ida Sawyer. Anneke was born in the Netherlands, raised in Canada, and educated in Britain. She thought nothing of riding a motorbike for hours through jungle paths in eastern Congo to interview the survivors of the latest massacre. Ida, an American who had worked as a journalist, brought a determined equanimity to her work, which ultimately got her expelled from Congo.

At one of Mobutu's ornate palaces on the shores of Lake Kivu, we were ushered through a waiting room filled with people in business attire and led to a white tent with no sides on a lawn leading down to the lake. Three officials in business suits sat opposite us, with a chair at the end of the table for the president. There was no security. Goma was in the middle of an active war zone, and there was nothing to stop gunmen from swooping in from the lake.

After a few minutes, a young man in blue jeans walked up and sat down in the presidential chair. It took me a moment to realize it was Kabila. We had a constructive conversation about the rape problem, during which I outlined three things that I hoped he would do to curb it: (1) Announce a "zero-tolerance" policy; (2) prosecute any rapist; and (3) dismiss commanders who tolerated rape. In a speech two days later, he announced a plan to pursue all three recommendations. Within a short period, two senior army officers had been convicted of rape, and two others were arrested. These initial steps sent the message that there would be consequences for using rape as a weapon of war, even if Kabila's follow-through was, as typical for him, less than vigorous.

The oddest but perhaps most important meeting I had with Kabila was in 2015 in Kinshasa. His two constitutionally permitted terms as president had ended, but he resisted stepping down. He did not have the political clout to change the constitution to permit a third term, as some African leaders had done, so he was engaged in what the Congolese called *"glissement"*—sliding into a third term. Protests were mounting, and protesters were being shot. Diplomats had been pressing him to move on, but I suspected they had been doing so, well, diplomatically. Our strategy for the meeting was guided by our research, which revealed that Kabila was not necessarily intent on becoming president for life but was worried about his security and future should he step down.

Kabila received Ida and me cordially. I laid out two possible paths that I saw for him. He could allow elections to proceed and hand power to a successor in what would be the first democratic transition in the country's history. He would be celebrated as the father of Congolese democracy and could look forward to many years as a respected statesman. I said this knowing that Kabila liked mainly to spend time on his ranch playing video games, but I tried to make the option sound attractive.

The other path was to continue his *glissement*. There would be more protests, more security-force shooting of protesters. Ultimately, despised, he would be forced to resign. Prosecution and imprisonment would be real possibilities.

We discussed the two options for the good part of an hour. At one point, he joked: "You say 'father of democracy.' You're not the first one to say this and you won't be the last." As we were leaving, he made a point of saying that he had not yet decided anything. As he shook our hands, he said, "As for my future, continue to pray for me."

After significant international, regional, and domestic pressure, Kabila eventually allowed an election in December 2018 and stepped down. The winner, Martin Fayulu, whom Kabila thought too much a foe, was robbed of victory. Realizing that he could not get away with giving the presidency to his preferred candidate, Emmanuel Ramazani Shadary, who received less than 20 percent of the vote, Kabila made a deal with another opposition candidate, Félix Tshisekedi, who also polled less than 20 percent. Kabila and his coalition still exercised considerable influence, but a peaceful transition, of sorts, had occurred. Tshisekedi was reelected in December 2023.

Hungary and Poland

Along-standing priority for Human Rights Watch had been curbing the democratic backsliding in Hungary and Poland, both members of the European Union. This topic was a major focus of visits I made to the two countries as well as two meetings that I had with then German chancellor Angela Merkel. The EU had the necessary tools for the defense of democratic values on its own turf, but, to my frustration, was often hamstrung by bureaucratic procedures and a disinclination to get too tough with a fellow member.

Hungarian prime minister Viktor Orbán was our primary concern. Early in his career, Orbán seemed like a classic post-Soviet Eastern European democrat. He was the beneficiary of a scholarship from George Soros, and in 1989, issued a call to remove Soviet troops from Hungary. But when he lost a bid for reelection in 2002, he took a big step to the right and became Europe's leading autocrat.

Starting in 2014, Orbán promoted his "illiberal democracy," which retained the veneer of democracy—periodic elections—but lacked its substance. He chipped away at the checks and balances on his executive power. He hijacked public institutions, curbed the power of the courts and appointed loyalists, criminalized basic activities of civil-society organizations, and left almost no independent media standing. (The government-controlled public broadcaster had instructions not to refer to our reporting.) He built a largely rural, conservative power base by demonizing certain minorities. He attacked the rights of LGBT people and banned same-sex unions. He made it virtually impossible to seek asylum in Hungary, encouraged abusive treatment of migrants and refugees, and criminalized those who helped them. And with thinly disguised antisemitism, he attacked Soros.

Orbán also grew closer to Putin and promoted pro-Russia positions at odds with EU policy in defense of democracy worldwide. At the UN Human Rights Council, instead of stating a common position, the EU was forced to announce the position of "a group of twenty-six countries" (meaning all EU countries other than Hungary) or "the EU members of the council" (Hungary was not a member).

There was no workaround for Orbán's growing autocracy within Hungary. His moves were rarely dramatic. When the EU protested too vociferously, he backed off, complying but only briefly. Stopping Orbán's autocratic drift was essential for preserving the EU as a club of democracies rather than allowing it to devolve into a mere trading bloc.

The EU has notoriously tough standards regarding the rule of law and fundamental rights for countries that want to enter it but has never made good use of its tools for reining in existing members that deviate from the EU's democratic principles. The EU's founding treaty does have a provision for members that fail to uphold core values of human rights and democracy. Under Article 7, sanctions, such as the suspension of voting rights, can be imposed. But that can occur only by a unanimous vote of all EU members other than the government in question. With Hungary and Poland both facing possible sanctions, they could cover for each other, nullifying this option.

An easier approach under Article 7 would be to declare an underperforming member in breach of the EU treaty—a significant stigma. That requires approval by four fifths of EU members, a plausible goal. But Merkel told me in October 2018 that she feared it would be counterproductive to invoke Article 7 if there were no concrete consequences. That is undoubtedly why, as she told me in October 2020, Orbán went along with proceedings under Article 7 once they began.

As a result, we started to look for other ways for European leaders to take a stand against Orbán's attacks on democracy. One strategy involved his political party, Fidesz, which was a member of the

European Parliament's center-right alliance, the European People's Party. The EPP, which included Merkel's Christian Democrats, was the largest and most powerful alliance in the European Parliament. But as Merkel told me at our October 2018 meeting, the EPP was reluctant to suspend Fidesz for fear it would join a competing alliance of parties on the far right. In our view, it was wrong to maintain friendly relations with Fidesz as Orbán undermined European democracy. We pushed for the EPP to expel Fidesz.

I traveled to Budapest in March 2019 to press the issue, joining our researcher on Hungary, Lydia Gall, a determined, no-nonsense Swedish-Hungarian lawyer based in Budapest. The government would not meet with us, so I spoke to the handful of independent media still operating in Hungary, including Klubrádió, which was later forced off the air. Lydia filmed me for a video along the banks of the Danube, which we posted on social media. And I gave a lecture at Central European University, the Soros-created institution of liberal education where Michael Ignatieff then served as rector.

At CEU, I figured I could say things about Orbán that Michael, who was then trying (ultimately unsuccessfully) to stop Orbán from expelling CEU from Budapest, could not. Orbán wanted CEU closed not only because of the Soros connection but also because he saw its liberal education as a threat to his autocratic rule. I called for EU hearings on Orbán's attacks on democracy, and the use of financial pressure by attaching conditions to Hungary's EU budgetary subsidies.

In March 2019, under continuing pressure from Human Rights Watch and others, the EPP finally "suspended" Fidesz. Rather than face further humiliation, Fidesz ultimately quit the alliance in March 2021. Contrary to Merkel's fears, it then had trouble finding another alliance to join. The point was made: Fidesz was an inappropriate partner of democratic political parties in Europe when, under Orbán, it was sabotaging democracy. That was important in ratcheting up the pressure on Orbán.

—

If Orbán was the foremost threat to democracy within the EU, the then-ruling Polish Law and Justice (PiS) party was a close second. While, as I said, Orbán's attacks tended to be subtle and incremental, the Polish government's attacks were frontal. Jarosław Kaczyński, the de facto though behind-the-scenes leader of PiS, followed a personal trajectory toward autocracy similar to Orbán's. Kaczyński was one of the founding members of the Helsinki Foundation for Human Rights before leading PiS in its anti-democratic direction.

PiS came to power in 2015, after it defeated the centrist Civic Platform party, which had ruled since 2007. PiS was determined to undermine the independence of the judiciary so the courts would stop serving as a check on its efforts to compromise basic rights in the name of its conservative Catholic vision, whether it was further restricting women's (already limited) right to an abortion, allowing Polish municipalities and regions to declare themselves "LGBT-free zones," or blocking disfavored asylum seekers. Unlike Poland's welcoming of some 1.3 million Ukrainian refugees, who were mainly white Christians, the government rejected darker-skinned, non-Christian asylum seekers from Syria, Afghanistan, Iraq, and elsewhere.

Much of the battle centered around the moves by PiS to control the appointment and removal of judges. Once reconfigured by PiS, the Constitutional Tribunal even ruled that the EU treaty's standards for judicial independence were unconstitutional in Poland. This was contrary to the most basic precept of the EU that no national law could supersede EU law.

I began monitoring developments in Poland as a young volunteer. The heady days of the Solidarity trade-union movement had given way to martial law, declared in December 1981 to avert a Soviet intervention. The Polish leader, General Wojciech Jaruzelski, imprisoned thousands of opposition activists. Despite my utter lack of qualifications, I was assigned to monitor martial law and to draft a report on Polish government repression. Given the initial lack of physical access to the country, most of my early "research" was reading an English translation of *Tygodnik Mazowsze*, the underground Polish publication that later evolved into the respected nationwide daily newspaper *Gazeta Wyborcza*. After several years of following events from afar, I traveled to the country in November 1986.

It was my first time behind the Iron Curtain. It was the dead of winter, which only added to the dark, foreboding feel of Warsaw. There was no reason to think that the crushing of the Solidarity movement in Poland would end any differently from the snuffing out of brief openings for reform in Hungary in 1956 and Czechoslovakia in 1968.

I spent a lot of time with a physicist who had become the country's principal human-rights defender, Zbigniew Romaszewski. He had been one of the organizers of the Workers' Defense Committee, known by its Polish initials KOR, that had served as an intellectual adviser to Solidarity. He then founded the Polish Helsinki Committee, one of several groups spawned by the 1975 Helsinki Accords. He had been imprisoned for a couple of years following martial law but was once again defending human rights.

Romaszewski showed remarkable patience as he walked me, a young and inexperienced lawyer, through the battles being waged by the determined activists in Poland. I learned far more from him in a few days in Warsaw than I did from months of reading journalistic accounts from afar. It gave me an immediate appreciation of the importance of local activists as "partners" (today's terminology) in helping international groups determine the best way to contribute positively to the evolution of human rights in a country.

I concluded in a December 1986 report that, while the Polish government had formally lifted martial law, many of its provisions had been written into the country's regular laws. One example allowed suspects to be arrested, charged, tried, convicted, and sentenced within forty-eight hours for political offenses. Unsurprisingly, these procedures produced a 100 percent conviction rate.

I traveled to Warsaw again three times between 2016 and 2021 to address PiS's attacks on the judiciary. Poland had become far more open and vibrant, but a retrenchment was under way.

In May 2018, I met with Małgorzata Gersdorf, then First President of Poland's Supreme Court, which is distinct from the Constitutional Tribunal. We discussed the government's desire to control the court's membership and stymie its work, including its efforts to force judges to retire, limit judicial oversight of the government, and discipline judges who ruled against it.

I also met with Jacek Czaputowicz, the minister of foreign affairs, who had a pro-democracy past as a member of the Solidarity-era Workers Defense Committee. He was well placed to appreciate the consequences for Poland if the government continued along its illiberal path, which I spelled out, and to convey that to others in the government.

In January 2020, I had a long video discussion with the deputy justice minister, Sebastian Kaleta, about the government's efforts to control the judiciary. We had asked to talk with his boss, Justice Minister Zbigniew Ziobro, the architect of these efforts, but were denied. Kaleta said that his government's treatment of the judiciary was no different from the actions of other European governments, picking examples out of context to suggest that ordinary bureaucratic regulations, such as those in Spain, were comparable. If I accomplished anything in this contentious meeting, it was to sap the minister of confidence that others would find his twisted analogies persuasive.

The European Commission initiated Article 7 proceedings against Poland in December 2017, but as in the case of Hungary, member states were reluctant to move things forward. As a result, for both Hungary and Poland, our most powerful weapon was to try to condition the European Union's generous subsidies on an end to their anti-democratic moves, particularly their attacks on the rule of law. One of the compromises involved in forming the EU is that its budget allows for subsidies to poorer regions or countries. At the time, Hungary was the third largest net recipient of those funds, and Poland was the largest.

Orbán notoriously used many of those subsidies to reward his cronies by hiring them to build low-priority projects such as football stadiums or even a "treetop walkway" over a forest that was cut down to help pay for it. Meanwhile, Hungarian hospitals were decrepit, with patients literally having to bring their own toilet paper and other necessities. So much for the claim that autocrats deliver better than democracies.

Angela Merkel was in a key position to condition these subsidies because, in the second half of 2020, as the next EU seven-year budget was being finalized, she was still chancellor of Germany, and Germany held the EU six-month rotating presidency.

Merkel was one of my favorite interlocutors among heads of state. Like Macron, she wanted a real conversation. Over the years, I met with her four times. One illustration of the candor that I so liked in her occurred when Wenzel Michalski, our Germany director, and I visited her in March 2014, a few months after it was revealed that the

U.S. government had been tapping her mobile phone. In response, she was toying with creating a "Euronet," a requirement that all data collected in Europe be stored in Europe. I explained that her proposal was the opposite of the advice we gave to internet companies operating in China. There, we insisted that companies not store any data in the country to reduce the risk of being forced to hand it over to the government (as Yahoo said it had been compelled to do, leading to a ten-year prison sentence for Chinese journalist Shi Tao). If Merkel endorsed a Euronet, I said, China would soon insist on a Chinanet. "I never thought of that," Merkel conceded. And the Euronet never happened.

Merkel at times showed herself to be a courageous defender of human rights. In 2015 and 2016, she famously admitted one million mainly Syrian refugees to Germany, stating, "We can do it!" The far-right Alternative for Germany (AfD) party made gains by campaigning against her decision, but her move ultimately was seen by many as positive, given Germany's success in integrating the refugees and the German economy's need for workers. In June 2016, during a trip to Berlin, I visited a large facility housing some of the refugees in Berlin's Spandau borough and was impressed by the respectable housing conditions and the intensive efforts to provide language training and other skills for the refugees.

When Wenzel and I met Merkel in October 2018 in anticipation of Germany holding the EU presidency, she seemed willing to use the subsidies to the Hungarian and Polish governments as leverage to end their attacks on democracy. But two years later, in October 2020, when the COVID-19 pandemic initially postponed my meeting with her and then forced us to meet by video, she made clear that she wanted conditionality but worried out loud that she would not be able to insist. Adoption of the seven-year EU budget required unanimity among all member states, and she feared that Orbán, who opposed conditionality on his subsidies, would veto it.

In my video meeting, I tried to convince Merkel to take a tougher stand. I said that Hungary desperately needed ongoing subsidies and so was in no position to block the entire EU budget. I reminded her that the four largest alliances in the European Parliament insisted on conditionality, and that the Netherlands and Luxembourg might even veto a budget without conditionality. But with her term as chancellor ending—she had already announced she would not seek reelection—her main concern seemed to be reaching an agreement on the budget during her EU presidency.

In the end, she compromised by tossing the matter to the EU's Court of Justice to determine whether conditioning subsidies on respect for the rule of law was legal. In February 2022, the court ruled that it was. Then, Ursula von der Leyen, the European Commission president (and a close Merkel ally, having previously served as her defense minister), stalled a bit longer in implementing this unprecedented step. It was only in December 2022 that member states approved a suspension of 55 percent of the EU's 6.3 billion euro budgetary commitments to Hungary based on rule-of-law problems. In addition, the European Commission withheld 5.8 billion euros' worth of subsidies related to the COVID-19 pandemic, also because of rule-of-law and corruption concerns. Orbán resorted to blackmail to try to get these decisions reversed, variously threatening to veto certain sanctions on Russia for its invasion of Ukraine, aid to Ukraine, and the entrance of Finland and Sweden into NATO.

Similarly, Poland used its acceptance of millions of Ukrainian refugees in 2022 to try to fend off efforts to condition its subsidies. The Polish government was a strong supporter of Ukraine, having had more than its share of life under Russian rule. Sebastian Kaleta, the deputy justice minister with whom I had met, trumpeted the Polish government's defense of democracy against the Russian invasion of Ukraine as if that sufficed, and the EU should not bother about the state of democracy in Poland.

I had an opportunity to address this argument at the World Economic Forum in Davos in May 2022. For several years at Davos, the Forum had invited me to attend what it called an Informal Gathering of World Economic Leaders, or an IGWEL. Unlike the many public sessions in Davos, IGWELs are private, limited to some thirty people, mostly heads of state. I was one of a handful of civic-group leaders thrown in. At this IGWEL, I was seated next to Poland's president, Andrzej Duda. When it was my turn to speak to the group, I made the case to the many European leaders in the room that what ultimately was at stake in the war between Russia and Ukraine was the fate of democracy in Europe. It was wrong, I said, for European nations to compromise their commitment to democracy at home to build and maintain a coalition against Russia.

Beginning in 2021, the EU withheld from Poland 35 billion euros in COVID-19 relief funds and loans because of concerns about the independence of Poland's judiciary. During the summer of 2022, with the Ukraine war under way and refugees fleeing to Poland, Ursula von der Leyen seemed inclined to release the funds despite the absence of genuine progress on the judiciary until protests by a range of senior EU officials stopped her. In July 2023, the European Commission announced that it would continue to withhold funds from Hungary and Poland because of their failure to uphold the rule of law. PiS lost the October 2023 elections when a large voter turnout returned Poland to a governing coalition that was committed to democracy and the rule of law, leading to the resumption of EU funding.

Hungary was a different story. In December, Orbán used the EU's desire to begin negotiations to admit Ukraine into the bloc as a bargaining chip to restore a 10 billion euro portion of Hungary's EU subsidies. However, in February 2024, the European Union resisted further blackmail and, with the new Polish government no longer covering for him, finally threatened Orbán with stripping Hungary's voting rights in the EU if he didn't agree to a new funding package for Ukraine, which he quickly accepted. The result of this ongoing struggle will determine whether the EU is as willing to defend democracy at home as it has been in Ukraine.

13

The United States

Our effort to shape U.S. foreign policy to better promote human rights has been central to our efforts from the outset. But early on, our initial inclination for U.S. domestic rights issues was to defer to organizations such as the ACLU and the NAACP Legal Defense Fund that litigate in U.S. courts. Over time, however, we came to recognize that litigation, despite its importance in the United States, has its limits. Our investigations, reports, and advocacy directed at the political branches of government could address problems that lawsuits had difficulty reaching. In 2001, we formally created a U.S. program. When I left Human Rights Watch, it had become the organization's largest country program.

Despite the strength of the U.S. judicial system, there are areas where U.S. courts are less effective. One obvious area is immigration. Unauthorized immigrants are reluctant to go to court for fear of deportation. Demonstrating patterns of abuse, using an investigative and reporting methodology, was often the only way to address their mistreatment. We also were able to contribute by deploying our capacity to conduct investigations in other countries—enabling us, among other things, to examine conditions for asylum seekers forced to wait along the U.S.-Mexican border due to Trump's "Remain in Mexico" program, or to speak to parents in Central America whose children were being held in the United States under Trump's family-separation program.

The biggest part of our U.S. work addressed the criminal justice system. Even when people charged with crimes receive due process during their trials, they can face abusive or unfair police or prosecutorial practices that are more difficult to challenge in court. Low-income Black and Latino men are disproportionately prosecuted in the United States, yet they are the least likely to have the means to address these practices. In addition, there is a legal complexity in addressing racial discrimination in the United States. Under the U.S. Constitution, as the courts have interpreted it, racial discrimination is prohibited only if it can be shown to have been intentional, which is difficult to prove. Under international human-rights law, unwarranted racial disparities in government practices are prohibited regardless of intent. Although the U.S. government has not implemented as part of U.S. law the more stringent international standard, making reliance on it in court difficult, that did not stop us from applying it in our reporting and generating pressure based on our findings directed at the political branches of government—another example of how public expectations, as shaped in part by our reporting, matter more than the letter of the law.

The criminal justice system was a major focus of our domestic U.S. work because of the magnitude of its problems. I appointed Jamie Fellner, an American lawyer, as our U.S. program's first director to address it. The United States is notorious for its extraordinarily high rates of incarceration, its excessively long prison sentences, the wretched conditions of many of its jails and prisons, and the disproportionately large number of Black males in particular who are incarcerated. The "war on drugs" greatly aggravated these problems. To make matters worse, "law and order" politicians had succeeded in making many of these policies popular. When Human Rights Watch started to address these issues, there was far less political pressure than today to change them.

We used our investigations and reports to try to raise their visibility. We interviewed people with information of direct relevance—victims of abusive treatment, prosecutors, judges, corrections officials, policymakers, and medical and mental-health experts. In addition, we did statistical analyses of government data—a new methodology for us at the time—to demonstrate unwarranted racial disparities. We called attention to the devastating effects of mandatory minimum prison sentences and lengthy incarceration for minor drug offenses. We addressed discriminatory practices in the setting of bail and the way it created unfair pressure to plead guilty. And we examined how police practices, and the deployment of police resources, contributed to racial disparities in arrests.

We spotlighted the immense psychological damage of prolonged solitary confinement, especially the growing trend toward confining inmates who were seen as difficult or dangerous in supermaximum security prisons with inhumanely limited contact with other inmates and access to exercise and other activities. We showed that many of the people placed in these institutions had mental-health problems, which their isolation only worsened. Ordinary prisons were used to warehouse people rather than provide them with treatment. We also attacked the shocking tolerance of rape in prisons.

Today, these problems are broadly acknowledged, and some of the many relevant jurisdictions in the United States—federal, state, and local—are addressing them. But when we started raising them, the "law and order" perspective was still dominant among the public and the media. Many Black leaders at the time were reluctant to address "war on drugs" issues because they saw the devastation that illicit drugs were causing their communities. We helped to promote an appreciation of the arguably even greater devastation done by discriminatory police practices and lengthy prison sentences imposed disproportionately on Black men.

The value of the investigative and reporting methodology came to be broadly recognized. Even traditional litigating organizations such as the ACLU came to use it. So did a good number of the proliferating community-level organizations that emerged to address these problems, many of which we worked with.

We helped to end the appalling practice of imposing life sentences without parole on offenders who were under eighteen years of age when they committed their crime. Such young people were particularly capable of reform. Elizabeth Calvin, a Human Rights Watch lawyer and specialist on children's rights based in Los Angeles, enlisted families of people subjected to these sentences, as well as some victims of their crimes, to obtain legislation ending the practice in California. The U.S. Supreme Court, in turn, severely limited the ability of courts nationwide to impose life imprisonment without parole on child offenders. In addition, Elizabeth helped to secure a series of reforms in California to reduce the prosecution of child offenders as if they were adults.

In recent years, the dimension of the criminal system that has emerged most prominently in the public's consciousness is the problem of police brutality. When we could successfully gather the facts about an incident, the problem lent itself to our methodology. During the Black Lives Matter protests following the murder of George Floyd in May 2020, New York City police engaged in the practice of "kettling"—they surrounded protesters, assaulted them with batons and pepper spray, and detained or arrested them. We documented one egregious instance in the Mott Haven section of the South Bronx. No Human Rights Watch researcher was present at the time, but many of the protesters took video images of the protest and the police response. We collected these videos, corroborated them, and used a graphic reconstruction to help people visualize what had happened. This reconstruction was so powerful that the New York City mayor was forced to address it. Ultimately, New York City paid a settlement of $21,500 to each protester. In September 2023, it announced an end to the practice of kettling.

Despite our initial hesitation, our work on serious U.S. abuses made an important contribution to curtailing them. It was also essential for the organization's global credibility. One of the classic ploys of repressive governments trying to deflect criticism was to suggest that we should focus instead on abuses in the United States. That is not a defense to a human-rights violation, but it changes the subject. A good way to silence that dodge was to show up with a stack of Human Rights Watch reports on the United States and place them with a good thump on the official's desk.

Foreign-Policy Double Standards

The U.S. government, among others, has a long history of promoting human rights among its adversaries while downplaying abuses among its friends. That double standard played a central role in our evolution.

When in 1981 the Reagan administration took office, its UN ambassador, Jeane Kirkpatrick, a former academic, had developed the theoretical distinction between what she called totalitarian and authoritarian governments. Totalitarian governments—or "revolutionary 'socialist' or Communist" ones, essentially Soviet-backed governments—were deemed immune to autonomous reform ("the history of this century provides no grounds for expecting that radical totalitarian regimes will transform themselves"), so their human-rights violations, in her view, should be confronted directly. On the other hand, authoritarian governments—or "right-wing autocracies," meaning mostly the military governments of Latin America that were U.S. allies—were deemed reformable ("more susceptible of liberalization"), so, she opined, their human-rights violations should be treated more gently, through engagement rather than confrontation.

It was a fancy academic justification for a blatant double standard. To show that we did not subscribe, we added Americas Watch to Helsinki Watch. Helsinki Watch continued to focus mainly on the Soviet-dominated governments of Eastern Europe (plus Turkey), while Americas Watch addressed mainly the military dictatorships of Latin America (plus Cuba and Nicaragua). We applied the same standards everywhere regardless of the political leanings of the government or its friendliness toward the United States. We added Asia Watch, Africa Watch, and Middle East Watch, before I consolidated them in 1995 under the name, which we had also begun using, of Human Rights Watch.

Pressing the U.S. government to promote human rights more consistently—as well as to respect human rights in its own overseas operations—continued to be a central part of our work, led by our Washington office. The U.S. government has enormous potential influence on human-rights practices because of its ability to condition military or economic assistance and to apply diplomatic pressure. Even when Washington was reluctant to act, our ability to direct public and media attention to U.S. support for an abusive regime could force U.S. officials to press a repressive ally to curb its abuse as a way of quelling the political storm back home.

Mike Pompeo, when Trump's secretary of state, tried to resurrect a Kirkpatrick-like reinterpretation of universal human-rights standards. He wanted to downplay rights that in his view were less essential (such as LGBT rights and reproductive freedom) while promoting rights that he saw as important (such as religious freedom).

To pursue his idea, he established a Commission on Unalienable Rights, which published a glossy brochure outlining his approach.

I had been the primary public critic of Pompeo's proposal, writing opinion articles in *The Washington Post* and *Foreign Policy*. I also testified before the commission. This pick-and-choose approach to human rights, I explained, would be welcomed by the world's autocrats. The Chinese government might choose to ignore the rights of free speech and association; the Saudi monarchy, the rights of women; the Indian government, religious freedom, and so on.

As a result of my criticisms, Pompeo reached out to me. His office initially proposed that we meet shortly before the November 2020 election. Not wanting to be instrumentalized for electoral purposes, I suggested that we speak later. We arranged to chat a month after Trump's electoral loss—ironically, on December 10, 2020, Human Rights Day, the anniversary of the Universal Declaration of Human Rights, which does not permit selective respect for them.

We spoke by video. After some perfunctory compliments from him about Human Rights Watch, he asked, in reference to the commission, "Did we get anything right?" I had not anticipated the question and had to scramble for an answer. The commission in its glossy brochure had linked international human-rights standards to the U.S. Constitution and Declaration of Independence. I suspect its purpose was to spotlight the ways in which international human-rights law had extended beyond U.S. constitutional law and thus should be rejected, but I saw one advantage in the linkage: it helped Americans understand, I told Pompeo, that "human rights" were not foreign concepts but directly related to the terminology of civil or constitutional rights that Americans more typically use to describe domestic rights. He accepted the answer and said he hoped we would find ways to work together.

Although Pompeo's selection of rights reflected his conservative ideology, his commission did raise an important question: Are we in danger of having too many rights? In my view, yes and no. Giving people more rights sounds great, but the more things that are recognized as rights—the more issues that are transformed from a political option to a government obligation—the more likely it is that some of those rights will generate opposition. In principle, that could jeopardize the entire human-rights enterprise by giving human rights a bad name. It also risks rights inflation—cheapening the meaning of all rights by turning everything into a right.

Yet even if there is a practical (or political) limit to how many things can be labeled a "human right," I do not view that label as essential to our methodology. We could gain traction by showing that a government was violating a treaty it had accepted, but as I have mentioned, the power of the methodology is not the ability to cite chapter and verse of a particular legal standard but to demonstrate that a government's conduct falls short of the standards that the public expects it to follow. Calling something a human right can help to build public opinion around a particular standard of conduct, but it is not a prerequisite.

I do not want to suggest that the problem of double standards is limited to Republican administrations. Jimmy Carter made human rights a priority in his foreign policy, but the reality was filled with exceptions. Clinton and Obama were little better. Biden came into office with his secretary of state, Antony Blinken, stating in February 2021 that "President Biden is committed to a foreign policy that unites our democratic values with our diplomatic leadership, and one that is centered on the defense of democracy and the protection of human rights." Biden reiterated the point in August 2022: "I've been clear that human rights will be the center of our foreign policy." But the emptiness of that vow became a standing joke within the Washington foreign-policy community. The inconsistency of the U.S. government's support for human rights—Biden's attempts to target Russia or China for their repression when, say, the Middle East had largely become a human-rights black hole for U.S. foreign policy— undermined Washington's credibility.

Domestic Rights Issues

As I mentioned, many Americans tend to think of domestic issues in terms of "constitutional" or "civil" rights rather than human rights. That orientation is only compounded by the way the U.S. government ratified the handful of human-rights treaties that it formally joined. Although Washington often plays a leading, if inconsistent, role in promoting human rights around the world, it is a relative laggard when it comes to ratifying the most important treaties—far fewer than most established democracies. To its credit, the U.S. government takes the treaties relatively seriously. Unlike some governments that pay them only lip service, Washington does not sign up to standards that it intends to ignore. But it allows itself to succumb to domestic right-wing attacks on treaties that most everyone else finds perfectly acceptable. The United States is the only government in the world not to have ratified the Convention on the Rights of the Child—ostensibly because the treaty interferes with parental authority. Nor has the U.S. government ratified the Convention on the Elimination of All Forms of Discrimination against Women, largely because the treaty recognizes the right to reproductive freedom.

Of the two treaties that initially codified the broad terms of the Universal Declaration of Human Rights, the U.S. government has ratified the International Covenant on Civil and Political Rights (joined by 174 governments), but not the International Covenant on Economic, Social and Cultural Rights (joined by 172). That selectivity parallels the U.S. Constitution—an old document among today's charters—which addresses only civil and political rights. Many economic and social rights are recognized in the United States (though often inadequately) by federal or state statutes, but that has not been enough to persuade the U.S. government in its treaty ratifications to recognize that economic and social rights deserve equal treatment to civil and political rights.

Even when the U.S. government does ratify a treaty, it typically enters a series of "reservations, understandings, and declarations" designed to ensure that the treaty does not oblige it to do anything that domestic law does not already require. In other words, instead of upgrading its conduct to meet the standards of the treaty, it downgrades the treaty to meet its conduct. It then declares the treaty "non-self-executing," meaning that, unlike regular legislation, no one can go to court to enforce it should, despite the government's intention, it prove more protective of rights than regular U.S. law.

This approach renders ratification a statement for the rest of the world but not something that improves the rights of people in the United States. By ratifying a treaty, the U.S. government does typically subject itself to periodic review by a committee established under the treaty to scrutinize compliance, but unlike a court, that committee has no enforcement power. The U.S. government never ratifies portions of treaties that would give individuals the right to file complaints for adjudication with an international body.

One stated rationale for this superficial approach to treaty ratification is that the U.S. government does not want to legislate by treaty. Under the U.S. Constitution, treaties require approval of only the Senate (by a two-thirds majority), plus the president, but unlike regular legislation, there is no role for the House of Representatives. But that rationale begs the question of why the U.S. government could not, parallel with ratifying a treaty, adopt legislation incorporating it and bringing the United States into compliance with its terms. Congress could level up, not down.

There is only one case that I know of in which the U.S. government changed its practices to ratify a human-rights treaty. It involved a treaty that we played a central role in promoting—the treaty banning the use of child soldiers. Formally, it is an "optional protocol"—essentially, a separate treaty—to the Convention on the Rights of the Child. The original children's rights treaty, adopted in 1989, allows children to serve in the military beginning at age fifteen, which is anomalous because in other respects it deems children not to become adults until they turn eighteen.

Led by my colleague Jo Becker, we documented and reported on the enormous harm done to children when forced to serve as soldiers in Colombia, the Democratic Republic of Congo, Liberia, Sierra Leone, Sudan, and Uganda. Some forces find children useful as soldiers because they are easily manipulated and have a hard time resisting efforts to draw them into violence and atrocities or even appreciating the consequences of their actions. If they survive, the emotional toll can be horrendous. Jo helped to lead a global effort to outlaw any use of children under eighteen as soldiers.

With the United States having been in a small minority of governments to oppose the land mines treaty (1997) and the International Criminal Court (1998), U.S. secretary of state Madeleine Albright asked the Pentagon for a senior-level review of whether it could join a consensus on making eighteen the minimum age for participation in hostilities. It agreed.

During the final negotiations in January 2000, two key elements of the draft treaty remained unresolved—the minimum age for voluntary enlistment and for participation in direct hostilities. The U.S. government determined, after its review, that it could live with eighteen as the minimum age for participating in armed conflict—a red-line issue for the human-rights groups that were promoting the treaty. It vowed not to deploy under-eighteens to combat, and it already did not forcibly conscript under-eighteens, but it wanted, together with other countries, to be able to continue to voluntarily enlist children as they graduated from secondary school, when some were still seventeen. A "straight-eighteen" standard would have been simpler, but gaining the support of the powerful and trendsetting Pentagon was important. The states leading the negotiations agreed to this compromise, although they added certain safeguards for under-eighteens who were voluntarily recruited. In 2000, the protocol was adopted, and the U.S. government ratified it in 2002. The Pentagon then stopped its practice of deploying seventeen-year-old voluntary recruits without regard to whether their unit was heading to armed conflict.

Even without ratification, a treaty can have some influence in the United States, although right-wing forces have vehemently opposed such influence. For example, in *Roper v. Simmons,* the U.S. Supreme Court cited the Convention on the Rights of the Child for its prohibition of the death penalty for offenses committed by people below eighteen years of age—and then adopted the same standard. The court noted that after the last holdouts—Iran, Pakistan, Saudi Arabia, Yemen, Nigeria, the Democratic Republic of Congo, and China—had stopped executing youth offenders, the United States stood intolerably alone.

Still, because of the U.S. government's restrictive approach to ratifying human-rights treaties, we often did not compare U.S. government conduct to the language of treaties, because Washington had already made that legally, if not entirely politically, irrelevant. Nor did we much care whether Americans referred to abusive conduct as a problem of "human rights" or something else. Rather, we focused on what Americans thought, or could be persuaded to think, was wrongful government conduct. We then deployed our classic methodology—investigating that misconduct, measuring it against public expectations to shame the government when it fell short, publicizing that discrepancy, and meeting with officials to press them to change. Regardless of terminology, that generated pressure for reform.

Guantánamo

Human Rights Watch staff regularly traveled to the U.S. Naval Base at Guantánamo Bay to observe proceedings for the men detained there. In 2012, I traveled there for the arraignment—the formal pleading to official charges—of the five men accused of playing roles in the September 11, 2001, attacks. I was struck by the strange contrast—a prison of extraordinarily tight security set amid a seemingly ordinary middle-American town, complete with such amenities of life as an elementary school, a McDonald's, a shopping center stocked with souvenirs in its gift shop, and modest housing for servicemember families.

The U.S. military housed the observers—journalists and rights defenders—in tents on an abandoned runway, spartan accommodations. The journalists were naturally inclined to focus on the courtroom shenanigans of the accused men. My task was to redirect them to the question of whether the proceedings were fair.

We sat in a small gallery that was separated from the courtroom by a glass partition. The sound was delayed by a few seconds so that a censor could shut it off should someone blurt out something deemed classified, such as a reference to U.S. interrogators' torture. Inside the courtroom were the accused men dressed in their prison garb, their interpreters, their defense attorneys, and the prosecution team. It had elements of a regular trial, but it was nothing of the sort.

We shared the small gallery with some families of the September 11 victims. I felt resentment from some of them because I assumed they wanted to see expeditious punishment, while the rights observers were concerned with the fairness of the proceedings. In fact, our interests were more aligned than we realized.

The prosecution was taking place not in a regular court but before a military commission designed to avoid public disclosure of the torture. As originally established by the Bush administration (though slightly improved by Obama), the commissions allowed confessions that were the product of prohibited "cruel, inhuman or degrading treatment or punishment" (the Bush administration falsely denied using torture). They also allowed hearsay evidence, such as a law-enforcement agent describing what others reported someone had said during interrogation. That had the effect of limiting cross-examination about the circumstances of a confession, or of allowing testimony from someone in custody whom the prosecutor did not want to produce in court. Because the military commissions were tribunals designed on the fly, they were replete with procedural irregularities and legal challenges. More than two decades after the September 11 attacks, the trial of the five men accused of the September 11 attacks was far from beginning.

Had the five men been brought to regular federal court, the trials would have been completed long ago, but the Bush-Cheney crowd insisted that military commissions would be tougher. In fact, they proved to be a travesty, plagued by endless delays, unfair procedures, and little prospect of delivering justice while the people subject to them languished in detention. (In November 2024, it appeared that some of the September 11 suspects might plead guilty, avoiding the need for a military commission trial, in return for life in prison rather than a possible death sentence.)

More than fifty journalists had come to Guantánamo to report on the arraignment. My plan had been to speak with them at the U.S. military's postarraignment news conference. Yet just before its scheduled time, the military suddenly announced that the rights observers had to leave early and fly home. Only the Pentagon's views would be heard. As I sat fuming at the airport, an op-ed that I had written about the arraignment, "Justice Cheated," came up on the *New York Times* website. I promptly emailed and tweeted it to the journalists who had been at the news conference to provide a counterpoint to the military line.

The U.S. government prohibited rights observers and journalists from speaking to any detainee. The closest I came was when I traveled to Saudi Arabia and met former detainees. One described to me the utter lack of justice: "They captured us for no reason and they let us go without telling us the reason. No one apologized." I felt shame on behalf of my country.

Torture

To maintain credibility as an objective fact finder, an organization must report results even if they are unpopular. It now seems routine to talk about the U.S. government's human-rights violations during George Bush's "global war on terror," but in the early days after September 11, many Americans wanted the government to do whatever it took to ensure their safety. Bush administration officials took advantage of that fear to rip up basic rules, such as those against torture. Michael Ignatieff wrote in *The New York Times:* "The question after Sept. 11 is whether the era of human rights has come and gone."

On the morning of September 11, 2001, a beautiful crisp and clear day, I was attending a board meeting in the thirty-fourth-floor conference room of the Human Rights Watch headquarters in the Empire State Building in Manhattan. The room had an unobstructed view south to the World Trade Center and beyond. My back was to the window, but at 8:46 that morning, a colleague across from me cried out, "A plane just hit the World Trade Center!" As I swung around and saw smoke surging from a gaping hole—some ten floors high—my initial thought was that a small plane packed with explosives must have hit the tower. It never occurred to me that it might have been a commercial passenger jet. When the second tower was hit at 9:03, we knew for sure that it was an attack and not an accident and immediately evacuated our office, fearing that the Empire State Building, the third largest tower in Manhattan at the time, could be next. I still remember my utter shock that such an attack could happen, only compounded by the collapse of the two World Trade Center towers.

As is widely known, the September 11 attacks involved four hijacked planes—the two that hit the World Trade Center, a third that hit the Pentagon, and a fourth that crashed in rural Pennsylvania after the passengers, learning of the other attacks, tried to take control of the aircraft. Because al-Qaeda was known to plan attacks in tandem, and because no one knew whether it might count the four September 11 planes as one or multiple attacks, people were scared there might soon be more.

In November 2001, we held our annual fundraising dinner in New York as scheduled, at the American Museum of Natural History. By then the U.S. government had invaded Afghanistan but had not yet opened the Guantánamo detention facility. We knew nothing about the U.S. government's torture program, but we were worried about where the fervent counterterrorism efforts might lead. So when I gave the keynote address, I mentioned our concern and underscored the importance of opposing terrorism in a way that respected human rights. I said we would be monitoring the response to the September 11 attacks to ensure it was carried out lawfully.

One of our biggest donors at the time, a moderately conservative investor, came up to me afterward and was livid. "If terrorists ever got ahold of my daughters," he said, "I would want them tortured." He did not last long as a donor. Sadly, our fears were soon borne out by revelations about the Bush administration's euphemistically labeled "enhanced interrogation techniques."

I mentioned earlier that few governments question the law when Human Rights Watch spotlights their violations. We tend to focus on abuses when there is little doubt that human-rights standards have been violated or that the public's expectations for government conduct have been breached. Yet in light of the U.S. government's legalistic approach to its treaty obligations, and fearing court challenges, the George W. Bush administration did make legal arguments when facing criticism of its human-rights conduct. Because various treaties that the U.S. government had accepted prohibit torture unconditionally, it sought in the infamous "Torture Memos," produced at the request of senior Bush administration officials, to redefine the meaning of torture and other cruel, inhuman, and degrading treatment and punishment in an effort to justify interrogation techniques that clearly violated these standards. The legal theories advanced in those memos were laughable, but they had the insidious effect of enabling senior officials, should they ever face prosecution, to say they had relied in good faith on the legal approval of the Justice Department's Office of Legal Counsel—the lawyers' lawyers, who drafted the memos.

There are plenty of reasons to question whether any reliance on the Torture Memos was in good faith. The Senate Select Committee on Intelligence's report on the CIA's detention and interrogation program found that key aspects of the program were kept hidden from Justice Department lawyers. In addition, there is considerable evidence that the officials went shopping for the legal advice they wanted and found pliable lawyers who would twist the law to justify the unjustifiable. Still, the existence of the memos created a formidable obstacle to any potential prosecutorial effort, even though no such effort was ever seriously made.

Sadly, the absurdity of the Torture Memos was alone not enough to persuade the public that the Bush administration should end its "enhanced interrogation techniques." When word of the torture program broke, I immediately recognized its gravity, not only for the victims but also for the capacity of the U.S. government to defend human rights when it was breaching them so blatantly. I felt that, given the stakes, I needed to devote significant attention to the U.S. government's own human-rights practices. I gave many speeches and wrote many articles arguing that torture was wrong. It should have been enough to note, as I did, that torture is prohibited by various treaties as well as U.S. law, that no exceptions are permitted even in war, that it is a clear crime. But those legal arguments were not winning the day with a public that remained traumatized by September 11 and, in many cases, was willing to countenance any government conduct that could be portrayed as keeping it safe from further al-Qaeda attacks.

As a result, I needed to persuade people that torture was not going to make them safe, that it was likely to make them less secure. I argued that evidence produced by torture is unreliable, that torture enrages people who identify with the victims and probably produces more terrorists than it sidetracks, that torture abandons the moral high ground needed to enlist other countries and the general public to fight terrorism.

On NBC, CBS, and CNN, and in *The Washington Post,* I debated Alan Dershowitz, the Harvard Law professor. He pretended to take a "reasonable" approach to torture, arguing that because torture inevitably happens, the U.S. government should ask a judge to supervise it—to issue a "torture warrant" for times when it might (supposedly) be appropriate. A similar proposal was made by Phil Heymann, a Harvard Law professor, and Juliette Kayyem, a Harvard Kennedy School resident scholar, to allow "cruel, inhuman or degrading treatment" upon presidential authorization.

I saw this as a dangerous legitimization of torture—license for a despicable act that should never be allowed. If U.S. judges might sometimes authorize torture, what message would that send to other countries? Would you want to be in an Egyptian or Chinese prison and depend on a local judge to determine whether you should be tortured? And how could the U.S. government ever condemn torture elsewhere if it openly practiced torture itself?

The hypothetical that Dershowitz cited—that torture proponents always cite—is the case of a ticking time bomb. Should not the interrogator be allowed to torture the suspect to save innocent people from being killed? But that rarely if ever happens in real life. Interrogators never know about a bomb before it goes off, let alone that a particular suspect knows about it. More likely, they know about a group that they suspect is engaged in acts of terrorism. If torture is allowed for a "ticking" bomb, why should it not also be allowed for a bomb that might go off tomorrow, or next month, or in a year? Are not those innocent victims just as worthy of saving? And why stop with a suspect who knows about the bomb? Why not torture people who might lead you to people who might know about the bomb? The hypothetical quickly becomes infinitely elastic.

In Israel, the 1987 Landau Commission authorized "a moderate measure of physical pressure" for suspects under interrogation in "ticking bomb" situations. Although the commission tried to keep the pressure short of torture, that limitation was quickly ignored in practice, and torture became routine. By 1996 and 1997, an astounding 85 percent of people interrogated by Israel's General Security Service, known as the Shin Bet, were being tortured. Methods included "violently shaking prisoners, depriving them of sleep, exposing them to loud music, tying them into painful positions for long periods, and covering their heads in foul-smelling sacks." In 1999, the Israeli Supreme Court banned further use of "moderate physical pressure," which reduced, though did not eliminate, the Israeli government's use of torture. (Israeli torture surged after Hamas's attack of October 7, 2023.)

There is plenty of evidence that people under torture will say whatever they think the torturer wants them to say, regardless of the truth. That creates false leads that divert investigative resources. It also discourages members of the public—often the key to early warning of a terrorist plot—from sharing their suspicions with law-enforcement agents, because many people will not want to send a suspect to be tortured.

Even the behavior of the CIA interrogators called into question the purpose of the torture. Did they really believe that Khaled Sheikh Mohammed, the alleged mastermind of the September 11 plot, who had revealed nothing of value during his first 182 times being waterboarded—mock execution by drowning—would suddenly say something useful on the 183rd try?

Despite the dubious benefits of torture, its damage can be immediate and real. There is nothing like being subject to torture to turn the victim, as well as family members and friends, into confirmed antagonists of the abusing government.

The torture also ended up undermining the prospects for prosecution. The Bush administration brought in "clean teams" of interrogators who were kept in the dark about what people had said under torture and tried to get them to talk again by treating them nicely (if that is even possible within the context of Guantánamo detention). But a military commission judge rejected the government's contention that a torture victim's later willingness to talk was not influenced by his earlier statements under torture.

Human Rights Watch—principally our Washington director at the time, Tom Malinowski—worked closely with the late Senator John McCain to secure legislation putting a definitive end to Bush's "enhanced interrogation techniques." Tom, a smart and articulate advocate and a beautiful writer, once served as Bill Clinton's foreign-policy speechwriter. He went on to serve as assistant secretary of state for human rights under Obama and as a two-term congressman from New Jersey. Sandy Berger, Clinton's national security adviser, made a point of calling me personally to say how talented Tom was and to urge me to hire him. I am glad I did.

A key actor in this effort was a young American captain, Ian Fishback, a West Point graduate who had served in Iraq and saw torture being used at a U.S. Army forward operating base near Fallujah. He tried to report this illegality up the chain of command but was ignored, so he contacted us, reaching Marc Garlasco. Later, he persuaded three other soldiers from his division to speak to us as well. They described orders and encouragement to beat prisoners and to employ sleep deprivation, exposure to extreme temperatures, and denial of food and water. All said that superior officers knew about the abuse but did nothing to stop it. We released their accounts in a September 2005 report entitled "Leadership Failure."

We introduced Fishback to McCain, an independently inclined Republican who carried moral authority on the issue of torture because he himself had been a victim of it while in captivity during the Vietnam War. McCain led the legislative effort to obtain passage of the Detainee Treatment Act of 2005, which prohibited not only torture but also "cruel, inhuman and degrading treatment or punishment," which the administration wrongly claimed the power to impose so long as the detainee was a non-American held outside the United States. The bill passed the Senate by a vote of 90 to 9 and the House by a three-to-one margin. McCain credited Fishback, whom we took around Capitol Hill, with helping to secure enough votes to make Bush's veto threat moot. *Time* magazine named Fishback one of the world's 100 most influential people of the year. Sadly, Fishback died in 2021 of cardiac arrest at age forty-two, clearly traumatized by his experience in Iraq. He was buried with full military honors in Arlington National Cemetery.

Obama, Torture, and Guantánamo

Upon becoming president, Barack Obama ordered Guantánamo closed within a year and suspended the use of military commissions. He soon retreated. I met with him in May 2009 in the White House Cabinet Room, where I was joined by colleagues from several major rights groups as well as a handful of academics. All of Obama's senior security officials were present, but none said a word during the hour-and-a-half meeting. Obama, impressively, had the confidence to handle the meeting on his own, armed with only a notepad.

It was not a satisfactory meeting. My colleagues and I pressed him to close the U.S. military prison at Guantánamo by either prosecuting suspects before a regular federal court or releasing them. In November 2009, the Obama administration announced plans to move the September 11 suspects to Manhattan for a federal trial, but to our great frustration, it did not promptly implement the plans. That gave Congress time to prohibit the move, in December 2010.

The men detained at Guantánamo had been characterized as the "worst of the worst," so there was little public sympathy for moving them to the United States, even though many of those held were later shown to have been rounded up on the basis of scanty evidence—sometimes in exchange for bounties—and had no known connection to al-Qaeda or the Taliban.

The ostensible reason for rejecting trials in the U.S. courthouse in Manhattan was security, but having worked in that same courthouse for four years as a prosecutor and one year as a law clerk, I knew it had a long history of handling dangerous cases with hardly a mishap, including those involving people charged with terrorism, accused mafia dons, and alleged heads of drug cartels. Before the congressional ban, one man who had been detained in Guantánamo, charged with the 1998 bombings of the U.S. embassies in Kenya and Tanzania, was even tried there. But Congress wanted to appear uncompromising by continuing to detain people at Guantánamo. That Guantánamo was at first deemed to be beyond the reach of the U.S. courts was also a factor, although the U.S. Supreme Court later repudiated that rationale.

We urged Obama to release the hundreds of men detained at Guantánamo whom the U.S. government claimed were too dangerous to release but could not, for lack of usable evidence, be charged with any crime. He resisted. According to secret determinations by U.S. intelligence agencies, these detainees posed an ongoing security threat to the United States. But Obama seemed mainly worried about being held politically responsible should he release a Guantánamo detainee who went on to commit an act of terrorism. That might be called the "Willie Horton problem," after the convicted felon who was released on furlough when Michael Dukakis was governor of Massachusetts. Horton proceeded to commit assault and rape, and George H. W. Bush tarred Dukakis repeatedly with the episode during the 1988 presidential campaign. Obama rejected the prosecute-or-release formula that we pressed upon him.

Like Bush, Obama did gradually release many of the men held at Guantánamo once they were deemed no longer to pose a threat. A total of some 780 men and boys, all Muslim, had been held in Guantánamo since 2002—656 at its peak in 2003. The vast majority were repatriated to their home countries or sent to a third country after years of detention without charges ever having been filed against them—more than 500 by Bush and about 200 by Obama.

At the very least, Guantánamo had become such a stain on America's reputation that even Trump never sent anyone there, despite threatening to do so. Of the thirty men who remained in Guantánamo in August 2024, only four were convicted, after pleading guilty before a military commission. Seven were charged years earlier and still awaited trial by military commission. Sixteen had been approved for transfer to another country if security requirements could be met. Three uncharged men had not been cleared for release despite spending almost two decades in custody.

Obama ended the torture but did not want to pay the political price of investigating and prosecuting the senior Bush administration officials who had authorized and directed it, despite a major Human Rights Watch report advocating it. He offered his familiar look-forward-not-back formula, and still hoped for cooperation from Congress in passing the Affordable Care Act (Obamacare), as well as on such issues as climate change and education. But because he would not prosecute the torturers, he (and then Biden) effectively left torture as a policy option—one that Trump in his first term suggested he would reinstate, although he never did. A future president might.

Obama's passivity was, ironically, aided by the revelations about the abuse of prisoners in Abu Ghraib, the U.S. military prison in Iraq. The photographs of that abuse, released in April 2004, remain the dominant picture that many people have of torture under the Bush administration, but they are deceptive. The abuse there was amateurish, inflicted by low-level servicemembers. That fed the myth that torture was the product of a few "bad apples," as Secretary of Defense Donald Rumsfeld claimed, rather than a deliberate U.S. policy. In fact, the CIA's torture was deliberate, organized, and approved at the highest levels of government. It involved the creation of an archipelago of secret CIA detention centers, or "black sites," in multiple countries where the torture took place and suspects "disappeared." Dana Priest revealed these centers in 2005 in a front-page *Washington Post* article. But, she wrote: "The Washington Post is not publishing the names of the Eastern European countries involved in the covert program, at the request of senior U.S. officials." Using infor-

mation that plane spotters posted on the internet, we had been track-
ing flights from Afghanistan suggesting that the Eastern European
secret detention centers were in Poland and Romania. We promptly
published our findings, and those black sites were quickly shut down.

The lawlessness of the CIA torture program was openly encouraged by winks and nods from senior U.S. government officials. In
reference to waterboarding, Vice President Cheney said that "a dunk
in water" was a "no-brainer." Porter Goss, the CIA director, included
waterboarding in a list of "professional interrogation techniques."
Michael Hayden, who served as CIA director from 2006 to 2009,
was known to want U.S. counterterrorism personnel "playing so close
to the line that you get chalk dust on your cleats." Statements of this
sort undoubtedly led the Abu Ghraib servicemembers to believe that
their abuse of prisoners would not be punished. Because they were
caught so publicly, their calculation proved wrong, and the embarrassment of the Abu Ghraib photographs ultimately contributed to
the Bush administration ending its torture program. But the U.S.
government, to its deep discredit, never held accountable the authors
of that systematic torture.

Donald Trump

Trump in his first term presented a different challenge for the
human-rights movement, which began with his embrace of friendly
autocrats, like Putin, whom Trump treated as an admirable strong-
man rather than a despicable dictator. Trump was also a threat to
human rights because he relished breaking taboos.

He broke taboos on the treatment of women, immigrants, and
people of color. In the eyes of his ardent followers, he provided an
imprimatur of propriety for discriminatory and abusive practices that
had been considered indecent or beyond the pale. Many others still
viewed these practices as wrong; Trump was hardly a standard-setter
for them. But among his most committed followers, Trump's behavior had the effect of weakening the stigma attached to such conduct.

Our task was not to persuade every last Trump supporter that
his human-rights abuses were wrong. On the other hand, there was

little point in singing to the progressive choir. To build the pro-rights majority needed to change government policy, we needed to convince the people in the center of the political spectrum that the government's conduct was wrong.

Annie and I took on a personal crusade that highlighted the arbitrariness of Trump's "Muslim Ban," imposed on immigrants from a group of Muslim-majority countries, including Syria, at the outset of his first presidency. Trump's aim was to curtail immigration to the United States by pandering to Americans' lingering fear of terrorists who had acted in the name of Islam. Annie and I found ourselves in the middle of a case that spotlighted just how wrong this Islamophobia was.

Khaled Almilaji is a Syrian doctor whom I first met in 2014 in Gaziantep, Turkey, where he was directing a network of doctors and thousands of health-care workers in rebel-held parts of Syria. (Before he fled Syria, the authorities had arrested, tortured, and imprisoned him for six months.) It was tough work. When his network discovered that, due to the Syrian government's poor vaccination program, polio had broken out among children in Deir Ezzor in eastern Syria—a fact that the government covered up for months—he organized a massive vaccination campaign that treated nearly two million Syrian children. He also led a task force documenting the Syrian government's chemical-weapon attacks and training health-care workers how to respond.

Khaled felt that a master's degree in public health would help his work, so I approached Brown University, where after my attendance as an undergraduate I continued to be involved as a member of the board of governors of its Watson Institute for International and Public Affairs. Brown agreed to admit and fund Khaled with a full scholarship in its public-health school. In September 2016, he and his wife, Jehan Mouhsen, also a doctor, moved to Providence. Their first semester went well. Beginning in December, during the winter holiday break, Khaled returned to Gaziantep to ensure that his organization was still running smoothly. Unfortunately, his visit corresponded with Trump's January 2017 inauguration and the prompt imposition of his Muslim Ban.

Jehan, who by then was pregnant with their first child, moved in with Annie and me in our New York apartment. Khaled and Jehan, an extraordinarily sympathetic couple, could not have been further from the terrorist stereotype that Trump was trying to promote and exploit. We started a media campaign on their behalf. The media immediately latched on to their story, *The New York Times* running a major piece entitled "Love, Interrupted: A Travel Ban Separates Couples." The lead photograph featured Jehan, sitting on our couch, holding a laptop showing Khaled on the other end of a video chat.

Trump never relented. Khaled and Jehan were forced to move to Canada. He resumed his studies at the University of Toronto. But the attention that we were able to draw to the case of Khaled and Jehan contributed in a modest way to the broad outcry against Trump's Muslim Ban and the pressure for it to be limited. It also helped to undermine the climate of fear toward Muslims that underlay so many of the U.S. government's abusive counterterrorism policies.

Joe Biden

Biden's assumption of the presidency was a welcome reprieve from the Trump years. He understood human rights as an important moral issue but did not see them as necessarily serving the U.S. national interest, leading to a mixed performance. As he reversed Trump's policies, the U.S. government rejoined the UN Human Rights Council, reengaged with the World Health Organization, supported global efforts to fight climate change, and ended sanctions on the International Criminal Court prosecutor. He performed masterly on Ukraine, immediately recognizing the threat that Putin posed to Ukraine's democratic aspirations (and the rest of Europe) and building a strong multilateral consensus behind the country's defense.

Biden, at least initially, seemed to appreciate the threat to human rights posed by the Chinese government. His administration helped to lead the world toward broad recognition of Beijing's persecution of Uyghur and other Turkic Muslims in Xinjiang, its crackdown on all independent voices across China including Hong Kong, and its efforts to challenge the global enforcement of human rights. There were positive steps as well in trying to stop the Ethiopian government's atrocities in Tigray, the Myanmar junta's repression of pro-democracy voices, and the Rwandan government's renewed support for the M23 rebels in Congo.

But seeing the world largely through the prism of great-power competition, Biden gradually resurrected the double standards of his predecessors. In his quest to build a coalition in defense of Ukraine, he toned down his public references to democracy as a motivating factor for his foreign policy and increasingly acted without regard to democratic principles—as when he turned himself into a supplicant of the ruthless Saudi crown prince. His desire to build an alliance against China led him to close his eyes to Indian prime minister Narendra Modi's Hindu-nationalist attacks on Muslims and his suppression of critical voices—even honoring him with a June 2023 state visit at the White House. That left Biden open to the charge of defending democracy in Taiwan from a possible Beijing attack while ignoring Modi's attacks on democracy in India.

Biden's desire for help in curbing the arrival of asylum seekers at the southern U.S. border led him to soft-pedal the autocratic tendencies of Mexican president Andrés Manuel López Obrador and to revive some of Trump's policies. In the name of stability, Biden was far too soft on Egyptian president Sisi. And to avoid backlash from a powerful domestic constituency, Biden treated far too gingerly Israeli prime minister Benjamin Netanyahu as his far-right government deepened the apartheid that Washington would not name and pummeled and starved Palestinian civilians in Gaza after Hamas had killed and abducted civilians in Israel.

The selectivity of America's defense of human rights weakened U.S. influence on a set of values that are foundational at home, that Biden claimed to rely on abroad, and that are America's strongest asset in the geopolitical contests with Russia and China. The autocratic threat to democracy is the human-rights challenge of our time. Biden's inconsistency in meeting that threat, his failure to make the defense of human rights not only an important end but also an indispensable means, risked long-term damage to the human-rights cause in the name of short-term political calculations. It also makes it easier for a transactional Trump as he returns to the White House to abandon democracy—for example, as an essential part of Ukraine's future.

14

International Criminal Justice

There is much debate in international human-rights circles about what kind of sanctions should be imposed to deter or punish the most serious violators. The consensus today is that broad trade sanctions are insufficiently focused on the perpetrators and cause too much harm to ordinary citizens. We agreed and pursued more targeted efforts, whether blocking the means of abuse (military aid or arms sales) or pinpointing the perpetrator (for travel bans or asset freezes). By far the most targeted of sanctions, and the one that perpetrators are most likely to fear, is criminal prosecution.

Human Rights Watch has long understood that some prosecutions are essential for the defense of human rights. Justice is important as a matter of respect for the victims and their families. It represents a statement that society takes seriously their plight, that it will not sweep their suffering under the rug. The precedent or prospect of justice can deter would-be offenders from committing an atrocity and marginalize those who have been charged. Prosecutions individualize responsibility for atrocities, undercutting the tendency to blame entire ethnic or religious groups and hence the incentive for broad revenge. Perhaps most important, justice represents an effort to repair the moral fabric when it has been shredded.

Criminal justice works best when it takes place locally, but the more violent and abusive a government is, the less likely that local judges and prosecutors will dare to bring perpetrators to justice, let alone survive an attempt. International justice is admittedly a second-best option, but it is an essential backstop, one that came a long way during my time as a human-rights activist. In my early days, there was no prospect of it. The important World War II precedents, the Nuremberg and Tokyo tribunals, were ancient history. Although the UN Security Council theoretically could have created additional tribunals, the Cold War precluded the necessary consensus for decades. Over time, however, the opportunities to pursue international justice grew considerably. This, in turn, had a positive effect on national prosecutions.

Truth Commissions

Early on, in the absence of international options, efforts to bring abusive officials to justice occurred solely at the domestic level. The only post–World War II prosecutions of serious human-rights crimes until the 1980s were in Greece and Portugal after the overthrow of their repressive governments in 1975. In our initial years, efforts to establish accountability for mass atrocities often took the form not of prosecutions but of truth commissions. Because these were national institutions, and the perpetrators were frequently still around, the latitude for action was limited. The initial truth commissions, which arose mainly in Latin America as transitions occurred from abusive military dictatorships to more democratic rule, described the atrocities that had been committed but often did not even name the perpetrators. The Argentine National Commission on the Disappeared, for example, begun with the 1983 transition to civilian rule, published *Nunca Más* (Never Again) in 1984. It described the forced disappearances and torture of the 1976–1983 military dictatorship but did not assign responsibility for any of these crimes.

My colleague at the time, Juan Méndez, an Argentine human-rights lawyer who himself had been tortured by the military junta and later went on to become the UN special rapporteur on torture, argued that truth was often the only form of accountability that we could hope for, and its pursuit should not be compromised even if criminal prosecution was politically impossible. In the case of Argentina, the leading commanders were prosecuted, but only after having been discredited by their initiation and loss of the 1982 Malvinas/Falklands war.

In Chile, the 1991 report of the "Truth and Reconciliation Commission" (known as the Rettig Commission, after its chairman) on the atrocities committed by the military dictatorship of General Augusto Pinochet was similarly limited: it described many of the abuses but did not name the perpetrators. José "Pepe" Zalaquett, a respected Chilean human-rights lawyer who served on the commission and is credited as the report's principal author, felt that naming names would be too dangerous for an emerging democracy. Although a truth commission identifying someone as responsible for an atrocity was not the same as a criminal conviction, Zalaquett also felt that, because the commission was an official body, it was unfair to name names without due process.

The 1992–93 truth commission for El Salvador after that country's civil war did name names despite intense opposition from the government. A parallel Ad Hoc Commission called for the dismissal or transfer of 103 officers. Under pressure from the U.S. and European governments, the Salvadoran government was forced to comply. All the officers were soon dismissed from the military and barred from public office. That was an important step toward accountability. It foreshadowed the "lustration," or purification by removal of tainted officials, used in various post-Soviet Eastern European countries.

The South African Truth and Reconciliation Commission, which began in 1995 and examined repression under apartheid, offered formal amnesty to individuals if they described truthfully the full extent of their criminality. If they did not, they could, at least in theory if not always in practice, be prosecuted. Because South Africa's transition from apartheid was widely seen as successful, its truth commission for many years was cited as a model, sometimes in lieu of prosecution. In fact, the parallel emergence of international tribunals in the mid-1990s opened the door for not only truth but also justice, changing public expectations and political possibilities for how to respond to mass atrocities.

The Anfal

My first stab at international justice took place at a time when there was no available international criminal tribunal. It occurred in the aftermath of a 1988 genocide in which Iraqi forces under Saddam Hussein rounded up and executed between fifty thousand and one hundred thousand Kurdish men, women, and children. The Iran-Iraq War was coming to an end, and Saddam sought revenge because Kurdish rebels had collaborated with Iran. His forces used chemical weapons to chase rebels and villagers from the mountains of northern Iraq, collected them on the paved roads in valleys, trucked them to Iraq's western desert, and executed them, dumping their bodies in mass graves. The campaign was called the Anfal after a Koranic verse justifying pillage of the property of infidels.

During the 1991 uprising that followed Saddam's defeat in the first Gulf War, the Kurds secured eighteen tons of Iraqi secret police documents. With the help of Peter Galbraith, then a staff member of the U.S. Senate Foreign Relations Committee, we persuaded the U.S. military to transport these documents to the United States. Working with a small team, my colleague Joost Hiltermann, an experienced Dutch researcher and Middle East expert, spent two years combing through them to compile a detailed account of how the genocide was carried out. We also collected soil samples revealing chemical-weapons use, forensic evidence from mass graves, and testimony from some 350 survivors and witnesses. In 1993, Human Rights Watch issued a major report on the Anfal.

With no prospect of prosecution, and working with my colleague Richard Dicker, an American attorney whom I would later name to direct our new international justice program, we focused on the International Court of Justice in The Hague, often called the World Court. Unlike the later International Criminal Court, which is also in The Hague, the ICJ is a civil tribunal, which can render only civil judgments but not determinations of individual guilt or punishment. Moreover, the ICJ is empowered to resolve mainly disputes between states. No private individual can bring a case before it, and only states, not individuals, can be sued.

We invoked the widely ratified Genocide Convention, which

empowers the ICJ to resolve disputes between state parties concerning responsibility for genocide. Our goal was to obtain an ICJ ruling that the Iraqi government had committed genocide against the Kurds. That formal acknowledgment would be an important form of accountability. It might also be preceded by a protective order ("provisional measures") against ongoing Iraqi government persecution of the Kurds. But to obtain such a judgment, we needed a government willing to bring the case, which was easier said than done. Governments feared Saddam Hussein, who was seen as ruthless enough to retaliate through acts of terrorism. Governments also worried about the reaction of other Arab governments that might sympathize with Saddam—and wanted continued access to his and the region's oil.

Richard and I visited a series of capitals trying to find a government willing to serve as plaintiff. We carried the Human Rights Watch report detailing the genocide as well as a legal memorandum prepared by Lori Damrosch, a Columbia Law professor, which made the case that the Anfal campaign met the treaty definition of a genocide. We did not want to enlist the U.S. government for fear that its actions would be seen as a continuation of the Gulf War rather than a principled quest for justice. In addition, the U.S. government in ratifying the Genocide Convention had entered a reservation requiring Washington's consent before any ICJ case could be brought against it. Under rules for interpreting treaty obligations known as reciprocity, Iraq could have insisted on its own consent if the U.S. tried to bring a case against it.

We got furthest with the Netherlands, working through Foreign Minister Pieter Kooijmans and his colleagues. Because of the ICJ's location in The Hague, the seat of the Dutch government, it had a special interest in international justice, and it seemed willing to take the case, but not on its own. It wanted us to cobble together a consortium of governments willing to act in unison, and it wanted those governments to include some from the Global South.

We tried mightily. Among governments willing to consider the effort were several Scandinavian states, as well as Canada, Chile, and Costa Rica. But we were unable to find a government in Asia, Africa, or the Middle East, which is what the Dutch felt they needed for political cover. So, the effort died.

After the U.S. invasion of Iraq in 2003 and the capture of Saddam, an Iraqi special tribunal charged him with the Anfal genocide. But the case was never completed because he was convicted and executed after an unfair trial for the 1982 massacre of some 150 residents of the Iraqi town of Dujail following an assassination attempt. In a separate Iraqi trial, also unfair, Ali Hasan al-Majid, a cousin of Saddam known as "Chemical Ali" for his use of chemical weapons against the Kurds, was convicted, among other things, for his role in directing the Anfal genocide, sentenced to death, and executed.

Pinochet and Universal Jurisdiction

As noted, the doctrine of universal jurisdiction allows many of the most serious human-rights crimes to be prosecuted in any national court that is empowered to pursue such cases by its government. It was envisioned in the widely ratified Geneva Conventions of 1949, which require state parties to "search for" persons who have committed war crimes and to "bring such persons, regardless of nationality, before its own courts." The Convention Against Torture of 1994 requires state parties either to prosecute any suspected torturer found on their territory, regardless of where the torture took place, or to extradite the suspect to a country that will do so. Universal jurisdiction is what allowed the Israeli government in 1961 to try Adolf Eichmann in Jerusalem for Nazi-era atrocities.

The highest-profile universal jurisdiction case more recently was the October 1998 arrest in London of Chile's former dictator, Augusto Pinochet. The arrest occurred just months after the July 1998 adoption of the Rome Statute, the treaty creating the International Criminal Court, which provided an international forum when national prosecutors lacked the means or inclination to pursue a case. The ICC's statute made clear that once the court had jurisdiction, which would occur only for future crimes, a suspect's position as a government official would provide no defense against prosecution of atrocity crimes. But what about people like Pinochet, whose crimes preceded the ICC?

Pinochet's arrest came upon a warrant under the powers of universal jurisdiction issued by a Spanish judge, Baltasar Garzón, mainly for the Pinochet government's alleged torture and forced disappearances. When the British House of Lords, then Britain's top court, ruled that Pinochet was not immune from prosecution despite his status as a former head of state, my colleague Reed Brody, an American lawyer whom I had assigned to the case, called it a "wake-up call to tyrants everywhere." Although the British home secretary at the time, Jack Straw, ultimately cited health grounds to allow Pinochet to return to Chile rather than face extradition to Spain—a reason also later used by the Chilean Supreme Court to halt his prosecution—Pinochet's arrest and sixteen-month detention in London made clear that a tool had been revived to prosecute the most serious human-rights offenders even for crimes that fell outside the new ICC's jurisdiction.

Within Chile, the Pinochet case opened the door for hundreds of domestic prosecutions of Pinochet-era offenders. As Reed wrote, "Pinochet returned home to a changed Chile, one in which previously timid judges no longer regarded him as untouchable and were willing to look for the many chinks in his legal armor." Most important, the Chilean Supreme Court ruled that Pinochet's 1978 self-amnesty did not preclude prosecution of the crime of forced disappearance, of which there were more than one thousand victims, because disappearance is a continuing crime that does not benefit from an amnesty adopted before the missing person had been accounted for. By the time Pinochet died in 2006, he was under house arrest, having been investigated for both disappearances and corruption. Hundreds of his agents were convicted of human-rights crimes.

Initially, many universal jurisdiction statutes allowed considerable powers of prosecution. But in 2001, witnesses and survivors of the 1982 massacre of Palestinians at the Sabra and Shatila refugee camps in Beirut used Belgium's broad universal jurisdiction law to try to bring Israel's then prime minister, Ariel Sharon, to justice for having allowed the massacre by allied Lebanese militia to proceed when he had been a general commanding Israeli troops in Lebanon.

There was a strong reaction. After the Sharon case as well as a 2003 one against a U.S. military commander for civilian casualties in Iraq, Defense Secretary Donald Rumsfeld threatened that NATO headquarters would be moved from Belgium if the government did not repeal its universal jurisdiction law. Some European governments pared back their courts' authority to pursue universal jurisdiction cases. In addition, the International Court of Justice pronounced in 2002 that Sharon as a head of government had immunity from prosecution under universal jurisdiction. The court applied a ruling from 2000 that, unlike in proceedings before international tribunals, sitting heads of state and government, as well as foreign ministers, enjoy immunity before national courts applying universal jurisdiction to allow them to fulfill their functions as representatives of their state.

For many years, the United States permitted prosecution for crimes committed abroad only if the victim or perpetrator was a U.S. national. Non-Americans who committed war crimes against other non-Americans overseas could not be prosecuted in U.S. courts even if they were found in the United States. Putin's invasion of Ukraine prompted the U.S. government to accept universal jurisdiction to allow prosecution of anyone found in the United States who is accused of war crimes.

In recent years, a number of European prosecutors, aided by specialized war-crime units that we encouraged governments to establish, have begun to pursue universal jurisdiction cases against Syrian officials who are found in their country, usually after they snuck in as would-be refugees. One prominent case took place in the German city of Koblenz, where a former Syrian intelligence officer was convicted of crimes against humanity and sentenced to life in prison. Evidence and analysis from the International, Impartial, and Independent Mechanism, the international prosecutor without a court that we helped to establish for Syria, enabled local prosecutors to master the complexities of the Syrian repressive apparatus. Prosecutors also relied on the photographs taken by the former Syrian military photographer "Caesar," the work of exiled Syrian lawyers, and two of our reports. By February 2024, according to the UN's Commission of Inquiry on Syria, "diligent prosecutors in Europe have convicted more than 50 perpetrators of war crimes and crimes against humanity committed in Syria."

Similarly, French and Swiss prosecutors pursued universal jurisdiction cases against former commanders of Liberian armed groups. These were modest steps toward filling a complete justice void in Liberia, which had not prosecuted a single person for atrocities committed during its two civil wars of 1989–1996 and 1999–2003. In both cases, the suspects were found in the prosecuting country. (In May 2024, Liberia finally moved to establish a domestic war-crimes court for these atrocities.)

Even countries where universal jurisdiction laws allow charges against a suspect who remains abroad, most prosecutors have not filed such charges. In absentia trials are best avoided because their one-sided nature seems unfair, at least in the absence of a waiver by the suspect, but presence in a country should not be a prerequisite for investigations, charges, and arrest warrants. People who might be captured inside a country with a universal jurisdiction statute are rarely the most senior commanders responsible for mass atrocities. Where there is no International Criminal Court jurisdiction—such as for Syria, when the country in question has not joined the court, and the UN Security Council will not provide jurisdiction—the only way to pursue these more senior figures is for national prosecutors to use universal jurisdiction despite the suspect's lack of physical presence.

That has begun to happen. In June 2018, the German Federal Court of Justice issued an arrest warrant for Jamil Hassan, at the time the head of the Syrian Air Force Intelligence Service, who was accused of overseeing torture, rape, and murder of "at least hundreds of people between 2011 and 2013." Hassan was not in custody and his alleged crimes had no connection to Germany; this was a pure universal jurisdiction case. In February 2019, Hassan was discovered to have traveled to Lebanon for medical care, but he was under Hezbollah's protection, so Lebanese authorities ignored a German request for his extradition.

In April 2023, French authorities charged three Syrian nationals, all existing or former senior advisers to Assad, for war crimes and crimes against humanity. However, two of their alleged victims had been a French father and son, providing a connection to France that obviated the need for universal jurisdiction. Similarly, federal prosecutors near Chicago were reported in April 2023 to be investigating senior Syrian officials for the torture and execution of an American aid worker.

French investigative judges in November 2023 charged Assad and other senior Syrian officials with war crimes and crimes against humanity for the August 2013 sarin attack in Eastern Ghouta. A lawyer in the case told me he hoped to avoid the International Court of Justice ruling rejecting universal jurisdiction charges for sitting heads of state by using "extraterritorial" rather than universal jurisdiction, based on a French group that was affected by the sarin attack. Even if that strategy fails, the French case provides an opportunity to reconsider the ICJ ruling. Although the capture and trial of senior Syrian officials does not seem imminent, the charges send an important signal of international determination to apply the rule of law to their mass atrocities.

Imagine if senior officials around Putin had been charged, and arrest warrants issued, as a result of universal jurisdiction investigations into the war-crime bombing of hospitals, schools, and other civilian institutions in Syria's Idlib province. We found evidence supporting such a case. Would that clear statement of disapproval have deterred Putin from pursuing the same war-crime strategy in Ukraine? In any event, Germany now seems to be pursuing universal jurisdiction investigations of Russian war crimes in Ukraine, supplementing the International Criminal Court charges.

Hissène Habré and Alberto Fujimori

After the Pinochet case demonstrated the power of universal jurisdiction to pursue dictators who had once seemed untouchable, Reed Brody, whom I had appointed as the organization's advocacy director, sought to apply it to Hissène Habré, the president of Chad from 1982 to 1990. Working closely with Chadian rights groups, Reed, beginning in 1999, played a key role in driving forward the prosecution of Habré.

A Chadian truth commission found that during Habré's eight-year rule his government tried to eliminate perceived opponents, killing some forty thousand people, and committing systematic torture. Because Habré was seen as a useful ally against Libya's Gaddafi, the French and U.S. governments, the latter under Ronald Reagan, supported him.

Souleymane Guengueng, a mild-mannered, deeply religious civil servant, barely survived three years of imprisonment while watching dozens of his cellmates succumb to torture and disease. He vowed that if he ever emerged alive, he would bring his tormentors to justice. He founded a victims' association and compiled hundreds of case files on Habré's victims. In 2001, Reed and Souleymane discovered an abandoned cache of political-police records, which, together with the testimony of Souleymane and other survivors, formed the foundation of the case against Habré.

When an insurgency ousted Habré from power, he fled to Senegal, reportedly with $12 million from the Chadian treasury. He used the funds to build a network of supporters in Senegal, particularly among Islamic religious groups. As a result, the Senegalese government was not eager to prosecute him. Reed and his partners led a complicated campaign that enlisted, at various stages, Senegal, Belgium, the UN Committee against Torture, the African Union, and, with the support of Belgium, the International Court of Justice.

Senegal's president from 2000 to 2012, Abdoulaye Wade, was uninterested in pursuing the case. Things changed when Macky Sall assumed the Senegalese presidency in 2012. His first justice minister, Aminata Touré, made the Habré case a cornerstone of her campaign against official impunity. Other key actors in the case included Jacqueline Moudeina, a Chadian lawyer who survived a 2001 grenade attack from a Habré henchman to lead the victims in battle, shrapnel still in her leg, and Clément Abaifouta, who had been forced to bury detainees in mass graves and took over the victims' association when death threats forced Souleymane into exile.

Finally, in July 2015, a special court in Senegal began Habré's trial, which provided a rare opportunity for victims to confront their perpetrator. One woman described how Habré had raped her. Habré was convicted and sentenced to life in prison for crimes against humanity. His conviction showed the importance of persistence (and of Human Rights Watch being willing to stick for the long term with efforts like this when I felt there was a sufficient chance of success to warrant the investment). The trial was also the first time that the domestic court of one country had convicted the former leader of another country for human-rights crimes. Habré died in custody in August 2021 at the age of seventy-nine. Reed wrote a compelling book about the lengthy campaign, *To Catch a Dictator*.

We also played a central role in the Peruvian government's conviction of Alberto Fujimori, who served as president from 1990 to 2000. He was notorious for his 1992 self-coup, in which he overturned the constitutional order and proceeded down a path of massive corruption and serious abuses, including allowing a death squad, the Colina Group, to operate out of the Army Intelligence Service. His main accomplice was Vladimiro Montesinos, who served both as a personal adviser and as head of the National Intelligence Service.

Fujimori was of Japanese ancestry, so when evidence emerged in 2000 implicating him and Montesinos in large-scale corruption, he fled to Japan, where he claimed citizenship and evaded extradition back to Peru on human-rights and corruption-related charges. However, overconfident, he arrived in Chile in November 2005, intending to make a triumphal return to neighboring Peru. Instead, Chilean authorities detained him. The big issue was whether firm evidence could be produced that demonstrated Fujimori's personal responsibility for the corruption and atrocities of his government.

José Miguel Vivanco and I dispatched to Peru Maria McFarland Sánchez-Moreno, at the time a researcher with Human Rights Watch's Latin American program. Maria is a Peruvian American lawyer who grew up in Peru, in part under Fujimori's presidency. She compiled a report detailing evidence that implicated him personally in both corruption and death-squad murders. In September 2007, Chile's Supreme Court, known for its high standards, ordered Fujimori extradited to Peru, relying on much of the evidence and analysis that Maria had supplied. In April 2009, Fujimori became the first civilian president in the world to be tried and convicted of human-rights violations by his country's national court. He was convicted for the killing of twenty-five people in two separate massacres carried out by the Colina Group, in 1991 and 1992, and sentenced to twenty-five years in prison. In December 2023, he was released at age eighty-five on a humanitarian pardon. He died in September 2024.

Bosnia, Rwanda, and Cambodia

The Pinochet, Habré, and Fujimori cases show the importance of national courts for bringing abusive officials to justice, but often, as I said earlier, national courts are too weak or compromised to play this role. In those cases, international tribunals are essential. The first two since Nuremberg and Tokyo were for the former Yugoslavia and Rwanda.

The genocides in Bosnia and Rwanda occurred at a time when the fissures of the Cold War were healing. For the first time in its history, the UN Security Council was acting in relative harmony. With our active encouragement, the council established international criminal tribunals for each situation. We became an important source of evidence and analysis for their prosecutors.

Both tribunals were remarkably successful. The International Criminal Tribunal for the former Yugoslavia obtained custody of all 161 people whom it charged. It convicted and sentenced 90 of them, including the former Bosnian Serb military and political leaders, Ratko Mladic and Radovan Karadzic, both sentenced to life imprisonment for genocide, among other crimes. The former Serbian leader, Slobodan Milosevic, was put on trial but died of natural causes before his prosecution was completed. The International Criminal Tribunal for Rwanda, as I said, convicted and sentenced sixty-two people, including former prime minister Jean Kambanda (life imprisonment for genocide).

International jurists were fully in charge of both tribunals, but sometimes the UN has set up hybrid courts involving a mixture of national and international jurists. The tribunal set up in 2006 to address the mass atrocities—the "killing fields"—of the Khmer Rouge from 1975 to 1979 was largely unsuccessful because the Cambodian government of Prime Minister Hun Sen was allowed a controlling role. Hun Sen had been a Khmer Rouge commander, so he was determined to block any broad judicial inquiry that could implicate him. In 2014, the court convicted two senior Khmer Rouge officials, Nuon Chea and Khieu Samphan, and sentenced them to life in prison. Hun Sen had offered each de facto amnesty but reversed course under domestic and international pressure. Two others were charged but did not stand trial. One, Ieng Sary, died, and the other, Ieng Thirith, was released with dementia. Pol Pot, the Khmer Rouge leader, died before the tribunal was created.

The only other person convicted by the tribunal was Kaing Guek Eav, known as Duch, the head of the notorious Tuol Sleng interrogation center in Phnom Penh, where at least fourteen thousand people were detained and tortured before being murdered. He was sentenced to life in prison in February 2012 and died in custody in 2020. I visited Tuol Sleng during an Asia Watch visit to Cambodia in 1990. Our delegation was told we were the first human-rights group to visit the country since the fall of the Khmer Rouge. Thousands of inmates were photographed upon arrival at Tuol Sleng, and their faces and fearful stares covered the walls. I found the experience haunting, a chilling reminder of the utter ruthlessness of the Khmer Rouge.

Hun Sen in effect allowed many mass murderers complete impunity. Given that the Khmer Rouge were responsible for an estimated two million of Cambodia's eight million people having been killed or having died from disease, starvation, or forced labor, the handful of convictions were not enough. Nor did they justify the $330 million spent on the tribunal. The lesson is that a partisan, or implicated, government cannot be entrusted with control of a justice institution, even when the tribunal has significant international participation.

Charles Taylor

A more successful hybrid model was the Special Court for Sierra Leone, established in January 2002 as a joint endeavor between the United Nations and the government of Sierra Leone but with international jurists having a majority vote in decision-making. The court charged thirteen people, four of whom died before proceedings could be completed. The remaining nine were convicted. Its most prominent defendant was the former president of neighboring Liberia, Charles Taylor. We played an important role in documenting his crimes, promoting the establishment of the Special Court, and pressing for his arrest.

Taylor had served in the government of the prior Liberian president, Samuel Doe, before fleeing to the United States in 1983 after allegedly embezzling nearly $1 million. He was held in a Massachusetts county jail but escaped a year later, allegedly with help from the U.S. government because he was seen as more pro-American than the Soviet-leaning Doe. In 1989, he launched a rebellion to topple Doe. The ensuing seven-year civil war was estimated to have killed up to two hundred thousand people. In 1997, Taylor was elected president of Liberia. Reflecting a remarkable resignation to his atrocities when there was no prospect of justice, his supporters' rallying cry was: "He killed my ma, he killed my pa, I don't wanna know. I'm still gunna vote for him."

Taylor ultimately did face criminal charges, but for his role in Sierra Leone, where he backed a rebel group known as the Revolutionary United Front (RUF) that was notorious for cutting off the limbs of its captives. Its atrocities were carefully documented, despite significant risk, by Corinne Dufka, an American former war photojournalist who wanted to try to help the people she photographed. She became a Human Rights Watch researcher who was based for many years in Freetown, the capital of Sierra Leone. With her upbeat personality and seeming fearlessness, she had a remarkable ability to talk her way past dangerous checkpoints to reach key victims and witnesses. Taylor sold the RUF arms in return for diamonds it mined. In June 2003, the Special Court unsealed charges against him for war crimes and crimes against humanity for aiding and abetting RUF atrocities.

Two months later, the deeply discredited Taylor resigned as president of Liberia, facing both military pressure in Liberia and political pressure from the George W. Bush administration. He fled to Nigeria, where President Olusegun Obasanjo had offered him exile, ostensibly to stop the bloodshed in Liberia. Taylor seemed to envision a comfortable retirement at a seaside villa. We launched a campaign, led by my colleagues Richard Dicker and Elise Keppler in close coordination with Corinne, to press Obasanjo to surrender Taylor for trial before the Special Court.

In June 2004, I met with Obasanjo and a bevy of his ministers at his residence in Abuja, the Nigerian capital, over a sumptuous breakfast. We discussed a range of topics constructively, but when it came to Taylor, Obasanjo, sitting at the head of the long table, shut the conversation down. He similarly dismissed a media campaign that we mounted in Nigeria, as I made the rounds of the leading newspapers and broadcast outlets. I felt like I was hitting my head against the wall.

We set about trailing Obasanjo whenever he traveled outside Nigeria, distributing press releases on the need for Taylor's surrender. We worked with West African and international human-rights groups to spur debate across the region about the importance of bringing Taylor to justice. We urged officials from the U.S. government and the European Union to raise the issue with Obasanjo. When he appeared at the Council on Foreign Relations in New York during the annual September opening of the UN General Assembly, we peppered him with questions about Taylor. At one such appearance, he looked at my colleague Minky Worden and asked, "Didn't you ask that last year?" We tried to make it impossible for him to go anyplace without confronting the Charles Taylor question.

Finally, Obasanjo suggested he would consider turning Taylor over to Liberia in response to a request from the "duly elected government" there, referencing Ellen Johnson Sirleaf, Liberia's new president and Africa's first female president. Through numerous press releases, letters, and meetings, we encouraged her to request Taylor's surrender. She hesitated out of fear for Liberia's precarious security situation, but in early March 2006, she did what we had asked, citing enormous international pressure. A week later, the Nigerian government announced that Taylor could be turned over to Liberia, but said that the Liberian government would have to fetch him. Taylor disappeared two days later.

The key to Obasanjo relenting was his desire to visit the White House to see George W. Bush, whose acquiescence he wanted to his plan to amend the Nigerian constitution to permit him to run for a third presidential term. Obasanjo was scheduled to meet with Bush two days after Taylor absconded, so we urgently pressed the White House, directly and through congressional allies, to condition the meeting on Taylor's arrest and surrender for trial. Just hours before the scheduled meeting, vigilant guards at a remote border post between Nigeria and Cameroon were said to have noticed Taylor in the back seat of a Range Rover with Nigerian diplomatic plates (and large quantities of cash and drugs) and arrested him. Taylor was soon on a plane to The Hague, where, for security reasons, the Special Court held his trial.

Corinne testified as a witness, describing the pattern of RUF atrocities as it benefited from Taylor's weapons. The Special Court convicted him of eleven counts of planning, aiding, and abetting war crimes and crimes against humanity. He was sentenced to a fifty-year prison term, which he is serving in a British prison. He was the first former head of state to be convicted by an international or hybrid tribunal since the Nuremberg trials.

The Taylor trial was enormously significant for West Africans who had long believed that the powerful, no matter how murderous, were above the law—that, as described by a youth who had witnessed his father murdered by the RUF, "justice is not meant for people like us." Moreover, that Taylor was convicted of "aiding and abetting" atrocities by arming an abusive force in another country should stand as a warning to officials in such countries as Iran, Belarus, and North Korea who have been providing arms or support to the Russian military as it commits war crimes in Ukraine—or, for that matter, to U.S. officials for having transferred arms to Saudi Arabia when they were used to bomb civilians in Yemen or to Israel as it bombed Palestinian civilians in Gaza.

The International Criminal Court

Today, the most important institution of international justice is the International Criminal Court. Its founding treaty was finalized in 1998 after five weeks of difficult negotiations in Rome. My colleagues and I were deeply involved in the process, our contributions led masterfully by Richard Dicker. The challenge we faced was that many of the world's major powers—especially the United States, Russia, and China—did not want a court that might prosecute their own citizens.

Under what is known as the principle of complementarity, the ICC was designed as a backstop, obtaining jurisdiction only if national governments are unable or unwilling to prosecute a suspect. This was different from the Yugoslav and Rwandan tribunals, which had the authority to override national prosecutorial efforts. As a result, governments could in theory avoid ICC prosecution of their citizens by prosecuting their own serious offenders. But because they might differ about when prosecutions were warranted, the strongest military powers did not want to risk being restrained by the ICC. They were unwilling to move beyond the victors' justice of the Nuremberg and Tokyo tribunals.

The U.S. government, in particular, claimed to want an ICC but, as I said, was determined to avoid the possibility of the ICC ever pursuing a U.S. citizen. It proposed requiring that a government give its consent before one of its nationals could be prosecuted (which Washington was unlikely to provide), insisting that the UN Security Council (where the U.S. government had veto power) must approve any investigation of prosecution, or demanding that only nationals of countries that had ratified the ICC treaty could be prosecuted (U.S. ratification was improbable). All were recipes for impunity. As Bill Clinton's secretary of defense, William Cohen, told Richard and me in May 1998 in his Pentagon office, he would oppose the U.S. government joining the ICC "unless there was an ironclad guarantee that no U.S. servicemember would ever be tried by the Court." Needless to say, that was not our conception of justice.

Richard followed the blueprint established during the land mines campaign by building a broad coalition of governments and civic groups that were committed to a court that would apply equally to everyone. The land mine campaign operated outside the United Nations to avoid the paralysis of its "consensus" rules, while the ICC campaign stayed under UN auspices but under a decision-making process that allowed votes. Initiated by the small World Federalist Movement, the coalition of nongovernmental groups became known as the Coalition for the International Criminal Court, a network with members in 150 countries. Richard also helped to promote an informal collection of more than 60 small and medium-sized governments from all parts of the world, known by the bland name of the "like-minded group," which included most of the established democracies—all European Union states except France (and Britain until Tony Blair's election in May 1997), as well as Canada, Australia, and New Zealand. It also included many newer or emerging democracies, among them Argentina, Chile, South Korea, Malawi, Senegal, and South Africa. Many of these younger democracies, having recently made the transition from authoritarian rule, appreciated the importance of an international institution of justice that by operating beyond the coercive reach of local tyrants could serve as an insurance policy against future abuse.

The Clinton administration's efforts to exempt U.S. nationals from the ICC's jurisdiction led to four points of contention during the Rome negotiations. The big question was whether the like-minded states would withstand pressure from Washington and insist on a court that did not exempt Americans and nationals of other nonmember states.

The first controversy concerned whether the UN Security Council should be permitted to halt an ICC prosecution. The U.S. delegation, you will remember, proposed that before the ICC could begin an investigation, the Security Council would have to expressly authorize it. Because the United States, as a permanent Security Council member, could block approval by exercising its veto, this proposal would have allowed Washington to prevent any investigation, including of its own soldiers and citizens and those of its allies. The other four permanent members—Britain, France, China, and Russia—would have had the same veto power. As a result, only nationals of a handful of pariah states would have been likely to face prosecution. The Security Council's historic inability to establish even temporary tribunals for such mass murderers as Saddam Hussein or Idi Amin suggested that many obvious candidates for prosecution would escape justice.

In negotiating sessions prior to Rome, the Singaporean government offered a compromise that ultimately prevailed. It granted the Security Council the power to halt an ICC prosecution but only if it acted in its usual manner—by the vote of nine of its fifteen members and acceptance of that vote by *all five* permanent members. As a result, no single permanent member could use its veto to block a prosecution. A Canadian amendment that was accepted limited this power to one-year renewable periods.

A second controversy: Most governments in Rome agreed that a prosecution could begin after a case was referred to the court either by the Security Council or by a government that had ratified the ICC treaty. But, as we've seen, the Security Council had often been unwilling to act even in the face of horrendous atrocities, and individual governments at that stage (though less so later) were notoriously reluctant to formally accuse one another of serious human-rights abuses (as I discovered in trying to convince a government to mount even a civil case of genocide against Iraq). That reluctance would be all the greater if the nationality of a suspect was American. In addressing the Rome conference in June 1998, I cited my frustrating experience with Iraq to stress the importance of the ICC prosecutor being empowered to initiate prosecutions even when states might find it inconvenient. The like-minded governments agreed.

Clinton officials objected. They cited Ken Starr, the U.S. independent counsel whose investigation led to the impeachment of Clinton, as an example of a "rogue prosecutor" who might unjustly pursue an American. At first, they were joined by the British and French governments, but both were satisfied by an Argentine-German proposal, ultimately adopted, that all decisions by the prosecutor to launch an investigation or prosecution on his or her own would be subject to review by a three-judge panel of the court.

The third controversy involved whether restrictions should be placed on the ICC's definition of war crimes. Because genocide and crimes against humanity involve by their nature widespread or systematic atrocities, the U.S. government was less worried about being accused of committing them. But given the frequent deployment of U.S. military personnel in armed conflicts overseas, they might commit a war crime—if, for example, a soldier killed a prisoner, a pilot deliberately bombed civilians, or an artillery gunner fired indiscriminately on a civilian neighborhood. In most such cases, the Pentagon could avoid ICC jurisdiction under the principle of complementarity by prosecuting members of its own forces, since U.S. military doctrine clearly prohibits these acts. But the Pentagon worried about conduct that was less clearly criminal.

Of special concern was the rule of proportionality, which prohibits a military attack anticipated to cause incidental civilian loss of life that is "excessive" compared to the expected "concrete and direct military advantage." This imprecise rule could implicate activity that U.S. military commanders considered lawful, but the ICC might not. The Gulf War bombing of Iraq's electrical grid arguably killed a disproportionate number of civilians, including the thousands said to have died because of the resulting loss of refrigeration, water purification, and other necessities of modern life. No one was ever prosecuted for it, but if the ICC had existed, might it have found that someone should have been?

To avoid prosecution in borderline situations, U.S. negotiators successfully redefined the proportionality rule for ICC purposes to prohibit attacks that injure civilians only when such harm is "*clearly* excessive" in relation to "the concrete and direct *overall* military advantage anticipated" [my italics]. The effect was to tip the balance considerably against the ICC finding a proportionality violation, though that didn't stop the ICC in March and June 2024 from charging four Russian military commanders with causing disproportionate harm to Ukrainian civilians by attacking electrical infrastructure.

The United States, joined by France, also proposed that governments be allowed to join the ICC while specifying that their citizens would be exempt from war-crime prosecutions. Since many governments could be expected to exercise this option, the Rome delegates rejected it. But as a compromise, a "transitional provision" in the treaty was adopted allowing governments upon joining the court to exempt their citizens from the court's war crimes jurisdiction for seven years. That allowed a hesitant government to reassure itself about the court's treatment of war crimes without permanently denying the court jurisdiction over its citizens for these crimes. Only France and Colombia ever availed themselves of it.

The most divisive issue faced by the Rome delegates was the question of which situations would give rise to ICC jurisdiction. The U.S. government was content with the Security Council being able to impose jurisdiction on a nonmember state because it could block action with its veto, but what rules should govern when a situation is referred by another government or an investigation is initiated by the prosecutor?

The German delegation noted that genocide, crimes against humanity, and war crimes are crimes of universal jurisdiction, meaning that those who commit them can be tried in any authorized court worldwide, even if the court has no connection to the crime. Germany argued that governments should be able to delegate to the ICC the power that universal jurisdiction confers in principle on their own courts. This was entirely sensible—and it would have ensured ICC jurisdiction wherever the most serious crimes occurred—but it was a step too far for the Rome delegates.

South Korea put forward a more limited proposal that gained broad support. It would have granted the ICC jurisdiction when any one of four governments concerned with a crime had ratified the ICC treaty or accepted the court's jurisdiction over the crime. Those were: (1) the government of the suspect's nationality; (2) the government of a victim's nationality; (3) the government that gained custody of the suspect, or (4) the government on whose territory the alleged crime took place. Each category would increase the possibility that the court could act.

Speaking for the Clinton administration, Ambassador David Scheffer, who as the nation's first ambassador-at-large for war crimes led the U.S. delegation in Rome, insisted, as I mentioned, that the court should be empowered only if the government of the suspect's nationality had accepted its jurisdiction, which would have allowed the U.S. government to prevent ICC prosecution of Americans. And because most abusive governments also would probably not ratify the treaty, the ICC would have been unable to prosecute many of the most important suspects.

Clinton administration officials were not mollified by the fact that, under the doctrine of universal jurisdiction, American soldiers are already vulnerable to prosecution in foreign courts. Washington has many ways to dissuade individual governments from attempting to prosecute an American—from diplomatic and economic pressure to the threat of military force. But the administration feared such deterrents would be less effective against an international institution like the ICC. Instead, Defense Secretary William Cohen met with his German counterpart to discuss it. We do not know what he said, but according to his leaked talking points, he was prepared to threaten to reduce the number of U.S. troops in Europe if the South Korean proposal gained support.

The Rome delegates agreed to eliminate two of Korea's proposed routes for ICC jurisdiction—when the treaty is ratified by the state of the victim's nationality or by the state that gains custody of the suspect—and that concession was damaging. Because a state could not confer jurisdiction on the ICC by arresting a suspect, a leader who commits atrocities against his own country's citizens might travel widely without being brought before the ICC—so long as his own government had not ratified the treaty (and assuming the Security Council did not act). One can imagine a genocidal killer free to shop in Milan, seek medical treatment in London, or vacation in the south of France, while the ICC stood by powerlessly. And if the victim's nationality could not be used for ICC jurisdiction, the ICC could not act against the leader of a nonratifying government that slaughters refugees from a ratifying state who seek shelter on its territory (again, assuming Security Council inaction). The Rome delegates retained two grounds for ICC jurisdiction: that the government of the suspect's nationality had ratified the treaty, which the U.S. government accepted, or that the government on whose territory the crime took place had ratified it, which it did not. The territorial "hook" could catch a leader who is responsible for atrocities abroad.

In weakening the Korean proposal, the Rome delegates felt the need to make concessions to Washington in the hope that the U.S. government would at least tolerate the court. Instead, the court was weakened, and Washington still opposed it. When the negotiations in Rome concluded in July 1998 without an effective exemption for Americans, the U.S. government stood in embarrassing isolation. The vote in favor of the statute for this historic institution of justice was 120 to 7. The only governments to join the United States in opposing it were China, Iraq, Israel, Libya, Qatar, and Yemen.

As occurred with the land mines and cluster-munitions treaties, the like-minded states ended up having enough clout, determination, and moral authority to prevail, though the final treaty adopted in Rome was full of compromises.

One of my early contributions to the ICC was by happenstance. I was in Ottawa in 1998 to see Lloyd Axworthy, the Canadian foreign minister who was a key ally for, among other things, securing the land mines treaty and advancing the ICC. He later joined our board of directors. After the meeting, while in the Foreign Ministry building, I took the opportunity to visit Philippe Kirsch, the ministry's legal adviser, who had played a helpful role during the initial stages of the ICC negotiations. The final negotiations in Rome were soon to take place, and I asked him whether he planned to attend. To my horror, he said no, he would have to be in The Hague at the time to argue a dispute with Spain before the International Court of Justice about fishing off Canada's eastern shore. I understood that fishing is big business in Canada, but I was nonetheless appalled. Could he not manage to spend a few days in The Hague, I asked, before going to Rome for the final ICC negotiations? He not only made it to Rome, but when the designated Dutch chair of the negotiations fell ill, Kirsch was chosen to replace him—a task that he handled with great skill. In tribute, he was then named the first president of the ICC, meaning its chief judge.

—

In a series of debates sponsored by the Council on Foreign Relations, I discussed the merits of the ICC with John Bolton. A fellow graduate of Yale Law School, John thought the possibility of an American being prosecuted by the ICC was anathema; so did Henry Kissinger, whose views I challenged in *Foreign Affairs*.

I said it was not obvious why it would be so objectionable for the ICC to be allowed to prosecute an American. For example, if a U.S. citizen were to murder someone on the streets of London, Washington could hardly object if British authorities prosecuted the American. So why should Washington object if British authorities, unable for whatever reason to prosecute the kinds of atrocities handled by the ICC, were to send an American suspect to The Hague? The U.S. government and its backers rejected that analogy. Washington clearly preferred to deal with national prosecutors, who, as I said, it evidently felt would be easier to cajole and pressure.

As for fears that dictators might take over the ICC and politicize it, the incentives worked in the opposite direction, because joining the ICC requires submitting to its jurisdiction.

Although the ICC does not offer jury trials, as constitutionally required for trials in the United States, it does provide all the elements of a fair trial as defined by international human-rights law. U.S. courts have not objected to extraditing suspects to the many countries that offer fair trials without juries. Fears that U.S. troops might not take part in humanitarian interventions if they were subject to scrutiny by an international prosecutor had already been undermined by the 1999 intervention on behalf of Kosovo, where NATO troops acted despite being subject to scrutiny by the international Yugoslav tribunal.

In the end, as in Rome, Washington seemed to be worried most not about war crimes committed at the initiative of low-level soldiers, which Pentagon lawyers would presumably prosecute, but war crimes that might be authorized on high. That possibility is hardly farfetched because it happened with the George W. Bush administration's torture policy. U.S. justice authorities are reluctant to prosecute senior officials, so there might well be reason for the ICC to step in. Indeed, the scenario might even be more likely for the United States, where all federal prosecutors report to the president through the attorney general, than in countries where prosecutors are treated as judicial officials independent of the executive.

On December 31, 2000, in the waning days of the Clinton administration, David Scheffer, acting on Clinton's direction, went to the UN in New York to sign the treaty, although the administration never submitted it to the Senate for ratification. Given the requirement of a positive vote by two-thirds of the Senate, that would have been futile. After George W. Bush came to office in January 2001, he named Bolton an under secretary of state and later U.S. ambassador to the UN. In May 2002, Bolton "unsigned" the treaty—something that we did not even know was possible. I imagined Bolton arriving at the UN with a big eraser to remove Scheffer's signature, although in fact he sent a letter. No succeeding president ever disowned that letter.

The signing of a treaty means that a government vows not to undermine it. The Bush administration did the opposite. The treaty gained the requisite sixty adherents for the court to be formally launched in July 2002. The next month, the Bush administration pushed through Congress the American Servicemembers' Protection Act, which authorized the U.S. president to use "all means necessary and appropriate" (including military force) "to bring about the release of any U.S. or allied personnel being detained" by the ICC. Allies were defined broadly to include personnel from any "NATO member country, a major non-NATO ally (including Australia, Egypt, Israel, Japan, Jordan, Argentina, the Republic of Korea, and New Zealand), or Taiwan." Because the ICC is based in The Hague, detractors dubbed the law the Hague Invasion Act.

The Russian government seemed to use this outrageous law as a precedent when in March 2023 the ICC charged Putin for war crimes in Ukraine. Former Russian president Dmitry Medvedev, who had become the deputy chairman of Russia's Security Council, threatened ICC judges with "a surgical application of a hypersonic" missile.

The Hague Invasion Act also provided for the withdrawal of U.S. military assistance from countries that ratify the ICC treaty and restricted U.S. participation in UN peacekeeping efforts unless U.S. personnel were given immunity from ICC prosecution. In June 2002, as the ICC treaty was about to come into force, the Bush administration vetoed continuation of the UN peacekeeping force in Bosnia in a quest to obtain permanent immunity for UN peacekeepers. Then, under a U.S. threat to veto all UN peacekeeping operations, the UN Security Council felt compelled to dictate that no UN peacekeeper who was the national of a state that had not joined the ICC could be sent to the ICC for a renewable period of one year. The U.S. government stopped seeking renewal of that exemption when it feared it would lose the vote shortly after it was revealed in April 2004 that U.S. soldiers had abused prisoners at Abu Ghraib in Iraq.

In July 2002, U.S. officials launched a global campaign to arm-twist governments to promise to send any American wanted by the ICC to the United States, not The Hague. These bilateral immunity agreements violated the legal obligations of ICC states to cooperate with the ICC. Ultimately, 102 governments signed them, although many never legally adopted them.

In September 2002, I addressed the first meeting of the ICC's Assembly of States Parties. At that stage, the ICC members—many of whom were close U.S. allies—were still trying to figure out how to address Washington's hostility to the court, particularly given the Bush administration's preoccupation with responding to the September 2001 terrorist attacks. I said:

> If the Bush administration has its way, it would rip up the Rome Treaty and substitute its own version—what we might call the Washington Treaty. The Rome Treaty reflects a vision of universal justice. The Washington Treaty reflects the view that justice is for everyone else, not the superpower. The Rome Treaty reflects a global order maintained by troops operating under enforceable international standards. The Washington Treaty sees no role for enforceable international standards. The Rome Treaty recognizes the need for an independent court of last resort when national justice systems fail. The Washington Treaty sees the superpower's justice system as infallible. . . .

> What is at stake is the very legitimacy of the ICC. As the

Bush administration is fully aware, a court that exempts the world's superpower risks losing its legitimacy. That is the goal of certain extremists in Washington who seek to exercise the United States' unprecedented military power without the inconvenient constraints of international law—or at least international law interpreted by anyone other than themselves.

I concluded by reminding the delegates that they had the power to stand up to the Bush administration. Bush was trying to rally support for his planned invasion of Iraq: "At a time when the U.S. government is the supplicant," I said, "when it is seeking global support for its military plans, the nations of the world should at the very least insist that military action by anyone be waged under independently enforceable human-rights standards."

—

Domestic politics helped to ease the Bush administration's frontal attack on the ICC. We began reporting on atrocities in the Darfur region of Sudan beginning in 2004. I traveled there that year with Jemera Rone, our researcher. I was able to speak with the victims of ethnic cleansing—people who were homeless, destitute, and very afraid. I saw many of them in the vast Kalma camp for displaced people, and watched as new tents were added on the periphery for expected arrivals. About fifty thousand people lived there at the time, and the population soon would more than double.

At one point, Jemera and I were surrounded by some two hundred people who had just fled an attack on their village by the notorious Janjaweed militia. The villagers described how, after so much ethnic cleansing, the militia members seemed surprised to find anyone still there. The attack on the village began a short time later. The Janjaweed murdered three men, sending the rest of the villagers fleeing. Over the next few days, the Janjaweed systematically looted the village of every valuable possession.

The Janjaweed clearly were operating with Sudanese government acquiescence, but when at the end of our trip Jemera and I visited Khartoum and pressed for an end to these attacks, government officials pretended that they had nothing to do with them. Sudanese officials grew visibly agitated when I told them that they could be prosecuted for their crimes if they did not stop the killing. We deployed the evidence of government sponsorship that we unearthed to build pressure on the UN Security Council to deploy peacekeeping troops in Darfur to protect civilians and to refer the situation in Darfur to the ICC.

Sudan never joined the ICC, so the only way that the ICC could obtain jurisdiction over the atrocities being committed in Darfur was by referral from the UN Security Council. Because the conflict in Darfur came to be understood in the United States as an attack by "Arab" Muslim pastoralists on "African" Christian and animist agriculturalists, the Christian evangelical community became deeply concerned about Darfur. That being an important part of Bush's political base, his administration in March 2005 allowed a referral to proceed, forswearing a veto (abstaining) in the Security Council.

It helped that, as Bush's second term began in January 2005, Condoleezza Rice had taken over as secretary of state. She sidelined Bolton, allowing a more moderate view of the ICC to be asserted by John Bellinger, who became the State Department's legal adviser. As Bellinger later wrote, "President Bush decided to agree to refer the Darfur situation to the ICC because he was more concerned about the atrocities in Darfur than the theoretical possibility of prosecutions of Americans in the future." The ICC, in turn, charged various Sudanese officials including then president Omar al-Bashir.

President Obama took this a step further. In February 2011, as troops under Libyan leader Muammar Gaddafi were firing upon peaceful protesters, the U.S. government voted *in favor* of a unanimous UN Security Council resolution referring Libya to the ICC. The Obama administration also lent U.S. support to securing the surrender to the ICC of Bosco Ntaganda, who fought with the M23 rebel group in eastern Congo, and Dominic Ongwen, of the Uganda-based Lord's Resistance Army, known for kidnapping children and forcing them to become soldiers.

Things got considerably worse under President Trump. ICC plans to move forward on an investigation of war crimes by Israeli and Palestinian forces set him off. His objection was consistent with long-time U.S. efforts to protect Israeli forces from any accountability for their war crimes. He was also upset by an announced investigation of war crimes in Afghanistan. The Trump administration feared that it might address torture there by U.S. forces under Bush, where several early detainees died in CIA custody, and some of the most brutal and dehumanizing mistreatment of detainees occurred.

Any war crime committed in these two situations was eligible for ICC action because Israeli and American prosecutors had not addressed them, so the principle of complementarity was not implicated. As I described, the court had jurisdiction over crimes committed in Israeli-occupied territory because in November 2012 the UN General Assembly had recognized "Palestine" as a nonmember observer state; Palestine in January 2015 accepted the ICC's jurisdiction for crimes committed on its territory; and in May 2018, Palestine referred the situation in its territory to the ICC for investigation. Similarly, Afghanistan acceded to the ICC's treaty in February 2003. Neither the United States nor Israel has joined the court, but American and Israeli offenders could still be prosecuted under the long-feared territorial jurisdiction.

Even the Yugoslav Tribunal, which the UN Security Council created with U.S. support, exercised territorial jurisdiction. The chief prosecutor decided not to formally investigate NATO's bombing campaign in Serbia, noting that "although some mistakes were made by NATO, the Prosecutor is satisfied that there was no deliberate targeting of civilians or unlawful military targets by NATO during the campaign." U.S. lawyers probably had not focused on the possibility of American suspects when authorizing the Yugoslav Tribunal, giving primary attention to the ethnic cleansing then under way. Regarding the ICC, the concern was front and center.

As I mentioned, Trump was so exercised by the ICC prosecutor's actions that in September 2020 he imposed financial sanctions on the prosecutor, Fatou Bensouda, and a deputy—outrageous interference in the independence of a justice institution. It was surpassed only by the Russian government under Putin, which in May 2023 issued an arrest warrant for Bensouda's successor as chief prosecutor, Karim Khan, in retaliation for Khan having charged Putin with war crimes in Ukraine.

Biden ended Trump's sanctions, and the Ukraine war led to an evolution in the U.S. position on territorial jurisdiction. The Biden administration was so enraged by Russian war crimes in Ukraine that it endorsed an ICC investigation of those crimes, even though Russia never joined the court. The Ukrainian government had granted the court jurisdiction for crimes committed on its territory. When in March 2023 the ICC charged Putin and his children's rights commissioner with forcibly deporting Ukrainian children to Russia, Biden called the charges "justified." But if such territorial jurisdiction is acceptable for a Russian suspect, it should also be acceptable for an American or Israeli one. The Biden administration has not explicitly embraced that logical conclusion, but a major shift seemed to have occurred.

During a March 2022 video conversation, I mentioned this apparent shift to Antony Blinken, Biden's secretary of state, noting that I appreciated the evolution. He obviously understood what I meant—and, I suspect, agreed with it—but did not respond. Even prominent Republicans such as Senator Lindsey Graham, one of the foreign-policy leaders in the Senate, shifted. Joined by a long bipartisan list of sponsors, he secured unanimous adoption in March 2022 of a resolution endorsing the ICC prosecution of war crimes in Ukraine. Graham said that Putin's "war crimes spree" had "rehabilitate[d] the I.C.C. in the eyes of the Republican Party and the American people." Other Republicans visited the ICC prosecutor to support the prosecution of Putin. In July 2023, Biden overrode Pentagon objections and ordered the U.S. government to share evidence of Russian war crimes in Ukraine with the ICC. As I described, when in May 2024 Khan sought arrest warrants for Israeli ministers Netanyahu and Gallant, Blinken claimed summarily that the court lacked jurisdiction but, to his credit, didn't press the point, and the White House rejected a congressional effort to impose sanctions on Khan. A senior Biden official told me off the record that objections to territorial jurisdiction had been abandoned.

—

One major test of the ICC was its efforts to secure the arrest of Omar al-Bashir while he was president of Sudan. The ICC had charged Bashir with genocide, crimes against humanity, and war crimes committed during the conflict in Darfur. To show his contempt, Bashir attempted to travel a good deal, mostly to other African nations. Many African states were ICC members and thus obliged to arrest him and send him to The Hague should he show up. Accordingly, some African leaders shut the door on him, but others allowed him to visit when he played on their fears that they might someday also face prosecution.

My colleague Elise Kepler, an American attorney, led Human Rights Watch's campaign to counter his efforts to undermine the ICC. She worked with a broad coalition of African civic groups that banded together to defend the court. They made clear that while abusive African leaders might not like the court's attention, their victims, existing and would-be, applauded it, even as many of these groups also encouraged the court to expand its work outside of Africa.

When it became known that Bashir was planning to attend an African Union conference in Nigeria in 2013, local activists held public protests and sued in the domestic courts to compel the government to arrest him. Working with these activists, we pitched in with a media campaign. Bashir left the country less than twenty-four hours after arriving without giving his scheduled speech.

When Bashir visited South Africa in 2015 for an African Union summit, the South African president at the time, Jacob Zuma, welcomed him. But local activists persuaded a South African court to order the government to arrest him. South African officials claimed they did not know where he was, until he had left the country. Zuma then announced that South Africa would withdraw from the court, but the South African High Court ruled that Zuma would first have to consult parliament. South Africa stayed a member.

Bashir was overthrown in a 2019 coup and imprisoned on corruption charges. Joined by Mausi Segun, the thoughtful, principled Nigerian lawyer who was our Africa director, I traveled to Khartoum in February 2020 to meet with the military coup leader, General Abdel Fattah al-Burhan, who at the time was chairing the Sovereign Council of Sudan, the collective body running the country. We also met with various civilian officials. It was my first trip to Sudan since my 2004 visit to Darfur. In the interim, the various Janjaweed militia had been combined and renamed the Rapid Support Forces, under the command of General Mohamed Hamdan Dagalo, known as "Hemedti." They rivaled in power the formal Sudanese army under General Burhan and would soon descend into armed conflict with it.

The meeting with Burhan took place when he was trying to present a friendly face to potential Western donors, so when I asked him whether he would be willing to surrender Bashir to the ICC, he promised cooperation—which I immediately repeated to the media to try to cement it. For a while, Burhan allowed ICC investigators to enter Sudan and collect evidence in Darfur to bolster their case, but the cooperation later waned. In April 2023, Bashir was reported to have been transferred from a Sudanese prison to a military hospital.

—

Many of the shortcomings attributed to the court—such as the failure to prosecute the officials responsible for war crimes in Syria or the Chinese government's persecution of Uyghurs in Xinjiang—are due to its lack of jurisdiction. Those governments never ratified the Rome Treaty, and referral by the UN Security Council was blocked by the Chinese and Russian vetoes. But even when the court has had jurisdiction, it has not done enough. The ICC remains an important global statement, a warning to would-be perpetrators of mass atrocities that their ability to compromise their national justice systems is no guarantee against prosecution. That has helped to push some national governments, such as Colombia and Guinea, to pursue prosecutions that they otherwise might have ignored. Yet there have been too few prosecutions by the ICC itself. As of November 2024, after more than two decades, the ICC had issued arrest warrants for only fifty-six people and convicted just eleven. Twenty-seven suspects remained at large. And the ICC had not convicted a single government official, whether current or former. All of those convicted had been members of nongovernmental armed groups—essentially, warlords.

Although the judges of the court render verdicts and make legal rulings, the most important ICC official is the chief prosecutor, of whom there have been three. The first, during the court's initial decade, was an Argentine lawyer, Luis Moreno Ocampo. He saw his job primarily as defending the court from attacks by the U.S. government, which he did with eloquence, spending much time touring the world to promote the court. He was a less successful prosecutor. He lacked the patience to conduct the detailed investigations needed to prove guilt beyond a reasonable doubt. While that is not the standard for filing a charge—"substantial grounds to believe that the person committed the crimes charged" is sufficient—a wise prosecutor has the trial in mind before filing charges. Moreno Ocampo was willing to proceed with only the evidence needed to charge. As a result, several of his most high-profile cases fell apart.

His successor, for the next decade, was the Gambian jurist Fatou Bensouda, who had served as Moreno Ocampo's deputy. She was more sober, less flamboyant, and devoted her attention to improving the professionalism of the office. Yet she proved incapable of bringing investigations to completion.

Moreno Ocampo was criticized for charging only Africans—a fact that, as I said, some African leaders exploited to undermine support for the court—but that focus was primarily the product of referrals by African governments and the UN Security Council. To minimize opposition in the court's early years, he pursued mainly these government-backed cases rather than starting prosecutions on his own initiative. Bensouda opened several investigations outside of Africa, including ones in Afghanistan and Palestine—the two that led Trump to impose sanctions on her—as well as the Philippines, Venezuela, Georgia, and Bangladesh (focusing on the Rohingya refugees from Myanmar). But by the time her tenure concluded, she had not brought charges against any non-Africans. However, she showed herself willing to assert her independence and resist pressure from the major powers by pursuing inquiries that they did not want.

The current prosecutor is a British barrister, Karim Khan. Of the three chief prosecutors, he is the most experienced inside an international courtroom, having served as both a prosecutor and a defense attorney. He therefore has a clearer sense of the investigative work required. When I met him in The Hague in June 2022, he told me that he recognized the office was spread too thin and vowed to close certain investigations that seemed less fruitful. He brought charges against three people for alleged war crimes as part of Russia-backed forces in Georgia during the 2008 armed conflict over South Ossetia. Most significant, he launched a major investigation of war crimes in Ukraine and, as I said, charged Putin and another Russian official for the war crime of abducting Ukrainian officials, and four Russian military commanders for the crime of targeting Ukraine's electrical infrastructure. More charges were expected.

Khan was regarded as attentive to the views of Western powers, particularly London and Washington. An indication of that came early in his tenure when he revived his office's investigation in Afghanistan after the Taliban retook power in August 2021. Aware of the sensitivity of a possible investigation of U.S. torture in Afghanistan (even though Biden had lifted Trump's sanctions), Khan announced that his investigation would prioritize crimes by the Taliban and the Islamic State.

Yet Khan did better on the other major test of his independence: the Palestine investigation. Despite the U.S. government's expressed outrage, he sought arrest warrants for, as I mentioned, Israeli ministers Netanyahu and Gallant, as well as three senior Hamas officials. I expect the move will go a long way toward quieting critics who claimed the ICC was for only non-Western powers. I can only hope that the U.S. government comes around to recognizing the importance of that development for the rule of law.

—

The minority that may be most despised by the people of its country is the Rohingya of Myanmar, a population that until a few years ago had numbered some one and a half million people, mostly in Myanmar's western Rakhine State. Their persecution stems from their religion—they are Muslims in a largely Buddhist nation—and their skin color, which is darker than most others in Myanmar. Even though many Rohingya families have been in Myanmar for generations, the Rohingya were excluded from Myanmar's list of 135 officially recognized ethnic groups and denied citizenship. Many people in Myanmar insisted on calling them Bengalis, suggesting that they were not really from Myanmar but had immigrated from Bangladesh.

I tried to address their plight during a February 2014 visit to Myanmar, joined by a delegation of our board members, at a time when we thought the days of military rule were waning. Among various government officials with whom we met was then president Thein Sein, a former general. The meeting took place at the luxurious presidential palace (Myanmar is a poor country) in the surreal, recently constructed capital of Naypyidaw. The capital was built in the middle of nowhere to maintain a distance from more populated parts of the country in the event the people revolted.

Dressed in a simple tunic amid the gold-plated splendor of a large meeting room, Thein Sein was polite in receiving us. We discussed the importance of constitutional reform to ease military control of the ostensibly civilian government and to permit Aung San Suu Kyi, the Nobel Peace Prize laureate and opposition leader, to run for president despite her British husband. Neither occurred. Three years later, the Myanmar army went on a rampage of murder, rape, and arson to chase 730,000 Rohingya to Bangladesh. Then, in February 2021, the army ended the country's short period of elected government with a coup, followed by a ruthless crackdown.

At first glance, the ICC seemed to have no jurisdiction to address the plight of the Rohingya. Myanmar never ratified the ICC treaty, and China as well as possibly Russia would have vetoed any attempt at the UN Security Council to refer Myanmar to the ICC. But ICC prosecutors pursued a novel argument for jurisdiction. One of the crimes that the ICC can prosecute as part of a widespread or systematic attack on a civilian population is deportation. Although the arson, rape, and murder that forced the Rohingya to flee took place in Myanmar, the process of deportation was not completed until they stepped foot in neighboring Bangladesh, meaning that Bangladesh's ratification of the ICC treaty could provide the court with jurisdiction. In November 2019, the court authorized an investigation.

The authors of those atrocities were the same ones who carried out the 2021 coup. Although the ICC does not have jurisdiction over the crimes that followed the coup, it will be heartening to see the same military leaders prosecuted for whatever crime they can be pursued for. In July 2023, Karim Khan visited the Rohingya refugee camps in Bangladesh and promised justice.

In a parallel effort, my colleague Pam Singh supported the government of the tiny West African state of Gambia to frame Myanmar's atrocities against the Rohingya as genocide before the International Court of Justice. That lawsuit used the same theory that Richard Dicker and I tried but failed to invoke in the case of Saddam Hussein's genocide against Iraqi Kurds. That is, under the Genocide Convention, the ICJ is empowered to resolve disputes relating to the responsibility of a state for genocide and to order provisional (meaning protective) measures. Again, this was not a criminal case against individuals but a civil suit against the government.

Gambia played this role as a member of the Organisation of Islamic Cooperation—a collection of Muslim-majority states. The

OIC rarely stood up for human rights, given that many of its members were highly abusive, including its most dominant members, Saudi Arabia and Pakistan. It thus had been deplorably apathetic before the Chinese government's persecution of Uyghur and other Turkic Muslims in Xinjiang. But with the far less powerful government of Myanmar, the OIC was willing to defend Rohingya Muslims. And Gambia, despite its small size and distance from Myanmar, had just emerged from a repressive dictatorship and was eager to play a positive human-rights role. Gambia's justice minister, Abubacarr Tambadou, had worked as a prosecutor on the Rwanda Tribunal and said that the atrocities against the Rohingya reminded him of the genocide against the Tutsi in Rwanda.

Gambia sought immediate court action to stop potential ongoing genocide against the six hundred thousand Rohingya who still lived in Myanmar, many confined to poorly supplied camps that we found were characterized by apartheid. In December 2019, Aung San Suu Kyi, to her discredit, defended the military before the court, evidently hoping that the army would then countenance her candidacy for president in November 2020 elections. It never did, and then detained her after the coup and lodged numerous criminal charges against her. In January 2020, the court unanimously ordered the Myanmar military not to resume its persecution of the Rohingya.

The Netherlands and Canada drew on the Myanmar precedent to try something similar for Syria. With ICC jurisdiction barred by the Russian and Chinese vetoes, they sued the Syrian government before the International Court of Justice for violating the Convention Against Torture. The convention provides that any dispute between states concerning its "interpretation or application"—meaning whether it is being violated—can be resolved by the ICJ after attempted negotiation and arbitration. Such a suit has been tried only once before, in Belgium's 2009 suit against Senegal to force it to extradite or prosecute Hissène Habré for overseeing large-scale torture. That was part of what pushed Senegal to prosecute Habré. In November 2023, the court issued a preliminary ruling against Syria and ordered it to take steps to prevent further torture.

The UN Human Rights Council in September 2018 created an Independent Investigative Mechanism for Myanmar, modeled on the IIIM set up by the UN General Assembly for Syria. Like its

Syrian counterpart, the IIMM will collect and preserve evidence and build cases for wherever prosecution ultimately can take place, such as in national courts pursuing universal jurisdiction. It has already indicated that military atrocities since the coup amount to crimes against humanity. A criminal case for genocide has been filed in Argentina under its universal jurisdiction law, similar to the brief effort that my colleagues and I made in Argentina to pursue the Saudi crown prince for torture and war crimes.

In January 2024, in a case brought by South Africa, the ICJ ordered Israel to refrain from various acts that might implicate the rights of Palestinians in Gaza under the Genocide Convention. The court focused on Israel's bombing and besieging of Palestinian civilians as well as inflammatory statements made by certain senior Israeli officials. The ICJ issued additional protective orders in March and May 2024.

—

Although it would seem inherently desirable to bring the perpetrators of mass atrocities to justice—a right to which victims and their families are entitled—that pursuit has its detractors. Some object to its considerable expense. One need not advocate the kinds of summary executions meted out to the likes of Muammar Gaddafi or former Romanian president Nicolae Ceaușescu to suggest that a less refined procedure might suffice. People carrying out mass atrocities do not accord their victims anything remotely like a fair trial, so why are they entitled to one? But once the international community is involved, it does not want to cut human-rights corners; delivering justice requires not only a verdict but also a process that is fair, one that reaffirms human rights rather than violating them anew.

Some critics of international justice, such as the writer David Rieff, suggested that prosecutions do more harm than good—that if the primary aim is to end human suffering, it might be better to forgive and forget, to give perpetrators an effective amnesty. Henry Kissinger made a similar argument in the name of "national reconciliation." In the case of dictators, the argument goes, the threat of prosecution pushes them to cling to power longer than they might have. Gareth Evans, the former Australian minister and CEO of the International Crisis Group, made this contention with respect to the former Zimbabwean dictator Robert Mugabe, claiming that if not for the capture and prosecution of former Liberian president Charles Taylor, Mugabe might have resigned earlier.

But it is rare for dictators to step down before they have lost all capacity to cling to power. There is a long list of tyrants who were forced to relinquish power without an amnesty, among them Philippine president Ferdinand Marcos, Haitian president Jean-Claude Duvalier, Ethiopian president Mengistu Haile Mariam, Ugandan president Idi Amin, Paraguayan president Alfredo Stroessner, and Zairian president Mobutu Sese Seko. The most that some could do was to flee the country and hope that justice would not catch up with them. Granting amnesty suggests that dictators can get away with mass atrocities simply by insisting that amnesty is the price for stepping down. Calling that "national reconciliation" ignores the coercion behind it. As Reed Brody often put it, with Hissène Habré's forty thousand victims in mind, "If you kill one person, you go to jail. If you kill forty people, they put you in an insane asylum. You kill forty thousand people, you get a comfortable exile with your bank account in another country."

Even the failure to prosecute can send that signal. To use Gareth's example, when in 2017 an elderly Robert Mugabe was forced to resign under threat of impeachment (for having tried to arrange for his wife to succeed him), he was replaced by Emmerson Mnangagwa, a senior Mugabe lieutenant. But because Mugabe had never been prosecuted for his brutality, Mnangagwa largely continued it. In any event, the creation of the ICC rendered this debate largely moot. A national government might grant amnesty for crimes, but the ICC has no duty to respect it unless the UN Security Council orders it to defer prosecution.

The argument for amnesty has slightly more weight in the context of an armed conflict, but in my view, not enough to prevail. The unconditional surrenders that led to the Nuremberg and Tokyo trials are rare. More commonly, both sides decide at some stage that the human and economic costs of continued battle are not worth it. At that point, it is conceivable that one warring faction might insist on amnesty as a condition for laying down its arms. But as in the case of dictatorships, sending the signal that atrocities can be bargained away with an amnesty only encourages more.

By contrast, the threat of prosecution can deter war crimes. In 2007 and 2008, Laurent Nkunda, at the time the leader of a Rwandan-backed rebel group in eastern Congo, regularly called our Congo researcher, Anneke Van Woudenberg, to discuss his concern that the ICC might be targeting him because of abuses by his troops. The ICC never seriously investigated him, but his worry illustrated precisely the kind of deterrent effect that international justice can have. Similarly, in 2013, the Obama administration reportedly warned Rwandan officials that they could face ICC prosecution if they did not stop supporting the murderous M23 rebel group in eastern Congo. That helped persuade the Rwandan government to stop for nearly a decade.

Criminal charges can also delegitimize and marginalize a leader, as occurred with Charles Taylor in Liberia, Omar al-Bashir in Sudan, and the Lord's Resistance Army in Uganda. The LRA largely disappeared as a force once its leaders were charged.

In the case of Ukraine, French president Macron suggested that it may be necessary to halt the ICC's prosecution of Putin as the price of a peace agreement. But Putin has shown himself utterly untrustworthy. Would his word on a peace agreement mean anything when he had already ripped up the Budapest Memorandum of 1994, in which the Russian government agreed to recognize Ukraine's sovereignty within its existing borders in return for it relinquishing Soviet nuclear weapons on its soil? A de facto ceasefire should suffice.

—

The involvement of the ICC, with its refusal to countenance amnesty, can also exert useful pressure for justice, as illustrated in Colombia. One horrible element of the country's decades-long civil war was the phenomenon of "false positive" executions. Between 2002 and 2008, army brigades across Colombia, under pressure from superiors to show results, lured young men to remote locations, often with promises of work, executed them, and then dressed them up as rebels, pretending they had been enemy combatants killed in action. At least three thousand and possibly sixty-four hundred were killed, one of the worst mass atrocities in the Western Hemisphere in recent decades.

These killings occurred under the right-wing government of

President Álvaro Uribe Vélez, with whom we understandably had a contentious relationship. My colleague José Miguel Vivanco was one of the most prominent critics of Uribe's deplorable human-rights record and pressed him on the false-positive killings repeatedly in one-on-one meetings. Uribe agreed to the meetings because of José Miguel's regional stature and our international influence. I saw Uribe only during public appearances, such as at the Council on Foreign Relations in New York, when I probed him on the issue to no good effect.

A better interlocutor was Juan Manuel Santos, who succeeded Uribe as president in 2010. He had been defense minister under Uribe starting in 2006, as credible reports of false-positive killings mounted. Although Santos at first was slow to recognize and investigate these executions, he ultimately did, and the Defense Ministry made some policy changes to reduce body-count incentives.

I had constructive meetings with Santos twice during that period at the Munich Security Conference. But the killings started to decline only with a major media scandal about them in late 2008. Based on the investigations that Santos had supported, the government dismissed twenty-seven army officers, and a key general was forced to resign. After our 2015 report implicated top army generals in these executions, then president Santos fired the head of the army.

When our board of directors visited Colombia in 2011, Santos and I, seated at the front of a Presidential Palace auditorium in Bogotá, had a lengthy discussion about human-rights issues in the country. The false-positive killings had stopped by the time he became president, but would he pursue prosecution? In June 2004, the ICC prosecutor had initiated a preliminary examination in Colombia. Because of the nature of Colombia's ratification, the ICC had jurisdiction over war crimes committed only since November 2009, although it could address earlier crimes against humanity. Still, the ICC's move exerted positive pressure for prosecution.

Santos's biggest achievement as president was to oversee a 2016 peace agreement with the main rebel group, the FARC, for which he won the Nobel Peace Prize that year. Under the deal, rebels who confessed to their crimes would serve no prison time but instead be sentenced to two to eight years of community service, while subject to modest and vaguely defined "restraints on rights and liberties." This soft-glove treatment was deemed necessary to secure rebel agreement to the accord. Santos insists he would never have countenanced an amnesty, but the fear that an amnesty would have sparked closer involvement by the ICC prosecutor helped him to maintain that position.

The deal applied the same treatment to military officials who were responsible for war crimes, including the false-positive killings. That was not necessary to induce the Colombian government to sign the accord—Santos had the authority to do that on his own—but he feared military opposition if he did not act as he did. His administration at first proposed to move the false-positive cases from the civilian to the military justice system but backed down after criticism from us. But he acquiesced to pressure from the military to allow a watered-down definition of command responsibility that had the effect of shielding senior officers.

The deal was far from ideal, and we complained about its relatively soft version of justice. But it was better than using the military justice system or allowing those "most responsible" for atrocities to escape with no restriction on their liberties, both of which we opposed. The key leverage we had was to point out that the lack of prosecution might trigger ICC action. Fatou Bensouda, the ICC chief prosecutor at the time, had even written to the Colombian Constitutional Court with these concerns in mind. In October 2021, with the peace deal including its justice provisions being implemented, Karim Khan, the current ICC chief prosecutor, formally closed the preliminary examination.

—

Perhaps the most prominent example of the tension between peace and justice arose in the context of the November 1995 Dayton peace negotiations over the Bosnian conflict. These negotiations were led by Richard Holbrooke, Bill Clinton's envoy, who was a diplomat of enormous energy and intellect. I was fortunate to befriend him before his sudden death in 2010. (Holbrooke could be surprisingly witty: when I brought one of my daughters to a Christmas party that he hosted with his wife, the author and former Human Rights Watch board member Kati Marton, he observed that my daughter had combined "two impossible things"—she was beautiful and looked like me.)

As the Dayton negotiations were about to begin, I met with Holbrooke to urge him to resist an amnesty. He was sympathetic—as was U.S. secretary of state Warren Christopher—but he worried that he might have to offer an amnesty to secure an accord. The U.S. government shared that concern. Although Madeleine Albright, when she was U.S. ambassador to the UN in New York, helped to persuade the UN Security Council to create the Yugoslav Tribunal in May 1993, Western support for it once it was established was initially tepid out of fear that prosecutions would obstruct efforts to negotiate a peace agreement. In fact, even though in July 1995 the Yugoslav Tribunal had already filed charges against the Bosnian Serb military leader, Ratko Mladic, and the Bosnian Serb political leader, Radovan Karadzic, Serbian president Slobodan Milosevic never insisted on an amnesty, and the Dayton Peace Accord made no mention of one. That was arguably made possible only because the indictment of Mladic and Karadzic had marginalized these two extremist figures, who might have demanded an amnesty. They didn't dare attend the negotiations for fear of arrest. That enabled Holbrooke to insist on negotiating with only Milosevic.

The Dayton accord did not end Western governments' skepticism about justice. NATO troops deployed in Bosnia as peacekeepers were at first reluctant to arrest people whom the Yugoslav Tribunal had charged, for fear of retaliation. Through early 1997, NATO troops had failed to arrest a single suspected war criminal. As a result, we launched an "Arrest Now!" campaign that helped to bolster those within the Clinton administration who wanted arrests and contributed to changing NATO policy. The ensuing arrests, far from disrupting peace, removed from the scene some of the figures who were most likely to cause problems. It took years, but ultimately even Karadzic and Mladic were located in hiding, arrested, sent to The Hague, and, as we've seen, convicted.

In 1999, during the NATO bombing campaign against Serbian and Yugoslav forces, the Yugoslav Tribunal charged Milosevic for crimes against humanity in Kosovo. Human Rights Watch provided evidence for six of the seven incidents of mass murder for which

Milosevic was originally charged. It was the first indictment by a fully international tribunal of a sitting head of state. Because the armed conflict in Kosovo was still raging at the time, the tribunal also became, by its own description, "the first international law enforcement agency to respond to massive crimes in real-time," an act repeated by the ICC for Ukraine and Palestine.

In 2000, Milosevic resigned the presidency in the face of protests over his refusal to accept that he had lost the election that year. We urged the U.S. government to condition financial assistance to the former Yugoslavia on its cooperation with the Yugoslav Tribunal. When the new Yugoslav government of Prime Minister Vojislav Kostunica resisted sending indicted suspects to The Hague, we pressed high-ranking members of the U.S. Congress, the National Security Council, and the State Department not to let aid go forward until those conditions were met.

In early 2001, with U.S. aid at risk, the Yugoslav government authorized Milosevic's arrest on domestic corruption charges. The U.S. government then decided to disburse its bilateral aid but postponed deciding whether to participate in a multilateral donors' conference at which much larger amounts of aid were at stake until the Yugoslav government surrendered Milosevic to The Hague. On June 28, one day before the donors' conference, Milosevic was handed to the tribunal.

His trial began in 2002, and Fred Abrahams, the Human Rights Watch researcher who had led an investigative team that posted some fifty "flash" bulletins during the Kosovo war, was one of the witnesses against him. Cross-examined directly by Milosevic, Fred dramatically recounted how he had sent Milosevic copies of our reports about atrocities being committed by Serbian forces against Kosovar Albanians. That helped to establish that Milosevic was on notice of the crimes being committed by troops under his command. Milosevic died in 2006, as I said earlier, while his trial was still under way.

Because of the net-positive effect of prosecution on the prospects for peace, UN guidelines adopted under Secretary-General Ban Ki-moon provide that UN mediators "cannot endorse peace agreements that provide for amnesties" for the most serious human-rights crimes. That is the right call.

Reflections and the Challenges Ahead

Among the many human-rights challenges that I have described, the contest between autocracy and democracy is now at the forefront of the modern human-rights struggle. Autocrats claim that democracies are too slow, too messy, too divisive to address today's challenges. Strongmen, they say, can act decisively without the delays and diversions of democratic debate. They would have us believe that autocracy is ascendant, democracy is in decline.

That is wrong. Indeed, if you put yourself in the shoes of an autocrat, it is a hostile world out there. To begin with, the dangers of autocratic rule have become starkly apparent. Autocrats tend to surround themselves with sycophants. They discourage debate, let alone dissent. They want an echo chamber, not a public discussion. As a result, they are prone to make big mistakes.

The world's two most prominent autocrats, Vladimir Putin and Xi Jinping, have become Exhibits A and B for the perils of unchecked power. The images of yes-men surrounding Putin and Xi have been on full display. For Putin, it was his Security Council members shaking in their seats as they tried to parrot his lines to justify the invasion of Ukraine. For Xi, it was the seeming automatons at stiff attention during the October 2022 Communist Party Congress, the antithesis of a deliberative chamber.

With no one close to these tyrants apparently willing to disagree or deliver bad news, Putin invaded Ukraine, thinking it would be a picnic. The Russian military, riddled by corruption, turned out to be adept mainly at targeting civilians and civilian structures. Unchallenged by a free opposition, Putin focused on enriching himself and his cronies at the expense of building an economy that was not primarily dependent on oil and gas extraction. In the case of China, there were Xi's lengthy, rigid "zero-COVID" lockdowns, abruptly reversed after nationwide protests, with no preparation and attendant substantial loss of life. Xi's prioritization of the Chinese Communist Party's power led him to disfavor independent parts of the economy needed to drive growth, from elements of the tech sector to ordinary consumers.

Democracy is no guarantee against poor governance, but it at least allows policy decisions to be publicly considered. Decisions are more likely to be wise when informed by the free flow of information and unfettered debate. That is true for ordinary decisions of government. It is all the more true for some of the major political challenges facing the world today, including climate change, poverty and inequality, and artificial intelligence.

As people see that unaccountable rulers prioritize their own interests over the public's, the popular demand for rights-respecting democracy remains strong. In country after country—Iran, Sri Lanka, Myanmar, Thailand, Sudan, Russia, Belarus, Nicaragua, Poland, Uganda, Venezuela—large numbers of people in recent years have taken to the streets, even at the risk of being arrested or shot. There are few popular rallies for autocratic rule.

It used to be that autocrats would hold "managed elections"—electoral contests in which some political competition was allowed, but the playing field was so tilted in favor of the autocrat that his victory was largely ensured. These were not terribly credible events, but they helped the autocrat maintain a veneer of electoral legitimacy. The small chance of losing a managed election was worth taking as a way to defuse protests against a government that simply clung to power without any pretense of a popular mandate. Some autocrats—including Viktor Orbán of Hungary and Recep Tayyip Erdogan of Turkey—still manage to pull off these exercises. But these days, most autocrats do not even risk managed elections. Poland's autocratic party, PiS, tried and failed in October 2023. Venezuela's Nicolás Maduro tried in July 2024 and, when he apparently lost, covered up the results.

By locking up most political opponents, preventing opposition political parties from operating, blocking rallies, and censoring the media, autocrats increasingly resort to zombie elections. That was the desperate strategy of Putin in Russia, Museveni in Uganda, Daniel Ortega in Nicaragua, Hun Sen in Cambodia, Alexander Lukashenko in Belarus, Abdel Fattah El-Sisi in Egypt, and Kais Saied in Tunisia. Their victory was assured, but they gained no legitimacy from the charade. That is a risky long-term strategy.

Yet if democracies are to prevail, democratic leaders must do more than spotlight the autocrats' shortcomings. They must make a stronger, positive case for democratic rule. That means doing a better job of meeting national and global challenges, of ensuring that democracy delivers on its promised dividends for all parts of society. It means standing up for democratic institutions such as independent courts, a free press, robust legislatures, and vibrant civil societies, even when that brings unwelcome scrutiny. And it demands elevating, rather than degrading, public discourse; acting on, rather than flouting, democratic principles; and unifying, rather than dividing, citizens. But if democratic officials are unable to summon the visionary leadership that this era requires, they risk fueling the frustration and despair that are fertile ground for autocrats.

It is sadly ironic that as autocratic rulers discredit themselves in the eyes of their people, a contingent of far-right politicians in established democracies is embracing autocratic platforms. A disturbing number of politicians are gaining electoral support with autocratic-like, anti-rights platforms. Often affirming "traditional values" or advancing a narrow definition of "the nation," they might decry the dangers of immigration, to the point of shredding the right of people fleeing war and persecution to have their claims to asylum fairly considered. They might find it politically profitable to demonize LGBT people as threats to traditional values, articulate a retrograde vision for women, or indulge racist theories that the white population is being "replaced."

Such programs of intolerance would exclude significant segments of society from the basic rights that are essential to democracy. After all, democracy requires not only elections but also government that is limited and directed by people who are free to exercise their rights.

Human-rights defenders like to point out that none of our rights are secure if the rights of anyone are being violated. But a disturbing number of Western politicians do not accept that syllogism. By portraying segments of society as threats to the community rather than members of it, autocrats seek to justify depriving them of their rights, assuming that mistreating these supposed outsiders will not affect the rights of people still deemed on the inside—indeed, that it is necessary to protect them. In part this reflects a more materially advanced Western world, in which people are less concerned about obtaining the physical necessities of life and so give greater priority to cultural or identity issues that often lie behind these claimed threats. In part it reflects the attributes of the modern era—the greater mobility, the faster pace of change, the parallel social isolation—which can be disconcerting, leaving people open to messages that their community is endangered. In part it reflects a growing sense by some people that they are being left behind, that opportunities for a better life have become constricted, that members of the governing elite are ignoring them, that they are regarded with contempt rather than the respect they seek and deserve. People who feel snubbed by democracy are ripe for the autocrat's appeal. Ironically, this trend is abetted by the identity politics that has come to dominate much progressive thought, because that, too, prioritizes differences in securing respect for rights over membership in a community.

None of these developments is easy to remedy. The forces that rend our society are powerful. In deeply divided societies, it can be difficult to secure the governing majority needed to address major problems effectively, which only aggravates the sense that democracy is not delivering. To defend democracy, we must address this threat at its core. It is not enough to speak about the importance of rights. We must also repair the social fabric on which rights depend. To regard even unpopular minorities as worthy of rights requires countering the autocrats' politics of fear to promote recognition that we are all members of a national or political community. It requires progressives, too, to affirm a national community even as they defend parts of that community whose rights are neglected or suppressed.

Yet there are few places where this vital work can be done. We seem to live in silos, where we talk to people who share our political views but ignore, or even demonize, those who differ. People self-divide by the television they watch, the social media they consume, the religious institutions they frequent (or not), even the places where they live. There seem to be fewer civic spaces that cross these divides. Our challenge is to find opportunities to build ties with those who differ from us, to reconstruct the sense of community that is a prerequisite to democracy.

The methodology that I've outlined here is useful for exerting pressure on governments that fall short of public expectations for moral conduct. But as shown by our work to ban land mines and cluster munitions or to uphold the rights of women and LGBT people, the methodology can also be used to shape public morality. That requires fighting demonization of unpopular minorities by giving them a human face, challenging their asserted otherness by spotlighting a common humanity. It requires critiquing the autocrats' self-serving sleights of hand, such as their creation of enemies and their rhetoric of hate as substitutes for practical programs of governance or positive visions for the future. It requires elaborating what returning to supposed traditional values would mean for the vast majority who do not sit atop the social hierarchy that is being eulogized. And it requires reminding people of the dangers to everyone from the tyranny of an asserted majority, not by demonizing that majority, but by stressing a commonality of fundamental interest in all of our rights.

We must also resist those who would substitute propaganda and censorship for facts. Facts are the key to accountability. A fact-free world is an autocrat's dream. The risks are only increasing as we face the prospect of disinformation enhanced by artificial intelligence. The best way to fight lies and spin is with a renewed commitment to facts. People who do not want to know the truth will fall back on the facile claim that truth is unknowable, but most people still live in a reality-based world. Fact-based discourse remains powerful, but it requires our defense and participation. The methodology that I describe can be an important tool in that endeavor.

The challenges to human rights are great, but they are not beyond our capacity to meet. Indifference is the enemy of democracy. Despair is the accomplice of the autocrat. If we throw up our hands, the enemies of rights prevail. It is the very magnitude of the challenges that compels a solution involving us all. "What can I do?" should be a question of action, not resignation. "What difference can I make?" An enormous difference. In today's world, where trust is in short supply, our influence increases the closer we are to our audience. People often trust family and friends more than distant pundits and institutions. That places a responsibility on all of us to use that trust—to add our voice—to the defense of rights. We each have a duty to affirm the facts and defend the values that are the foundation of a society built on rights.

—

As I look back on my time at Human Rights Watch, I feel tremendously fortunate to have been able to devote the bulk of my career to a cause in which I believed so profoundly. That is no small thing. Even though I long ago had to give up the frontline work of a researcher, I met enough of the people whose rights were violated that it remained profoundly gratifying to be able to do my part to defend them. I knew that my work with governments and the media made a difference in their lives and I felt lucky to take on that role.

As I've tried to illustrate here, I also relished the battle. It can be infuriating to watch powerful officials trample on people. I took great satisfaction in fighting back, in deploying my skills and abilities to raise the cost of their callousness, to make them less oblivious to the harm they inflicted, to push back in a way that they felt.

The more I saw the results of our work, the more I felt a special responsibility, and desire, to continue it. Even when I left Human Rights Watch, I realized that, because of my years of experience, my voice continued to carry moral authority, which encouraged me to continue using it even without an institution behind me.

The satisfaction that I least anticipated was from building an institution. It was the part of my responsibilities that I was least trained to carry out. I learned it entirely on the job. But it meant that I left a legacy not simply of particular campaigns and strategies but of an institution capable of carrying on even as I departed. The elements of that task—hiring a top-notch staff, managing an organization, building a community of donors—were not the reasons I joined Human Rights Watch, but I hope they will be my most lasting legacy.

There is something inherently frustrating about the defense of human rights. It is not the kind of job that lets you close a chapter and move on. Defending human rights is never done. Victories can be ephemeral. Problems can ease in one part of the world and intensify elsewhere. It is an incessant struggle.

But once I accepted that reality, it was easier to manage my expectations. Ultimately, what made upholding human rights rewarding was not simply the successes, wonderful as they were, but the defense itself. Our fight for human rights, our determination not simply to stand for our cause but to escalate the cost of violating these basic standards of humanity, made the values we defended stronger. To forsake the battle, to resign in despair, was a sure route to a crueler world. To persevere for these rights, to exert as much pressure as we could in their defense, did not guarantee that we won, but it was the best we could do to strengthen our rights. I found that process deeply fulfilling.

This book is not only a history of the part of the movement that I was privileged to join for most of my professional life. It is also a guide for action. The tools outlined, as I hope I have shown, are powerful. We should all find ways to deploy them. I believe deeply in the importance of rights. But the best defense should not be left to a handful of institutions. The best defense demands action from all of us. From you.

Acknowledgments

The views expressed in this book are entirely my own. This is not a Human Rights Watch publication, even though I am deeply indebted to the staff of Human Rights Watch for contributing their creativity and energy to the defense of human rights that I outline. As I drafted the book, many of those staff, current and former, kindly reviewed drafts and contributed their thoughts and recollections, including Fred Abrahams, Brad Adams, Michele Alexander, William Arkin, Laetitia Bader, Heather Barr, Shantha Rau Barriga, Jo Becker, Reed Brody, Maria Laura Canineu, Cassandra Cavanaugh, Lou Charbonneau, Philippe Dam, Clementine de Montjoye, Rachel Denber, Richard Dicker, Corinne Dufka, Lama Fakih, Jamie Fellner, John Fisher, Lydia Gall, Arvind Ganesan, Meenakshi Ganguly, Giorgi Gogia, Eric Goldstein, Steve Goose, Joost Hiltermann, Bénédicte Jeannerod, LaShawn Jefferson, Sara Kayyali, Elise Keppler, Jan Kooy, Leslie Lefkow, Lotte Leicht, Tanya Lokshina, Maria McFarland Sánchez, Wenzel Michalski, Lewis Mudge, Anna Neistat, Alison Parker, Laura Pitter, Andrew Prasow, Graeme Reid, Sophie Richardson, Kathleen Rose, James Ross, Ida Sawyer, Max Schoenig, Mausi Segun, Omar Shakir, Emma Sinclair Webb, Param-Preet Singh, Bruno Stagno Ugarte, Tamara Taraciuk Broner, Letta Tayler, Nisha Varia, José Miguel Vivanco, Yaqiu Wang, Mary Wareham, Joanna Weschler, Sarah Leah Whitson, Daniel Wilkinson, and Sarah Yager.

I am deeply grateful to my wife, Annie Sparrow, who beyond herself reviewing certain chapters provided the emotional support, and patience, that I needed to complete the book.

I express my gratitude to Kathryn Sikkink and Mathias Risse at the Harvard Kennedy School for their help in developing ideas for the book and to the Rockefeller Foundation's Bellagio Center for providing an idyllic retreat for writing parts of the book. I appreciate the assistance of William Brennan with fact-checking and Greg Carr for enabling that work.

A special thanks to Tina Bennett, my agent, for having faith in a first-time book writer, and Jon Segal, my editor at Knopf, for his enormous skill in helping me to shape and tighten the book.

Notes

Preface

ix "The arc of the moral universe": Dr. Martin Luther King, Jr., "Remaining Awake Through a Great Revolution," speech delivered at the National Cathedral, Washington, DC, March 31, 1968, https://www.seemeonline.com/history/mlk-jr-awake.htm.

ix [H]uman progress never rolls in: King, Jr., "Remaining Awake Through a Great Revolution."

xi "Never doubt that": First quoted in Donald Keys, *Earth at Omega: Passage to Planetization* (Brookline, MA: Branden Press, 1982), epigraph of chapter 6. On the murky origins of this quote, see https://quoteinvestigator.com/2017/11/12/change-world/.

Chapter 1: Idlib, Syria

3 Instead, it targeted civilians: A good summary can be found in Independent International Commission of Inquiry on the Syrian Arab Republic, "Civilians Under Attack in Syria," June 2022.

3 It dropped barrel bombs: Syrian Network for Human Rights, "In Nine Years, the Syrian Regime Has Dropped Nearly 82,000 Barrel Bombs, Killing 11,087 Civilians, Including 1,821 Children," April 2021.

3 oil drums filled: "Syria War: What Are Barrel Bombs and Why Are They So Deadly?," NBC News, February 2015.

3 deployed chemical weapons: Syrian Network for Human Rights, "On the Day of Remembrance for All Victims of Chemical Warfare," November 2023.

3 starved them: Amnesty International, "Syria: 'We Leave or We Die': Forced Displacement Under Syria's 'Reconciliation' Agreements," November 2017.

3 and forcibly disappeared, tortured: Amnesty International, "Syria: UN Member States Must Support Institution for Conflict's Disappeared," June 2023;

"Syria Accused of 'Pervasive' Torture in First Global Case over Civil War," *The Guardian,* October 2023.

3 and executed them: Human Rights Watch ("HRW"), "'No One's Left,'" September 2013.

4 One anesthesiologist who had: Faoud M. Faoud et al., "Health Workers and the Weaponisation of Health Care in Syria," *The Lancet,* December 2017; "UN, Arab League Appoint Veteran Diplomat to Take Over Annan's Role on Syrian Crisis," UN News, August 2012; "Syria Envoy Lakhdar Brahimi on First Visit to Damascus," BBC, September 2012.

4 Even though international humanitarian law: International Committee of the Red Cross, "The Protection of Hospitals During Armed Conflicts: What the Law Says," November 2023.

4 they were a favorite target: Physicians for Human Rights, "Illegal Attacks on Health Care in Syria"; Leonard S. Rubenstein and M. Zaher Sahloul, "In Syria, Doctors Become the Victims," *New York Times,* November 2014.

4 The doctors moved: Syrian American Medical Society, "Impacts of Attacks on Healthcare in Syria," October 2018.

4 When the UN Office: Stephanie Nebehay, "U.N. Shares Locations of Idlib Hospitals and Schools, Hoping to Protect Them," Reuters, September 2018; "Summary by the Secretary-General of the Report of the United Nations Headquarters Board of Inquiry into Certain Incidents in Northwest Syria Since 17 September 2018 Involving Facilities on the United Nations Deconfliction List and United Nations Supported Facilities," April 2020, paragraphs 25–26; Annie Sparrow, "Health Care Under Fire," *New York Review of Books,* June 2022.

4 Nearly one thousand: Physicians for Human Rights, "Attacks on Health Care in Syria," March 2022.

4 Government forces gradually retook: Kenneth Roth, "Russia's Responsibility in the Syrian Reconquest of Idlib," *New York Review of Books,* July 2018. At various points I cite my own articles for factual support. In some cases, I was an eyewitness to the events described, in which case the publication serves as an earlier recording of these observations. More typically, when I describe broader developments, my articles were all vetted by Human Rights Watch staff and so have the same factual foundation as a regular Human Rights Watch report.

5 By 2020, three million civilians: "'A Horrifying New Level': UN Says 900,000 Displaced in Northwest Syria Since December," France 24, February 2020.

5 When these areas fell: Roth, "Russia's Responsibility in the Syrian Reconquest of Idlib."

5 At least one million: Ayhan Simsek, "Merkel, Macron Urge Putin to Stop Attacks in Idlib, Syria," Anadolu Ajansı, February 2020; OCHA, "2020 Humanitarian Needs Overview: Syrian Arab Republic (April 2020)," https://reliefweb.int/.

5 number of Syrian refugees: UN Refugee Agency, "Refugees and Asylum Seekers in Turkey"; Center for American Progress, "Turkey's Refugee Dilemma," March 2019.

5 Those bombers deliberately: HRW, "'Targeting Life in Idlib,'" October 2020.

5 Pursuing the classic: Kenneth Roth, "Syria: What Chance to Stop the Slaughter?" *New York Review of Books,* November 2013.

5 Russia's and China's vetoes: Julian Borger and Bastien Inzaurralde, "Russian Vetoes Are Putting UN Security Council's Legitimacy at Risk, Says US," *The Guardian,* September 2015; Dag Hammarskjöld Library, "UN Security Council Meetings & Outcomes Tables," https://research.un.org/.

6 a commission of inquiry: UN Human Rights Council, "Independent International Commission of Inquiry on the Syrian Arab Republic," https://www.ohchr .org/en/hr-bodies/hrc/iici-syria/independent-international-commission.

6 Human Rights Watch: HRW, "Syria," https://www.hrw.org/middle-east/n -africa/syria.

6 and allied organizations: Syrian Network for Human Rights, https://snhr.org/; The Syria Campaign, https://thesyriacampaign.org/; Amnesty International, "Syria," https://www.amnesty.org/en/location/middle-east-and-north-africa /syria/.

6 That gave us leverage: Roth, "Russia's Responsibility in the Syrian Reconquest of Idlib."

6 Turkey was a difficult: HRW, "Türkiye," https://www.hrw.org/europe/central -asia/turkey.

7 After the flight: UN Refugee Agency, "Over One Million Sea Arrivals Reach Europe in 2015," December 2015; International Rescue Committee, "What Is the EU-Turkey Deal?," March 2022.

9 In September 2018, Erdogan warned: "Idlib: Turkey's Ceasefire Call Rejected by Russia, Iran," Al Jazeera, September 2018; "Turkey Calls for Ceasefire in Syria's Idlib but Russia Opposes," France 24, September 2018.

9 However, a few days later: "Idlib Assault on Hold as Russia, Turkey Agree on Buffer Zone," Al Jazeera, September 2018.

9 Macron, supported by Merkel: "Syria Summit: Call for 'Lasting Ceasefire' at Last Rebel-Held Stronghold, Idlib," *The Guardian,* October 2018.

9 But even the buffer-zone: "Fighting in Idlib Threatens Fragile Ceasefire," Deutsche Welle, May 2019; "Idlib Air Raids Kill Several amid Heaviest Fighting in Months," Al Jazeera, May 2019. For a broader perspective, see International Crisis Group, "Silencing the Guns in Syria's Idlib," May 2020; Faysal Abbas Mohamad, "The Astana Process Six Years On: Peace or Deadlock in Syria?," Carnegie Endowment for International Peace, August 2023.

9 On February 20, 2020: "Merkel, Macron Urge Putin to End Conflict in Syria's Idlib," Reuters, February 2020; Rym Momtaz, "Macron and Merkel Call Putin over Syria," *Politico,* February 2020; Bulent Aliriza, "Idlib Test for Erdogan-Putin Relationship," Center for Strategic and International Studies, February 2020.

9 a Syrian airstrike killed: Carlotta Gall, "Airstrike Hits Turkish Forces in Syria, Raising Fears of Escalation," *New York Times,* February 2020.

9 The Turkish military: Carlotta Gall, "Turkey Declares Major Offensive Against Syrian Government," *New York Times,* March 2020.

9 Erdogan and Putin agreed to a ceasefire: Andrew Roth, "Russia and Turkey agree Ceasefire in Syria's Idlib Province," *The Guardian,* March 2020; "Russia's

Putin Says Agreed Deal with Turkey's Erdogan That Lays Ground for Syria Ceasefire," Reuters, March 2020.

9 Only in 2023: Sarah Dadouch, "Syrian Military Academy in Homs," *Washington Post*, October 2023; Syrian Network for Human Rights, "Approximately 45 Civilians Killed, Including 13 Children, and 51 Vital Civilian Facilities Targeted," from October 5–12, 2023," October 2023; Sam Hamad, "Assad Regime Calls for Ceasefire After Brutal and 'Systematic' Idlib Bombing Kills 46 Civilians," *New Arab*, October 2023; Hadia Al Mansour, "Life Grinds to a Halt in Syria's Idlib amid Assad Bombing Campaign," *New Arab*, December 2023; Paulo Pinheiro, Hanny Megally, and Lynn Welchman, "Under Gaza's Shadow, Syria Faces a New Welter of Conflict," *New York Times*, February 2024.

Chapter 2: Formative Years

12 still letting Jews leave: Gordon F. Sander, "Inside America's Failed, Forgotten Conference to Save Jews from Hitler," *Washington Post*, July 2023.

12 U.S. government reluctantly allowed: U.S. Holocaust Memorial Museum, "What Did Refugees Need to Obtain a US Visa in the 1930s?"

14 had made human rights: Office of the Historian, U.S. Department of State, Remarks by President Carter, December 1978; Aryeh Neier, "The Power of Jimmy Carter's Vision for Universal Human Rights," *Just Security*, April 2023.

15 Amnesty International had 150: Amnesty International, "Amnesty International Annual Report 1980," October 1980.

15 I monitored events: Lawyers Committee for Human Rights, "Repression Disguised as Law: Human Rights in Poland," 1987.

17 analyzed my professional life: Malcolm Gladwell, *Outliers* (New York: Little, Brown, 2008).

17 They came of age: Gladwell, *Outliers*, 64-68.

17 He writes of the need: Gladwell, *Outliers*, 40.

Chapter 3: Pressure for Change

20 trial of the "Jazz Section": Michael T. Kaufman, "Trial in Prague: Five Jazz Fans vs. State Power," *New York Times*, March 1987; Jonathan Bousfield, "The Soap Opera Story of Jazz Section, Czechoslovakia's Unintended Cultural Rebels," New East Digital Archive, February 2022.

20 Its publications became: Michael T. Kaufman, "Trial in Prague: Five Jazz Fans vs. State Power," *New York Times*, March 1987; Kenneth Roth, "Prague & the Perils of Jazz," *Commonweal*, June 1987.

21 The government responded: Roth, "Prague & the Perils of Jazz."

21 Vaclav Havel, the dissident: Declaration of Charter 77, January 1977, https://www.files.ethz.ch/isn/125521/8003_Charter_77.pdf; "Timeline—Vaclav Havel, Playwright and President," Reuters, December 2011.

21 Havel summed up: Roth, "Prague & the Perils of Jazz."

21 I wrote about: Roth, "Prague & the Perils of Jazz."

22 The judge conceded: Roth, "Prague & the Perils of Jazz."

22 Helsinki Watch, a member: Aryeh Neier, *The International Human Rights Movement: A History* (Princeton, NJ: Princeton University Press, 2020), 212–13.

22 They described beatings: For background, see Helsinki Watch, Albania, April 1991, https://www.hrw.org/.

23 At least we were able: Helsinki Watch, Albania, April 1991, https://www.hrw.org/.

23 The would-be emigrants: Helsinki Watch, Albania, April 1991, https://www.hrw.org/.

24 Twenty-four people: John Arundel, "Defense Attorney Wants New Trials for Convicted Collaborators," UPI, May 1991.

24 Yasser Arafat, the leader: Jack Anderson and Dale Van Atta, "Why Arafat Backed Saddam," *Washington Post,* August 1990.

24 Palestinians in Kuwait: Caryle Murphy, "Kuwaitis, Feeling Sense of Betrayal, Ponder Future Ties with Palestinians," *Washington Post,* March 1991.

25 I published an op-ed piece: Kenneth Roth, "Mass Graves in Kuwait," *New York Times,* June 1991.

25 and my colleagues: HRW, "A Victory Turned Sour: Human Rights in Kuwait Since Liberation," September 1991.

25 It murdered fourteen: Kenneth Roth, "Haiti: The Shadows of Terror," *New York Review of Books,* March 1992.

25 I visited the Casernes Dessalines: U.S. Citizenship and Immigration Services, "Resource Information Center: Haiti," May 1998.

26 Paul died in his home: "Poison Suspected in Death of Haiti's Powerful Col. Paul," *Washington Post,* November 1998.

26 He escaped and went into hiding: Roth, "Haiti: The Shadows of Terror."

26 Aristide applauded students: Roth, "Haiti: The Shadows of Terror."

27 Difficult as it was: Americas Watch, National Coalition for Haitian Refugees, Caribbean Rights, "Haiti: The Aristide Government's Human Rights Record," November 1991.

27 I published a critical article: Roth, "Haiti: The Shadows of Terror."

27 met with Aristide: Howard W. French, "Meetings with Aristide Emphasize Human Rights," *New York Times,* June 1992.

27 The Cuban leadership: Don Podesta, "Cuba, Facing a U.N. Probe, Acts to Improve Rights Record," *Washington Post,* April 1988.

28 By speaking to the occupants: Podesta, "Cuba, Facing a U.N. Probe, Acts to Improve Rights Record"; Aryeh Neier, "In Cuban Prisons," *New York Review of Books,* June 1988; "Human Rights in Cuba: Report of a Delegation of the Association of the Bar of the City of New York," October 1988, https://repository.law.miami.ed; HRW, "Cuba's Repressive Machinery: Human Rights Forty Years After the Revolution," June 1999.

29 This is not a matter: "Macron Avoids 'Lecturing' Egypt on Rights, Sisi Defends His Record," Reuters, October 2017; C. K. Tan and Pak Yiu, "Xi Tells U.N. Rights Chief That China Doesn't Need Lectures," Nikkei Asia, May 2022; Samuel Moyn, "How the Human Rights Movement Failed," *New York Times,* April 2018.

30 First, they tried: See chapter 5.

30 Often, they started: See chapter 6.

30 Governments accused us: See chapter 9.

31 Five years later: International Criminal Court, "Saif Al-Islam Gaddafi," https://www.icc-cpi.int/defendant/saif-al-islam-gaddafi; "Global Centre for the Responsibility to Protect, Statement on the Situation in Libya, February 2011," February 2011.

31 As a condition: HRW, "Libya: Words to Deeds," January 2006.

32 Five weeks later: HRW, "Libya: HRW Report Helps in Pardon of Political Prisoners," April 2006.

34 She also wrote: Jeri Laber, *The Courage of Strangers: Coming of Age with the Human Rights Movement* (New York: PublicAffairs, 2002).

35 When we found: David Rieff, "The Precarious Triumph of Human Rights," *New York Times Magazine,* August 1999.

35 "That helped to give": Aryeh Neier, "The Attack on Human Rights Watch," *New York Review of Books,* November 2006.

35 Sadly, she was: Sam Roberts, "Jemera Rone, Investigator Who Bared Human Rights Abuses, Dies at 71," *New York Times,* August 2015; HRW, "Remembering Jemera Rone," August 2015.

36 War correspondents' accounts: Aryeh Neier, *War Crimes: Brutality, Genocide, Terror, and the Struggle for Justice* (New York: Times Books, 1998), 13–14; International Committee of the Red Cross, "Instructions for the Government of Armies of the United States in the Field (Lieber Code), 24 April 1863."

36 Amnesty began issuing: Amnesty International, "Amnesty International Marks 40 Years of Urgent Actions," March 2013.

37 The Chinese government is: Yaqiu Wang, "As US Tech Firms Bow to China's Censorship, Chinese Users Risk Everything to Defy It," *The Diplomat,* April 2024; Amnesty International, "Pho Noodles and Pandas: How China's Social Media Users Created a New Language to Beat Government Censorship on COVID-19," March 2020; Meaghan Tobin and Katherine Lee, "How Chinese Citizens Use Puns to Get Past Internet Censors," Rest of World, October 2022.

37 Even as the war in Ukraine raged: Adam Satariano, Paul Mozur, and Aaron Krolik, "Russia Strengthens Its Internet Controls in Critical Year for Putin," *New York Times,* March 2024; Lee Hockstader, "In Exile, Russian Journalists Battle the Kremlin's Goliath," *Washington Post,* February 2024; Anatoly Kurmanaev, Alina Lobzina, and Tomas Dapkus, "For Lithuania, Unease over a Growing Russian-Speaking Diaspora," *New York Times,* April 2024.

37 I recall being transfixed: HRW, "Libya: Bodies Uncovered Near Gaddafi's Compound," August 2011.

39 I had been criticizing: E.g., Kenneth Roth @KenRoth, "Fifty Governments Just Pressed China to Implement the Damning UN Rights Office Report on Beijing's Crimes Against Humanity Against Uyghur/Turkic Muslims in Xinjiang . . . ," Twitter post, November 1, 2022, 4:10 AM, https://x.com/KenRoth/status/1587358729888043009?s=20.

40 My first report: "A Human Rights Group Criticizes Polish Regime," *New York Times,* March 1983.

40 An illustration of the power: HRW, "Up in Flames: Humanitarian Law Violations and Civilian Victims in the Conflict over South Ossetia," January 2009.

40 Two Human Rights Watch researchers: HRW, Russia/Georgia: "Militias Attack Civilians in Gori Region," August 2008.

40 Russian forces immediately: Author interview with Tanya Lokshina, associate director, HRW Europe and Central Division, March 2023.

41 After a global search: HRW, "Tirana Hassan to Lead Human Rights Watch," March 2023.

41 a partnership with Planet: HRW, "New Satellite Imagery Partnership," November 2017.

42 ethnic cleansing of Rohingya: HRW, "Myanmar: No Justice, No Freedom for Rohingya 5 Years On," August 2022.

42 The imagery clearly showed: HRW, "Burma: Scores of Rohingya Villages Bulldozed," February 2018.

43 Their efforts to gather: Katy Chevigny and Ross Kaufman, *E-Team* (Los Gatos, CA: Netflix, 2013), documentary.

44 I learned early in: John G. Koeltl, "Reflections on Judge Edward Weinfeld," *Judicature*, 2016, https://judicature.duke.edu/; William E. Nelson, *In Pursuit of Right and Justice: Edward Weinfeld as Lawyer and Judge* (New York: NYU Press, 2004).

45 "First they came for": Holocaust Memorial Day Trust, "First They Came, by Pastor Martin Niemöller," https://www.hmd.org.uk/resource/first-they-came -by-pastor-martin-niemoller/.

45 The same is true: Rochelle Terman, "The Shame Weapon," *Foreign Affairs*, March 2024.

46 That gave rise: See chapter 12.

46 Human Rights Watch thus: See chapter 5.

46 discrimination on the basis: United Nations Free & Equal, "International Human Rights Law and Sexual Orientation & Gender Identity," https://www .unfe.org/.

46 We tried to fight: HRW, "Human Rights Watch Letter to the Pope Regarding Violence, Bias Against LGBT People," October 2013.

46 That is how: "Vatican Calls for Homosexuality to Be Decriminalized," *National Catholic Reporter*, December 2008; Carol Glatz, "Pope Clarifies Remarks About Homosexuality and Sin," U.S. Conference of Catholic Bishops, January 2023.

46 He used the occasion: UN Office of the High Commissioner for Human Rights, "Secretary-General Ban Ki-moon, Pledges Support for Decriminalization of Homosexuality," December 2010.

46 This was a remarkable step: Raphael Rashid, "A Small Group in South Korea Has a Big Homophobic Agenda," *New York Times*, April 2024.

46 In 2014, we adopted: HRW, "UN: Landmark Resolution on Anti-Gay Bias," September 2014.

47 In 2007, Argentina: "The Yogyakarta Principles," https://yogyakartaprinciples .org/.

47 Brazil, Chile, Colombia: HRW, "UN: Landmark Resolution on Anti-Gay Bias," September 2014.

47 We also fought hard: Claudia Zygmunt, "Polish Activists Win Cases Against 'LGBT-Free Zones,'" HRW, May 2023; "Polish Court Rules That Four 'LGBT-Free Zones' Must Be Abolished," Reuters, June 2022.

47 the "sodomy" laws: HRW, "This Alien Legacy: The Origins of 'Sodomy' Laws in British Colonialism," December 2008.

47 We pursued a particularly: HRW, "'No Longer Alone': LGBT Voices from the Middle East, North Africa," April 2018.

47 We did something similar: Rothna Begum, "The Brave Female Activists Who Fought to Lift Saudi Arabia's Driving Ban," HRW, September 2017; HRW, "Boxed In: Women and Saudi Arabia's Male Guardianship System," July 2016.

48 This paralleled our larger: Graeme Reid, "Russia, Homophobia and the Battle for 'Traditional Values,'" *Social Europe,* May 2023.

48 I traveled to Egypt: HRW, "Egypt: Crackdown on Homosexual Conduct Exposes Torture Crisis," February 2004; HRW, "In a Time of Torture: The Assault on Justice in Egypt's Crackdown on Homosexual Conduct," February 2004.

48 He was to emerge: Amnesty International, "Egypt: End Harassment of Rights Activist and Journalist Hossam Bahgat," November 2021.

48 we arranged for forty-four: HRW, Annual Report 2004; HRW, "'All This Terror Because of a Photo': Digital Targeting and Its Offline Consequences for LGBT People in the Middle East and North Africa," February 2023.

48 I made a significant mistake: Alex Emmons, "Human Rights Watch Took Money from Saudi Businessman After Documenting His Coercive Labor Practices," *The Intercept,* March 2020; Tamara Straus, "What Happened to George Soros's $100 Million Bet? How Human Rights Watch Went Global," *Chronicle of Philanthropy,* February 2024.

50 David Rieff wrote: David Rieff, "The Precarious Triumph of Human Rights," *New York Times Magazine,* August 1999.

52 appearances on *The Colbert Report: The Colbert Report*, "Kenneth Roth," episode 1288, Comedy Central, January 6, 2014.

52 I chose Liu Xiaobo: HRW, "Liu Xiaobo"; HRW, "Bahrain: Prominent Activist Nabeel Rajab Freed from Prison," June 2020.

52 Aleksei Navalny, a charismatic: Paul Sonne and Ivan Nechepurenko, "From Frigid Cells to Mystery Injections, Prison Imperiled Navalny's Health," *New York Times,* February 2024.

52 Jamal Khashoggi, the opposition: "Jamal Khashoggi: All You Need to Know About Saudi Journalist's Death," BBC, February 2021.

52 Narges Mohammadi served: Nobel Peace Prize, "Narges Mohammadi," February 2024, https://www.nobelprize.org/prizes/peace/2023/summary/.

52 Twice they honored: "*In the Now* S03E01—Holy Moly," RT, November 2015, https://www.youtube.com/watch?v=22ZDLvsdrZQ.

53 I subjected myself: E.g., *HARDtalk*, "Kenneth Roth," BBC, February 2015, https://www.bbc.co.uk/programmes/n3csw9ln; *HARDtalk*, "Kenneth Roth: Is

the Fight for Human Rights Being Lost?," BBC, February 2013, https://www .bbc.co.uk/programmes/w3ct32mq.

53 Sophie Richardson, our China director: HRW, "UN: Act to End China's Mass Detentions in Xinjiang," February 2019.

53 As Chinese authorities were forcibly: Rob Schmitz, "Reporter's Notebook: Uighurs Held for 'Extremist Thoughts' They Didn't Know They Had," NPR, May 2019.

53 I was appearing: *Roda Viva*, "Kenneth Roth," June 2016, https://www.youtube .com/watch?v=TQxpNgMopDg.

53 My most rewarding: HRW, "'I Had to Run Away': The Imprisonment of Women and Girls for 'Moral Crimes' in Afghanistan," March 2012.

53 These supposed crimes: HRW, "Afghanistan: Hundreds of Women, Girls Jailed for 'Moral Crimes,'" March 2012.

55 As he settled into: HRW, "Guinea: High-Level Charges in 2009 Massacre," July 2013.

56 Many of the perpetrators: HRW, "Guinea: Landmark Verdict in Stadium Mass Killings Trial," July 2024.

56 Torture was rampant: HRW, "World Report 2001: Uzbekistan."

57 demeaning "virginity tests": Xan Rice, "Egyptians Protest over 'Virginity Tests' on Tahrir Square Women," *The Guardian*, May 2011.

57 His excuse played so poorly: HRW, "Egypt: Military 'Virginity Test' Investigation a Sham," November 2011.

57 Meles, seen as: Adekeye Adebajo, "Meles Zenawi: Ethiopia's Pragmatic Philosopher-King or Cruel Despot?," *The Guardian*, August 2012.

57 Although it was: HRW, "Ethiopian Dictator Mengistu Haile Mariam," November 1999.

57 Critics faced harassment: Center for Strategic & International Studies, "Assessing the Legacy of Ethiopian Prime Minister Meles Zenawi," August 2012.

57 The government was committed: HRW, "Ethiopia: Donor Aid Supports Repression," October 2010.

57 his government expelled: "Government Denies Food Aid 'Manipulated' for Political Gain," *New Humanitarian*, June 2010.

58 Alas, he died: "Ethiopian PM Meles Zenawi Dies After Illness," BBC, August 2012.

58 The meeting stayed: Crispus Mugisha, "Museveni, US Human Rights Activist Exchange Hot Words in Ntungamo Meeting," *Nile Post*, June 2022.

58 After the meeting: "No One Can Teach Me About Human Rights: Museveni," *The Independent*, June 2022.

59 Our purpose was: HRW, "Neither Rights Nor Security Killings, Torture, and Disappearances in Mexico's 'War on Drugs,'" November 2011.

59 Gratifyingly, within weeks: HRW, "Power of Truth: Human Rights Watch Annual Report 2013."

60 I had recently visited: HRW, "Qatar: Take Urgent Action to Protect Construction Workers," September 2017.

60 Postings on Twitter: E.g., Mohamed AlMarshdi @m1990f1, "Mercenary with Qatar Money," Twitter post, January 22, 2020, 6:05 PM, https://x.com/m1990f1/status/1220120413944057862?s=20.

60 Under the leadership of: HRW, "Shackling," https://www.hrw.org/topic/disability-rights/shackling.

60 I joined her to address: Kriti Sharma, "Dispatches: Turning the Tide on Shackling in Indonesia," HRW, April 2016.

61 The ministry also rolled out: HRW, "Indonesia: Shackling Reduced, but Persists," October 2018.

61 reached roughly 70 percent: HRW, "Living in Chains: Shackling of People with Psychosocial Disabilities Worldwide," October 2020.

62 "as spiritual guardians": Stephen Hopgood, *The Endtimes of Human Rights* (Ithaca, NY: Cornell University Press, 2013). See also Kenneth Roth, "The End of Human Rights?," *New York Review of Books,* October 2014.

64 describing our campaign: Charles Trueheart, "Clout Without a Country: The Power of International Lobbies," *Washington Post,* July 1998.

65 People in the United States: Neier, *The International Human Rights Movement: A History,* 172–73.

65 Working with the European Union: EUR-Lex, "Unanimity," https://eur-lex.europa.eu/.

66 Although the high representative: European Commission, "Frequently Asked Questions: Restrictive Measures (Sanctions)," February 2022.

66 When we were only: Robert D. McFadden, "Robert L. Bernstein, Publisher and Champion of Dissent, Dies at 96," *New York Times,* May 27, 2019.

68 The gift was major news: Stephanie Strom, "Soros to Donate $100 Million to Rights Group," *New York Times,* September 2010; Ed Pilkington, "George Soros Gives $100 Million to Human Rights Watch," *The Guardian,* September 2010.

68 It was the largest gift: HRW, "George Soros to Give $100 Million to Human Rights Watch," September 2010; Open Society Foundations, "Soros and Open Society Foundations Give $100 Million to Human Rights Watch," September 2010.

68 It transformed the organization: Tamara Straus, "What Happened to George Soros's $100 Million Bet? How Human Rights Watch Went Global," *Chronicle of Philanthropy,* February 2024.

68 The one in Japan: UN Human Rights Council, "Commission of Inquiry on Human Rights in the Democratic People's Republic of Korea"; HRW, "Power of Truth: Human Rights Watch Annual Report 2013."

68 The Australia office: HRW, "Australia: Events of 2023," World Report 2024.

69 In 2012, the Indian government: United Nations, "Security Council Fails to Adopt Draft Resolution on Syria as Russian Federation, China Veto Text Supporting Arab League's Proposed Peace Plan," February 2012; United Nations, "Security Council Fails to Adopt Draft Resolution on Syria That Would Have Threatened Sanctions, Due to Negative Votes of China, Russian Federation," July 2012.

69 In 2012 and 2013: Mala Das, "India Votes Against Sri Lanka, UN Human

Rights Council Resolution Adopted," NDTV, March 2012; "India Votes Against Sri Lanka in UNHRC, 25 Votes in Favour of Resolution, 13 Against," *India Today*, March 2013.

69 Brazil had been pressing: Roth, "The End of Human Rights?"

69 For example, during the 2012: World Economic Forum, "Davos 2012—AP Debate on Democracy," January 2012, https://www.youtube.com/watch ?v=Dt7N1QVRbMU; United Nations, "Security Council Fails to Adopt Draft Resolution Condemning Syria's Crackdown on Anti-Government Protestors, Owing to Veto by Russian Federation, China," October 2011.

70 Were companies taking: Office of the UN High Commissioner for Human Rights, "Guiding Principles on Business and Human Rights," 2011.

70 We applied those principles: HRW, "Occupation, Inc.: How Settlement Businesses Contribute to Israel's Violations of Palestinian Rights," January 2016.

70 Taking a chapter from: H. Jeff Smith, "The Shareholders vs. Stakeholders Debate," *MIT Sloan Management Review*, July 2003.

70 After we published our: HRW, "No Guarantees: Sex Discrimination in Mexico's Maquiladora Sector," August 1996; Laurie J. Bremer, "Pregnancy Discrimination in Mexico's Maquiladora System: Mexico's Violation of Its Obligations Under NAFTA and the NAALC," *Law and Business Review of the Americas*, Autumn 1999, https://core.ac.uk/.

71 We found that the mine's: HRW, "Gold's Costly Dividend: Human Rights Impacts of Papua New Guinea's Porgera Gold Mine," February 2011.

71 It condemned the rape: "Statement by Barrick Gold Corporation in Response to Human Rights Watch Report," February 2011.

Chapter 4: Leading and Building an Organization

74 Each year, I wrote: HRW, "Previous World Reports," https://www.hrw.org /previous-world-reports.

78 The challenge was: Michelle Goldberg, "The Left's Fever Is Breaking," *New York Times*, December 2022; Ryan Grim, "Elephant in the Room," The Intercept, June 2022.

78 I understand the argument: Maurice Mitchell, "Building Resilient Organizations," The Forge, November 2022.

81 Malloch-Brown, a former president: Mark Malloch-Brown, "The UN Can No Longer Protect Human Rights by Itself," *Financial Times*, December 2023; Jack Snyder, "Why the Human Rights Movement Is Losing," *Foreign Affairs*, July 2022.

82 Many donors and supporters: Snyder, "Why the Human Rights Movement Is Losing."

82 The Brazilian human-rights: Lucia Nader, "Solid Organizations in a Liquid World," Sur, June/December 2014, https://sur.conectas.org/.

83 It later gave additional: Aryeh Neier, *The International Human Rights Movement: A History* (Princeton, NJ: Princeton University Press, 2020), 205; Ford Foundation, "Human Rights Watch," https://www.fordfoundation.org/work /our-grants/awarded-grants/grantee/human-rights-watch/.

84 Hillary Clinton would not: "First Lady Hillary Rodham Clinton Remarks for the United Nations Fourth World Conference on Women," September 1995.

84 Our first women's rights: HRW, "Criminal Injustice: Violence Against Women in Brazil," October 1991.

84 In 1990, we did it anyway: Neier, *The International Human Rights Movement: A History,* 228.

84 Humanitarian law provides: For an account of our early application of international humanitarian law, see HRW, "Monitoring Violations of the Laws of War," in HRW, World Report 1989.

84 Ford thought it would be impossible: Aryeh Neier led these conversations with Ford. He, in turn, described them to me.

85 Without drawing firm conclusions: I have a draft of the report, dated December 8, 1992, which I do not believe was ever published.

89 His government cut funding: Jillian Kestler-D'Amours, "'An Attack on Israel Would Be an Attack on Canada,'" *Briarpatch,* May 2010.

89 We also did not accept: HRW, "HRW Policies and Guidelines on Donations," December 2020.

91 We looked, for example: HRW, "'My Fear Is Losing Everything': The Climate Crisis and First Nations' Right to Food in Canada," October 2020; HRW, "How the Climate Crisis Affects Reproductive Rights," February 2023.

92 Human Rights Watch has pursued: HRW, "South Africa: Abandoned Coal Mines Risk Safety, Rights," July 2022; HRW, "Bosnia and Herzegovina: Deadly Air Pollution Killing Thousands," August 2022; HRW, "US: Louisiana's 'Cancer Alley,'" January 2024.

92 Our experience showed: Benji Jones, "Indigenous People Are the World's Biggest Conservationists, but They Rarely Get Credit for It," *Vox,* June 2021.

92 He sought to enable: Adam Popescu, "Guns, Gorillas and Netflix: A Belgian Prince in Congo," *New York Times,* September 2022; Capacity4dev, "Virunga: Preserving Africa's National Parks Through People-Centred Development," April 2018, https://capacity4dev.europa.eu/.

92 That is also the approach: Scott Pelley, "Restoring Gorongosa National Park After Decades of War," *60 Minutes,* CBS, June 2, 2024.

93 The lines often corresponded: HRW, "Rainforest Mafias: How Violence and Impunity Fuel Deforestation in Brazil's Amazon," September 2019; InfoAmazonia, "Four Years of Bolsonaro's Amazon Destruction, in Satellite Imagery," October 2022.

93 Bolsonaro favored the destruction: Jake Spring, "Brazil's Military Fails in Key Mission: Defending the Amazon," Reuters, March 2021.

93 The draft agreement stipulated: HRW, "EU/Brazil: Delay Trade Deal Pending Amazon Crisis Response," July 2020; European Commission, "EU-Mercosur: Text of the Agreement."

93 Another source of leverage: Lukas Berti and Jika, "Brazil Wants the OECD, but Does the OECD Want Brazil," The Brazilian Report, January 2022.

93 When his administration tried: Patricia Campos Mello, "Risco Ambiental do Governo Bolsonaro Freia Avanço do Brasil na OCDE," *Folha de S. Paulo,* February 2021; HRW, "Letter on the Amazon and Its Defenders to the Organ-

isation for Economic Cooperation and Development (OECD)," February 2021.

93 We also persuaded: David Biller and Joshua Goodman, "Senate Democrats Urge Biden to Condition Aid to Brazil," AP, April 2021.

94 And we helped convince: Mello, "Risco Ambiental do Governo Bolsonaro Freia Avanço do Brasil na OCDE"; Janaina Figueiredo, "OCDE Exige que Candidatos ao Bloco Apurem Violência Contra Ativistas Ambientais, Dificultando Acesso do Brasil," *O Globo*, October 2022.

94 During Lula's first year: Manuela Andreoni, "Global Forest Loss Remains High, Despite Recent Progress," *New York Times*, April 2024; "Brazil and Colombia Are Curbing Destruction of Amazon Rainforest," *The Economist*, April 2024.

95 I saw the possibility: International Covenant on Economic, Social and Cultural Rights, December 1966.

96 I wrote an article: Kenneth Roth, "Defending Economic, Social and Cultural Rights: Practical Issues Faced by an International Human Rights Organization," *Human Rights Quarterly*, February 2004, https://muse.jhu.edu/.

96 For years, academics: E.g., Lanse Minkler and Shawna Sweeney, "On the Indivisibility and Interdependence of Basic Rights in Developing Countries," *Human Rights Quarterly*, May 2011.

96 They also invoke: UN General Assembly, "Declaration on the Right to Development," Resolution 41/128, December 1986. A draft treaty, known as the International Covenant on the Right to Development, has been submitted by the UN Human Rights Council to the UN General Assembly for consideration. Resolution 54/18 adopted by the Human Rights Council on October 12, 2023.

97 As if in illustration: United Nations, "Third Committee Approves 12 Draft Resolutions, Including Texts on Mercenaries, Unilateral Coercive Measures, Indigenous Peoples and Right to Food," November 2023.

97 It is not a legally binding treaty: UN Office of the High Commission of Human Rights, "New Treaty Would Codify Right to Development," May 2023.

97 Philip Alston, a New York University: "LSE Events, Professor Philip Alston, The Populist Challenge to Human Rights," December 2016, https://www.youtube.com/watch?v=kAy4RUPVA2w.

97 Indeed, I pursued: HRW, "Human Rights and the AIDS Crisis: The Debate over Resources," July 2000; Kenneth Roth, "Human Rights and the AIDS Crisis: The Debate over Resources," National Library of Medicine, July 2000.

97 Samuel Moyn, in his book: Samuel Moyn, *Not Enough: Human Rights in an Unequal World* (Cambridge, MA: Harvard University Press, 2019), 195. See also Samuel Moyn, "How the Human Rights Movement Failed," *New York Times*, April 2018.

98 Through much of its history: HRW, "NGOs Urge Implementation of Wolfensohn Commitment to Human Rights," September 2000.

98 Those include the rights: World Bank, "Human Rights, Inclusion and Empowerment"; HRW, "Abuse-Free Development: How the World Bank Should Safeguard Against Human Rights Violations," July 2013.

99 For example, the British: HRW, World Report 2023, United Kingdom, January 2023. That effort was abandoned in June 2023. HRW, "World Report 2024, United Kingdom," January 2024.

99 Alston, the NYU: Alston, "LSE Events, Professor Philip Alston, The Populist Challenge to Human Rights"; see also UN Office of the High Commissioner for Human Rights, "Statement on Visit to the United Kingdom, by Professor Philip Alston, United Nations Special Rapporteur on Extreme Poverty and Human Rights," November 2018.

99 Deploying this insight: HRW, "Nothing Left in the Cupboards: Austerity, Welfare Cuts, and the Right to Food in the UK," May 2019.

Chapter 5: China

101 And no other government: Kenneth Roth, "How China Threatens Human Rights Worldwide," *New York Review of Books,* January 2020; Helen James, Pauline Turuban, and Dorian Burkhalter, "How China Is Rewriting Human Rights Norms," Swiss Info, September 2023.

101 Despite putting on airs: Vivian Wang, "China Wants to Look Open. Under the Surface, Xi's Grip Is Clear," *New York Times,* March 2024.

102 Officials from the: Christian Shepherd, "As China's Economy Slows, the Buck Stops with Leader Xi Jinping," *Washington Post,* August 2023; "Xi Jinping Reaches into China's Ancient History for a New Claim to Rule," *The Economist,* June 2023.

102 They also say: Austin Ramzy, "China's Cultural Revolution, Explained," *New York Times,* May 2016; Tom Phillips, "The Cultural Revolution: All You Need to Know About China's Political Convulsion," *The Guardian,* May 2016; Frank Dikotter, "Mao's Great Leap to Famine," *New York Times,* December 2010.

102 Hundreds of millions: Fareed Zakaria, "What the West Is Still Getting Wrong About the Rise of Xi Jinping," *Washington Post,* October 2022.

102 But large parts: Scott Rozelle and Matthew Boswell, "China's Marginalized Millions," *Foreign Affairs,* October 2022; Henry Storey, "Is China Finally Getting Serious About Hukou Reform?" The Interpreter, September 2023.

102 The party's wisdom: Ian Johnson, "Xi's Age of Stagnation: The Great Walling-Off of China," *Foreign Affairs,* August 2023; "Xi Is Tanking China's Economy. That's Bad for the U.S.," *Washington Post,* February 2024; Daisuke Wakabayashi and Mike Isaac, "Big American Tech Profits from Chinese Ad Spending Spree," *New York Times,* March 2024; Joe Leahy, "Why Xi Jinping Is Afraid to Unleash China's Consumers," *Financial Times,* May 2024.

102 And perhaps the biggest: Yi Fuxian, "The Long Reach of China's Demographic Destiny," Project Syndicate, July 2023.

103 Although the Chinese: E.g., The National Committee of the Chinese People's Political Consultative Conference, "Roles and Functions of Chinese People's Political Consultative Conference," August 2021, http://en.cppcc.gov.cn/.

103 As observers put it: Lingling Wei and Jonathan Cheng, "Why Xi Jinping Reversed His Zero-Covid Policy in China," *Wall Street Journal,* January 2023.

103 Using a variation of the: John Rawls, *A Theory of Justice* (Cambridge, MA: Belknap Press of the Harvard University Press, 1971).

103 By coming to the streets: Simon Scarr, Manas Sharma, Marco Hernandez, and Vimvam Tong, "Measuring the Masses: The Contentious Issue of Crowd Counting in Hong Kong," Reuters, June 2019.

103 That embarrassing, highly visible: HRW, "Dismantling a Free Society: Hong Kong One Year After the National Security Law," June 2021.

103 The people of Taiwan: Howard W. French, "Beijing's Blind Spot on Taiwan," *Foreign Policy,* January 2024; Sneha Gubbala and Janell Fetterolf, "Support for Democracy Is Strong in Hong Kong and Taiwan," Pew Research Center, March 2024.

103 Although per-capita: Dan Negrea and Matthew Kroenig, "Do Countries Need Freedom to Achieve Prosperity?," Atlantic Council Freedom and Prosperity Center, June 2022.

103 Xi Jinping's government: Wang Yi, "Pursuing a Country-Specific Path to Human Rights Advancement and Jointly Promoting Worldwide Progress in Human Rights," December 2023, https://www.mfa.gov.cn/; Wang Yi, "A People-Centered Approach for Global Human Rights Progress," February 2021, http://geneva.china-mission.gov.cn/; Shannon Tiezzi, "Can China Change the Definition of Human Rights?," The Diplomat, February 2021; Kenneth Roth, "How Putin and Xi Are Trying to Break Global Human Rights," *Foreign Policy,* October 2022.

103 At times it promotes: Institute for Security & Development Policy, "Human Rights in China," March 2017.

104 It rejects universal: Ministry of Foreign Affairs of the People's Republic of China, "Proposal of the People's Republic of China on the Reform and Development of Global Governance," September 2023, https://www.fmprc.gov.cn/.

104 This view accords: "China's Message to the Global South," *The Economist,* July 2023.

104 The exiled Chinese: Ai Weiwei, "The Artwork That Made Me the Most Dangerous Person in China," *The Guardian,* February 2018.

104 In addition, Beijing hides: Kenneth Roth, "China's Global Threat to Human Rights," HRW, World Report 2020, January 2020.

104 Beijing does not want: Li Yuan, "Why China's Censors Are Deleting Videos About Poverty," *New York Times,* May 2023.

105 Using the testimony: HRW, "Death by Default: A Policy of Fatal Neglect in China's State Orphanages," January 1996.

105 The embarrassed Chinese: HRW, "Chinese Orphanages: A Follow-Up," March 1996.

105 He stayed in the square: Nicholas Bequelin, "Robin Munro Obituary," *The Guardian,* July 2021.

105 Many local governments: HRW, "'My Children Have Been Poisoned': A Public Health Crisis in Four Chinese Provinces," June 2011.

105 We also investigated: HRW, "'One Year of My Blood': Exploitation of Migrant Construction Workers in Beijing," March 2008; "'Swept Away': Abuses

Against Sex Workers in China," May 2013; "'As Long as They Let Us Stay in Class': Barriers to Education for Persons with Disabilities in China," July 2013; "'Have You Considered Your Parents' Happiness?': Conversion Therapy Against LGBT People in China," November 2017.

106 Revealing the range: HRW, "China's Algorithms of Repression: Reverse Engineering a Xinjiang Police Mass Surveillance App," May 2019.

106 Checkpoints there were: Kenneth Roth and Maya Wang, "Data Leviathan: China's Burgeoning Surveillance State," *New York Review of Books*, August 2019.

106 the "social credit system": Maya Wang, "China's Chilling 'Social Credit' Blacklist," *Wall Street Journal*, December 2017; Roth, "China's Global Threat to Human Rights."

106 As the Chinese government blocked: "It Is Getting Even Harder for Western Scholars to Do Research in China," *The Economist*, April 2023.

106 Finding nuggets of information: E.g., HRW, "'Only Men Need Apply': Gender Discrimination in Job Advertisements in China," April 2018.

106 The blanked-out spots: Alison Killing, Megha Rajagopalan, and Christo Buschek, "Blanked-Out Spots on China's Maps Helped Us Uncover Xinjiang's Camps," *BuzzFeed News*, August 2020.

107 Allegations of torture: HRW, "Tiger Chairs and Cell Bosses: Police Torture of Criminal Suspects in China," May 2015.

107 Over time, the Chinese: Alison Killing, "The Challenges of Conducting Open Source Research on China," Bellingcat, April 2023.

107 My pretext was: United Nations, "UN Global Compact Convenes Summit in China," November 2005; "United Nations Global Compact to Convene 'Global Compact Summit: China' in Shanghai (30 November–1 December 2005)," CSR Wire, November 2005.

107 He had been allowed: UN Office of the High Commissioner for Human Rights, "Special Rapporteur on Torture Highlights Challenges at End of Visit to China," December 2005.

107 So they sent "retrievers": HRW, "'An Alleyway in Hell': China's Abusive 'Black Jails,'" November 2009.

108 A few days later: HRW, "'We Could Disappear at Any Time': Retaliation and Abuses Against Chinese Petitioners," "China: Rampant Violence and Intimidation Against Petitioners," December 2005.

108 He said that the country's: HRW, "Promises Unfulfilled: An Assessment of China's National Human Rights Action Plan," January 2011.

108 He said that any: This account of the meeting is drawn from contemporary notes taken by Peter Huvos.

108 However, Beijing's willingness: Michael J. Green and Paul Haenle, "What the Bush-Obama China Memos Reveal," *Foreign Policy*, April 2023.

108 Beginning in 2009: National Committee on U.S.-China Relations, "U.S.-China Track II Dialogue on the Rule of Law & Human Rights."

109 He refused to meet the Dalai Lama: Matthew Weaver, "Barack Obama Accused of Bowing to Beijing with Dalai Lama 'Snub,'" *The Guardian*, Octo-

ber 2009; Tania Branigan, "Clinton Seeks Consensus with China on Tackling Global Economic Woes," *The Guardian,* February 2009.

109 Needless to say: HRW, "Letter to President Obama Ahead of His Visit to China," November 2009.

109 Before the Chinese leader: Chris McGreal and Bobbie Johnson, "Hillary Clinton Criticises Beijing over Internet Censorship," *The Guardian,* January 2010.

109 Mentioning freedoms of speech: The White House, "Press Conference with President Obama and President Hu of the People's Republic of China," January 2011.

109 In response, Hu: The White House, "Press Conference with President Obama and President Hu of the People's Republic of China."

110 a statement that would: The National Bureau of Asian Research, "Understanding Chinese 'Wolf Warrior Diplomacy,'" October 2021.

110 The administration underscored: Sheryl Gay Stolberg, "Business Leaders Make Cut at State Dinner with Hu," *New York Times,* January 2011.

110 Joined by Annie: "Michelle in McQueen: First Lady's Daring British Choice as She Represents America at China State Dinner (and That's Not the Only Controversial Item on the Menu)," *Daily Mail,* January 2011.

110 I was seated: "Dinner & Diplomacy: Top Human Rights Executive Joins Hu at White House," Voice of America, January 2011.

110 Now he launched: Kenneth Roth, "Eat, Drink, Human Rights," *Los Angeles Times,* January 2011.

110 In 2017, Liu died: HRW, "China: Democratic Voice Liu Xiaobo Dies in Custody," July 2017.

111 A postscript: Sophie Richardson: Veronica Toney, "Complete Guest List for the State Dinner in Honor of Chinese President Xi Jinping," *Washington Post,* September 2015.

111 During Bill Clinton's 1992 presidential: Warren Christopher, *In the Stream of History: Shaping Foreign Policy for a New Era* (Stanford, CA: Stanford University Press, 1998), 152.

111 In 1993, Clinton: USCAnnenberg US-China Institute, "Statement by the President Clinton on Most Favored Nation Status for China, 1993," May 1993, https://china.usc.edu/statement-president-clinton-most-favored-nation-status-china-1993.

112 That began an intense discussion: HRW, "President Clinton's Visit to China in Context," 1998.

112 Human Rights Watch argued: HRW, "China: The Cost of Putting Business First," July 1996.

112 But instead of making: John M. Broder and Jim Mann, "Clinton Reverses His Policy, Renews China Trade Status: Commerce: President 'De-Links' Most-Favored-Nation Privilege from Human Rights. He Admits Failure of Earlier Course and Says Broader Strategic Interests Justify Switch." *Los Angeles Times,* May 1994.

112 He also noted: Steven Greenhouse, "Christopher Presses Policy of Engagement with Asia," *New York Times,* May 1994.

112 Everyone knew of: Daniel Williams, "Christopher Cites Progress on Human Rights in China," *Washington Post,* May 1994.

112 I made clear: Greenhouse, "Christopher Presses Policy of Engagement with Asia."

113 In his public: The White House, "Remarks by Vice President Biden and Chinese Vice President Xi at the State Department Luncheon," February 2012.

113 Given China's huge: The White House, "Remarks by Vice President Biden and Chinese Vice President Xi at the State Department Luncheon."

114 My colleagues and I: Roth, "China's Global Threat to Human Rights."

114 After I arrived: Neil Vigdor and Austin Ramzey, "Hong Kong Denies Entry to Human Rights Watch Director, Group Says," *New York Times,* January 2020.

114 Ibrahim then announced: Yousry al-Badri, "Minister of Interior: The Plan Succeeded 100%," *Al-Masry Al-Youm,* August 2013 (translated from the Arabic).

114 After a detailed investigation: HRW, "All According to Plan: The Rab'a Massacre and Mass Killings of Protesters in Egypt," August 2014.

115 She smiled and returned: Kenneth Roth, "Egypt's Tiananmen," *Foreign Policy,* August 2014.

115 The government's refusal: Kareem Fahim, "'Systematic' Killings in Egypt Are Tied to Leader, Group Says," *New York Times,* August 2014; Erin Cunningham, "Human Rights Watch Executives Barred from Entering Egypt to Present Report," *Washington Post,* August 2014; "Human Rights Watch Staff Denied Entry to Egypt," *The Guardian,* August 2014; "HRW Chief Denied Entry to Egypt," Al Jazeera, August 2014; HRW, "Egypt: Human Rights Watch Delegation Refused Entry," August 2014.

115 I had released: HRW, World Report 2012, January 2012, https://www.hrw.org/video-photos/video/2012/05/02/world-report-2012.

115 At the time: Vigdor and Ramzy, "Hong Kong Denies Entry to Human Rights Watch Director, Group Says."

115 The month before: Amy Qin, "China Hits Back at U.S. over Hong Kong Bill in a Mostly Symbolic Move," *New York Times,* December 2019; Gerry Shih, "China Announces Sanctions Against U.S.-Based Nonprofit Groups in Response to Congress's Hong Kong Legislation," *Washington Post,* December 2019.

116 My somewhat disheveled: Kenneth Roth (@KenRoth), "I Flew to Hong Kong to Release @HRW's New World Report. This Year It Describes How the Chinese Government Is Undermining the International Human Rights System," Twitter post, January 12, 2020, 9:02 AM, https://x.com/KenRoth/status/1216359911690514433.

116 That I was barred: Vigdor and Ramzy, "Hong Kong Denies Entry to Human Rights Watch Director, Group Says"; Shibani Mahtani, "Hong Kong Denies Entry to Human Rights Watch Head Kenneth Roth," *Washington Post,* January 2020; "Head of Human Rights Watch Denied Entry to Hong Kong," *The Guardian,* January 2020; "Hong Kong Denies Entry to Human Rights Watch Director," Al Jazeera, January 2020; HRW, "Hong Kong Bars Human Rights Watch Head," January 2020.

116 He made clear that: Austin Ramzy, "China Uses Growing Clout to Stifle Critics Abroad, Rights Group Says," *New York Times,* January 2020. See also Sophie Richardson, "Why China's Move to Bar Human Rights Watch Chief from Hong Kong Was Contrary to the City's Basic Law," *Hong Kong Free Press,* January 2020.

116 It did that when: Richard Milne, "Norway Sees Liu Xiaobo's Nobel Prize Hurt Salmon Exports to China," *Financial Times,* August 2013.

116 When upon an extradition request: Amy Hawkins and Leyland Cecco, "New Allegations and a Resignation Strain Already Fraught China-Canada Relations," *The Guardian,* March 2023.

116 It also detained: Leyland Cecco and Helen Davidson, "Meng and the Michaels: Why China's Embrace of Hostage Diplomacy Is a Warning to Other Nations," *The Guardian,* September 2021.

116 After the COVID-19: Fergus Hunter, Daria Impiombato, Yvonne Lau, and Adam Triggs, "Countering China's Coercive Diplomacy," Australian Strategic Policy Institute, 2023.

116 Beijing did not want: "In Wuhan, Doctors Knew the Truth. They Were Told to Keep Quiet," *Washington Post,* August 2023; Annie Sparrow, "The Chinese Government's Cover-Up Killed Health Care Workers Worldwide," *Foreign Policy,* March 2021.

117 That accounts for: "China to Stop Testing Chilled, Frozen Foods for COVID from Jan. 8," Reuters, December 2022.

117 And it certainly: Alina Chan, "Why the Pandemic Probably Started in a Lab, in 5 Key Points," *New York Times,* June 2024; Michael R. Gordon and Warren P. Strobel, "Lab Leak Most Likely Origin of Covid-19 Pandemic, Energy Department Now Says," *Wall Street Journal,* February 2023; Benjamin Meuller, "New Data Links Pandemic's Origins to Raccoon Dogs at Wuhan Market," *New York Times,* March 2023; Jimmy Tobias, "The Rise and Fall of the Racoon Dog Theory of Covid-19," The Intercept, May 2023. If COVID-19 leaked from the Wuhan lab, it could have been because that is where samples of coronavirus collected from bats in Yunnan were stored, Jane Qiu, "How China's 'Bat Woman' Hunted Down Viruses from SARS to the New Coronavirus," *Scientific American,* June 2020, or due to "gain of function" research done in the lab, Nicholas Wade, "Where Did Covid Come From?" *Wall Street Journal,* February 2024.

117 He had shared: Sopan Deb and Marc Stein, "N.B.A. Executive's Hong Kong Tweet Starts Firestorm in China," *New York Times,* October 2019.

117 NBA broadcasts in China: Sopan Deb, "After a Boycott, Chinese Television Is Again Airing N.B.A. Games," *New York Times,* March 2022.

117 When the clothing: Ravi Mattu, "'Cherry on the Cake': How China Views the U.S. Crackdown on TikTok," *New York Times,* March 2024.

117 Hollywood increasingly censored: Michelle Toh and Wayne Chang, "'Top Gun: Maverick' Brings Back the Taiwan Flag After Controversy," CNN, June 2022.

117 Companies abiding by censorship: Natasha Piñon, "Here's a Growing List of Companies Bowing to China Censorship Pressure," Mashable, October 2019;

U.S. International Trade Commission, "Foreign Censorship, Part 2: Trade and Economic Effects on U.S. Businesses," July 2022.

118 Beijing also conducts: Maya Wang, "China's Techno-Authoritarianism Has Gone Global," *Foreign Affairs,* April 2021.

118 Hong Kong authorities: Tiffany May, "Hong Kong Offers Bounties as It Pursues Dissidents Overseas," *New York Times,* July 2023; "Hong Kong Puts Arrest Bounties on Five Overseas Activists Including US Citizen," *The Guardian,* December 2023.

118 Meta, the parent: HRW, "Hong Kong: Tech Firms Should Oppose Protest Song Ban," June 2023.

118 In July 2019, we attracted: HRW, "UN: Unprecedented Joint Call for China to End Xinjiang Abuses," July 2019; International Service for Human Rights, "HRC41, 25 States Jointly Condemn China's Suppression of Minorities in Xinjiang," July 2019.

118 In October 2019: "Joint Statement on Human Rights Violations and Abuses in Xinjiang," October 2019, https://www.gov.uk/.

118 Fifty governments were willing: U.S. Mission to the UN, "Joint Statement on Behalf of 50 Countries in the UN General Assembly Third Committee on the Human Rights Situation in Xinjiang, China," October 2022; Louis Charbonneau, "Record Number of States Condemn China's Persecution of Uyghurs," HRW, October 2022.

118 Beijing responded to each group condemnation: Permanent Mission of the People's Republic of China to the UN, "Joint Statement of 69 Countries at the Interactive Dialogue on High Commissioner's Annual Report at the 47th Session of the Human Rights Council," June 2021, http://geneva.china-mission.gov.cn/.

118 But about half: Roth, "China's Global Threat to Human Rights."

119 I asked whether: "40th Session of the Human Rights Council, UPR Outcome of China, Statement by Pakistan," March 2019.

119 He agreed to: "Pakistan's Khan Backs China on Uighurs, Praises One-Party System," Al Jazeera, July 2021.

119 Beijing's effort to buy: Tola Amusan, "The Belt and Road Initiative's Impact Depends on the Recipient Country," The Diplomat, December 2023; Selina Sykes, "'No Strings Attached' to Africa Investment, Says China's Xi," France 24, September 2018.

119 The secrecy also: "The Path Ahead for China's Belt and Road Initiative," *The Economist,* September 2023; Mark A. Green, "Debt Distress on the Road to 'Belt and Road,'" Wilson Center, January 2024.

119 Some BRI projects: Rupert Stone, "China Is Losing Ground in Sri Lanka," Lowy Institute; Duncan Miriri, "Kenya Forcing Importers to Use Costly New Chinese Railway, Businessmen Say," Reuters, December 2019.

119 BRI projects also: "Nairobi's New Expressway May Ease Traffic Woes—but Mostly for the Wealthy," The Conversation, November 2021.

120 But there was one big: Karen Gilchrist, "China's Growing Influence Threatens to Undermine Global Human Rights, New Research Finds," CNBC, March 2023.

120 It prevented domestic: HRW, "The Costs of International Advocacy: China's Interference in United Nations Human Rights Mechanisms," September 2017.

120 She died in custody: Sophie Richardson, "The Death of a Defender in China," HRW, March 2014; UN Office of the High Commissioner for Human Rights, "China: UN Experts Renew Calls for Probe into Death of Cao Shunli," March 2019.

121 For example, as Gaddafi: UN Security Council Resolution 1970 (2011), February 2011; HRW, "UN: Security Council Refers Libya to ICC," February 2011.

121 In Beijing's view: Permanent Mission of the People's Republic of China to the UN Office at Geneva, "Remarks by H. E. Wang Yi, State Councilor and Foreign Minister of the People's Republic of China, at the High-Level Segment of the 46th Session of the United Nations Human Rights Council," February 2021, http://geneva.china-mission.gov.cn/; Helen James, Pauline Turuban, and Dorian Burkhalter, "How China Is Rewriting Human Rights Norms," Swiss Info, September 2023.

121 It urged "win-win": Sophie Richardson, "China's Influence on the Global Human Rights System," Brookings, September 2020; Amnesty International and Urgewald, "'Mutually Beneficial Cooperation' or 'Win-Win Cooperation,'" in "What China Says, What China Means," https://whatchinasays.org/; "Rana Siu Inboden, "Defending the Global Human Rights System from Authoritarian Assault," National Endowment for Democracy, July 2023.

121 It wanted governments: "China's Latest Attempt to Rally the World Against Western Values," *The Economist,* April 2023.

121 Bachelet had rightly: Nick Cumming-Bruce, "U.N. Human Rights Chief to Make First Trip to China Since 2005," *New York Times,* May 2022.

122 She added considerably more: Stephanie Nebehay, "U.N. Says to Publish Findings Soon on Abuses in Xinjiang," Reuters, December 2021.

122 My greatest frustration: Kenneth Roth, "Why the U.N. Chief's Silence on Human Rights Is Deeply Troubling," *Washington Post,* April 2019.

122 His timidity came: HRW, "'Break Their Lineage, Break Their Roots': China's Crimes Against Humanity Targeting Uyghurs and Other Turkic Muslims," April 2021.

122 In Beijing, he announced: Michelle Nichols, "U.N. Chief to China's Leaders: Allow 'Credible' Visit by Rights Envoy," Reuters, February 2022.

123 She refused to: Helen Davidson, "UN Human Rights Chief Could Not Speak to Detained Uyghurs or Families During Xinjiang Visit," *The Guardian,* June 2022; Benedict Rogers, "Michelle Bachelet's Failed Xinjiang Trip Has Tainted Her Whole Legacy," *Foreign Policy,* June 2022; Austin Ramzy, "U.N. Human Rights Chief Tempers Criticism at End of China Trip," *New York Times,* May 2022.

123 She finally did: UN Office of the High Commissioner for Human Rights, "OHCHR Assessment of Human Rights Concerns in the Xinjiang Uyghur Autonomous Region, People's Republic of China," August 2022.

123 Türk had never: Kenneth Roth, "The U.N. Gave a Quiet Diplomat the Wrong Job," *Foreign Policy,* September 2022.

123 "come out swinging": Imogen Foulkes, "Is It the Toughest Job at the UN?,"

Swiss Info, June 2020; Suzanne Nossel, "The Job of Human Rights Chief Isn't What You Think," *Foreign Policy*, August 2018.

123 He never explicitly: Imogen Foulkes, "Can the UN Hold China to Account?," Swiss Info, March 2023.

123 Rather than contribute: Nick Cumming-Bruce, "Meet the World's New Human Rights Crisis Manager. He Has a Lot to Do," *New York Times*, November 2022; Lizzy Davies, "Volker Türk: The Man Charged with Protecting the World's Human Rights," *The Guardian*, January 2023.

123 On the most challenging: See, e.g., UN Office of the High Commissioner for Human Rights, "Türk's Global Update to the Human Rights Council," March 2024.

123 Through a spokesperson: UN News, "China Responsible for 'Serious Human Rights Violations' in Xinjiang Province: UN Human Rights Report," August 2022.

124 We lost the vote: Nick Cumming-Bruce, "China Turns Back Move for U.N. Debate on Abuse of Uyghurs," *New York Times*, October 2022.

124 But those that voted: Jamey Keaten, "UN Rights Body Rejects Western Bid to Debate Xinjiang Abuses," AP, October 2022; International Federation for Human Rights, "UN Human Rights Council Voted Against Debate on Human Rights Violations in China's Xinjiang Region," October 2022.

124 To illustrate how much: "China May Face More Embarrassment over Its Human-Rights Record," *The Economist*, March 2023.

124 Sophie Richardson, our China: U.S. Customs and Border Protection, "Uyghur Forced Labor Prevention Act."

124 It presumptively bars: Antony J. Blinken, "Implementation of the Uyghur Forced Labor Prevention Act," U.S. Department of State, June 2022.

124 The industries affected: Stuart Lau and Antonia Zimmermann, "Forced Labor Still Haunts China's Xinjiang, Report Finds," *Politico*, March 2024; Xiaoyan Kang et al., "The 10-m Cotton Maps in Xinjiang, China During 2018–2021," *Nature*, October 2023; Thomas Kaplan, Chris Buckley, and Brad Plumer, "U.S. Bans Imports of Some Chinese Solar Materials Tied to Forced Labor," *New York Times*, August 2021; Ji Siqi, "Why Has the US Ban on Xinjiang's Tomato Exports Had Such Limited Effect?," *South China Morning Post*, October 2022; Edward White, "China's Xinjiang Aluminium Boom Exposes Global Carmakers to Forced Labour," *Financial Times*, February 2024.

125 If firmly implemented: Laura T. Murphy et al., "Laundering Cotton: How Xinjiang Cotton Is Obscured in International Supply Chains," Sheffield Hallam University, Helena Kennedy Centre for International Justice, November 2021, https://www.shu.ac.uk/.

125 That pressure would: Antonia Zimmermann, "On Chinese Forced Labor, Europe Plays Catch-up with the US," *Politico*, March 2024; Jim Wormington, "Xinjiang Abuses Show Need for Robust EU Forced Labor Law," HRW, February 2024.

125 While exports from Xinjiang: "China Wants the World to Forget About Its Crimes in Xinjiang," *The Economist*, March 2023; János Allenbach-Ammann, "EU Imports from Xinjiang Rose by 34% in 2022," Euractiv, February 2023.

125 She conditioned the deal: European Commission, "EU and China Reach Agreement in Principle on Investment," December 2020; Lily McElwee, "The Rise and Demise of the EU-China Investment Agreement: Takeaways for the Future of German Debate on China," Center for Strategic & International Studies, March 2023.

125 Although Beijing later: International Labour Organization, "China Ratifies the Two ILO Fundamental Conventions on Forced Labour," August 2022.

125 Shortly after Olaf Scholz: "In the Spotlight: Germany on the International Stage," Munich Security Conference, February 2022, https://security conference.org/msc-2022/agenda/event/in-the-spotlight-germany-on-the-in ternational-stage/.

125 His defense ignored: Kenneth Roth, "The China Challenge for Olaf Scholz," *Internationale Politik Quarterly*, May 2022.

126 That led the European Parliament: "China Wants the World to Forget About Its Crimes in Xinjiang," *The Economist*, March 2023; "EU Ratification of China Investment Deal Put on Ice," Deutsche Welle, May 2021.

126 It seemed to hope: Steven Erlanger and Matina Stevis-Gridneff, "Even as U.S. Beckons, European Leaders Head to Beijing," *New York Times*, March 2023.

126 But with the Chinese: Suzanne Lynch, "European Commission Signals Game Over for China Investment Deal," *Politico*, April 2023.

126 Some were released: Yuan Yang, "Muddled Engagement with China Leaves Xinjiang in the Lurch," *Financial Times*, March 2023; Alice Su, "Chinese Policemen Are Gaslighting Uyghurs in Exile," *The Economist*, June 2023; "China Wants the World to Forget About Its Crimes in Xinjiang," *The Economist*, March 2023.

126 Others were placed: "The Evolution of Forced Labour in Xinjiang," *The Economist*, May 2024; U.S. Department of Labor, Bureau of International Labor Affairs, "Against Their Will: The Situation in Xinjiang"; Adrian Zenz, "Forced Uyghur Labor Undergirds Xinjiang's Export Boom," *The Hill*, November 2023.

126 These shifts suggested: Adrian Zenz, "How Beijing Forces Uyghurs to Pick Cotton," *Foreign Policy*, May 2023.

127 Because of its policies: Alicia García-Herrero and Alessio Terzi, "China's Economy Cannot Export Its Problems Away," Project Syndicate, May 2024; Nicole Hong, "Why China's Shrinking Population Is a Problem for Everyone," *New York Times*, April 2023; Christian Shepherd, "China's Quandary: Bail Out Debt-Laden Cities, or Risk Disruptive Defaults?," *Washington Post*, June 2023; Marius Zaharia and Kevin Yao, "Xi Faces Painful Gear Shift as China's Investment-Led Growth Sputters," Reuters, October 2022; Roland Rajah and Robert Walker, "China's Troubles May Well Get Worse Before They Get Better," Lowy Institute, September 2023; Iori Kawate, "China's Favored State-Owned Companies Squeeze Private Sector," Nikkei Asia, February 2024.

127 Many of the protesters: Kelly Ng and BBC Chinese, "The Young Chinese Who Stood Up Against Xi's Covid Rules," BBC, December 2023.

127 When one province: Muyi Xiao, Mara Hvistendahl, and James Glanz, "Official Data Hinted at China's Hidden Covid Toll. Then It Vanished," *New York Times*, July 2023.

128 Xi's attacks on: Jennifer Conrad, "China Cracks Down on Its Tech Giants. Sound Familiar?," *Wired*, July 2021; Lilian Zhang, "A Timeline of China's 32-Month Big Tech Crackdown That Killed the World's Largest IPO and Wiped Out Trillions in Value," *South China Morning Post*, July 2023.

128 While seeking foreign investment: Elaine Yu and Dan Strumpf, "U.S. Companies in China Worry Due Diligence Will End in Spy Dramas," *Wall Street Journal*, May 2023; Rebecca Feng and Chun Han Wong, "China Blocks Executive at U.S. Firm Kroll from Leaving the Mainland," *Wall Street Journal*, September 2023.

128 Most economists view: Paul Lin, "Xi Unable to Solve Economic Woes," *Taipei Times*, September 2023; Michael Schuman, "The China Model Is Dead," *The Atlantic*, September 2023; Daniel H. Rosen and Logan Wright, "China's Economic Collision Course," *Foreign Affairs*, March 2024.

128 With the economy: Alexandra Stevenson, "China's Male Leaders Signal to Women That Their Place Is in the Home," *New York Times*, November 2023; "China Wants Women to Stay Home and Bear Children," *The Economist*, November 2023.

Chapter 6: Russia and Syria

129 Initially facing: Serge Schmemann, "Things in Russia Aren't as Bad as the Bad Old Soviet Days. 'They're Worse,'" *New York Times*, May 2023.

129 He never made: Stephen Kotkin, "The Five Futures of Russia," *Foreign Affairs*, April 2024; "Russia Built an Economy Like a Fortress but the Pain Is Real," AP, March 2022; Congressional Research Service, "Russia's Trade and Investment Role in the Global Economy," January 2023.

129 He extols the family: Anton Troianovski, "Playing to Western Discord, Putin Says Russia Is Battling 'Strange' Elites," *New York Times*, October 2022; Anthony Faiola, "How Putin Is Weaponizing 'Traditional Values' to Defend Russian Aggression in Ukraine," *Washington Post*, March 2022.

129 His nostalgic veneration: Andrei Kolesnikov, "The End of the Russian Idea," *Foreign Affairs*, August 2023.

130 Putin has resurrected: Robert Coalson, "The Monster Returns: Stalin Looms Large Over Putin's Russia," Radio Free Europe Radio Liberty, January 2024; Andrew Roth, "Russian Court Orders Closure of Country's Oldest Human Rights Group," *The Guardian*, December 2021.

130 Instead, the Kremlin's strategies: Mikhail Zygar, "Putin's New Story About the War in Ukraine," *Foreign Affairs*, November 2023.

130 It is as if: Anastasia Edel, "A Day Inside Putin's Surreal Television Empire," *Foreign Policy*, May 2023.

130 The Kremlin's social media trolls: Marek N. Posard, James Marrone, and Todd Helmus, "How You Can Fight Russia's Plans to Troll Americans During Campaign 2020," *Los Angeles Times*, July 2020; Tom McCarthy, "How Russia Used Social Media to Divide Americans," *The Guardian*, October 2017; "How Russian Trolls Used Meme Warfare to Divide America," *Wired*, December 2018.

130 The Kremlin seeks both: Catherine Belton, "Secret Russian Foreign Policy Document Urges Action to Weaken the U.S.," *Washington Post,* April 2024.

130 This propaganda goes beyond: E.g., Neil MacFarquhar and Ivan Nechepurenko, "Rocked by Deadly Terror Attack, Kremlin Amps Up Disinformation Machine," *New York Times,* March 2024.

131 In Ukraine, the Kremlin: Amanda Seitz, Arijeta Lajka, "Amid Horror in Bucha, Russia Relies on Propaganda and Disinformation," *PBS Newshour,* April 2022; Jim Heintz, "Russia's War with Ukraine Has Generated Its Own Fog, and Mis- and Disinformation Are Everywhere," AP, August 2023. See also Anastasia Edel, "A Day Inside Putin's Surreal Television Empire," *Foreign Policy,* May 2023.

131 Human Rights Watch and others: HRW, SITU, and Truth Hounds, "'Our City Was Gone': Russia's Devastation of Mariupol, Ukraine," February 2024; HRW, "Ukraine: Russian Forces' Trail of Death in Bucha," April 2022.

131 Those who sought: Lee Hockstader, "Russian Journalists in Exile Are Sending a Critical Message," *Washington Post,* February 2024. Increasing restrictions on access to VPNs emerged before the March 2024 presidential election. Adam Satariano, Paul Mozur, and Aaron Krolik, "Russia Strengthens Its Internet Controls in Critical Year for Putin," *New York Times,* March 2024.

131 Yet, given the significant number: Marco Hernandez, "Decoding the Anti-war Messages of Miniature Protesters in Russia," *New York Times,* June 2023; "Russia Protests: More Than 1,300 Arrested at Anti-War Demonstrations," *The Guardian,* September 2022; Amos Chapple, "Writing on the Wall: The Activists Tallying Russia's Anti-War Protests," Radio Free Europe Radio Liberty, July 2023.

131 Putin tried to build: Mikhail Zygar, "Putin's New Story About the War in Ukraine," *Foreign Affairs,* November 2023.

131 But overwhelming majorities: UN News, "General Assembly Resolution Demands End to Russian Offensive in Ukraine," March 2022; UN News, "Ukraine: UN General Assembly Demands Russia Reverse Course on 'Attempted Illegal Annexation,'" October 2022; UN News, "UN General Assembly Calls for immediate End to War in Ukraine," February 2023.

132 The General Assembly: UN News, "UN General Assembly Votes to Suspend Russia from the Human Rights Council," April 2022; UN News, "UN General Assembly Elects 15 New Members to Human Rights Council," October 2023; United Nations, "General Assembly Suspends Libya from Human Rights Council," March 2011.

132 The UN Human Rights Council: UN Office of the High Commissioner for Human Rights, "Human Rights Council Adopts Resolution on the Deteriorating Human Rights Situation in Ukraine and Closes Special Session," May 2022; UN Office of the High Commissioner for Human Rights, "Human Rights Council Adopts Six Resolutions, Appoints Special Rapporteur on Situation of Human Rights in Russian Federation, Extends Mandates on Afghanistan and Right to Health," October 2022.

132 Forty-three states: International Criminal Court, "Ukraine."

132 The ICC was: International Criminal Court, "Ukraine."

132 Within days of Russia's invasion: International Criminal Court, "Statement of ICC Prosecutor, Karim A. A. Khan QC, on the Situation in Ukraine: Receipt of Referrals from 39 States Parties and the Opening of an Investigation," March 2022.

132 In March 2023, he filed: International Criminal Court, "Situation in Ukraine: ICC Judges Issue Arrest Warrants Against Vladimir Vladimirovich Putin and Maria Alekseyevna Lvova-Belov," March 2023.

132 In March and June 2024, he charged: International Criminal Court, "Situation in Ukraine: ICC Judges Issue Arrest Warrants Against Sergei Ivanovich Kobylash and Viktor Nikolayevich Sokolov," March 2024; International Criminal Court, "Situation in Ukraine: ICC Judges Issue Arrest Warrants Against Sergei Kuzhugetovich Shoigu and Valery Vasilyevich Gerasimov," June 2024.

132 Putin remained vulnerable: Kenneth Roth, "Building a War-Crimes Case Against Vladimir Putin," *Globe and Mail,* April 2022; Thomas S. Warrick, "Perseverance Can Bring Russian War Criminals Including Putin to Justice," Atlantic Council, April 2022.

132 In addition, Ukrainian: "War-Crimes Prosecutions in Ukraine Are a Long Game," *The Economist,* April 2023.

132 Several European governments: Bojan Pancevski, "Germany Opens Investigation into Suspected Russian War Crimes in Ukraine," *Wall Street Journal,* March 2022; HRW, "Q&A: Justice Efforts for Ukraine," March 2023.

132 That principle, established: International Justice Resource Center, "Universal Jurisdiction"; Joshua M. Goodwin, "Universal Jurisdiction and the Pirate: Time for an Old Couple to Part," *Vanderbilt Journal of Transnational Law,* May 2006.

132 Just as the Serbian: "Milosevic Sent to Hague," *The Guardian,* June 2001; R. Jeffrey Smith, "Serb Leaders Hand Over Milosevic for Trial by War Crimes Tribunal," *Washington Post,* June 2011.

133 The August 2023 summit: Andrew Roth, "Vladimir Putin to Miss South Africa Summit Amid Row over Possible Arrest," *The Guardian,* July 2023.

133 When Omar al-Bashir: Norimitsu Onishi, "Omar al-Bashir, Leaving South Africa, Eludes Arrest Again," *New York Times,* June 2015.

133 As a matter of principle: HRW, "Ukraine: Banned Landmines Harm Civilians," January 2023.

133 Indiscriminate bombing is: International Committee of the Red Cross, "Indiscriminate attacks."

133 To make these findings: HRW, SITU, and Truth Hounds, "The Devastation of Mariupol, Ukraine," February 2024.

133 The organization also: HRW and SITU, "Death at the Station: Russian Cluster Munition Attack in Kramatorsk," February 2023.

133 Cluster munitions open: International Committee of the Red Cross, "Cluster Munitions: What Are They and What Is the Problem?"

133 At the time, Ida Sawyer: HRW, "United Nations Security Council Arria-Formula Meeting," April 2022.

134 The ICC's Assembly: Rome Statute of the International Criminal Court, July 1998 as amended June 2010, Articles 13, 15*bis* and 15*ter*.

134 At best, the UN General Assembly: Oona A. Hathaway, "Russia's Crime and Punishment," *Foreign Affairs,* January 2023; Dawn Clancy, "Ukraine Warns the World: It's Now or Never for Prosecuting Putin," PassBlue, February 2024.

134 An international tribunal: Dawn Clancy, "The Divide Hardens on What a Special Court for the Crime of Aggression by Russia Should Look Like," PassBlue, May 2023.

134 These Western governments: Glenn Thrush and Charlie Savage, "State Dept. Proposes Joint Tribunal to Try Russian Leaders," *New York Times,* March 2023.

134 A key moment for: "Conference on Security and Co-operation in Europe Final Act, Helsinki 1975."

134 It also confirmed: "Conference on Security and Co-operation in Europe Final Act, Helsinki 1975."

134 The Accords marked: Aryeh Neier, *The International Human Rights Movement: A History* (Princeton, NJ: Princeton University Press, 2020), 144–45.

134 The Soviet government: Neier, *The International Human Rights Movement: A History,* 144.

135 Soon afterward, in 1976: Aryeh Neier, "Putin's Brezhnev Moment," Project Syndicate, February 2023.

135 Many of them: Natan Sharansky, "Why Putin's Repression Is Worse Than What I Endured Under the Soviets," *Washington Post,* May 2023.

135 Their call to the West: HRW, "History," https://www.hrw.org/about/about-us/history.

135 I saw that relative: HRW, "Confessions at Any Cost: Police Torture in Russia," "Police Torture Epidemic in Russia Today," November 1999.

135 Over the next decade: Details provided by Tanya Lokshina.

135 During the most atrocity-filled: HRW, "A Voice for Justice: Annual Report 2000."

136 Grozny, the Chechen capital: David Von Drehle, "Putin Should Know: There's More Than One Way for a Bloody Siege to End," *Washington Post,* March 2022; "Putin's First Invasion: The 1999 Invasion of Chechnya," History on the Net.

136 Based largely on our evidence: HRW, "U.N. Resolution on Chechnya Welcomed," April 2001.

136 The Council of Europe's: Joel Blocker, "Europe: Council's Assembly Acts to Suspend Russia over Chechnya," Radio Free Europe Radio Liberty, April 2000.

136 The court, in turn, issued: HRW, "Update on European Court of Human Rights Judgments Against Russia Regarding Cases from Chechnya," March 2009.

136 In Moscow, senior officials: HRW, "A Voice for Justice: Annual Report 2000."

136 By 2003, Putin: Vladimir Kara-Murza, "The West Deserves Much of the Blame for Putin's Rise to Unchecked Power," *Washington Post,* June 2023.

136 But the rest: HRW Annual Report 2005.

137 Within a month: HRW, "'Bullets Were Falling Like Rain': The Andijan Massacre," "Uzbekistan: New Report Documents Massacre," May 2005; "Human Rights Watch: Uzbeks Hiding 'Massacre,'" NBC News, June 2005.

137 More than four hundred: Anna Neistat, "Massacre in Andijan," *London Review of Books,* July 2015.

137 Natalia gave an interview: As recounted by Tanya Lokshina.

137 Unidentified security personnel: Luke Harding, "Who Shot Natalia Estemirova?," *The Guardian,* July 2009; HRW, "Russia: A Decade On, No Justice for Natalia Estemirova," July 2019. For our tribute to Natalia in 2007, see HRW, "Honoring Natalia Estemirova," https://www.youtube.com /watch?v=H4cgvLWx6tc.

138 "Thousands of Russian": Anna Neistat, "In Chechnya," *London Review of Books,* July 2006.

138 Anna took "tremendous": Tanya Lokshina, "Why Anna Politkovskaya Still Inspires," CNN, October 2016.

138 In 2006, she was killed: Shaun Walker, "The Murder That Killed Free Media in Russia," *The Guardian,* October 2016; "Working for Novaya Gazeta Puts Its Journalists in the Crosshairs," Radio Free Europe Radio Liberty, October 2021.

138 The violence in Chechnya: Anna Neistat, "In Chechnya," *London Review of Books,* July 2006.

138 The texts included: Andrew E. Kramer, "Rights Group Says Its Researcher in Moscow Is Threatened," *New York Times,* October 2012.

138 I said that threats: HRW, "Russia—Threats to Human Rights Watch Researcher," October 2012, https://www.youtube.com/watch?v=Z8Y-mOoODfI.

139 In response, Ahmadinejad claimed: "Ahmadinejad and the CFR," *Jewish Current Issues,* September 2006, https://jpundit.typepad.com/.

139 Putin also was: Historical Speeches, "Putin's Famous Munich Speech 2007," https://www.youtube.com/watch?v=hQ58Yv6kP44; Thom Shanker and Mark Landler, "Putin Says U.S. Is Undermining Global Stability," *New York Times,* February 2007; Ian Traynor, "Putin Hits at US for Triggering Arms Race," *The Guardian,* February 2007.

139 Putin's answer was: American Rhetoric, "Vladimir Putin: Keynote Address and Q&A on Security Policy at the 43rd Munich Security Conference," February 2007, https://www.americanrhetoric.com/speeches/vladimirputin43rdm unichsecurityconference2007.htm.

139 Russia's September 2015: Fiona Hill, "The Real Reason Putin Supports Assad," Brookings, March 2013.

140 undoubtedly wanted to: Anne Barnard and Neil MacFarquhar, "Vladimir Putin Plunges into a Caldron in Syria: Saving Assad," *New York Times,* October 2015.

140 Putin pretended to be: "Vladimir Putin: 'The Syrian People Will Determine Their Future Themselves,'" France 24, November 2017; "Only Syrian People Should Determine the Future of Their Country, Putin Renews," Syrian Arab News Agency, January 2016.

140 When the Syrian people: HRW, "Syria," https://www.hrw.org/middle-east /n-africa/syria; United State Department of State, *Country Reports on Human Rights Practices for 2015,* "Syria," https://2009-2017.state.gov/.

140 With so many doctors having been killed: Omer Karasapan, "The War on Syria's Health System," Brookings, February 2016.

140 Annie was one: Syrian American Medical Society, "Turkey Medical Missions."

140 The world's failure: Kenneth Roth, "Putin Has a History of Atrocities. Just How Far Will Russian Forces Go in Ukraine?," *The Guardian,* March 2022.

141 With the residents suffering: HRW, "Russia/Syria: War Crimes in Month of Bombing Aleppo," December 2016; HRW, "Syria: Civilians at Risk as Aleppo Siege Tightens," July 2016; "Syria's Government Recaptures All of Aleppo City," Al Jazeera, December 2016.

141 Journalists at the time: As recalled by Tanya Lokshina.

141 With equally devastating results: HRW, "Russia Backs Syria in Unlawful Attacks on Eastern Ghouta," March 2018; HRW, "'Targeting Life in Idlib': Syrian and Russian Strikes on Civilian Infrastructure," October 2020.

141 Human Rights Watch researchers: HRW, "Ukraine: Rebel Forces Detain, Torture Civilians," August 2014; Yulia Gorbunova, "Mass Grave Found in Eastern Ukraine," HRW, July 2014.

142 I spent a lot: Charles Lister, "Normalizing Assad Has Made Syria's Problems Even Worse," *Foreign Policy,* July 2023.

142 The Russian government: UN Security Council Resolution 2139, February 2014.

142 But the Kremlin: Miriam Elder, "Syria Will Receive Attack Helicopters from Russia, Kremlin Confirms," *The Guardian,* June 2012; Syrian Network for Human Rights, "The Syrian Regime Has Dropped Nearly 70,000 Barrel Bombs on Syria," December 2017.

142 Perhaps the most notorious: HRW, "Russia: Reject Proposed Changes to Rules on Foreign-Funded NGOs," July 2012; Ellen Barry and Michael Schwirtz, "After Election, Putin Faces Challenges to Legitimacy," *New York Times,* March 2012; Ellen Barry and Michael Schwirtz, "Arrests and Violence at Overflowing Rally in Moscow," *New York Times,* May 2012.

142 The charge was applied: HRW, "Russia: New Restrictions for 'Foreign Agents,'" December 2022; Sonia Phalnikar, "Russia's Sweeping Foreign Agent Law," Deutsche Welle, March 2022.

143 The law was also: HRW, "Russia: Bill Bans Work with Most Foreign Groups," July 2023; Damelya Aitkhozhina, "New 'Undesirables' Law Expands Activists' Danger Zone," HRW, June 2021. For a timeline and list of Putin's increasingly repressive laws, see Yuras Karmanu and Dasha Litvinova, "A Timeline of Restrictive Laws That Authorities Have Used to Crack Down on Dissent in Putin's Russia," AP, March 2024.

143 In February 2015: Andrew E. Kramer, "Boris Nemtsov, Putin Foe, Is Shot Dead in Shadow of Kremlin," *New York Times,* February 2015.

143 "In the months": "Boris Nemtsov: Murdered Putin Rival 'Tailed' by Agent Linked to FSB Hit Squad," BBC News, March 2022.

143 The European Court: "A Murder at the Kremlin Walls: Who Ordered Boris Nemtsov Dead?" *Washington Post,* July 2023.

143 Before he died: Valerie Hopkins and Andrew E. Kramer, "Aleksei Navalny, Russian Opposition Leader, Dies in Prison at 47," *New York Times,* February 2024; Luke Harding, "Navalny Says Russian Officer Admits Putting Poison in Underwear," *The Guardian,* December 2020.

143 The FSB also poisoned: "After Being Poisoned, Vladimir Kara-Murza Deserves Answers," *Washington Post,* June 2022.

143 For example, our 2013 report: HRW, "Russia: Migrant Olympic Workers Cheated, Exploited," February 2013; HRW, "Russia: IOC Acts on Sochi Abuses," February 2014.

143 When we issued: HRW, "Russia: Children with Disabilities Face Violence, Neglect," September 2014; description by Rachel Denber.

143 Our reporting in 2017: Tanya Lokshina, "Chechen Leader Denies Anti-Gay Purge in Putin Meeting," HRW, April 2017; Tanya Lokshina, "Anti-LGBT Violence in Chechnya: When Filing 'Official Complaints' Isn't an Option," *Open Democracy,* April 2017; description by Tanya Lokshina.

143 In January 2023, it would shut down: Kathryn Armstrong, "Moscow Helsinki Group: Russia's Oldest Human Rights Organisation Told to Close," BBC News, January 2023.

143 The previous year's Nobel Peace Prize: "Russia's Novaya Gazeta Paper Suspends Activity After Second Warning," Reuters, March 2022.

144 Hundreds of journalists: Matthew Luxmoore, "The Independent Journalists Risking Their Freedom to Keep Reporting from Russia," *Wall Street Journal,* May 2023.

144 Amnesty International and: HRW, "Russia: Government Shuts Down Human Rights Watch Office," April 2022; "Russia Revokes Registrations of Pro-Democracy, Human Rights Groups," Radio Free Europe Radio Liberty, April 2022.

144 In May 2022, the Kremlin: Timothy Bella, "Russia Bans 963 Americans, Including Biden and Harris—but Not Trump," *Washington Post,* May 2022; "Complete List of 963 Americans Banned from Russia Forever," *Times-Tribune,* November 2023.

144 In May 2014, a resolution: United Nations, "Referral of Syria to International Criminal Court Fails as Negative Votes Prevent Security Council from Adopting Draft Resolution," May 2014.

144 I had proposed: Kenneth Roth, "What Trump Should Do in Syria," *New York Review of Books,* December 2016.

145 After months of advocacy: HRW, "Letter to Foreign Ministers: Support UNGA Resolution on Accountability for Syria Crimes," December 2016.

145 By a vote of: UN News, "Syria: UN Approves Mechanism to Lay Groundwork for Investigations into Possible War Crimes," December 2016; International, Impartial and Independent Mechanism, "The IIIM," https://iiim.un.org/.

145 As of December 2023, the IIIM: International, Impartial and Independent Mechanism, "Bulletins," https://iiim.un.org/documents/bulletins/.

145 With our backing: UN News, "Top UN Human Rights Body Orders Inquiry into Syrian Violence," August 2011; UN Human Rights Council, "Independent International Commission of Inquiry on the Syrian Arab Republic."

146 He smuggled out: HRW, "Syria: Stories Behind Photos of Killed Detainees," December 2015.

146 None received the bodies: HRW, "If the Dead Could Speak: Mass Deaths and Torture in Syria's Detention Facilities," December 2015.

147 Syrian forces: Tobias Schneider and Theresa Lütkefend, "Nowhere to Hide: The Logic of Chemical Weapons Use in Syria," Global Public Policy Institute, February 2019.

147 When inhaled in large amounts: Agency for Toxic Substances and Disease Registry, "Medical Management Guidelines for Chlorine."

147 Sarin, an odorless nerve agent: Centers for Disease Control and Prevention, "Sarin: Exposure, Decontamination, Treatment."

147 Children, given their smaller stature: Kenneth Roth, "Syria: What Chance to Stop the Slaughter?," *New York Review of Books,* November 2013; HRW, Annual Report 2013.

147 Some fourteen hundred: Annie Sparrow, "Syria: Death from Assad's Chlorine," *New York Review of Books,* May 2015; Julian Berger, "Syria to Hand Over Chemical Weapons but Doubts Linger over Full Arsenal," *The Guardian,* April 2014; Arms Control Association, "Timeline of Syrian Chemical Weapons Activity, 2012–2022," February 2022.

147 A year before, in August 2012: The White House, "Remarks by the President to the White House Press Corps," August 2012.

147 Most people assumed: "Reassessing Obama's Biggest Mistake," *The Economist,* August 2023.

147 Putin published an op-ed: Vladimir V. Putin, "A Plea for Caution from Russia," *New York Times,* September 2013.

147 Anna Neistat responded: Anna Neistat, "What Vladimir Putin Didn't Tell the American People About Syria," *The Guardian,* September 2013.

147 ten to twelve were fired: "Reassessing Obama's Biggest Mistake," *The Economist,* August 2023.

147 And the trajectory: HRW, "Attacks on Ghouta: Analysis of Alleged Use of Chemical Weapons in Syria," September 2013. See also Civil Rights Defenders, Open Society Justice Initiative, Syrian Archive, Syrian Center for Media and Freedom of Expression, "Eastern and Western Ghouta Sarin Attack."

148 A UN investigation: Borger, "Syria to Hand Over Chemical Weapons but Doubts Linger over Full Arsenal"; see also UN News, "'Clear and Convincing' Evidence of Chemical Weapons Use in Syria, UN Team Reports," September 2013.

148 But the British: Nicholas Watt, Rowena Mason, and Nick Hopkins, "Blow to Cameron's Authority as MPs Rule Out British Assault on Syria," *The Guardian,* August 2013; Peter Baker and Jonathan Weisman, "Obama Seeks Approval by Congress for Strike in Syria," *New York Times,* August 2013.

148 At the G20 summit: Ben Rhodes, "Inside the White House During the Syrian 'Red Line' Crisis," *The Atlantic,* June 2018.

148 Days later in London: Patrick Wintour, "John Kerry Gives Syria Week to Hand Over Chemical Weapons or Face Attack," *The Guardian,* September 2013.

148 He and Russian foreign minister: Bill Chappell, "U.S. And Russia Form a Plan on Syria's Chemical Weapons," NPR, September 2013.

148 As a result, the Russian: UN News, "UN Security Council Agrees to Rid Syria of Chemical Weapons, Endorses Peace Process," September 2013.

148 Until then, whether: Kenneth Roth, "Syria: What Chance to Stop the Slaughter?," *New York Review of Books,* November 2013.

148 Although at various stages: HRW, "Statement on Possible Intervention in Syria," August 2013.

148 In addition to its videotaped executions: Belkis Wille, "ISIS Accused of Unleashing Chemical Weapons in Mosul," HRW, March 2017.

148 Syria, one of the world's: OPCW, "Syria's Accession to the Chemical Weapons Convention Enters into Force," October 2013.

148 By June 2014: OPCW, "Announcement to Media on Last Consignment of Chemicals Leaving Syria," June 2014.

148 But the Syrian military: HRW, "Syria: A Year On, Chemical Weapons Attacks Persist," April 2018.

148 The Kremlin claimed: Ken Bredemeier, "US Blasts Russian Denial That Syria Uses Chemical Weapons," Voice of America, April 2017.

149 As we showed: HRW, "Syria: New Evidence Shows Pattern of Nerve-Agent Use," May 2017. See also OPCW, "Report of the OPCW Fact-Finding Mission in Syria Regarding an Alleged Incident in Khan Shaykhun, Syrian Arab Republic," April 2017.

149 The massive negative publicity: Arms Control Association, "Timeline of Syrian Chemical Weapons Activity, 2012–2022," February 2022; HRW, "Syria: A Year On, Chemical Weapons Attacks Persist."

149 Under Western pressure: United Nations, "Security Council Unanimously Adopts Resolution 2235 (2015), Establishing Mechanism to Identify Perpetrators Using Chemical Weapons in Syria," August 2015; United Nations, "Unanimously Adopting Resolution 2319 (2016), Security Council Extends Mandate of Mechanism to Identify Perpetrators Using Chemical Weapons in Syria," November 2016.

149 After two years: "Timeline of Investigations into Syria's Chemical Weapons," Reuters, April 2018; UN News, "Security Council Fails at Fresh Attempt to Renew Panel Investigating Chemical Weapons Use in Syria," November 2017.

149 French and British government initiative: OPCW, "CWC Conference of the States Parties Adopts Decision Addressing the Threat from Chemical Weapons Use," June 2018. See also Ian Anthony, "Strengthening Global Regimes: Addressing the Threat Posed by Chemical Weapons," SIPRI, November 2020.

149 As a result, the OPCW: OPCW, "'Addressing the Threat from Chemical Weapons Use,' Ltamenah (Syrian Arab Republic) 24, 25, and 30 March 2017," April 2020; OPCW, "OPCW Releases Second Report by Investigation and Identification Team," April 2021.

149 In February and April 2017: "Russia and China Veto UN Resolution to Impose Sanctions on Syria," *The Guardian,* March 2017; United Nations, "Security Council Fails to Adopt Resolution Condemning Chemical Weapons Use in Syria, Following Veto by Russian Federation," April 2017.

149 a position that I had challenged: "Munich Security Conference, Conflict in Syria Panel," C-SPAN, February 2017, https://www.c-span.org/video /?424282-3/munich-security-conference-conflict-syria-panel.

150 suspend Syria's voting rights: OPCW, "Conference of the States Parties

Adopts Decision to Suspend Certain Rights and Privileges of the Syrian Arab Republic Under the CWC," April 2021.

150 It was important: Louis Charbonneau, "Suspend Syria's Rights Under Chemical Weapons Convention," HRW, April 2021.

150 The OPCW concluded: Louisa Loveluck, "Syrian Army Responsible for Douma Chemical Weapons Attack, Watchdog Confirms," *Washington Post,* January 2023.

150 A week after that: Helene Cooper, Thomas Gibbons-Neff, and Ben Hubbard, "U.S., Britain and France Strike Syria over Suspected Chemical Weapons Attack," *New York Times,* April 2018.

150 The Syrian government reportedly: Liz Sly and Louisa Loveluck, "Assad Is Defiant as U.S.-Led Strikes in Syria Show No Sign of Threatening His Hold on Power," *Washington Post,* April 2018.

150 With only one additional known case: Syrian Network for Human Rights, "The Syrian Regime Uses Chemical Weapons Again in Latakia and the United States, France, Britain, and the Civilized Countries of the World Must Fulfill Their Promises," May 2019.

150 Annie wrote in 2013: Annie Sparrow, "Syria's Assault on Doctors," *New York Review of Books,* November 2013.

150 In 2018, she explained: Annie Sparrow, "Hypocritic Oath," *Foreign Policy,* February 2018.

151 Because the UN is a club: OCHA, "What Is General Assembly Resolution 46/182?"; ReliefWeb, "OCHA on Message: General Assembly Resolution 46/182," March 2012. The annex to G.A. Resolution 46/182 states: "The sovereignty, territorial integrity and national unity of States must be fully respected in accordance with the Charter of the United Nations. In this context, humanitarian assistance should be provided with the consent of the affected country and in principle on the basis of an appeal by the affected country."

151 unable "to reach the vast majority": HRW, "Syria: Authorize Cross-Border Humanitarian Aid," February 2013.

151 Five days after: UN Security Council, "Statement by the President of the Security Council," October 2013. See also Roth, "Syria: What Chance to Stop the Slaughter?"

151 At the January 2014 meeting: UN News, "'World Must Do More' to Aid Besieged Communities in Syria, Urges Top UN Relief Official," January 2014.

151 Separately, she admitted: Annie Sparrow, "Syria's Polio Epidemic: The Suppressed Truth," *New York Review of Books,* February 2014.

151 I made it a major part: HRW, "World Report 2014 Release: Berlin Press Conference," January 2014.

151 In February, at the Munich Security Conference: Munich Security Conference 2014, "Night Owl Session 'The Syrian Catastrophe,'" February 2014, https://securityconference.org/en/medialibrary/asset/night-owl-session-the-syrian-catastrophe-0008-01-02-2014/.

152 The one drafted: UN Security Council Resolution 2139 (2014).

152 John Kerry, the U.S. Secretary: "What Is the Geneva II Conference on Syria?" BBC News, January 2014.

152 But on February 22: UN News, "Unanimously Approved, Security Council Resolution Demands Aid Access in Syria," February 2014.

153 July 2014 resolution "deploring": UN Security Council Resolution 2165 (2014), July 2014; United Nations, "With Millions of Syrians in Need, Security Council Adopts Resolution 2165 (2014) Directing Relief Delivery Through More Border Crossings, Across Conflict Lines," July 2014.

153 Russia's invasion of Crimea: Steven Lee Myers and Ellen Barry, "Putin Reclaims Crimea for Russia and Bitterly Denounces the West," *New York Times,* March 2014.

153 ouster of Ukraine's pro-Russian president: Alan Taylor, "Ukraine's President Voted Out, Flees Kiev," *The Atlantic,* February 2014.

153 reducing the number of border crossings: Security Council Report, "In Hindsight: Six Days, Five Resolutions, One Border Crossing," July 2020.

153 With the death: Andrew Wilks, "A Look at Events Surrounding the Devastating Earthquake That Hit Turkey and Syria a Year Ago," AP, February 2024.

153 The Syrian government thus: ReliefWeb, "North-west Syria Operational Update (September—October 2023)," November 2023.

153 This time, however, the others: United Nations, "Security Council Rejects Two Draft Resolutions Aimed at Renewing Cross-Border Humanitarian Operations in Syria's North-West," July 2023.

153 At the last minute: Farnaz Fassihi, "Humanitarian Aid to Syria Is Imperiled After Failed U.N. Security Council Votes," *New York Times,* July 2023.

154 In the prior two years: Charles Lister, "Normalizing Assad Has Made Syria's Problems Even Worse," *Foreign Policy,* July 2023.

154 Damascus backed off: Edith M. Lederer, "Agreement to Reopen Crossing to Syria's Northwest Will Safeguard Independent UN Operations, UN Says," AP, August 2023; ReliefWeb, "Aid Agencies Reiterate Call for Unimpeded Access of Aid Delivery in Northwest Syria," January 2024.

154 A broad range of: "There Is Still No Legal Barrier to UN Cross-Border Operations in Syria Without a UN Security Council Mandate," https://www.crossborderislegal.org/; see also "There Is No Legal Barrier to UN Cross-Border Operations in Syria," *The Guardian,* April 2014.

154 The alternative would be: Raja Abdulrahim, "With a Hand from the U.S. Military, Aid Finally Reaches a Syrian Camp," *New York Times,* June 2023; Syrian Emergency Task Force, "Breaking the Siege of Rukban."

154 In a reversion: Daniel Triesman, "Putin Unbound: How Repression at Home Presaged Belligerence Abroad," *Foreign Affairs,* April 2022.

155 Some backers of Ukraine: Jennifer Schuessler, "Journalist Resigns from Board After PEN America Cancels Russian Writers Panel," *New York Times,* May 2023; Marie Oleinik, "Russians Abroad Are Not the Enemy," Al Jazeera, March 2022.

155 I think a more productive: "Biden Speaks Directly to Russian People: 'You Are Not Our Enemy,'" NBC News, March 2022.

155 Having courageously returned: Paul Sonne and Ivan Nechepurenko, "From Frigid Cells to Mystery Injections, Prison Imperiled Navalny's Health," *New*

York Times, February 2024; Valerie Hopkins, "Thousands Turn Out for Navalny's Funeral in Moscow," *New York Times,* March 2024; Andrei Soldatov and Irina Borogan, "How Navalny Changed Russia," *Foreign Affairs,* February 2024.

Chapter 7: Saudi Arabia

156 He began showing his colors: Ben Hubbard, David D. Kirkpatrick, Kate Kelly, and Mark Mazzetti, "Saudis Said to Use Coercion and Abuse to Seize Billions," *New York Times,* March 2018; Martin Chulov, "'Night of the Beating': Details Emerge of Riyadh Ritz-Carlton Purge," *The Guardian,* November 2020.

156 He detained Lebanon's: Chandrika Narayan, "Lebanon's Prime Minister Resigns, Plunging Nation into New Political Crisis," CNN, November 2017; Anne Barnard and Maria Abi-Habib, "Why Saad Hariri Had That Strange Sojourn in Saudi Arabia," *New York Times,* December 2017.

156 Although he introduced: Steven A. Cook, "Saudi Arabia Is Extremely Popular in the Middle East," *Foreign Policy,* May 2023.

156 The women's-rights activists: Guy Davies, "Saudi Women's Driving Activist on Trial Almost 2 Years After Ban Was Lifted," ABC News, March 2020.

156 He wanted to ensure: Priyanka Boghani, "The Paradox of Saudi Arabia's Social Reforms," PBS Frontline, October 2019.

157 After considerable nudging: HRW, "Saudi Arabia Blocks Promised Access to Prisons," December 2006.

158 He was also said to have: Bruce Riedel, "The Case of Saudi Arabia's Mohammed bin Nayef," Brookings, February 2021.

158 The closest we have come: Government of Iceland, "Iceland Leads a Joint Initiative Calling on Saudi Arabia to Improve Its Human Rights Situation," March 2019.

158 at our active urging: UN General Assembly, "Election of the Human Rights Council (13 October 2020)"; HRW, "UN: Deny Rights Council Seats to Major Violators," October 2020; "Saudi Arabia Narrowly Fails in Bid to Win a Seat on UN Human Rights Council," *The Guardian,* October 2024.

159 The Saudi-led coalition: Kali Robinson, "Yemen's Tragedy: War, Stalemate, and Suffering," Council on Foreign Relations, May 2023.

159 Its bombers struck: HRW, World Report 2020, Yemen; HRW, "Yemen: Saudi-Led Funeral Attack Apparent War Crime," October 2016; HRW, "Yemen: Coalition Bus Bombing Apparent War Crime," September 2018; "Yemen: Saudi Coalition Air Raids Kill 20 at Wedding in Hajjah," Al Jazeera, April 2018.

159 An estimated nine thousand: "A Prisoner Swap Is a Symbolic Step Towards Ending the Saudi-Led War in Yemen," *The Economist,* April 2023.

159 The Saudi government: HRW, "Hiding Behind the Coalition: Failure to Credibly Investigate and Provide Redress for Unlawful Attacks in Yemen," August 2018; "UN: Suspected War Crimes in Yemen Committed by All Sides," Al Jazeera, August 2018.

159 The attacks contributed: UN Refugee Agency, "Yemen Crisis Explained," March 2023.

159 Naturally, I did: Nieuwsuur, "Kenneth Roth, Directeur HRW," September 2017, https://www.facebook.com/watch/?v=1643002579077939.

160 Just three days: Ben Hubbard, "Saudi Arabia Agrees to Let Women Drive," *New York Times,* September 2017.

160 We welcomed the move: HRW, "Saudi Arabia: As Women's Driving Ban Ends, Provide Parity," September 2017.

160 They agreed to call it: Rob Vreeken, "Mede dankzij Nederland komt er in Jemen een onderzoek naar mogelijke oorlogsmisdrijven," *de Volksrant,* September 2017; UN Human Rights Council, "Group of Eminent Experts on Yemen," https://www.ohchr.org/en/hr-bodies/hrc/yemen-gee/index.

160 Denmark, Finland Germany: Jon Stone, "Germany, Denmark, Netherlands and Finland Stop Weapons Sales to Saudi Arabia in Response to Yemen famine," *The Independent,* November 2018; "Norway Suspends Arms Sales to UAE over Yemen War," Reuters, January 2018.

160 The U.S. Congress voted: Catie Edmondson, "Senate Fails to Override Trump's Veto on Saudi Arms Sales," *New York Times,* July 2019; Ben Hubbard and Shuaib Almosawa, "Biden Ends Military Aid for Saudi War in Yemen. Ending the War Is Harder," *New York Times,* February 2021.

160 After we condemned: Cluster Munition Coalition, "Use of Cluster Bombs in Yemen."

160 terminate the GEE: Stephanie Kirchgaessner, "Saudis Used 'Incentives and Threats' to Shut Down UN Investigation in Yemen," *The Guardian,* December 2021.

161 Four countries that had: Kirchgaessner, "Saudis Used 'Incentives and Threats' to Shut Down UN Investigation in Yemen."

161 That was enough: UN Human Rights Council, "A/HRC/48/L.11—Situation of Human Rights in Yemen," September 2021.

161 It was the first time: "'We Have Failed Yemen': UN Human Rights Council Ends War Crime Probe," *The Guardian,* October 2021.

161 civilian casualties in Yemen: Norwegian Refugee Council, "Yemen: Civilian Casualties Double Since End of Human Rights Monitoring," February 2022; Yemen Data Project, "Saudi Coalition Bombings Surge Following End of U.N. War Crimes Investigations."

161 an agreement to a ceasefire: Sierra Ballard and Jacob Kurtzer, "The Humanitarian Influence of Yemen's Truce," Center for Strategic and International Studies, December 2022; Norwegian Refugee Council, "Yemen: Civilian Casualties Halved Since the Start of the Truce," May 2022.

161 A "list of shame": UN Security Council Resolution 1379 (2001); Jo Becker, "Experts Slam Double Standards in UN 'List of Shame,'" HRW, March 2019.

161 The list produced: "Secretary-General Annual Report on Children and Armed Conflict," June 2023.

161 "Listed parties may be": Jo Becker, "UN Chief Leaves Child Rights Violators Off 'List of Shame,'" HRW, July 2022.

161 Ban Ki-moon listed: HRW, "UN: Return Saudi-Led Coalition to 'List of Shame,'" June 2016; Allan Rock, "Saudi Arabia and the UAE Belong on the UN 'List of Shame,'" Al Jazeera, June 2019.

161 had acted under blackmail: "Content of Report on Conflict-Affected Children 'Will Not Change,' Asserts Ban," UN News, June 2016; Alex Emmons and Zaid Jilani, "U.N. Chief Admits He Removed Saudi Arabia from Child-Killer List Due to Extortion," The Intercept, June 2016.

162 "Children already at risk": "Content of Report on Conflict-Affected Children 'Will Not Change,' Asserts Ban," UN News, June 2016.

162 He created a new category: Rick Gladstone, "U.N. Draft Blacklist of Child Killers Includes Saudi Arabia," *New York Times,* October 2017.

162 was "largely ineffective": HRW, "UN's 'List of Shame' Goes Easy on Saudi-Led Coalition," June 2018; Kareem Fahim, "U.N. Probe Details Fallout of Proxy War in Yemen Between Saudi Coalition and Iran," *Washington Post,* January 2018.

162 "a significant decrease": HRW, "UN's 'List of Shame' Goes Easy on Saudi-Led Coalition," June 2018.

162 Guterres's action softened: Jo Becker, "The U.N. Secretary-General Is Letting Powerful Countries Get Away with Killing Kids," *Foreign Policy,* August 2020.

162 Guterres ignored what I told him: HRW, "UN: New 'List of Shame' Shortchanges Children," July 2019.

162 In 2020, Guterres removed: HRW, "UN Chief's 'List of Shame' Drops Saudi-Led Coalition," June 2020; Bethan McKernan, "Saudi-Led Coalition Forces in Yemen Taken off UN Rights Blacklist," *The Guardian,* June 2020.

163 In one positive reaction: Daniel Politi and David D. Kirkpatrick, "Argentine Prosecutors Consider Charges Against Saudi Crown Prince Ahead of G-20," *New York Times,* November 2018; María Manuela Márquez Velásquez, "The Argentinian Exercise of Universal Jurisdiction 12 Years After Its Opening," Opinio Juris, April 2022.

163 The judge approved: HRW, "G20: Argentine Probe of Saudi Crown Prince Advances," November 2018.

163 The decision made headlines: Daniel Politi and David D. Kirkpatrick, "Argentine Prosecutors Consider Charges Against Saudi Crown Prince Ahead of G-20," *New York Times,* November 2018; Anthony Faiola and Anne Gearan, "'We Don't Want Him Here': Saudi Crown Prince Is a Protected Pariah at G-20 Summit," *Washington Post,* December 2018; "MBS Arrives in Argentina in the Face of G20: Will He Be a Pariah?," Al Jazeera, November 2018.

164 He decamped to: José Miguel Vivanco, "Saudi Crown Prince Hiding in the Embassy?," HRW, November 2018; Faiola and Gearan, "'We Don't Want Him Here': Saudi Crown Prince Is a Protected Pariah at G-20 Summit."

164 Vladimir Putin gave him: Dan Mangan, "Watch Russian President Vladimir Putin and Saudi Crown Prince Mohammed bin Salman's Exuberant Handshake at G-20," CNBC, November 2018; James Landale, "G20 Argentina: Saudi Prince's International Standing Revealed," BBC News, December 2018.

164 the official photograph: Scott Squires and Maximilian Heath, "Saudi Crown Prince Sidelined in G20 Family Photo," Reuters, November 2018.

164 I quickly published: Kenneth Roth, "The Saudi Crown Prince Should Fear the Long Reach of Justice," *Washington Post,* November 2018.

164 When campaigning for: Alex Emmons, Aída Chávez, and Akela Lacy, "Joe Biden, in Departure from Obama Policy, Says He Would Make Saudi Arabia a 'Pariah,'" The Intercept, November 2019.

164 Emerging from a villa: The White House, "Remarks by President Biden in Press Conference," June 2021; David E. Sanger, Michael D. Shear, and Anton Troianovski, "Biden and Putin Express Desire for Better Relations at Summit Shaped by Disputes," *New York Times,* June 2021.

165 Biden apparently wanted: Chris Cillizza, "Why Joe Biden's Fist Bump with MBS Was Such a Disaster," CNN, July 2022.

165 He said he had: The White House, "Remarks by President Biden on His Meetings in Saudi Arabia," July 2022.

165 Bin Salman told: Mark Mazzetti, Edward Wong, and Adam Entous, "U.S. Officials Had a Secret Oil Deal with the Saudis. Or So They Thought," *New York Times,* October 2022; U.S. Energy Information Administration, "What Is OPEC+ and How Is It Different from OPEC?," May 2023.

165 That was a tiny percentage: Ellen R. Wald, "Why OPEC Is Cutting Oil Production (and Why There's Not Much the U.S. Can Do About It)," *New York Times,* October 2022.

165 Even that pathetic promise: Mazzetti, Wong, and Entous, "U.S. Officials Had a Secret Oil Deal with the Saudis. Or So They Thought."

165 Within a year: Alex Lawler, "Explainer: What New OPEC+ Oil Output Cuts Are in Place After Thursday Deal," Reuters, December 2023.

165 Biden threatened consequences: Steve Holland, "Biden Vows Consequences for Saudi Arabia After OPEC+ Decision," Reuters, October 2022; Karen DeYoung, "Biden's 'Consequences' for Saudi Arabia Are Reaping Quiet Results," *Washington Post,* November 2022.

165 reembraced the crown prince: Edward Wong and Vivian Nereim, "Blinken's Visit to Saudi Arabia Caps U.S. Effort to Rebuild Ties," *New York Times,* June 2023; Mark Mazzetti, Ronen Bergman, Edward Wong, and Vivian Nereim, "Biden Administration Engages in Long-Shot Attempt for Saudi-Israel Deal," *New York Times,* June 2023.

165 In August 2024, the administration: Karen DeYoung, "U.S. restarts Offensive Weapons Sales to Saudi Arabi After Lengthy Ban," *The Washington Post,* August 2024.

165 As *The New York Times:* Vivian Nereim, "'Equality of Injustice for All': Saudi Arabia Expands Crackdown on Dissent," *New York Times,* February 2023.

166 One retired teacher: Joey Shea, "Saudi Crown Prince Confirms Death Sentence for Tweets," HRW, September 2023; Aya Batrawy, "Saudi Man Sentenced to Death for Tweets in Harshest Verdict Yet for Online Critics," NPR, August 2023; Dania Akkad, "Saudi Court Overturns Death Sentence Against Retired Teacher over Posts on X," *Middle East Eye,* August 2024.

166 The crown prince also led: Emile Hokayem, "Assad Comes in From the Cold,"

Foreign Affairs, May 2023; David Batty and Jack Shenker, "Syria Suspended from Arab League," *The Guardian,* November 2011.

166 It ran a detention center: HRW, "Yemen: UAE Backs Abusive Local Forces," June 2017.

166 At least sixty: HRW, "The Persecution of Ahmed Mansoor," January 2021; HRW et al., "Joint Statement: UAE Human Rights Record Ahead of COP28," May 2023.

166 In July 2024, many: HRW, "UAE: Unfair Trial, Unjust Sentences," July 2024.

166 In addition, the UAE has: Declan Walsh, Christoph Koettl, and Eric Schmitt, "Talking Peace in Sudan, the U.A.E. Secretly Fuels the Fight," *The New York Times,* September 2023.

166 But she became: Heidi Blake, "The Fugitive Princess of Dubai," *New Yorker,* May 2023.

167 She was believed: Blake, "The Fugitive Princess of Dubai"; Madeleine Baran and Heidi Blake, "'The Runaway Princesses,' a New Yorker Podcast, Exposes the Plight of Dubai's Royal Women," *New Yorker,* January 2024; Jane McMullen, "Princess Latifa Urges UK Police to Reopen Sister's Kidnap Case," BBC, February 2021.

167 She had not been allowed: "#MissingPrincess: What Has Happened to Princess Latifa," BBC News, February 2021.

167 Before her flight: "Sheikha (Princess) Latifa Al Maktoum, FULL VIDEO— Escape from Dubai—#FreeLatifa," March 2018, https://www.youtube.com /watch?v=UN7OEFyNUkQ.

167 She said similar things: Bianca Britton, "Sheikha Latifa: Former UN Rights Chief Criticized for Calling Princess 'Troubled,'" CNN, December 2018.

167 She added that: "Dubai Princess Who Tried to Flee UAE 'Troubled': Ex-UN Human Rights Chief," NDTV, December 2018.

167 All of that sounded: "Mary Robinson 'Dismayed' over Comments on Her Visit to UAE Princess," Newstalk, December 2018.

167 Mohammed's treatment of his daughters: "#MissingPrincess: What Has Happened to Princess Latifa."

168 Major documentaries were produced: "#MissingPrincess: What Has happened to Princess Latifa"; "The Missing Princess: The Runaway Princess of Dubai," *60 Minutes Australia,* July 2018, https://www.youtube.com/watch ?v=TPuhzT47XWs.

168 Photographs began to appear: "Princess Latifa: Photo Appears to Show Dubai Ruler's Daughter in Spain," BBC News, June 2021.

168 That she remained: Blake, "The Fugitive Princess of Dubai."

168 In Saudi Arabia: International Labour Organization, "Making Decent Work a Reality for Domestic Workers in the Middle East," December 2021. At the time of Human Rights Watch's report, there were approximately 1.5 million migrant domestic workers in Saudi Arabia, HRW, "'As If I Am Not Human': Abuses Against Asian Domestic Workers in Saudi Arabia," July 2008.

169 they removed most: HRW, "Saudi Arabia Blocks Promised Access to Prisons," December 2006.

169 She showcased how: HRW, "'As If I Am Not Human': Abuses Against Asian Domestic Workers in Saudi Arabia."

169 employed the *kafala:* Kali Robertson, "What Is the Kafala System?" Council on Foreign Relations, November 2022.

169 Even if she could retrieve: Robertson, "What Is the Kafala System?"; Marie Dhumieres, "In Saudi Arabia, Indonesian Maids Are on Death Row for Sorcery," The World, March 2014; Abdul Hannan Tago, "Tortured Filipino Maid Faces Fresh Snag in Repatriation," *Arab News,* October 2014; Christian Lee & Telly Nathalia, "Saudi Arabia Releases Indonesian Maids Accused of Witchcraft," *Jakarta Globe,* April 2019; Ghazanfar Ali Khan, "On Death Row for Sorcery, Maid Spared by King," *Arab News,* February 2014.

170 After Nisha's further research: HRW, "Saudi Arabia: Domestic Workers Face Harsh Abuses," July 2008.

170 The report garnered: Peter Gelling, "Rights Group Urges Saudi Arabia to Protect Domestic Workers," *New York Times,* July 2008; Heba Saleh, "Call for Saudi Labour Law Reform," *Financial Times,* July 2008; Ian Black, "Human Rights: Saudis Treat Domestic Staff Like 'Virtual Slaves,'" *The Guardian,* July 2008; Nisha Varia, "Protecting Domestic Workers' Rights," HRW, July 2008.

170 Lacking decent employment: The World Bank, "Migration and Remittances Factbook 2008."

170 Workers who face abuse: International Labour Organization, "Regulatory Framework Governing Migrant Workers, Saudi Arabia," December 2023.

171 secure a landmark: International Labour Organization, "C189—Domestic Workers Convention, 2011 (No. 189)."

171 It entered into force: International Labour Organization, "Ratifications of C189—Domestic Workers Convention, 2011 (No. 189)."

171 The convention has: HRW, "Claiming Rights: Domestic Workers' Movements and Global Advances for Labor Reform," October 2013; International Labour Organization, "Making Decent Work a Reality for Domestic Workers in the Middle East: Progress and Prospects Ten Years After the Adoption of the ILO Domestic Workers Convention, 2011 (No. 189)," June 2021.

171 The Gulf Arab states: International Labour Organization, "Making Decent Work a Reality for Domestic Workers in the Middle East."

171 Ensuing national reforms: International Labour Organization, "Making Decent Work a Reality for Domestic Workers in the Middle East."

Chapter 8: War Crimes

172 By contrast, most people affected: Aryeh Neier, *The International Human Rights Movement: A History* (Princeton, NJ: Princeton University Press, 2020), 194.

173 "expected to cause": "Protocol Additional to the Geneva Conventions of 12 August 1949, and Relating to the Protection of Victims of International Armed Conflicts (Protocol I), 8 June 1977," "Article 51—Protection of the Civilian Population."

174 We published Jemera's: HRW, "Needless Deaths in the Gulf War: Civilian

Casualties During the Air Campaign and Violations of the Laws of War," November 1991.

174 We found that: Kenneth Roth, "Perspective on War: Civilians Are Off-Limits—Right?: Cheney Must Explain Why Populated Areas of Iraq Were Deliberately Bombed, a Violation of International Law," *Los Angeles Times,* February 1992.

174 But attacking forces: International Committee of the Red Cross, "International Humanitarian Law Databases—Article 57—Precautions in attack."

174 By exposing these situations: HRW, "Needless Deaths in the Gulf War: Civilian Casualties During the Air Campaign and Violations of the Laws of War," chapter 3.

175 Between two and three hundred: HRW, "Needless Deaths in the Gulf War: Civilian Casualties During the Air Campaign and Violations of the Laws of War."

175 Our report encouraged: HRW, "Needless Deaths in the Gulf War: Civilian Casualties During the Air Campaign and Violations of the Laws of War," chapter 4.

175 Our aim was: HRW, "'Between a Drone and Al-Qaeda': The Civilian Cost of US Targeted Killings in Yemen," October 2013. The U.S. government has held no one to account for these civilian deaths. Bonyan Jamal and Niku Jafarnia, "The US Is Failing Yemenis," The Hill, February 2024.

175 Amnesty International issued: Amnesty International, "'Will I Be Next?': US Drone Strikes in Pakistan," October 2013.

176 the meaning of "disproportionate": HRW, "Needless Deaths in the Gulf War: Civilian Casualties During the Air Campaign and Violations of the Laws of War," chapter 4.

176 Richard Cheney, then: Barton Gellman, "Allied Air War Struck Broadly in Iraq," *Washington Post,* June 1991.

176 When the Serbian: William M. Arkin, "Smart Bombs, Dumb Targeting?," *Bulletin of the Atomic Scientists,* May/June 2000. See also Peter Fairley, "An Essential Part of Modern Life That Armies Should Never Attack Again," *New York Times,* April 2024.

176 in March and June 2024: International Criminal Court, "Situation in Ukraine: ICC Judges Issue Arrest Warrants Against Sergei Ivanovich Kobylash and Viktor Nikolayevich Sokolov," March 2024; International Criminal Court, "Situation in Ukraine: ICC Judges Issue Arrest Warrants Against Sergei Kuzhugetovich Shoigu and Valery Vasilyevich Gerasimov," June 2024.

176 Bill uncovered ninety: HRW, "Civilian Deaths in the NATO Air Campaign," February 2000.

177 The most controversial: HRW, "Civilian Deaths in the NATO Air Campaign."

177 It was not: Montreal Institute for Genocide and Human Rights Studies, "Rwanda Radio Transcripts"; Scott Straus, "Rwanda and RTLM Radio Media Effects," June 2009, https://www.ushmm.org/.

177 While it did spew: International Committee of the Red Cross, "International Humanitarian Law Databases—Definition of Military Objectives."

177 At times, NATO: UN International Criminal Tribunal for the former Yugosla-

via, "Final Report to the Prosecutor by the Committee Established to Review the NATO Bombing Campaign Against the Federal Republic of Yugoslavia," June 2000.

177 NATO did warn them: HRW, "Civilian Deaths in the NATO Air Campaign."

177 Once the media: HRW, "Civilian Deaths in the NATO Air Campaign."

178 Yet the U.S.: UN Treaty Collection, "Convention on Cluster Munitions."

178 sent cluster munitions: Katie Rogers and Eric Schmitt, "Biden Defends 'Difficult' Decision to Send Cluster Munitions to Ukraine," *New York Times,* July 2023.

178 One element of that war: John M. Broder, "U.S. War Plan in Iraq: 'Decapitate' Leadership: Strategy: The Joint Chiefs Believe the Best Way to Oust the Iraqis Would Be Air Strikes Designed to Kill Hussein," *Los Angeles Times,* September 1990.

178 conducted fifty strikes: Marc Garlasco, "Twenty Years Ago the Invasion of #Iraq Began with Airstrikes on Dora Farms in an Attempt to Kill Saddam Hussein. I Was the Chief of High Value Targeting (HVT) in the Pentagon," Twitter post, March 19, 2023, 12:26 PM, https://twitter.com/marcgarlasco/status/1637490720008294402?s=20.

178 Many civilian lives: HRW, "Off Target: The Conduct of the War and Civilian Casualties in Iraq," December 2003.

178 Marc left Human Rights Watch: John Schwartz, "Rights Group Assailed for Analyst's Nazi Collection," *New York Times,* September 2009.

179 assisting the monitoring: Ben Birnbaum, "Minority Report," *New Republic,* April 2010.

179 One U.S. pilot: Randall Richard, "'Like Fish in a Barrel,' U.S. Pilots Say," *Washington Post,* February 1991; Kaleena Fraga, "How a Stretch of Road Between Kuwait and Iraq Became Known as the 'Highway of Death,'" All That's Interesting, January 2023; Rare Historical Photos, "Highway of Death, the Result of American Forces Bombing Retreating Iraqi Forces, Kuwait, 1991."

179 The sole exception: International Committee of the Red Cross, "International Humanitarian Law Databases—Rule 47. Attacks Against Persons Hors de Combat."

179 The Russian military: Olivia Yanchik, "Human Wave Tactics Are Demoralizing the Russian Army in Ukraine," Atlantic Council, April 2023; Nicolas Camut, "Over 20,000 Wagner Troops Killed, 40,000 Wounded in Ukraine: Prigozhin-Linked Channel," *Politico,* July 2023.

180 Another limitation of: International Committee of the Red Cross, "What Are Jus Ad Bellum and Jus in Bello?," January 2015.

180 We did not press: Kenneth Roth, "Saving Lives in Time of War," DAWN, August 2022.

180 Samuel Moyn of Yale: Samuel Moyn, *Humane: How the United States Abandoned Peace and Reinvented War* (New York: Farrar, Straus and Giroux, 2021).

180 He offered no: Dexter Filkins, "Did Making the Rules of War Better Make the World Worse," *New Yorker,* September 2021; Kenneth Roth, reply by Samuel Moyn, "Litigating the War on Terror: An Exchange," *New York Review of Books,* September 2021.

180 fought a "total war": Lawrence Freedman, "Kyiv and Moscow Are Fighting Two Different Wars," *Foreign Affairs,* February 2023.

181 Obviously, some groups: Samuel Moyn, "The Ethical and Political Stakes of Humanizing War," DAWN, August 2022.

181 David Kennedy, a Harvard Law: David Kennedy, "The International Human Rights Movement: Part of the Problem?," *Harvard Human Rights Journal,* 2002.

181 U.S. officials believed: HRW, " 'Between a Drone and Al-Qaeda': The Civilian Cost of US Targeted Killings in Yemen," October 2013.

182 A government is not allowed: Kenneth Roth, "What Rules Should Govern US Drone Attacks?," *New York Review of Books,* April 2013.

183 Once in custody: Kenneth Roth, "The Law of War in the War on Terror: Washington Abuse of 'Enemy Combatants,' " *Foreign Affairs,* January/February 2004.

183 What if a government: "How Mexico Has Become the 'Enemy' of America's Republicans," *The Economist,* July 2023.

183 That is what former: HRW, "Philippines' 'War on Drugs' "; International Criminal Court, "Republic of the Philippines."

183 That is why: Kenneth Roth, "Must It Always Be Wartime?," *New York Review of Books,* March 2017.

183 But the ICRC's: International Committee of the Red Cross, "International Humanitarian Law Databases—The Threshold of Non-International Armed Conflict."

183 President Biden imposed: Charles Savage, "Biden Rules Tighten Limits on Drone Strikes," *New York Times,* July 2023; "Biden Offers Smart Rules of Engagement for the Drone War," *Washington Post,* July 2023; Gia Kokotakis, "Biden Administration Declassifies Two Counterterrorism Memorandums," Lawfare, July 2023.

184 The clearest example: International Committee of the Red Cross, "International Humanitarian Law Databases—Rule 11. Indiscriminate Attacks."

184 A 1980 protocol: UN Office for Disarmament Affairs, "The Protocol on Prohibitions or Restrictions on the Use of Mines, Booby-Traps and Other Devices as Amended on 3 May 1996 (Amended Protocol II)"; International Committee of the Red Cross, "International Humanitarian Law Databases—Rule 81. Restrictions on the Use of Landmines"; UN Office for Disarmament Affairs, "High Contracting Parties and Signatories CCW"; Arms Project of HRW and Physicians for Human Rights, "Landmines: A Deadly Legacy," October 1993.

184 We called land mines: Arms Project of HRW and Physicians for Human Rights, "Landmines: A Deadly Legacy."

184 We cofounded a global: International Campaign to Ban Landmines, "20 Years in the Life of a Nobel Peace Prizewinning Campaign," May 2012.

184 Negotiations began at the UN: UN Office for Disarmament Affairs, "The Convention on Conventional Weapons."

184 The Canadian and Norwegian: "Jody Williams Nobel Lecture," Nobel Peace Prize 1997, December 1997.

184 The result was: "Convention on the Prohibition of the Use, Stockpiling, Production and Transfer of Anti-Personnel Mines and on Their Destruction"; International Committee of the Red Cross, "Overview of the Convention on the Prohibition of Anti-Personnel Mines," August 2007.

184 In 2022, land mines: HRW, "Landmines: Boost Support for Global Ban Treaty," November 2022; HRW, "Ukraine: Banned Landmines Harm Civilians," January 2023.

185 Moreover, many bomblets: HRW, "Cluster Munitions," 2014.

185 One would have thought: HRW, "Cluster Munitions and International Humanitarian Law: The Need for Better Compliance and Stronger Rules," July 2004.

185 We investigated and reported: HRW, "NATO's Use of Cluster Munitions in Yugoslavia," May 1999; HRW, "Fatally Flawed: Cluster Bombs and Their Use by the United States in Afghanistan," December 2002; HRW, "Flooding South Lebanon: Israel's Use of Cluster Munitions in Lebanon in July and August 2006," February 2008.

185 We were the first: HRW, "Cluster Bombs: Memorandum for Convention on Conventional Weapons (CCW) Delegates," December 1999; Steve Goose, "Cluster Munitions: Toward a Global Solution," HRW, World Report 2004.

185 So we moved: Cluster Munitions Coalition, "Global Ban."

185 We pushed for: "Cablegate: Arms Control Panel Ignores Real Issues at Munich Security," SCOOP Wikileaks, February 2008.

185 By 2023, 112: UN Treaty Collection, "Convention on Cluster Munitions."

185 There are still: HRW, "Cluster Munitions: Renew Global Momentum for Ban," May 2023; Cluster Munition Coalition, "Cluster Munition Monitor 2023," August 2023.

186 our Arms Project: "The Arms Project," HRW, World Report 1993.

186 Under Steve, it also led: HRW, "Blinding Laser Weapons: The Need to Ban a Cruel and Inhumane Weapon," September 1995; HRW, "Killer Robots"; Campaign to Stop Killer Robots, "Stephen D. Goose of Human Rights Watch," June 2016, https://www.youtube.com/watch?v=7_wpQehHkF0.

Chapter 9: Israel

188 We documented and denounced: HRW, "Civilians Under Assault: Hezbollah's Rocket Attacks on Israel in the 2006 War," August 2007; see also HRW, "Lebanon: Hezbollah Rocket Attacks on Haifa Designed to Kill Civilians," July 2006.

188 Hezbollah threatened demonstrations: HRW, "Lebanon/Israel: Hezbollah Smear Campaign Won't Silence Report," August 2007.

188 Hezbollah went so far: Yotam Berger and Jonathan Lis, "25 Years After Hebron Massacre, Debate Sparked over Burial Site of Murderer Baruch Goldstein," *Haaretz*, February 2019.

188 No one can: International Committee of the Red Cross, "Exploring Humanitarian Law," January 2009.

188 The Israeli military: International Committee of the Red Cross, "International Humanitarian Law Databases—Rule 22. Principle of Precautions Against the Effects of Attacks."

189 We investigated almost two dozen: HRW, "Fatal Strikes: Israel's Indiscriminate Attacks Against Civilians in Lebanon," August 2006.

189 The Israeli military also: HRW, "Flooding South Lebanon: Israel's Use of Cluster Munitions in Lebanon in July and August 2006," February 2008.

189 But shortly after: Israeli Missions Around the World, "Avihai Mandelblit."

189 In 2019, as Israel's: "Netanyahu Indicted on Corruption Charges, Says He Won't Resign," France 24, November 2019.

189 I said, as he knew: International Committee of the Red Cross, "What Is International Humanitarian Law?," April 2022.

190 I noted that: Nils Melzer, "The Principle of Distinction Under International Humanitarian Law," Chapter XI, in *Targeted Killing in International Law* (Oxford: Oxford University Press, 2008).

190 We had been highly critical: HRW, "Palestine: No Letup in Arbitrary Arrests, Torture," May 2019.

190 He vowed that: Dr. Mohammad Shtayyeh (@DrShtayyeh), "Today I Met with a Senior Delegation from HRW, Headed by @kenroth and Confirmed My Government's Commitment to/ Guarantee of the Right of Palestinian Citizens," Twitter post, July 27, 2019, 2:22 PM, https://twitter.com/DrShtayyeh/status/1155181803138949120?s=20.

190 He did not keep: HRW, "Palestine: Impunity for Arbitrary Arrests, Torture," June 2022.

191 Because Israel had: Robert L. Bernstein, "Rights Watchdog, Lost in the Mideast," *New York Times,* October 2009.

191 made these points: Jane Olson and Jonathan Fanton, "Crossfire: A Rights Group and Israel," *New York Times,* October 2009.

191 Nonetheless, partisan defenders: Alan M. Dershowitz, "Elon Musk Is Right About George Soros—and Not Anti-Semitic," *Wall Street Journal,* May 2023.

191 Shortly before he died: Robert D. McFadden, "Robert L. Bernstein, Publisher and Champion of Dissent, Dies at 96," *New York Times,* May 2019.

192 In a major report: HRW, "Occupation, Inc.: How Settlement Businesses Contribute to Israel's Violations of Palestinian Rights," January 2016.

192 The issue was sensitive: "BDS," https://bdsmovement.net/.

192 Two and a half years before: HRW, "Israel: Human Rights Watch Denied Work Permit," February 2017; Letter from Moshe Nakash to Emily Schaeffer Omer-Man, February 2017, https://www.hrw.org/.

192 They reversed course: HRW, "Israel: Human Rights Watch Granted Work Permit," April 2017; Ian Fisher, "Israel Denies a Work Visa to Human Rights Watch Researcher," *New York Times,* February 2017; Peter Beaumont, "Israel Denies Visas to Staff from 'Hostile' Human Rights Watch," *The Guardian,* February 2017; Oren Liebermann, Elise Labott, and James Masters, "Israel Denies Work Permit for Human Rights Watch Director," CNN, February 2017.

193 "no information has surfaced": HRW, "Israel Orders Human Rights Watch Official Deported," May 2018; Letter from Moshe Nakash to Michael Sfard, May 2018, https://www.hrw.org/.

193 I traveled to: HRW, "Israel Expels Human Rights Watch Director Today," November 2019; Isabel Kershner, "Israel to Expel Human Rights Worker, Citing Anti-Boycott Law," *New York Times,* November 2019; Oliver Holmes, "'Israel Is Joining an Ugly Club,' Says Rights Group as Director Expelled," *The Guardian,* November 2019; "Israel Expels HRW Country Director," Deutsche Welle, November 2019; UN Office of the High Commissioner for Human Rights, "UN Experts Condemn Israeli Decision to Expel Omar Shakir of Human Rights Watch," November 2019.

193 At the airport: "Israel's Deportation of Human Rights Watch Activist Condemned," BBC, November 2019.

193 The groups included: Zena Agha, "Israel Moves to Silence the Stalwarts of Palestinian Civil Society," *New York Times,* November 2021; Yuval Abraham, Oren Ziv, and Meron Rapoport, "Secret Israeli Dossier Provides No Proof for Declaring Palestinian NGOs 'Terrorists,'" *+972 Magazine,* November 2021; HRW, "Israel/Palestine: Designation of Palestinian Rights Groups as Terrorists," October 2021.

193 Human Rights Watch braced: HRW, "A Threshold Crossed: Israeli Authorities and the Crimes of Apartheid and Persecution," April 2021.

193 a "one-state reality": Michael Barnett, Nathan Brown, Marc Lynch, and Shibley Telhami, "Israel's One-State Reality," *Foreign Affairs,* April 2023.

193 but the conclusion: B'Tselem, "A Regime of Jewish Supremacy from the Jordan River to the Mediterranean Sea: This Is Apartheid," January 2021; Al-Haq, "Al-Haq Launches Landmark Palestinian Coalition Report: 'Israeli Apartheid: Tool of Zionist Settler Colonialism,'" November 2022; Amnesty International, "Israel's Apartheid Against Palestinians: Cruel System of Domination and Crime Against Humanity," February 2022; UN News, "Israel's Occupation of Palestinian Territory Is 'Apartheid': UN Rights Expert," March 2022.

194 For many years: Chris McGreal, "Amnesty Says Israel Is an Apartheid State. Many Israeli Politicians Agree," *The Guardian,* February 2022; Ofer Aderet, "Rabin in 1976 Interview: Settlements Are a Cancer," *Haaretz,* September 2015.

194 So had commentators: Thomas L. Friedman, "From Tel Aviv to Riyadh," *New York Times,* June 2023; Thomas L. Friedman, "How the Mideast Conflict Is Blowing Up the Region, the Democratic Party and Every Synagogue in America," *New York Times,* May 2021; Jimmy Carter, *Palestine: Peace Not Apartheid* (New York: Simon & Schuster, 2006); Carter Center, "Jimmy Carter Issues Letter to Jewish Community on Palestine Peace Not Apartheid," December 2006; Peter Beaumont, "Israel Risks Becoming Apartheid State if Peace Talks Fail, Says John Kerry," *The Guardian,* April 2014.

194 We also traveled: B'Tselem, "Settlements," January 2019, https://www.btselem.org/settlements.

194 It exists as: Mitch Potter, "The Toronto Man Who Saved Nazareth," *Toronto Star,* December 2015.

195 We analyzed these findings: Rome Statute of the International Criminal Court, July 1998, Article 7(1)(j); "International Convention on the Suppression and Punishment of the Crime of Apartheid," 1974.

195 We found that these elements: HRW, "A Threshold Crossed: Israeli Authorities and the Crimes of Apartheid and Persecution," April 2021.

196 Some of its partisans: Jennifer Schuessler and Marc Tracy, "Harvard Reverses Course on Human Rights Advocate Who Criticized Israel," *New York Times,* January 2023.

196 But that "defense": Tracey Wilkinson, "Is Israel's Treatment of Palestinians a form of Apartheid?," *Los Angeles Times,* January 2024.

196 Even a former head: Chris McGreal, "Israel Imposing Apartheid on Palestinians, Says Former Mossad Chief," *The Guardian,* September 2023.

196 Ritual invocations of the "peace process": Kenneth Roth, "Reassessing the Approach to Israel," Deutsche Welle, May 2023.

196 As we had urged: UN Human Rights Council, "The Independent International Commission of Inquiry on the Occupied Palestinian Territory, Including East Jerusalem, and Israel."

197 The International Court of Justice: International Court of Justice, "Legal Consequences Arising from the Policies and Practices of Israel in the Occupied Palestinian Territory, Including East Jerusalem," July 2024.

197 Netanyahu in February 2024: Isabel Kershner, "Israel's Government Formally Rejects the Unilateral Recognition of a Palestinian State," *New York Times,* February 2024.

197 obstruction of much food: Vivian Yee, Adam Sella, and Roni Caryn Rabin, "Inspections, Bottlenecks and Safety Concerns Hinder Gaza Aid," *New York Times,* January 2024; Liam Stack, "Parts of Gaza Are in Famine, World Food Program Chief Says," *New York Times,* May 2024; Jennifer Hansler, "USAID Administrator Says It Is 'Credible' to Assess Famine Is Already Occurring in Parts of Gaza," CNN, April 2024.

197 He also sought: Statement of ICC Prosecutor Karim A. A. Khan KC: Applications for Arrest Warrants in the Situation in the State of Palestine, International Criminal Court, May 2024.

197 In an interview: "ICC Prosecutor: UK Didn't Blitz the IRA—Israel Needs That Restraint," *Sunday Times,* May 2024; Robin Stein, Haley Willis, Ishaan Jhaveri, Danielle Miller, Aaron Byrd, and Natalie Reneau, "Visual Evidence Shows Israel Dropped 2,000-Pound Bombs Where It Ordered Gaza's Civilians to Move for Safety," *New York Times,* December 2023.

197 Attacks on civilians: International Committee of the Red Cross, International Humanitarian Law Databases, "Definition of Indiscriminate Attacks" and "Proportionality in Attack."

197 or the deliberate starving: Rome Statute of the International Criminal Court, Article 8(2)(b)(xxv).

197 prohibits transferring members: "Geneva Convention Relative to the Protec-

tion of Civilian Persons in Time of War of 12 August 1949," Articles 49 and 147.

197 The Rome Statute: Rome Statute of the International Criminal Court, Article 8(2)(b)(viii).

197 Under Netanyahu's far-right government: Isabel Kershner, "Israel's Push to Expand West Bank Settlements, Explained," *New York Times*, June 2023; Cate Brown, "Israel Announces Largest West Bank Land Seizure Since 1993 During Blinken Visit," *Washington Post*, March 2024.

197 The Israeli government denies: E.g., Dore Gold, "From 'Occupied Territories' to 'Disputed Territories,'" Jerusalem Center for Public Affairs, January 2002.

198 Few governments endorse: Chris McGreal, "Pompeo Says Israel Has Biblical Claim to Palestine and Is 'Not an Occupying Nation,'" *The Guardian*, February 2023.

198 The International Court of Justice rejected: Kenneth Roth, "The ICJ Has Demolished Israel's Claims That It Is Not Occupying Palestinian Territories," *The Guardian*, July 2024.

198 In a September 1967 memo: Gershom Gorenberg, "Israel's Tragedy Foretold," *New York Times*, March 2006; Gershom Gorenberg, "The Man Who Tried to Save Israel from Itself," *Foreign Policy*, June 2024.

198 The resolution provided: UN Security Council, Resolution 2334 (2016), December 2016; United Nations, "Israel's Settlements Have No Legal Validity, Constitute Flagrant Violation of International Law, Security Council Reaffirms," December 2016.

198 This was also: "Pompeo: US No Longer Considers Israeli Settlements Illegal," Al Jazeera, November 2019.

198 Blinken reinstated it: John Hudson and Karen DeYoung, "White House Reverses West Bank Policy, Calling Israeli Settlements Illegal," *Washington Post*, February 2024; Jonathan Weisman, "Biden's Reversal on Israeli settlements, Days Before the Michigan Primary, Shows the Political Bind He's In," *New York Times*, February 2024.

198 chief prosecutor, Fatou Bensouda: Julian Borger, "Trump Targets ICC with Sanctions After Court Opens War Crimes Investigation," *The Guardian*, June 2020; Julian Borger, "US Imposes Sanctions on Top International Criminal Court Officials," *The Guardian*, September 2020; Pranshu Verma, "Trump's Sanctions on International Court May Do Little Beyond Alienating Allies," *New York Times*, October 2020; HRW, "US Sanctions on the International Criminal Court," December 2020.

198 The Biden administration: U.S. Department of State, "Ending Sanctions and Visa Restrictions Against Personnel of the International Criminal Court," April 2021.

198 Still, Biden called: "Statement from President Joe Biden on the Warrant Applications by the International Criminal Court," White House, May 2024.

199 Antony Blinken said: "Warrant Applications by the International Criminal Court," U.S. Department of State, May 2024.

199 Biden called it "justified": Jeff Mason and Simon Lewis, "Biden Says Putin Committed War Crimes, Calls Charges Justified," Reuters, March 2023.

199 Blinken could have been referring: "ICC Pre-Trial Chamber I Issues Its Decision on the Prosecutor's Request Related to Territorial Jurisdiction over Palestine," International Criminal Court, February 2021; "General Assembly Votes Overwhelmingly to Accord Palestine 'Non-Member Observer State' Status in United Nations," United Nations, November 2012.

199 Blinken also mentioned: "Statement of ICC Prosecutor Karim A. A. Khan KC from Ramallah on the Situation in the State of Palestine and Israel," International Criminal Court, December 2023.

199 "callously pouring gasoline": Prime Minister of Israel, X, Twitter post, May 20, 2024, 2:46 PM, https://x.com/IsraeliPM/status/1792628054075883543.

199 Rather than investigate: Yuval Abraham and Meron Rapoport, "Surveillance and Interference: Israel's Covert War on the ICC Exposed," *+972 Magazine,* May 2024.

199 Israeli intelligence agents: Harry Davies, Bethan McKernan, Yuval Abraham, and Meron Rapoport, "Spying, Hacking and Intimidation: Israel's Nine-Year 'War' on the ICC Exposed," *The Guardian,* May 2024; Kenneth Roth, "The ICC Spying Revelations Show the Israeli Government to Be a Lawless Regime," *The Guardian,* May 2024.

200 Alan Dershowitz, the Harvard Law: Alan Dershowitz, "Dershowitz: Jews Shouldn't Be Defending George Soros Against Elon Musk," *Jerusalem Post,* June 2023; see also Alan M. Dershowitz, "Elon Musk Is Right About George Soros—and Not Anti-Semitic."

200 One of the leaders: Prof Gerald M Steinberg, "Roth Is the Most Powerful and Obsessive Israel-Basher (#antisemitism) of the 21st Century," Twitter post, March 5, 2023, 5:11 AM, https://x.com/GeraldNGOM/status/1632322856464859136?s=20.

200 The charge of antisemitism: Arsen Ostrovsky, "Just Your Daily Reminder That @KenRoth of @hrw Is an Unhinged Antisemite with a Pathological Obsession with Israel," Twitter post, July 27, 2022, 3:33 AM, https://x.com/Ostrov_A/status/1552195349498007558?s=20; Arsen Ostrovsky (@Ostrov_A), "You disgusting Jew hater. Can't even bring yourself to condemn Palestinian terror attack . . . @KenRoth @hrw," Twitter post, April 9, 2022, 7:13 AM, https://x.com/Ostrov_A/status/1512750581806469122; JCCWatch.org (@JCCWatch), "Dany, you are plain wrong: Jew Hate has no place at Harvard @KenRoth targets Jews and uses @hrw to falsely smear Israel to promote Jew Hatred," Twitter post, January 14, 2023, 1:33 AM, https://x.com/JCCWatch/status/1614148801731633153?s=20.

201 "An eye for an eye": Kenneth Roth, "Letter to the Editor, 'Getting It Straight,'" *New York Sun,* July 2006.

201 While defending the disproportionate: Abraham Foxman, "No Accident," *New York Sun,* August 2006.

201 To enhance the antisemitism charge: Prof Gerald M Steinberg, "Mike Offner: '@TheNation implying that Jews cannot be #antisemitic is itself #antisemitic'—on @kenroth's lame attempt to use of his (thin) Jewish roots," Twitter post, January 10, 2023, 3:03 AM, https://x.com/GeraldNGOM/status/1612721803939422208?s=20; Prof Gerald M Steinberg, "@kenroth

is significant—exploiting his nominal Jewish background and his father's stories from pre-Shoa Germany," Twitter post, January 27, 2023, 5:00 AM, https://x.com/GeraldNGOM/status/1618911897927180288?s=20; Prof Gerald M Steinberg, "My reading of ~25 yrs of Roth's obsession.... His only Jewish identity is to use his father's history in Nazi Germany as a shield," Twitter post, January 15, 2023, 9:59 AM, https://x.com/GeraldNGOM/status /1614638495053537283?s=20.

201 To challenge my Judaism: "Kenneth Roth," Wikipedia.

201 At one point: "Kenneth Roth: Revision history," Wikipedia.

201 My willingness to criticize: Democracy Now!, "'There is a real effort to redefine antisemitism to mean, essentially, criticism of Israel,' says @KenRoth," Twitter post, January 9, 2023, 9:02 AM, https://x.com/democracynow/status /1612449642800893952?s=20.

201 Other Jewish critics: Peter Beinart, "Has the Fight Against Antisemitism Lost Its Way?," *New York Times,* August 2022; Jeffrey Goldberg, "Goldblog vs. Peter Beinart, Part II," *The Atlantic,* May 2010.

201 and Richard Goldstone: Barry Bearak, "South African Judge May Be Kept from Grandson's Bar Mitzvah," *New York Times,* April 2010; UN Human Rights Council, "United Nations Fact Finding Mission on the Gaza Conflict."

201 He later retracted: Richard Goldstone, "Reconsidering the Goldstone Report on Israel and War Crimes," *Washington Post,* April 2011; see also Kenneth Roth, "Gaza: The Stain Remains on Israel's War Record," *The Guardian,* April 2011.

201 As one Australian journalist: John Lyons, "Touchy Subject: We Must End Self-Censorship on Israel and Palestine," *Sydney Morning Herald,* October 2021.

201 One working definition: International Holocaust Remembrance Alliance, "Working Definition of Antisemitism."

202 That example lies behind: World Jewish Congress, "Antisemitism Defined: Double Standards Against the State of Israel," May 2022; Echoes & Reflections, "The New Antisemitism and the Three Ds," 2020.

202 Although we did not address: HRW, "Erased in a Moment: Suicide Bombing Attacks Against Israeli Civilians," October 2002.

202 Some partisans claimed: Jonathan S. Tobin, "Harvard Surrenders to the Antisemites," Jewish News Syndicate, January 2023.

202 Some say: Denver Riggleman et al., "Memes, Missiles, and Mobilizations: An Analysis of the 2021 Israel/Hamas Conflict," Network Contagion Research Institute, January 2023; HRW, "'An Open Prison Without End': Myanmar's Mass Detention of Rohingya in Rakhine State," October 2020.

202 One prominent partisan: "Goal of IHRA Anti-Semitism Definition Is to Target Human Rights Groups, Says Proponent," *Middle East Monitor,* April 2023.

203 "It is not antisemitic": "The Jerusalem Declaration on Antisemitism," https:// jerusalemdeclaration.org/.

203 "Paying disproportionate attention": Nexus, "The Nexus Document," https:// nexusproject.us/the-nexus-document/.

203 Indeed, Kenneth Stern: Kenneth Stern, "I Drafted the Definition of Anti-semitism. Rightwing Jews Are Weaponizing It," *The Guardian,* December 2019; Elizabeth Williamson, "Preaching Tolerance Abroad, as Hatred Surges at Home," *New York Times,* May 2023.

203 More than one hundred: HRW, "UN: More Groups Address 'Antisemitism' Issue," April 2023.

203 "Calling out China": Gareth Evans, "Not Anti-Semitic," *Sydney Morning Herald,* June 2021.

204 "a slate of 169": Ron Kampeas, "Prominent Jewish Leaders Add to Drumbeat of Criticism of Israel's New Government," Jewish Telegraphic Agency, February 2023.

204 The signatories included: Mark I. Pinsky, "Is Our Fear of Antisemitism Poisoning Our Discussion of Israel?," *Moment,* February 2023.

204 In August 2023: "'Accusing Israel of Apartheid Is Not Anti-Semitic': Holocaust Historian," Al Jazeera, August 2023.

204 When I explained: Hilary Leila Krieger, "We Don't Do Comparisons," *Jerusalem Post,* November 2004.

204 To this day: E.g., Alicia Segovia, "Hey Ken don't you have ANY OTHER concern than Israel? Your excessive scrutiny is, itself, antisemitic," Twitter post, June 20, 2023, 7:41 AM, https://twitter.com/asegovia9/status/16674970916342 00578?s=46&t=gSyXb7sKiD3Vw2KlEZi5NQ.

205 To note this: Roger Cohen, "For Europe's Jews, a World of Fear," *New York Times,* October 2023; Kanishka Singh, "US Antisemitic, Islamophobic Incidents Surge with War, Advocates Say," Reuters, October 2023; Conference of Presidents of Major American Jewish Organizations, "Hatred of Israel Is Endangering American Jews," December 2023; see also Ayal K. Feinberg, "Homeland Violence and Diaspora Insecurity: An Analysis of Israel and American Jewry," in *Politics and Religion* (Cambridge: Cambridge University Press), July 2019.

205 As Jonathan Greenblatt: ADL, "ADL Records Dramatic Increase in U.S. Antisemitic Incidents Following Oct. 7 Hamas Massacre," October 2023.

205 "It is a universal": Jeffrey Goldberg, "Does Human Rights Watch Understand the Nature of Prejudice?," *The Atlantic,* September 2014.

205 It said that Amnesty's: ADL, "ADL Condemns Amnesty International's Latest Effort to Demonize Israel," January 2022.

205 The ADL, the American Jewish Committee: Conference of Presidents of Major American Organizations, "Jewish Organizations Condemn Inflammatory Amnesty International-UK Report on Israel," January 2022.

205 Another critic accused: Alexander Joffe, "Israeli Voices Get Silenced on Campus; Jew Haters Are Given 'Academic Freedom,'" *Algemeiner,* February 2023.

206 Netanyahu, for example: Zeev Sternhell, "Why Benjamin Netanyahu Loves the European Far-Right," *Foreign Policy,* February 2014; Ilan Ben Zion, "Netanyahu Greets Hungary's Orban as 'True Friend of Israel,'" AP, July 2018; Lili Bayer, "Hungarian Government Campaign Renews Antisemitism Concerns," *The Guardian,* November 2023.

206 As Peter Beinart pointed out: Peter Beinart, "Antisemitic Zionists Aren't a Contradiction in Terms," *Jewish Currents*, January 2023.

206 Indeed, the leading American Jewish: Peter Beinart, "Has the Fight Against Antisemitism Lost Its Way?," *New York Times,* August 2022.

206 So did Aharon Barak: Patrick Kingsley, "He's 86 and Long Retired. Why Are Israelis Protesting Outside His Home?," *New York Times,* May 2023.

207 As Netanyahu described it: Prime Minster of Israel, "The weak crumble, are slaughtered and are erased from history while the strong, for good or for ill, survive. The strong are respected, and alliances are made with the strong, and in the end peace is made with the strong." Twitter post, August 29, 2018, 1:05 PM, https://x.com/IsraeliPM/status/1034849460344573952?s=20.

207 "Israel had to make clear": Abraham Foxman, "No Accident."

207 Instead, he banks on: Thomas L. Friedman, "American Jews, You Have to Choose Sides on Israel," *New York Times,* March 2023; Ross Douthat, "The Israel-Hamas War Will Reshape Western Politics," *New York Times,* November 2023; Ishaan Tharoor, "It's the Republicans, Not the Democrats, Who Are Radical on Israel," *Washington Post,* July 2023; Chrissy Stroop, "Stop Gaslighting the Left About Evangelicals. They Believe Awful Things About Jews," *The Forward,* September 2019.

208 It later emerged: Emma Petit, "A Human-Rights Leader Was Denied a Harvard Post over Alleged 'Anti-Israel Bias.' Now a Dean Faces Calls to Resign," *Chronicle of Higher Education,* January 2023.

208 The journalist Michael Massing: Michael Massing, "Why the Godfather of Human Rights Is Not Welcome at Harvard," *The Nation,* January 2023.

208 At first, Elmendorf: Miles J. Herszenhorn and Asher J. Montgomery, "Hundreds Call for Resignation of Harvard Kennedy School Dean Accused of Blocking Fellowship over Israel Criticism," *Harvard Crimson,* January 2023.

209 Elmendorf justified his decision: Miles J. Herszenhorn, "Former Human Rights Watch Head Says Harvard Kennedy School Dean Blocked Fellowship over Israel Criticism," *Harvard Crimson,* January 2023.

209 That was an odd: Herszenhorn, "Former Human Rights Watch Head Says Harvard Kennedy School Dean Blocked Fellowship over Israel Criticism"; Harvard Kennedy School Center for Public Leadership, "Wexner Israel Fellowship"; Miles J. Herszenhorn, "Palestinian Advocacy Group Protests Former Israeli Military Official at Harvard Kennedy School," *Harvard Crimson,* February 2022.

209 On rare occasion: Herszenhorn, "Former Human Rights Watch Head Says Harvard Kennedy School Dean Blocked Fellowship over Israel Criticism."

209 It also yielded: "Harvard's Rejection of Human Rights Leader Sends Chilling Message," *Boston Globe,* January 2023; Michael Casey, "Harvard Rescinds Fellowship Offer to Leading Rights Activist," *Boston Globe,* January 2023; Hilary Burns, "Harvard's Decision to Not Offer Fellowship to Leading Human Rights Activist Brings Uproar," *Boston Globe,* January 2023.

209 In addition, I placed: Kenneth Roth, "Harvard Needs to Stand with Its Principles, Not with Israel—or Its Donors," *Boston Globe,* January 2023; Kenneth Roth, "I Once Ran Human Rights Watch. Harvard Blocked My Fellowship

over Israel," *The Guardian,* January 2023; Chris McGreal, "Harvard Blocks Role for Former Human Rights Watch Head over Israel Criticism," *The Guardian,* January 2023.

209 After two weeks: Jennifer Schuessler and Marc Tracy, "Harvard Reverses Course on Human Rights Advocate Who Criticized Israel," *New York Times,* January 2023; Travis Andersen and Hilary Burns, "Harvard Dean Reverses Decision Not to Offer Fellowship to Human Rights Activist Kenneth Roth," *Boston Globe,* January 2023.

210 He hid behind: Harvard Kennedy School, "Update Regarding Ken Roth as a Fellow at HKS," January 2023.

210 In September 2023: "Elmendorf to Step Down as Dean of Harvard Kennedy School," *Harvard Gazette,* September 2023.

210 For years, universities: Joseph Leone, "The Harvard Kennedy School's Anti-Palestinian Bias," *Jewish Currents,* January 2023.

210 I discovered that my efforts: Kenneth Roth, "Crimes of War in Gaza," *The New York Review of Books,* July 2024.

210 The media kept asking: Kenneth Roth, "The Law Limits Israel's Response to Hamas," *Daily Princetonian,* October 2023.

210 I explained that Hamas's initial attacks: Kenneth Roth, "The Attack on Israel Has Been Called a '9/11 Moment.' Therein Lies a Cautionary Tale," *The Guardian,* October 2023.

210 that humanitarian law requires: UNITAR, "35% of Buildings Affected in Gaza Strip," March 2024.

211 that even a military target: Robin Stein et al., "A Times Investigation Tracked Israel's Use of One of Its Most Destructive Bombs in South Gaza," *New York Times,* December 2023; Annie Sparrow and Kenneth Roth, "Destroying Gaza's Health Care System Is a War Crime," *Foreign Policy,* February 2024.

211 that Hamas's wrongful use: Kenneth Roth, "South Africa's Genocide Case Against Israel Is Imperfect but Persuasive. It May Win," *The Guardian,* January 2024.

211 that the Israeli warnings: Roth, "South Africa's Genocide Case Against Israel Is Imperfect but Persuasive. It May Win"; Kenneth Roth, "Israel Appears to Be on the Verge of Ethnic Cleansing in Gaza," *The Guardian,* October 2023; Kenneth Roth, "The ICJ Ruling Is a Repudiation of Israel and Its Western Backers," *The Guardian,* February 2024; "UN Chief Says Blocked Gaza Aid Is a 'Moral Outrage,' Calls for War to End," Al Jazeera, March 2024.

211 I noted that Hamas's: Roth, "South Africa's Genocide Case Against Israel Is Imperfect but Persuasive. It May Win"; Roth, "The ICJ Ruling Is a Repudiation of Israel and Its Western Backers."

211 I addressed the devastation: Roth, "Israel Appears to Be on the Verge of Ethnic Cleansing in Gaza"; Bethany Dawson, "EU and UK Slam Israeli Ministers' Call for 'Voluntary Emigration' from Gaza Strip," *Politico,* January 2024.

211 When Israel claimed: Kenneth Roth, "Israel's Attempt to Destroy Unrwa Is Part of Its Starvation Strategy in Gaza," *The Guardian,* March 2024.

211 I added that to discuss: Roth, "Israel's Attempt to Destroy Unrwa Is Part of Its

Starvation Strategy in Gaza"; Kenneth Roth, "Atrocities Seeks Extreme Reaction. Don't Give Hamas What It Wants," *Time,* October 2023.

212 And I decried the damage: Roth, "The ICJ Ruling Is a Repudiation of Israel and Its Western Backers."

Chapter 10: The United Nations

213 That began to change: United Nations, "The United Nations—Partner in the Struggle Against Apartheid."

213 Some governments, typically: Helen James, Pauline Turuban, and Dorian Burkhalter, "How China Is Rewriting Human Rights Norms," Swiss Info, September 2023.

214 The guardian of that status: United Nations, "Committee on Non-Governmental Organizations."

214 Some highly abusive: Dorian Burkhalter, "NGOs Face Uphill Battle to Gain Access to the UN," Swiss Info, March 2023.

214 operate by "consensus": United Nations, "Committee on Non-Governmental Organizations."

215 As *The New York Times:* "A Gang of Six at the U.N.," *New York Times,* February 1991.

215 The Iraqi delegate: Paul Lewis, "Faction in U.N. Panel Blocks a Rights Group," *New York Times,* February 1991.

215 Human Rights Watch was finally: Carter Center, "Human Rights, The United Nations, and Nongovernmental Organizations," 18.

215 high commissioner for human rights: UN Office of the High Commissioner for Human Rights, "High Commissioner."

216 A central reason: Suzanne Nossel, "The Job of Human Rights Chief Isn't What You Think," *Foreign Policy,* August 2018.

216 To the contrary: Paul Lewis, "Ecuadorean Nominated as U.N.'s New Human Rights Chief," *New York Times,* February 1994; Andrew Clapham, "Creating the High Commissioner for Human Rights: The Outside Story," *European Journal of International Law,* 1994.

216 Ayala-Lasso saw his role: Julia Preston, "First U.N. Commissioner for Rights Proves Low Key," *Washington Post,* December 1994; Imogen Foulkes, "Inside Geneva: Universal Human Rights at 75. Who Defends Them?," Swiss Info.

216 He managed to complete: Aryeh Neier, *War Crimes: Brutality, Genocide, Terror, and the Struggle for Justice* (New York: Times Books, 1998), 23–24; Reed Brody, "Give the World a Clear Voice for Human Rights," *International Herald Tribune,* March 1997.

216 He was so bad: Paul Lewis, "U.N. and U.S. Pressed on Rights Stance," *New York Times,* February 1997.

217 Aided by Annan: HRW, "Robinson Addresses Security Council: 'It's About Time,'" September 1999.

217 She spoke out: Mary Robinson, "Chechnya: Mary Robinson's Report," *New York Review of Books,* May 2000; "Robinson Again Seeks POW Status for Guantanamo Captives," Swiss Info, February 2002.

217 She visited China: HRW, "No Breakthrough Yet on Human Rights in China," September 1998.

217 Her most controversial: HRW, "Human Rights Developments," World Report 2002; Rachel L. Swarns, "The Racism Walkout: The Overview; U.S. and Israelis Quit Racism Talks over Denunciation," *New York Times*, September 2001; HRW, "Disappointment as U.S. Bolts Race Conference," September 2001; "Racism Summit Seeks Breakthrough," BBC News, September 2001; "Mixed Emotions as Durban Winds Up," BBC News, September 2001.

217 marred by intolerance: Mark McKinnon, "Israel Threatens to Pull Delegates," *Globe and Mail,* September 2001.

217 the concluding document: World Conference against Racism, Racial Discrimination, Xenophobia and Related Intolerance, "Declaration," September 2001; "Mixed Emotions as Durban Winds Up," BBC News, September 2001.

217 Yet pro-Israel partisans: Tom Lantos, "The Durban Debacle: An Insider's View of the UN World Conference Against Racism," *The Fletcher Forum of World Affairs,* Winter/Spring 2002.

217 He was faulted: Philip Gourevitch, "The Genocide Fax," *New Yorker,* May 1998.

217 "responsibility to protect": HRW, "Annan Blasts Global Failure on Darfur Horror," December 2006.

218 East Timor went on: UNTAET, "The United Nations and East Timor—A Chronology."

218 He dismissed the suggestion: "UN Reform Remains Work in Progress, Says Annan, Urging Group of 77 to Keep Up the Job," UN News, September 2006; United Nations, "Secretary-General Urges Human Rights Activists to 'Fill Leadership Vacuum,' Hold World Leaders to Account, in Address to International Day Event," December 2006.

218 "Justice has often bolstered": HRW, "Annan Blasts Global Failure on Darfur Horror," December 2006.

218 He forcefully criticized: United Nations, "Secretary-General's Address to the Commission on Human Rights," April 2005; The UN Office at Geneva, "Address of United Nations Secretary-General Kofi Annan to the Human Rights Council," June 2006.

218 He was also: United Nations, "Secretary-General Says Establishment of International Criminal Court Is Gift of Hope to Future Generations," July 1998.

218 "We need an anti-terrorism": HRW, "Annan Blasts Global Failure on Darfur Horror."

219 He turned into: United Nations, "Ban Calls for Efforts to Secure Equal Rights for LGBT Community," September 2016; Raphael Rashid, "How Religion Spurs Homophobia in South Korean Politics," Nikkei Asia, March 2021.

219 Working closely with: UN News, "'Human Rights up Front' Initiative Ever More Vital to Strengthen UN's Preventive Work, Says Deputy UN Chief," January 2016.

220 When security forces: UN Security Council, "Letter Dated 18 December 2009 Addressed to the President of the Security Council by the Secretary-General";

HRW, "Guinea: Stadium Massacre, Rape Likely Crimes Against Humanity," December 2009.

220 Britain and France have not used: Paul Lewis, "Fighting in Panama: United Nations; Security Council Condemnation of Invasion Vetoed," *New York Times,* December 1989.

220 The most active: Dag Hammerskjöld Library, "UN Security Council Meetings & Outcomes Tables"; Eric Alterman, *We Are Not One* (New York: Basic Books, 2022).

221 The Russian government: Security Council Report, "The Permanent Members and the Use of the Veto: An Abridged History," November 2013; Dag Hammerskjöld Library, "UN Security Council Meetings & Outcomes Tables."

221 In recent years: Global Centre for the Responsibility to Protect, "Political Declaration on Suspension of Veto Powers in Cases of Mass Atrocities," August 2015.

221 As the war in Gaza: "UN Security Council Meetings & Outcomes Tables," Dag Hammarskjöld Library.

221 Under an initiative: United Nations, "General Assembly Adopts Landmark Resolution Aimed at Holding Five Permanent Security Council Members Accountable for Use of Veto," April 2022; Ben Donaldson, "Liechtenstein's 'Veto Initiative' Wins Wide Approval at the UN. Will It Deter the Big Powers?," PassBlue, April 2022.

222 These actions provide: Joanna Weschler, "Human Rights and the Security Council: Practical Steps to Build Effectiveness," Universal Rights Group, December 2022.

222 In a May 2002: Kenneth Roth, "Where No Abuse Is Too Big to Be Ignored," *International Herald Tribune,* May 2002.

222 remarkable April 2005 address: United Nations, "Secretary-General's Address to the Commission on Human Rights," April 2005; Loubna Freih and Joanna Weschler, "Back Annan's Call for a New Human Rights Body," *New York Times,* April 2005.

222 jettisoned the commission: UN General Assembly Resolution 60/251, April 2006; The UN Office at Geneva, "Address of United Nations Secretary-General Kofi Annan to the Human Rights Council," June 2006; UN Human Rights Council, https://www.ohchr.org/en/hrbodies/hrc/home.

222 That change introduced: UN General Assembly Resolution 60/251, April 2006.

223 Several were rejected: Kenneth Roth, "How Not to Fix the U.N. Human Rights Council," *Foreign Policy,* December 2017.

223 Even Russia was defeated: Somini Sengupta, "Russia Loses Seat on U.N. Human Rights Council," *New York Times,* October 2016.

223 To circumvent a competitive election: Roth, "How Not to Fix the U.N. Human Rights Council."

223 In March 2011: United Nations, "General Assembly Suspends Libya from Human Rights Council," March 2011.

223 And in April 2022: UN News, "UN General Assembly Votes to Suspend Russia from the Human Rights Council," April 2022; "Russia Fails to Win

Back Seat on Human Rights Council After UN Vote," *The Guardian,* October 2023.

223 a two-thirds vote: UN General Assembly Resolution 60/251, April 2006.

223 for even a regional powerhouse: UN Human Rights Council, "International Commission of Human Rights Experts on Ethiopia."

224 Major Western powers: E.g., Claudio Francavilla, "EU Deal with Egypt Rewards Authoritarianism, Betrays 'EU Values,'" HRW, March 2024; U.S. Department of State, "U.S. Relations with Egypt," April 2022.

224 Sustaining that industry: Lucie Béraud-Sudreau, *French Arms Exports: The Business of Sovereignty* (Oxfordshire, UK: Routledge, 2020); Emmanuel Martin, "Macron and the European Strategic Autonomy Trope," GIS, June 2023.

224 Le Drian, longtime defense minister: Monique El-Faizy, "Egypt's Human Rights Record Casts a Shadow on Sisi's Visit to France," France 24, October 2017.

224 That was illustrated: "Macron Accueille d'une Longue Poignée de Mains le Prince Héritier Saoudien à l'Élysée," France 24, July 2022; Bénédicte Jeannerod, "France's Macron Ignores Violations During China Visit," HRW, April 2023; Giorgio Leali, "India Buys French Fighter Jets, Submarines as Modi Visits Macron," *Politico,* July 2023.

226 Macron had welcomed Sisi: "Macron Gave Sisi France's Highest Award on Paris Visit: Official," France 24, December 2020.

227 although it did: Permanent mission of France to the UN in New York, "Cross-Regional Joint Statement on Xinjiang," October 2021.

227 As Eric Alterman: Eric Alterman, *We Are Not One* (New York: Basic Books, 2022), 3. See also Dag Hammerskjöld Library, "UN Security Council Meetings & Outcomes Tables."

227 But they also object: Julian Borger, "US Quits UN Human Rights Council—'A Cesspool of Political Bias,'" *The Guardian,* June 2018.

227 We had long argued: Roth, "How Not to Fix the U.N. Human Rights Council."

227 Haley also complained: Borger, "US Quits UN Human Rights Council—'A Cesspool of Political Bias'"; U.S. Mission to International Organizations in Geneva, "Ambassador Nikki Haley: Remarks at the Graduate Institute of Geneva," June 2017.

227 The Trump administration: U.S. Mission to International Organizations in Geneva, "Remarks by Mike Pompeo, Secretary of State and Nikki Haley, U.S. Permanent Representative to the United Nations," June 2018; HRW, "UN: US Retreat from Rights Body Self-Defeating," June 2018.

228 No other government had ever voluntarily: Gardiner Harris, "Trump Administration Withdraws U.S. from U.N. Human Rights Council," *New York Times,* June 2018.

228 No other government had endorsed: Gardiner Harris, "Haley Blames Watchdog Groups for U.S. Withdrawal from U.N. Rights Council," *New York Times,* June 2018; Kenneth Roth, "Nikki Haley Blames Rights Groups for Her Misguided 'Reform," The Hill, July 2018; Kenneth Roth, "How Not to Fix the U.N. Human Rights Council," *Foreign Policy,* December 2017.

228 it condemned Venezuela: HRW, "Venezuela: Landmark UN Rights Council Resolution," September 2018; Kenneth Roth, "Biden Can't Make Washington a Beacon for Human Rights by Returning to Business as Usual," *Foreign Policy*, January 2021.

228 Iceland, which assumed: Nick Cumming-Bruce, "U.N. Rights Council to Investigate Killings in Philippine Drug War," *New York Times*, July 2019.

228 When Joe Biden: Michelle Nichols, "U.S. Elected Back to U.N. Human Rights Council That Trump Quit," Reuters, October 2021; White House, "Statement by President Joseph R. Biden, Jr. on the United States Election to the Human Rights Council (HRC)," October 2021; U.S. Department of State, "Election of the United States to the UN Human Rights Council (HRC)," October 2021.

228 Biden chose not to seek: Kenneth Roth, "The US Won't Run for Another Term on UN Human Rights Council. Israel Is Likely Why," *The Guardian*, October 2024.

Chapter 11: Rwanda and the Democratic Republic of Congo

229 When the rebel: International Rescue Committee, "Mortality in the Democratic Republic of Congo: An Ongoing Crisis," May 2007.

229 A year before the genocide: Africa Watch, Federation Internationale des Droits de l'Homme, Union Interafricaine des Droits de l'Homme et des Peuples, Centre International des Droits de la Personne et du Développement Démocratique, Report of the International Commission of Investigation of Human Rights Violations in Rwanda Since October 1, 1990, January 1993.

230 She later wrote: HRW, "Leave None to Tell the Story: Genocide in Rwanda," March 1999.

230 She died tragically: George Packer, "Alison Des Forges," *New Yorker*, February 2009.

230 We arranged for her: "Human Rights in the White House," *Washington Post*, December 1993.

230 She wrote a note: "'Take Care of My Children,'" *Washington Post*, April 1994.

230 Monique had miraculously escaped: Alison Des Forges, "A Life Saved," *Washington Post*, April 1994.

230 Monique's tale was covered: Steven Greenhouse, "One Rwandan's Escape: Days Hiding in a Ceiling, a Bribe and a Barricade," *New York Times*, April 1994; "'So That the World Does Not Forget Rwanda,'" *Washington Post*, April 1994; Lawrence Weschler, "Lost in Rwanda," *New Yorker*, April 1994.

231 We had an internal: Kenneth Roth, "War in Iraq: Not a Humanitarian Intervention," HRW, January 2004.

231 The treaty prohibiting genocide: "Convention on the Prevention and Punishment of the Crime of Genocide," December 1948.

231 In what might be called: Beth Van Schaack, "The Crime of Political Genocide: Repairing the Genocide Convention's Blind Spot," *Yale Law Journal*, May 1997; Cynthia Haven, "Stalin Killed Millions. A Stanford Historian Answers the Question, Was It Genocide?," *Stanford News*, September 2010.

231 In Alison's view: Jonathan Rauch, "Now Is the Time to Tell the Truth About Rwanda," *The Atlantic,* April 2001. See also Sylvie Corbet, "President Macron Says France and Its Allies 'Could Have Stopped' the 1994 Rwanda Genocide," AP, April 2024.

231 Instead, the French: UN Security Council Resolution 912 (1994), April 1994; Chris McGreal, "France's Shame?," *The Guardian,* January 2007; HRW, "Leave None to Tell the Story: Genocide in Rwanda"; HRW, "Rwanda: Genocide Archives Released," April 2024; Bronwen Everill, "The Long Cultural Legacy of the Rwandan Genocide," *Foreign Policy,* April 2024.

232 In the initial weeks: Alison Des Forges, "Quit the Foot-Dragging on Rwanda," *USA Today,* June 1994; Alison Des Forges, "The Method in Rwanda's Madness: Politics, Not Tribalism, Is the Root of the Bloodletting," *Washington Post,* April 1994. See also HRW, "Response to the New Times Article on Rwandan Genocide," May 2009; Philip Gourevitch, *We Wish to Inform You That Tomorrow We Will Be Killed with Our Families* (New York: Farrar, Straus and Giroux, 1998), 59; James C. McKinley, Jr., "Fighting Outlasts Defeat of Mobutu," *New York Times,* October 1997.

232 In fact, the genocide: "Rwanda's Genocide Is Not Random 'Tribal Violence,'" *Washington Post,* May 1994.

232 They whipped up: Montreal Institute for Genocide and Human Rights Studies, "Rwanda Radio Transcripts"; Scott Straus, "Rwanda and RTLM Radio Media Effects," June 2009.

232 After the October 1993: Philip Gourevich, "The Genocide Fax," *New Yorker,* May 1998; Rory Carroll, "US Chose to Ignore Rwandan Genocide," *The Guardian,* March 2004.

232 When Alison implored: White House Office of the Press Secretary, "Statement by the Press Secretary," April 1994.

232 Instead, he urged her: George Packer, "Alison Des Forges," *New Yorker,* February 2009.

232 The slaughter of Tutsi: When toward the end of the genocide, in June 1994, the French government toyed with a military intervention in Rwanda, the RPF opposed it, fearing that the government would reinstate the prior government. David Crary, "Mitterand Readies French Troops for Rwanda," *Washington Post,* June 1994.

233 Driven in part by widespread: HRW, "Rwanda: Genocide Archives Released," April 2024; Everill, "The Long Cultural Legacy of the Rwandan Genocide."

233 the R2P doctrine: UN Office on Genocide Prevention and the Responsibility to Protect, "Responsibility to Protect"; United Nations, "World Summit, 14–16 September 2005, New York."

233 The invasion of Libya: Global Centre for the Responsibility to Protect, "Statement on the Situation in Libya, February 2011," February 2011; David Rieff, "The End of Human Rights?," *Foreign Policy,* April 2018; Everill, "The Long Cultural Legacy of the Rwandan Genocide."

233 After President George W. Bush's: Roth, "War in Iraq: Not a Humanitarian Intervention"; see also HRW, "Human Rights Watch Policy on Iraq."

234 In addition to having tried: International Criminal Tribunal for Rwanda, "Key Figures of ICTR Cases"; "Theoneste Bagosora, Architect of Rwanda Genocide, Dies Aged 80," *The Guardian*, September 2021.

234 Alison served as a witness: HRW, "Annual Report 2009."

235 She rejected the false claims: HRW, "Human Rights Watch Mourns Loss of Alison Des Forges," February 2009; Declan Walsh, "From the Horror to the Envy of Africa: Rwanda's Ruler Holds Tight Grip," *New York Times*, April 2024.

235 He refused, instead deferring: Leslie Haskell and Lars Waldorf, "The Impunity Gap of the International Criminal Tribunal for Rwanda: Causes and Consequences," *Hastings International and Comparative Law Review*, Winter 2011; HRW, "Rwanda: Justice After Genocide—20 Years On, March 2014.

235 While purporting: UN International Residual Mechanism for Criminal Tribunals, "ICTR Prosecutor Meets Rwanda President," April 2001.

235 The Rwandan government: Security Council debate, November 8, 1994.

235 The government and its allies: Joseph Kamanzi, "Why Don't We Get Same Harvard Outrage Against Kenneth Roth over Genocide Against the Tutsi?," *New Times*, January 2023.

235 Nor did it endear: HRW, "Rwanda," https://www.hrw.org/africa/rwanda.

235 But while he indicated: Kenneth Roth, "Course Correction in Rwanda," *Washington Post*, July 1996.

236 Rwandan critics of Kagame: HRW, "Rwanda: Wave of Free Speech Prosecutions," March 2022.

236 Political opponents were: Ida Sawyer, "Rwandan Blogger to Stand Trial for Genocide Ideology," HRW, March 2017; Kenneth Roth, "The Power of Horror in Rwanda," *Los Angeles Times*, April 2009; HRW, "Response to the New Times Article on Rwandan Genocide."

236 When I raised: Roth, "The Power of Horror in Rwanda."

236 There was no independent media: HRW, World Report 2024—Rwanda, January 2024.

236 I later wrote: Roth, "Course Correction in Rwanda."

236 The executions occurred: HRW, "'All Thieves Must Be Killed': Extrajudicial Executions in Western Rwanda," July 2017.

237 Rwandan officials held: HRW, "Rwanda: Cover-Up Negates Killings," November 2017.

237 An investigation by the broadcaster: Thaïs Brouck, "HRW Controversy: Rwanda Rejects Accusations of Extrajudicial Killings," France 24.

237 As we reported: HRW, Annual Report 2013.

238 "among the worst perpetrators": UN Office of the High Commissioner for Human Rights, "Citing 'Appalling' Human Rights Record of Leaders of M23 Mutineers in DR Congo, Pillay Fears Further Abuses," June 2012.

238 Rwanda's military was: HRW, "DR Congo: M23 Rebels Committing War Crimes," September 2012.

238 In November 2012: ReliefWeb, "Final Report of the Group of Experts on the DRC Submitted in Accordance with Paragraph 4 of Security Council Resolution 2021 (2011) (S/2012/843)," November 2012.

238 We issued a second report: HRW, "DR Congo: War Crimes by M23, Congolese Army," February 2013.

238 A third report: HRW, "DR Congo: M23 Rebels Kill, Rape Civilians," July 2013.

238 Rwanda became known: USAID, "Political Economy Analysis of Decentralization and the Imihigo Process in Rwanda: A Review of the Literature," July 2021.

238 Key donors suspended: Michela Wrong, "Kagame's Revenge," *Foreign Affairs,* April 2023.

238 The top U.S. war-crimes official: Chris McGreal, "Rwanda's Paul Kagame Warned He May Be Charged with Aiding War Crimes," *The Guardian,* July 2012.

239 He asked to be sent: Audrey Kawire Wabwire and Ida Sawyer, "Congo Warlord Gets 30 Years: Persistence over Many Years Helps Bring Bosco Ntaganda to Justice," HRW, November 2019; International Justice Monitor, "Background Bosco Ntaganda."

239 He did not explicitly: Margaret Besheer, "Kerry Seeks End to Military Support for Congo Rebels," Voice of America, July 2013; "U.S. Says Rwanda Aids Congo Rebels," *New York Times,* July 2013.

239 The U.S. and various: Lesley Wroughton, "U.S. Tells Rwanda to Stop Support for M23 Rebels in Congo," Reuters, July 2013.

239 Then in October 2013: Mike Pflanz and David Blair, "DR Congo: M23 Rebels Close to Defeat After US and Britain Urge Rwanda to Stay Out," *The Telegraph,* October 2013; Ida Sawyer, "After the M23—Congo's Next Challenges," HRW, November 2013.

239 Given Rwanda's dependence: World Bank, "Results Profile: Rwanda," July 2012.

239 The M23 collapsed: Sawyer, "After the M23—Congo's Next Challenges."

239 To our chagrin: Michela Wrong, "Kagame's Revenge," *Foreign Affairs,* April 2023; Africa Center for Strategic Studies, "Rwanda and the DRC at Risk of War as New M23 Rebellion Emerges: An Explainer," June 2022.

239 Kagame's motive seemed: Comfort Ero and Richard Atwood, "10 Conflicts to Watch in 2023," *Foreign Policy,* January 2023; Wrong, "Kagame's Revenge."

239 Giving little credit: "US condemns Rwanda's Support of Armed M23 Rebels in Eastern Congo and Calls for Troop Withdrawal," AP, February 2024; Romain Gras and Julian Pecquet, "US Suspends Military Aid to Rwanda over Support for M23 Rebels in DRC," *Africa Report,* October 2023; Nicole Widdersheim, "US Sanctions Rights Abusers in Eastern Congo," HRW, August 2023; Thomas Fessy, "EU Sanctions Congo, Rwanda Army Officers," HRW, July 2023; "EU Sanctions Rwandan Army Officer over Involvement in Congo Rebellion." Reuters, July 2023; Andres Schipani, "Rwanda Criticised for Backing Rebels in DRC Accused of Atrocities," *Financial Times,* June 2023.

239 Now, given Kagame's: Wrong, "Kagame's Revenge"; Joe Penney, "Rwanda Helped Oust Jihadists in Mozambique. Can This Model Work in West Africa?," PassBlue, August 2023; Evan W. Nachtrieb, "America Must Act to Prevent a Rwanda-Congo War," *Foreign Policy,* April 2024; International Res-

cue Committee, "Rwanda Plan Explained: Why the UK Government Should Rethink the Scheme," June 2022; Christophe Châtelot, "DRC Foreign Minister: 'The European Union Is Complicit in the Plundering of Our Resources and the Aggression of Rwanda,'" *Le Monde,* February 2024.

240 The chief prosecutor: International Criminal Court, "Preliminary Examination: Democratic Republic of the Congo II"; "Congo Files New Complaint to ICC Against Rwanda's Military and M23 Rebels," Reuters, May 2023; Mike Corder, "International Court Prosecutor to Probe Crimes in Eastern Congo Following Government Request," AP, June 2023; International Criminal Court, "Statement of ICC Prosecutor Karim A.A. Khan KC on the Situation in the Democratic Republic of the Congo and Renewed Investigations," October 2024.

240 His father, Laurent-Désiré Kabila: Lynne Duke, "Rwanda Admits Its Troops Aid Congo Rebels," *Washington Post*, November 1998; HRW, "What Kabila Is Hiding: Civilian Killings and Impunity in Congo," October 1997.

240 but the elder Kabila: "Revealed: How Africa's Dictator Died at the Hands of His Boy Soldiers," *The Guardian,* February 2001.

240 The son, seen initially as a weak figure: Norimitsu Onishi with Ian Fisher, "Doubts on Whether Kabila's Son Can Lead Congo," *New York Times,* January 2001.

240 For example, he surrendered: Ida Sawyer and Kenneth Roth, "Joseph Kabila Forever," *Foreign Policy,* July 2015.

240 We had just published: HRW, "Soldiers Who Rape, Commanders Who Condone: Sexual Violence and Military Reform in the Democratic Republic of Congo," July 2009.

241 Within a short period: Sawyer and Roth, "Joseph Kabila Forever"; HRW, Annual Report 2009.

242 As he shook our hands: Sawyer and Roth, "Joseph Kabila Forever."

242 Realizing that he: Natasha Booty, "Emmanuel Ramazani Shadary: Kabila's Choice for DR Congo President," BBC, December 2018.

242 Kabila made a deal: Michelle Gavin, "Power-Sharing Agreement Breaks Down in DRC," Council on Foreign Relations, December 2020.

242 Kabila and his coalition: Tom Wilson and David Pilling, "How Joseph Kabila Lost Then Won Congo's Election," *Financial Times,* January 2019; NYU Center on International Cooperation, "Who Really Won the Congolese Elections?" January 2019.

242 Tshisekedi was reelected: Jean-Yves Kamale, "Congo's President Félix Tshisekedi Is Sworn into Office Following His Disputed Reelection," AP, January 2024; International Crisis Group, "DR Congo: A Full Plate of Challenges After a Turbulent Vote," January 2024.

Chapter 12: Hungary and Poland

243 He was the beneficiary: Michael Ignatieff, "Why the Populist Right Hates Universities," *The Atlantic,* August 2023.

243 But when he lost: "Socialists Set for Hungary Victory," CNN, April 2002.

243 Starting in 2014: Hungarian Government, "Prime Minister Viktor Orbán's Speech at the 25th Bálványos Summer Free University and Student Camp," July 2014.

243 He hijacked public: Lydia Gall, "Hungary's Authoritarian Leader Is No Gift to US Conservatives," The Hill, August 2022; Emily Bazelon, "In Israel, High Stakes for High Court: Democracy's Fate," *New York Times,* July 2023.

243 The government-controlled: Wirth Zsuzsanna, "'Ne írd meg semmilyen formában, köszi'—Így hallgatja el a kormánynak kínos híreket az állami hírügynökség," Direkt36, March 2022.

244 And with thinly disguised: Gall, "Hungary's Authoritarian Leader Is No Gift to US Conservatives"; Lili Bayer, "Hungarian Government Campaign Renews Antisemitism Concerns," *The Guardian,* November 2023.

244 Orbán also grew: E.g., Barbara Moens, Nicholas Vinocur, and Jacopo Barigazzi, "Putin's Buddy Orbán Pushes EU to the Brink over Ukraine," *Politico,* December 2023; Luke McGee, "How Orban's Ties to Putin Are Putting European Aid to Ukraine at Risk," CNN, January 2024.

244 When the EU protested: Elisabeth Zerofsky, "Poland's War on Two Fronts," *New York Times Magazine,* April 2023.

244 Stopping Orbán's autocratic drift: Kenneth Roth, "Stopping the Authoritarian Rot in Europe," *EUobserver,* April 2020.

244 With Hungary and Poland: David Martin, "What Is Article 7 of the EU Treaty?" Deutsche Welle, December 2018; Daniel Kelemen, "Poland's Constitutional Crisis," *Foreign Affairs,* August 2016.

244 That requires approval: HRW, "EU: Use Article 7 Now to Protect European Values," June 2021; EUR-Lex, "Suspension Clause (Article 7 of the Treaty on European Union)."

245 The government would not meet: Lydia Gall, "Hungary Forces Klubradio Off Air," HRW, February 2021.

245 Lydia filmed me: HRW, "Executive Director Kenneth Roth Calls for #ExpelFidesz," March 2019.

245 I called for EU hearings: Central European University, "Reasons for Hope—Human Rights: Still a Reason for Hope?," March 2019, https://www.youtube.com/watch?v=XPuMsg_k_6I; Central European University, "Kenneth Roth on Human Rights: Still a Reason for Hope?" March 2019, https://www.youtube.com/watch?v=z0blaYLfsAo; Shaun Walker, "Classes Move to Vienna as Hungary Makes Rare Decision to Oust University," *The Guardian,* November 2019.

245 In March 2019: European People's Party, "FIDESZ Membership Suspended After EPP Political Assembly," March 2019.

245 Fidesz ultimately quit: Maïa de la Baume, "Orbán's Fidesz Quits EPP Group in European Parliament," *Politico,* March 2021.

245 Contrary to Merkel's fears: Andrew Higgins, "Orban's Dream of an Illiberal Pan-European Alliance Is Fading," *New York Times,* November 2023.

246 Polish government's attacks: Zerofsky, "Poland's War on Two Fronts."

246 Kaczyński was one: Helsinki Foundation for Human Rights, "Advocating for Human Rights Since 1989: History."

246 Unlike Poland's welcoming: Zerofsky, "Poland's War on Two Fronts"; HRW, "Poland: Rule of Law Erosion Harms Women, LGBT People," December 2022.

246 This was contrary: Zerofsky, "Poland's War on Two Fronts."

246 The Polish leader: "Prisoners in Poland," *Washington Post,* March 1982.

247 He had been imprisoned: William Yardley, "Zbigniew Romaszewski, Physicist Who Resisted Poland's Communists, Dies at 74," *New York Times,* March 2014.

247 Unsurprisingly, these procedures: Kenneth Roth, *Repression Disguised as Law: Human Rights in Poland* (New York: Lawyers Committee for Human Rights, 1986); William G. Blair, "Report Says Poland Is Masking Rights Violations," *New York Times,* December 1986.

247 We discussed the government's: Emily Bazelon, "In Israel, High Stakes for High Court: Democracy's Fate," *New York Times,* July 2023; Philippe Dam, "Welcome New Monitoring for Poland," HRW, January 2020.

247 met with Jacek Czaputowicz: Quellen Zur Geschichte der Menschenrechte, "Jacek Czaputowicz."

248 We had asked: Zerofsky, "Poland's War on Two Fronts."

248 At the time, Hungary: Katharina Buchholz, "Which Countries Are EU Contributors and Beneficiaries?," Statista, June 2023; Matina Stevis-Gridneff, "E.U.'s Hungary Problem Looms Large Ahead of Crucial Ukraine Summit," *New York Times,* January 2024.

248 Meanwhile, Hungarian hospitals: Patrick Kingsley and Benjamin Novak, "In Hungary, Viktor Orban Showers Money on Stadiums, Less So on Hospitals," *New York Times,* October 2019; HRW, "Hungary: Health Care Failures Endanger Lives," August 2020; Andrew Higgins, "The Walkway to Nowhere: A Monument to Hungary's Patronage Politics," *New York Times,* March 2024; Szilvia Zsilák, "The Forest Was Cut to the Ground During the Construction of the EU-Funded Treetop Walkway in Nyírmártonfalva," *Atlatszo,* March 2023.

248 Angela Merkel was: European Council, "List of Presidencies of the Council of the European Union."

248 One illustration of the candor: "US Bugged Merkel's Phone from 2002 Until 2013, Report Claims," BBC News, October 2013.

249 creating a "Euronet": Leonid Bershidsky, "Bershidsky on Europe: Merkel Backs 'Euronet,'" Bloomberg, February 2014.

249 There, we insisted: Joseph Kahn, "Yahoo Helped Chinese to Prosecute Journalist," *New York Times,* September 2005.

249 she famously admitted: Bernd Riegert, "Merkel: Europe Can Do It," Deutsche Welle, October 2015.

249 The far-right Alternative for Germany: "Half of Germans Skeptical About Merkel's Migrant Stance," Deutsche Welle, August 2020.

250 In the end, she compromised: Kim Lane Scheppele and Laurent Pech, "Compromising the Rule of Law While Compromising on the Rule of Law," *Verfassungsblog,* December 2020.

250 In February 2022: Court of Justice of the European Union, "Measures for the Protection of the Union Budget: The Court of Justice, Sitting as a Full Court,

Dismisses the Actions Brought by Hungary and Poland Against the Conditionality Mechanism Which Makes the Receipt of Financing from the Union Budget Subject to the Respect by the Member States for the Principles of the Rule of Law," February 2022.

250 It was only in December: European Council, "Rule of Law Conditionality Mechanism: Council Decides to Suspend €6.3 Billion Given Only Partial Remedial Action by Hungary," December 2022.

250 the European Commission withheld: European Commission, "Commission Finds That Hungary Has Not Progressed Enough in Its Reforms and Must Meet Essential Milestones for Its Recovery and Resilience Funds," November 2022.

250 Orbán resorted to blackmail: Michael Weissenstein, "Hungary: Criticism Makes It Hard to Cooperate with West," AP, March 2023; Paola Tamma, "EU Strikes Deal with Hungary, Reducing Funding Freeze to Get Ukraine Aid Approved," *Politico,* December 2022; Steven Erlanger and Andrew Higgins, "Finland on Cusp of Joining NATO, but Maybe Not with Sweden," *New York Times,* March 2023; Elisabeth Braw, "It's Hungary's Turn to Undermine Sweden's NATO Accession," *Foreign Policy,* September 2023.

250 Sebastian Kaleta, the deputy: Zerofsky, "Poland's War on Two Fronts."

251 Beginning in 2021: "Poland Shows That Populists Can Be Beaten," *The Economist,* October 2023.

251 von der Leyen seemed inclined: Jorge Liboreiro, "Ursula von der Leyen Defends Controversial Approval of Polish Recovery Plan," Euronews, June 2022; Gabriela Baczynska, "EU Executive Tries to Reassure Angry Parliament: No Funds for Poland Without Reforms," Reuters, June 2022; "Poland Warns of Repercussions if Brussels Keeps Blocking Funds," Reuters, August 2022.

251 continue to withhold funds: Bernd Riegert, "Rule of Law: EU Reprimands Poland and Hungary," Deutsche Welle, September 2023.

251 PiS lost the October 2023 elections: Jan Cienski," Poland Election Results: Opposition Secures Win, Final Count Shows," *Politico,* October 2023; Anne Applebaum, "Poland Shows That Autocracy Is Not Inevitable," *The Atlantic,* October 2023; Raphael Minder and Barbara Erling, "Poland Puts Forward Justice Reform Needed to Unfreeze EU Funds," *Financial Times,* January 2024; Raf Casert, "EU Moves to End Standoff with Poland over Anti-EU Policies and Begins to Release Billions in Funds," AP, February 2024; European Commission, "Poland's Efforts to Restore Rule of Law Pave the Way for Accessing up to €137 Billion in EU Funds," February 2024.

251 Orbán used the EU's desire: Jorge Liboreiro, "Brussels Releases €10 Billion in Frozen EU Funds for Hungary Amid Orbán's Threats," Euronews, December 2023; Nicolas Camut, Hans von der Burchard, and Clea Caulcutt, "Orbán's Walkout Was Planned, Macron Says," *Politico,* December 2023; Matina Stevis-Gridneff and Monika Pronczuk, "The E.U.'s $54 Billion Deal to Fund Ukraine, Explained," *New York Times,* February 2024.

251 European Union resisted further blackmail: Matina Stevis-Gridneff, Monika Pronczuk, and Jason Horowitz, "How a Game of Good Cop-Bad Cop Sealed the E.U. Ukraine Fund Deal," *New York Times,* February 2024.

Chapter 13: The United States

252 conditions for asylum seekers: HRW, "'Like I'm Drowning': Children and Families Sent to Harm by the US 'Remain in Mexico' Program, January 2021; HRW, "US: Separated Families Report Trauma, Lies, Coercion," July 2018.

253 Under the U.S. Constitution: *Washington v. Davis,* 426 U.S. 229 (1976). For an illustration of the U.S. Department of Justice's Broader Understanding of the requirement of discriminatory intent under U.S. law, see U.S. Department of Justice Civil Rights Division, "Section VI—Proving Discrimination—Intentional Discrimination."

253 Under international human-rights law: "International Convention on the Elimination of All Forms of Racial Discrimination," December 1965.

253 U.S. government has not implemented: Jamie Fellner, "Race, Drugs, and Law Enforcement in the United States," *Stanford Law & Policy Review,* June 2009.

253 The "war on drugs": HRW, "A Nation Behind Bars: A Human Rights Solution," May 2014.

253 unwarranted racial disparities, we: HRW, "Targeting Blacks: Drug Law Enforcement and Race in the United States," May 2008; HRW, "United States: Punishment and Prejudice: Racial Disparities in the War on Drugs," May 2000.

253 We called attention: HRW, "Human Rights Violations in the United States: Cruel and Unusual: Disproportionate Sentences for New York Drug Offenders," March 1997.

254 We addressed discriminatory practices: HRW, "The Price of Freedom: Bail and Pretrial Detention of Low Income Nonfelony Defendants in New York City," December 2010.

254 And we examined: HRW, "Targeting Blacks: Drug Law Enforcement and Race in the United States," May 2008.

254 We spotlighted the immense: HRW, "Cold Storage: Super-Maximum Security Confinement in Indiana," October 1997.

254 had mental-health problems: Jeffrey L. Metzner and Jamie Fellner, "Solitary Confinement and Mental Illness in U.S. Prisons: A Challenge for Medical Ethics," *Journal of the American Academy of Psychiatry and the Law,* March 2010.

254 Ordinary prisons were used: HRW, "Ill-Equipped: U.S. Prisons and Offenders with Mental Illness," October 2003.

254 tolerance of rape: HRW, "No Escape: Male Rape in U.S. Prisons," 2001.

254 Many Black leaders: David Remnick, "Ten Years After 'The New Jim Crow,'" *New Yorker,* January 2020; Yolanda Young, "Analysis: Black Leaders Supported Clinton's Crime Bill," NBC News, April 2016.

254 life sentences without parole: HRW, "'When I Die, They'll Send Me Home': Youth Sentenced to Life Without Parole in California," January 2008.

254 Elizabeth Calvin, a Human Rights Watch: Campaign for the Fair Sentencing of Youth, "California Becomes 20th State to Abolish Life-Without-Parole Sentences for Children," October 2017.

254 severely limited the ability of courts: Joshua Rovner, "Juvenile Life Without Parole: An Overview," Sentencing Project, April 2023.

254 secure a series of reforms: HRW, "Elizabeth Calvin."

255 the practice of "kettling": HRW, "US: New York Police Planned Assault on Bronx Protesters," September 2020.

255 Ultimately, New York City: Daniel Wu, "NYC to Pay $21,500—per Person—to Protesters 'Kettled' by Police," *Washington Post,* March 2023; "Meet the Bronx Activists Who Won a Historic Settlement for NYPD's Violent Attack at 2020 BLM Protest," Democracy Now!, March 2023; Laura Pitter, "New York Taxpayers Foot Bill for Abusive Police," HRW, March 2023.

255 it announced an end: Maria Cramer, "N.Y.P.D. Must Rewrite Rules for Policing Protests After Sweeping Deal," *New York Times,* September 2023. See also Bahar Ostadan, "The NYPD Is Now Legally Mandated to Respond to Protests Differently," *Gothamist,* March 2024.

255 developed the theoretical distinction: Jeane J. Kirkpatrick, "Dictatorships & Double Standards," *Commentary,* November 1979.

256 we added Americas Watch: Aryeh Neier, *The International Human Rights Movement: A History* (Princeton, NJ: Princeton University Press, 2020), 206–7.

257 To pursue his idea: U.S. Department of State, "Report of the Commission on Unalienable Rights," August 2020.

257 the primary public critic: Kenneth Roth, "Beware the Trump Administration's Plans for 'Fresh Thinking' on Human Rights," *Washington Post,* July 2019; Kenneth Roth, "Pompeo's Commission on Unalienable Rights Will Endanger Everyone's Human Rights," *Foreign Policy,* August 2020.

257 I also testified: HRW, "Submission to Commission on Unalienable Rights," May 2020; U.S. Department of State Commission on Unalienable Rights Meeting, Featuring Kenneth Roth, January 10, 2020," https://video.state.gov /detail/video/6163108495001.

258 "President Biden is committed": Antony J. Blinken, "Putting Human Rights at the Center of U.S. Foreign Policy," U.S. Department of State, February 2021.

258 "I've been clear": "Remarks by President Biden on the End of the War in Afghanistan," White House, August 2021.

259 The United States is the only: "Convention on the Rights of the Child," November 1989; UNICEF, "Frequently Asked Questions on the Convention on the Rights of the Child."

259 Nor has the U.S.: "Convention on the Elimination of All Forms of Discrimination against Women," December 1979; "Access to Safe and Legal Abortion: Urgent Call for United States to Adhere to Women's Rights Convention, UN Committee," UN Office of the High Commissioner for Human Rights, July 2022.

259 Of the two treaties: "International Covenant on Civil and Political Rights"; "International Covenant on Economic, Social and Cultural Rights."

260 U.S. government never ratifies portions: Kenneth Roth, "The Charade of US Ratification of International Human Rights Treaties," *Chicago Journal of International Law,* 2000.

260 It is an "optional protocol": "Optional Protocol to the Convention on the Rights of the Child on the Involvement of Children in Armed Conflict," May 2000.

260 The original children's rights: "Convention on the Rights of the Child," Article 38.

260 we documented and reported: Jo Becker, "Children as Weapons of War," HRW, World Report 2004.

260 outlaw any use of children: "Coalition to Stop the Use of Child Soldiers," Amnesty International, January 2004.

260 Albright asked the Pentagon: Jo Becker, *Campaigning for Justice: Human Rights Advocacy in Practice* (Stanford, CA: Stanford University Press, 2013), 24.

261 continue to voluntarily enlist: Elizabeth Olson, "U.S. Fights Tide on a Move to Raise the Military Service Age," *New York Times,* January 2000.

261 A "straight-eighteen": Becker, *Campaigning for Justice*, 22–24.

261 The states leading: "Optional Protocol to the Convention on the Rights of the Child on the Involvement of Children in Armed Conflict," May 2000, Article 3.

261 The Pentagon then stopped: Becker, *Campaigning for Justice,* 25.

261 The court noted: *Roper v. Simmons*, 543 U.S. 551 (2005); "Convention on the Rights of the Child," Article 37.

262 The journalists were: Jane Sutton, "Accused 9/11 Plotters Defiant at Guantanamo Arraignment," Reuters, May 2012; Chris Lawrence and Larry Shaughnessy, "9/11 Suspects Ignore, Disrupt Guantanamo Arraignment," CNN, May 2012.

262 The sound was delayed: Carol Rosenberg, "At Guantánamo's Court Like No Other, Progress Is Frustrated by State Secrets," *New York Times,* May 2023.

263 They also allowed hearsay: HRW, "Q and A: Military Commissions Act of 2006"; ACLU, "President Obama Signs Military Commissions Changes into Law," October 2009.

263 Because the military commissions: Gary D. Brown, "Another Decade of Military Commissions," American Bar Association, January 2023.

263 More than two decades: Carol Rosenberg, "Trial Guide: The Sept. 11 Case at Guantánamo Bay," *New York Times,* February 2024.

263 proved to be a travesty: HRW, "Q&A: Guantanamo Bay, US Detentions, and the Trump Administration," June 2018.

263 In November 2024, it appeared: Carol Rosenberg, "Plea Deals for Accused 9/11 Plotters Are Valid, Judge Rules," *The New York Times,* November 2024.

263 More than fifty journalists: Peter Finn, "9/11 Detainees Work to Disrupt Opening of Arraignment at Guantanamo Bay," *Washington Post,* May 2012.

263 an op-ed that I had written: Kenneth Roth, "Justice Cheated," *New York Times,* May 2012.

264 Michael Ignatieff wrote: Michael Ignatieff, "Is the Human Rights Era Ending?" *New York Times,* February 2002.

264 the September 11 attacks: Jane Meyer, *The Dark Side: The Inside Story of How the War on Terror Turned into a War on American Ideals* (New York: Doubleday, 2008), 3.

265 "enhanced interrogation techniques": "Report of the Senate Select Committee on Intelligence: Committee Study of the Central Intelligence Agency's Detention and Interrogation Program," December 2014.

265 infamous "Torture Memos": "A Guide to the Memos on Torture," *New York Times*. The key treaties are: "International Covenant on Civil and Political Rights," December 1966, Article 7; "Convention Against Torture and Other Cruel, Inhuman or Degrading Treatment or Punishment," December 1984; Geneva Conventions of 1949, common Article 3.

265 The legal theories advanced: Jeffrey Rosen, "Conscience of a Conservative," *New York Times Magazine,* September 2007.

265 The Senate Select Committee: "Report of the Senate Select Committee on Intelligence: Committee Study of the Central Intelligence Agency's Detention and Interrogation Program"; Rebecca Kaplan, "Senate Report: CIA Misled Lawmakers, Public on Enhanced Interrogation," CBS News, December 2014.

265 considerable evidence that: Meyer, *The Dark Side*, 7–8, chapter 9.

266 On NBC, CBS: "Legal Torture?" *60 Minutes,* CBS News, January 2002; "Dershowitz: Torture Could Be Justified," CNN, March 2003; "For the Defense," *Washington Post,* February 2005.

266 A similar proposal: Philip B. Heymann and Juliette N. Kayyem, *Protecting Liberty in an Age of Terror* (Cambridge, MA: MIT Press, 2005).

267 The hypothetical that: Kenneth Roth, "Who Profits from Torture?," *The Independent,* July 2006.

267 the 1987 Landau Commission: Yuval Ginbar, *Why Not Torture Terrorists?* (Oxford: Oxford University Press, 2008), chapter 12; HRW, "Israeli Interrogation Methods Under Fire After Death of Detained Palestinian," March 1992.

267 Although the commission tried: B'Tselem, "Legitimizing Torture: The Israeli High Court of Justice Rulings in the Bilbeisi, Hamdan and Mubarak Cases," January 1997.

267 astounding 85 percent: B'Tselem, "Routine Torture: Interrogation Methods of the General Security Service," February 1988.

267 Methods included "violently shaking": Ilene Prusher, "Israeli Court Outlaws Torture," *The Guardian,* September 1999.

267 Israeli Supreme Court banned: Prusher, "Israeli Court Outlaws Torture."

267 Which reduced, though: Public Committee Against Torture in Israel, "Torture in Israel Today," 2022.

267 Israeli torture surged: B'Tselem, "Welcome to Hell: The Israeli Prison System as a Network of Torture Camps," August 2024.

268 Did they really believe: Carol Rosenberg, "Chains, Shackles and Threats: Testimony on Torture Takes a Dramatic Turn," *New York Times,* January 2020; Carol Rosenberg, "C.I.A. Violently Cut Off 9/11 Suspect When He Tried to Talk About Attacks," *New York Times,* February 2024.

268 But a military commission: Carol Rosenberg, "How a Judge's Ruling on Torture Imperils a Guantánamo Prosecution Strategy," *New York Times,* August 2023; ACLU, "ACLU Says 'Clean Teams' Cannot Wash Away Dirty Interrogation Tactics," February 2008.

268 A key actor: C. J. Chivers, "Ian Fishback's American Nightmare," *New York Times Magazine,* February 2023.

269 We released their accounts: HRW, "Leadership Failure: Firsthand Accounts

of Torture of Iraqi Detainees by the U.S. Army's 82nd Airborne Division," September 2005.

269 We introduced Fishback: Capt. Ian Fishback, "A Matter of Honor," *Washington Post*, September 2005; Tom Malinowski, "Ian Fishback: A Whistleblower Who Reminded the U.S. Military of Its Values," *Politico*, December 2021.

269 McCain credited Fishback: Quil Lawrence, "The Final, Anguished Years of a Warrior-Scholar Who Exposed Torture by U.S. Troops," NPR, December 2021; "Senate Ignores Veto Threat in Limiting Detainee Treatment," CNN, October 2005.

269 *Time* magazine named: Coleen Rowley, "Ian Fishback," *Time*, May 2006.

269 Sadly, Fishback died: Sam Roberts, "Maj. Ian Fishback, Who Exposed Abuse of Detainees, Dies at 42," *New York Times*, November 2021.

269 He was buried: C. J. Chivers, "Soldier Who Called Out Torture in Iraq Is Laid to Rest at Arlington," *New York Times*, August 2023.

269 Upon becoming president: Jonathan Masters, "Guantanamo Bay: Twenty Years of Counterterrorism and Controversy," Council on Foreign Relations, September 2022.

269 He soon retreated: "Why Obama Failed to Close Guantanamo," *PBS NewsHour*, January 2017.

269 In November 2009: Charlie Savage, "Accused 9/11 Mastermind to Face Civilian Trial in N.Y.," *New York Times*, November 2009.

269 That gave Congress time: Peter Landers, "Congress Bars Gitmo Transfers," *Wall Street Journal*, December 2010; HRW, "US: Detainee Transfer Ban Will Hinder Terror Fight," December 2010.

270 The men detained at: Carol Rosenberg, "They Were Guantánamo's First Detainees. Here's Where They Are Now." *New York Times*, March 2021; "The Guantánamo Papers," *New York Times*, April 2011; Mark Denbeaux, Joshua W. Denbeaux, John Gregorek, "Report on Guantánamo Detainees: A Profile of 517 Detainees Through Analysis of Department of Defense Data," Seton Hall Law, February 2006; Jonathan Masters, "Guantanamo Bay: Twenty Years of Counterterrorism and Controversy," Council on Foreign Relations, September 2022.

270 The ostensible reason: HRW, "It Happened Here: New Yorkers for 9/11 Justice," November 2010.

270 Before the congressional ban: U.S. Department of Justice, "Ahmed Ghailani Transferred from Guantanamo Bay to New York for Prosecution on Terror Charges," June 2009.

270 That Guantánamo was: HRW, "The Road to Abu Ghraib," June 2004; "The Supreme Court Rejects Military Tribunals," *PBS NewsHour*, June 2006; "Biden Can Close the Extrajudicial Prison at Guantánamo," *New York Times*, April 2023; Jonathan Masters, "Guantanamo Bay: Twenty Years of Counterterrorism and Controversy," Council on Foreign Relations, September 2022.

270 Horton proceeded to commit: U.S. Department of Justice Office of Justice Programs, "Willie Horton Case," 1988; Kenneth Roth, "Obama & Counterterror: The Ignored Record," *New York Review of Books*, February 2015.

270 A total of some 780: "The Guantánamo Docket," *New York Times,* February 2024; Masters, "Guantanamo Bay: Twenty Years of Counterterrorism and Controversy."

270 The vast majority: Masters, "Guantanamo Bay: Twenty Years of Counterterrorism and Controversy."

271 Three uncharged men: "The Guantánamo Docket," *New York Times;* Carol Rosenberg, "Malaysian Prisoners Plead Guilty to Conspiring in 2002 Bali Bombing," *New York Times,* January 2024.

271 Obama ended the torture: HRW, "Getting Away with Torture? Command Responsibility for the U.S. Abuse of Detainees," April 2005.

271 He offered his familiar: David Johnston and Charlie Savage, "Obama Reluctant to Look into Bush Programs," *New York Times,* January 2009.

271 cooperation from Congress: "Remarks of President Barack Obama—Address to Joint Session of Congress," White House, February 2009.

271 But because he: Matthew Weaver and Spencer Ackerman, "Trump Claims Torture Works but Experts Warn of Its 'Potentially Existential' Costs," *The Guardian,* January 2017.

271 The photographs of that abuse: "The Abu Ghraib Pictures," *Der Spiegel* International, February 2008.

271 That fed the myth: HRW, "The Road to Abu Ghraib."

271 In fact, the CIA's torture: "Report of the Senate Select Committee on Intelligence: Committee Study of the Central Intelligence Agency's Detention and Interrogation Program."

271 Dana Priest revealed: Dana Priest, "CIA Holds Terror Suspects in Secret Prisons," *Washington Post,* November 2005.

272 We promptly published: HRW, "Human Rights Watch Statement on U.S. Secret Detention Facilities in Europe," November 2005. A third Eastern European black site was in Lithuania. "Another Secret CIA Prison Found," ABC News, December 2011; Andrew Higgins, "A C.I.A. Black Site Remains a Touchy Subject for Lithuania," *New York Times,* April 2024.

272 In reference to waterboarding: Mark Tran, "Cheney Endorses Simulated Drowning," *The Guardian,* October 2006.

272 Porter Goss, the CIA director: Douglas Jehl, "Questions Are Left by C.I.A. Chief on the Use of Torture," *New York Times,* March 2005.

272 Michael Hayden, who served: Jeff Stein, "'Playing to the Edge,' by Michael V. Hayden," *New York Times,* February 2016.

272 Because they were caught: "Iraq Prison Abuse Scandal Fast Facts," CNN, February 2024.

273 Trump's "Muslim Ban": Michael D. Shear and Helene Cooper, "Trump Bars Refugees and Citizens of 7 Muslim Countries," *New York Times,* January 2017.

273 massive vaccination campaign: Bachir Tajaldin, Khaled Almilaji, Paul Langton, and Annie Sparrow, "Defining Polio: Closing the Gap in Global Surveillance," *Annals of Global Health,* November 2015; Annie Sparrow, "Syria's Polio Epidemic: The Suppressed Truth," *New York Review of Books,* February 2014.

274 The lead photograph: Jack Healy and Anemona Hartocollis, "Love, Interrupted: A Travel Ban Separates Couples," *New York Times,* February 2017. See also "Newlyweds from Syria, Separated by Travel Ban," *New York Times,* https://www.facebook.com/watch/live/?ref=search&v=10151079247759999.

274 But the attention: ACLU Washington, "Timeline of the Muslim Ban."

274 As he reversed: Kenneth Roth, "Democracy and Human Rights," *Just Security,* February 2022.

274 His administration helped: John Hudson, "As Tensions with China Grow, Biden Administration Formalizes Genocide Declaration Against Beijing," *Washington Post,* March 2021; White House, "FACT SHEET: New U.S. Government Actions on Forced Labor in Xinjiang," June 2021; Aamer Madhani, "Biden in Call with China's Xi Raises Human Rights, Trade," AP, February 2021.

274 There were positive steps: White House, "FACT SHEET: Biden-Harris Administration Actions in Response to Ongoing Crisis in Northern Ethiopia," September 2021; Humeyra Pamuk and Simon Lewis, "Biden Administration Rules Myanmar Army Committed Genocide Against Rohingya," Reuters, March 2022; Romain Gras and Julian Pecquet, "US Suspends Military Aid to Rwanda over Support for M23 Rebels in DRC."

275 In his quest: Peter Baker, "Biden Is Caught Between Allies as Canada Accuses India of Assassination," *New York Times,* September 2023.

275 His desire to build: "Biden to Host India's Modi for State Visit Despite Concerns over Human Rights," *The Guardian,* May 2023.

275 That left Biden open: Howard French, "Why Does the U.S. Care More About Taiwan's Democracy Than India's?" *Foreign Policy,* April 2023.

275 Biden's desire for help: Jorge G. Castañeda, "Biden Should Not Ignore Mexico's Turn to Authoritarianism," *New York Times,* April 2021; Tyler Mattiace and Vicki B. Gaubeca, "Biden Expands Trump-Era Border Restrictions Once Again," HRW, January 2023.

275 In the name of stability: Michael Crowley and Vivian Yee, "Choosing Security over Rights, U.S. Approves $235 Million in Egypt Aid," *New York Times,* September 2023.

275 And to avoid backlash: Nahal Toosi, "Biden's Never Been Driven by Human Rights. This Time, It Might Cost Him," *Politico,* February 2024; Kenneth Roth, "Biden's Sanctions on Israeli Settlers Are an Important Step—but Not Nearly Enough," *The Guardian,* February 2024; Kenneth Roth, "Biden's Response Harms U.S. Interests," *Washington Post,* May 2024; Kenneth Roth, "Why Is the West Defending Israel After the ICC Requested Netanyahu's Arrest Warrant?," *The Guardian,* May 2024.

Chapter 14: International Criminal Justice

276 The consensus today: Peter Beinart, "America's Other Forever War," *New York Times,* February 2021.

277 The only post–World War II: Kathryn Sikkink, *The Justice Cascade* (New York: W. W. Norton, 2011), chapter 2.

277 The Argentine National Commission: National Commission of the Disappeared, *Nunca Mas*, 1984, http://www.desaparecidos.org/.

277 It described the forced disappearances: Ronald Dworkin, "Report from Hell," *New York Review of Books*, July 1986.

277 Juan Méndez, an Argentine: Americas Watch, "Truth and Partial Justice in Argentina: An Update," April 1991.

278 In the case of Argentina: Dworkin, "Report from Hell."

278 In Chile, the 1991 report: "Report of the Chilean National Commission on Truth and Reconciliation," U.S. Institute of Peace; HRW, World Report 1992, "Chile: Human Rights Developments."

278 José "Pepe" Zalaquett: Aryeh Neier, *War Crimes: Brutality, Genocide, Terror, and the Struggle for Justice* (New York: Times Books, 1998), 80–83; Neil Genzlinger, "José Zalaquett, Leader in Chile's Search for Truth, Dies at 77," *New York Times*, February 2020; Emily Langer, "José Zalaquett, Champion of Human Rights in Pinochet's Chile and Around the World, Dies at 77," *Washington Post*, February 2020; University of Michigan Ford School, "Jose Zalaquett: Moral and Political Reconstruction in Post-Conflict Societies," October 2010.

278 Although a truth commission: Priscilla B. Hayner, *Unspeakable Truths: Transitional Justice and the Challenge of Truth Commissions* (New York and London: Routledge, 2011), 139.

278 All the officers: Neier, *War Crimes: Brutality, Genocide, Terror, and the Struggle for Justice*, 28–29: Hayner, *Unspeakable Truths: Transitional Justice and the Challenge of Truth Commissions*, 128; Americas Watch, "El Salvador—Accountability and Human Rights: The Report of the United Nations Commission on the Truth for El Salvador," August 1993; "Truth Commission: El Salvador," U.S. Institute of Peace, July 1992.

278 It foreshadowed the "lustration": HRW, World Report 1993, "Czechoslovakia: Human Rights Developments."

278 South African Truth: Hayner, *Unspeakable Truths: Transitional Justice and the Challenge of Truth Commissions*, 135; "Truth Commission: South Africa," U.S. Institute of Peace, December 1995; Truth and Reconciliation Commission, https://www.justice.gov.za/trc/.

279 The campaign was called: Kanan Makiya, "The Anfal: Uncovering an Iraqi Campaign to Exterminate the Kurds," *Harper's Magazine*, May 1992; Kenneth Roth, "Indict Saddam," *Wall Street Journal*, March 2002.

279 In 1993, Human Rights Watch: HRW, "Genocide in Iraq: The Anfal Campaign Against the Kurds," July 1993; Patrick E. Tyler, "U.S. to Help Retrieve Data on Iraqi Torture of Kurds," *New York Times*, May 1992.

279 No private individual: International Court of Justice, "How the Court Works."

279 We invoked the widely: "Convention on the Prevention and Punishment of the Crime of Genocide," 1948.

280 We did not want: Joost Hiltermann, "Elusive Justice: Trying to Try Saddam," *Middle East Report*, Summer 2000.

280 Under rules for: "Reservations to Treaties—4.2.4 Effect of an Established Reservation on Treaty Relations"; International Court of Justice, "How the Court Works."

281 After the U.S. invasion: Edward Wong, "Saddam Charged with Genocide of Kurds," *New York Times,* April 2006.

281 But the case was: Kirk Semple, "Saddam Hussein Is Sentenced to Death," *New York Times,* November 2006; Marc Santora, James Glanz, and Sabrina Tavernise, "Dictator Who Ruled Iraq with Violence Is Hanged for Crimes Against Humanity," *New York Times,* December 2006; International Crimes Database, "Al Anfal"; Philip Alston, the Special Rapporteur on extrajudicial, summary or arbitrary executions, "Tragic Mistakes Made in the Trial and Execution of Saddam Hussein Must Not Be Repeated."

281 In a separate Iraqi trial: International Crimes Database, "Al Anfal"; Charles Tripp, "Ali Hassan al-Majid Obituary," *The Guardian,* January 2010; Kevin Jon Heller, "Convictions in the Anfal Trial," Opinio Juris, June 2007.

281 It was envisioned: "The Geneva Conventions of 12 August 1949" (the language is repeated in the section on penal sanctions in each of the four conventions); Kenneth Roth, "The Case for Universal Jurisdiction," *Foreign Affairs,* September 2001.

281 The Convention Against Torture: "Convention Against Torture and Other Cruel, Inhuman or Degrading Treatment or Punishment," December 1984.

281 Universal jurisdiction is what: Devika Hovell, "The Authority of Universal Jurisdiction," *European Journal of International Law,* 2018.

281 The highest profile: HRW, "The Pinochet Precedent: How Victims Can Pursue Human Rights Criminals Abroad," November 1998.

281 The ICC's statute: Rome Statute of the International Criminal Court, Article 27, July 1998.

281 Pinochet's arrest: Wolfgang Kaleck, "From Pinochet to Rumsfeld: Universal Jurisdiction in Europe 1998–2008," *Michigan Journal of International Law,* June 2009; Baltasar Garzón, "Pinochet's Arrest"; International Crimes Database, "Regina v. Bartle and the Commissioner of Police for the Metropolis and Others Ex Parte Pinochet"; David Connett, John Hooper, and Peter Beaumont, "Pinochet Arrested in London," *The Guardian,* October 1998.

282 When the British: Amnesty International, "Chronology of the Case of Augusto Pinochet," October 2008.

282 my colleague Reed Brody: Reed Brody, *To Catch a Dictator* (New York: Columbia University Press, 2022), 33; International Commission of Jurists, "ICJ Commissioner Reed Brody: 'Twenty Years Later, Pinochet's Arrest Remains an Inspiration,'" September 2018.

282 Although the British: Nicholas Watt, "Pinochet to Be Set Free," *The Guardian,* January 2000; Warren Hoge, "After 16 Months of House Arrest, Pinochet Quits England," *New York Times,* March 2000; HRW, "Chile: Pinochet Escapes Justice," July 2002.

282 Within Chile, the Pinochet case: Gram Slattery, "Chile Doubles Down on Prosecutions for Pinochet-Era Crimes," Reuters, November 2015.

282 As Reed wrote: Brody, *To Catch a Dictator,* 33.

282 self-amnesty did not preclude prosecution: Jose Miguel Vivanco, "Ready for Justice," *New York Times,* October 1999; Carrie Kahn, "Chile Will Search for

1,000+ Victims of Forced Disappearance by Pinochet Dictatorship," NPR, August 2023.

282 By the time Pinochet died: Gideon Long, "Chile's Pinochet Again Put Under House Arrest," Reuters, August 2007.

282 Hundreds of his agents: Slattery, "Chile Doubles Down on Prosecutions for Pinochet-Era Crimes."

282 But in 2001, witnesses: Campaign for Justice for the Victims of Sabra and Shatila, "Belgian Court Case Charging Ariel Sharon with War Crimes Enters New Stage: Lawyer Affirms That 'Principles, Not Politics, Undergird This Case,'" November 2001.

282 After the Sharon case: Craig S. Smith, "Rumsfeld Says Belgian Law Could Prompt NATO to Leave," *New York Times,* June 2003; Kathleen Moore, "Iraq: Civilians Filing War Crimes Suit in Belgium Against U.S. Commander Franks," Radio Free Europe Radio Liberty, May 2003.

282 Some European governments: Wolfgang Kaleck and Patrick Kroker, "Syrian Torture Investigations in Germany and Beyond: Breathing New Life into Universal Jurisdiction in Europe?," *Journal of International Criminal Justice,* March 2018; HRW, "Belgium: Universal Jurisdiction Law Repealed," August 2003; HRW, "Israel: Ariel Sharon's Troubling Legacy," January 2014.

283 in addition, the International: Andrew Osborn, "Sharon Cannot Be Tried in Belgium, Says Court," *The Guardian,* February 2002.

283 The court applied: International Court of Justice, "Case Concerning the Arrest Warrant of 11 April 2000 (*Democratic Republic of the Congo v. Belgium*), February 2002."

283 Putin's invasion of Ukraine: Aishvarya Kavi, "Congress Votes to Expand U.S. Power to Prosecute International War Crimes," *New York Times,* December 2022; "18 U.S. Code § 2441—War Crimes."

283 In recent years: Wolfgang Kaleck and Patrick Kroker, "Syrian Torture Investigations in Germany and Beyond: Breathing New Life into Universal Jurisdiction in Europe?," *Journal of International Criminal Justice,* March 2018; Trial International, "Universal Jurisdiction Interactive Map."

283 One prominent case: HRW, "Germany: Conviction for State Torture in Syria," January 2022.

283 Evidence and analysis: International, Impartial and Independent Mechanism, "IIIM-Syria Welcomes German Court's Crimes Against Humanity Verdict," January 2022.

283 Prosecutors also relied: European Union Agency for Criminal Justice Cooperation, "Syrian Official Sentenced to Life for Crimes Against Humanity with Support of Joint Investigation Team Assisted by Eurojust," January 2022; Kenneth Roth, "Mazen Darwish and Anwar Al Bunni," *Time,* May 2022; HRW, Annual Report 2022.

283 "diligent prosecutors in Europe": Paulo Pinheiro, Hanny Megally, and Lynn Welchman, "Under Gaza's Shadow, Syria Faces a New Welter of Conflict," *New York Times,* February 2024.

283 Similarly, French and Swiss: Kim Willsher, "French Court Convicts Former

Liberian Rebel Commander over Atrocities," *The Guardian,* November 2022; "Swiss Court Upholds Ruling Against Former Liberian Warlord," Swiss Info, June 2023; HRW, "France: Liberia Atrocity Trial," October 2022; HRW, "Switzerland: Liberian War Crimes Trial Resumes," February 2021.

283 These were modest steps: HRW, "France's Trial for Atrocities Committed in Liberia," October 2022; Dounard Bondo, "It Is High Time for Liberia to Conduct Its Own War Crimes Trials," Al Jazeera, December 2022. In May 2024, Liberia finally moved to establish a national war crimes court. Dounard Bondo and Ruth Maclean, "Liberia Moves to Create War Crimes Court, Decades After Civil Wars Ended," *New York Times,* May 2024.

284 In May 2024, Liberia: Dounard Bondo and Ruth Maclean, "Liberia Moves to Create War Crimes Court, Decades After Civil Wars Ended," *The New York Times,* May 2024.

284 Even countries where: Eurojust, "At a Glance: Universal Jurisdiction in EU Member States"; Wolfgang Kaleck and Patrick Kroker, "Syrian Torture Investigations in Germany and Beyond: Breathing New Life into Universal Jurisdiction in Europe?," *Journal of International Criminal Justice,* March 2018.

284 the German Federal Court: "Germany Issues International Arrest Warrant for Top Assad Officer," Reuters, June 2018; European Center for Constitutional and Human Rights, "German Authorities Issue Arrest Warrant Against Jamil Hassan, Head of the Syrian Air Force Intelligence."

284 In February 2019, Hassan was discovered: Anchal Vohra, "Germany 'Seeks Extradition' of Syria's Jamil Hassan from Lebanon," Al Jazeera, February 2019.

284 two of their alleged victims: Rina Bassist, "Three Assad Advisers Indicted in France for Syria War Crimes," *Al-Monitor,* April 2023; International Federation for Human Rights, "Syria/Dabbagh Case—French Justice Orders the Trial of Ali Mamlouk, Jamil Hassan and Abdel Salam Mahmoud," April 2023; HRW, "France: Court Ruling Win for Syrian Victims," May 2023.

284 Similarly, federal prosecutors: Katie Benner and Adam Goldman, "After American's Killing in Syria, F.B.I. Builds War Crimes Case Against Top Officials," *New York Times,* April 2023.

284 French investigative judges: Marlise Simons, "French Judges Issue Warrant for Assad in Syria War Crimes Case," *New York Times,* November 2023; Kim Willsher, "French Court Issues Arrest Warrant for Bashar al-Assad for Complicity in War Crimes," *The Guardian,* November 2023.

285 A lawyer in the case: Syrian Center for Media and Freedom of Expression, "French Magistrates Issue Arrest Warrants for the Syrian President and Three Associates for Chemical Weapons Attacks," November 2023.

285 We found evidence: HRW, "'Targeting Life in Idlib': Syrian and Russian Strikes on Civilian Infrastructure," October 2020.

285 Germany now seems: Bojan Pancevski, "Germany Opens Investigation into Suspected Russian War Crimes in Ukraine," *Wall Street Journal,* March 2002.

285 Working closely with Chadian: Much of this account is drawn from Brody's book, *To Catch a Dictator: The Pursuit and Trial of Hissène Habré.* See also Reed Brody, "Hissène Habré Sentenced to Life for Atrocities," HRW, May 2016.

285 Because Habré was seen: Doug Merlino, "Staying the Course: On Reed Brody's 'To Catch a Dictator,'" *Los Angeles Review of Books*, April 2023.

286 Habré died in custody: "Convicted ex-Chadian Leader Hissène Habré Dies at 79," BBC, August 2021.

286 Reed wrote: Brody, *To Catch a Dictator: The Pursuit and Trial of Hissène Habré*.

287 He was notorious: Maxwell A. Cameron, "Self-Coups: Peru, Guatemala, and Russia," *Journal of Democracy*, January 1998.

287 His main accomplice: Scott Wilson, "Peru's Ex-Intelligence Chief Is Sentenced," *Washington Post*, July 2002.

287 Fujimori was of Japanese ancestry: Jonathan Watts, "Fujimori Clings to Haven in Japan," *The Guardian*, September 2001.

287 Instead, Chilean authorities: "Peru's ex-President Arrested in Chile," Al Jazeera, November 2005.

287 She compiled a report: HRW, "Probable Cause: Evidence Implicating Fujimori," December 2005.

287 ordered Fujimori extradited: Jonathan Franklin, "Chile Orders Fujimori Back to Peru," *The Guardian*, September 2007.

287 He was convicted: HRW, "Peru: Fujimori Verdict a Rights Victory," April 2009.

287 he was released: Mitra Taj and Genevieve Glatsky, "Peru's Top Court Orders Fujimori Released from Prison," *New York Times*, December 2023; Dan Collyns, "Alberto Fujimori, Peru's Divisive Former President, Released from Jail," *The Guardian*, December 2023; Maria McFarland Sánchez-Moreno, "Ex-President's Release Raises a Red Flag on Peru's Democracy," Just Security, December 2023.

287 He died in September: Sewell Chan, "Alberto Fujimori, 86, Leader of Peru Imprisoned for Rights Abuses, Dies," *The New York Times*, September 2024.

288 With our active encouragement: Aryeh Neier, *War Crimes: Brutality, Genocide, Terror, and the Struggle for Justice* (New York: Times Books, 1998), 120, 265.

288 obtained custody of all 161 people: UN International Criminal Tribunal for the former Yugoslavia, "The Fugitives."

288 It convicted and sentenced: Holocaust Memorial Day Trust, "International Criminal Tribunal for the former Yugoslavia"; Marlise Simons, "Radovan Karadzic Sentenced to Life for Bosnian War Crimes," *New York Times*, March 2019; Marlise Simons and Marc Santora, "Ratko Mladic Loses Final Appeal in Genocide Conviction," *New York Times*, June 2021.

288 The former Serbian leader: Marlise Simons and Alison Smale, "Slobodan Milosevic, 64, Former Yugoslav Leader Accused of War Crimes, Dies," *New York Times*, March 2006.

288 sentenced sixty-two people: Cornell Law School Legal Information Institute, "International Criminal Tribunal for Rwanda"; James C. McKinley Jr., "Ex-Rwandan Premier Gets Life in Prison on Charges of Genocide in '94 Massacres," *New York Times*, September 1998.

288 Hun Sen had been: Charlie Campbell, "Cambodia's Khmer Rouge Trials Are a Shocking Failure," *Time*, February 2014.

288 the court convicted two senior: HRW, "Cambodia: Khmer Rouge Convictions 'Too Little, Too Late,'" August 2014.

288 Pol Pot, the Khmer Rouge leader: "Cambodia: Tribunal Upholds Conviction of Khmer Rouge Leader," Deutsche Welle, September 2022.

288 The only other person: Extraordinary Chambers in the Courts of Cambodia, "Kaing Guek Eav"; Seth Mydans, "Duch, Prison Chief Who Slaughtered for the Khmer Rouge, Dies at 77," *New York Times,* September 2020.

289 Thousands of inmates: Yale University Genocide Studies Program, "Tuol Sleng Image Database."

289 the handful of convictions were not enough: HRW, "Cambodia: 30 Years After Fall of the Khmer Rouge, Justice Still Elusive," January 2009; "Cambodia: Tribunal Upholds Conviction of Khmer Rouge Leader," Deutsche Welle, September 2022; Ben Kiernan, "The Demography of Genocide in Southeast Asia," *Critical Asian Studies,* 2003.

289 A more successful hybrid: "Residual Special Court for Sierra Leone"; Lansana Gberie, "The Special Court for Sierra Leone Rests—for Good," *Africa Renewal,* April 2014.

289 Its most prominent: HRW, "Bringing Justice: the Special Court for Sierra Leone," September 2004; HRW, "The Special Court for Sierra Leone," April 2012.

290 In 1997, Taylor was elected: Xan Rice, "Liberia's Ex-Leader Handed Over for War Crimes Trial," *The Guardian,* March 2006; HRW, "Charles Taylor"; Joshua Keating, "Charles Taylor Says U.S. Helped Him Break Out of Jail," *Foreign Policy,* July 2009.

290 Reflecting a remarkable: Several variations of this chant have been published. For the precise wording used here, I rely on Corinne Dufka's description.

290 Taylor ultimately did face: HRW, "Getting Away with Murder, Mutilation, and Rape: New Testimony from Sierra Leone," June 1999.

290 Its atrocities were: Corinne assembled her photographs from Sierra Leone and other conflicts she covered in a compelling book, Corinne Dufka, *This Is War* (New York: G Editions, 2023).

290 Special Court unsealed charges: Residual Special Court for Sierra Leone, "Charles Taylor."

290 Two months later: HRW, "Selling Justice Short: Why Accountability Matters for Peace," July 2009.

290 He fled to Nigeria: "Liberia's Taylor Begins Exile in Nigeria," *PBS NewsHour,* August 2003; "Questions Raised over Taylor's Exile in Nigeria," *New Humanitarian,* August 2003.

291 We worked with West African: HRW, "Nigeria: Surrender Taylor to War Crimes Court," August 2005.

291 Finally, Obasanjo suggested: "Nigerian President Is Under Pressure to Turn Over Former Liberian President Charles Taylor to the UN Backed Court in Sierra Leone," Voice of America, November 2009.

291 Through numerous press releases: HRW, "U.S. Should Press Liberian Leader on Taylor's Surrender," December 2005; HRW, "Liberia: New President Must Act Now on Taylor," January 2006.

291 She hesitated out of fear: Warran Hoge, "Liberia Wants Exile Handed Over," *New York Times,* March 2006; HRW, "Liberia: President Requests Surrender of Taylor," March 2006.

291 A week later: "Obasanjo Agrees to Hand Over Taylor," *New Humanitarian,* March 2006.

291 Taylor disappeared two days later: "Liberian Warlord Taylor Vanishes While in Exile," NBC News, March 2006.

291 Obasanjo was scheduled: HRW Annual Report 2012.

291 Just hours before: Xan Rice, "Liberia's Ex-Leader Handed Over for War Crimes Trial," *The Guardian,* March 2006; Corinne Dufka, "Charles Taylor's Trail of Carnage," HRW, April 2006.

291 Taylor was soon: HRW, "'Even a "Big Man" Must Face Justice': Lessons from the Trial of Charles Taylor," July 2012.

291 Corinne testified as a witness: HRW Annual Report 2012.

291 He was sentenced: Owen Bowcott, "War Criminal Charles Taylor to Serve 50-Year Sentence in British Prison," *The Guardian,* October 2013.

292 He was the first former head: HRW, "Charles Taylor"; David M. Crane, "We Must Put the Power of International Law to Work in Ukraine," The Hill, March 2023.

292 The Taylor trial was: Dufka, "Charles Taylor's Trail of Carnage."

292 that Taylor was convicted: David Crane, "Aiding and Abetting Russian International Crimes: The Crocodiles Are Watching," *Jurist,* January 2023.

292 to U.S. officials: Connor Echols, "Will the Human Rights Movement Survive the Gaza War?," Responsible Statecraft, December 2023.

292 Today, the most important: For an overview of the court, see International Criminal Court, "How the Court Works."

293 Initiated by the small: Coalition for the International Criminal Court, "About the Coalition"; HRW, World Report 1999, "Special Issues and Campaigns"; Claude E. Welch, Jr. & Ashley F. Watkins, "Extending Enforcement: The Coalition for the International Criminal Court," *Human Rights Quarterly,* 2011.

293 Richard also helped: HRW, World Report 1999, "Special Issues and Campaigns."

294 The big question: HRW, World Report 1999, "Special Issues and Campaigns." I am indebted to Richard Dicker for many of these details, which I outlined in Kenneth Roth, "The Court the US Doesn't Want," *New York Review of Books,* November 1998.

294 As a result, no single: Rome Statute of the International Criminal Court, Article 16.

294 In addressing the Rome conference: Intervention of Kenneth Roth, Diplomatic Conference of Plenipotentiaries on the Establishment of an International Criminal Court, June 1998.

295 They cited Ken Starr: Neil King Jr., "U.S. Defeat in Global Court Creation Shows Diffusion of International Power," *Wall Street Journal,* July 1998; Benjamin R. Dolin, Government of Canada, "The International Criminal Court: American Concerns about an International Prosecutor," May 2022.

295 At first, they were joined: Rome Statute of the International Criminal Court, Article 15.

295 Of special concern: International Committee of the Red Cross, "Proportionality in Attack."

295 The Gulf War bombing: HRW, "Needless Deaths in the Gulf War," June 1991.

296 The effect was to tip: Rome Statute of the International Criminal Court, Article 8.

296 though that didn't stop: International Criminal Court, "Situation in Ukraine: ICC Judges Issue Arrest Warrants Against Sergei Ivanovich Kobylash and Viktor Nikolayevich Sokolov," March 2024; International Criminal Court, "Situation in Ukraine: ICC Judges Issue Arrest Warrants Against Sergei Kuzhugetovich Shoigu and Valery Vasilyevich Gerasimov," June 2024.

296 a "transitional provision": Rome Statute of the International Criminal Court, Article 124.

296 Only France and Colombia: Shana Tabak, "Article 124, War Crimes, and the Development of the Rome Statute," *Georgetown Journal of International Law,* 2009.

296 The German delegation: International Justice Resource Center, "Universal Jurisdiction."

297 Speaking for the Clinton administration: David Scheffer describes the internal deliberations of the Clinton administration in *All the Missing Souls: A Personal History of the War Crimes Tribunals* (Princeton, NJ: Princeton University Press, 2013), chapter 8.

297 The Rome delegates: Rome Statute of the International Criminal Court, Article 12.

298 The only governments: HRW, "Q&A: The International Criminal Court and the United States," September 2020.

298 To my horror: International Court of Justice, "Fisheries Jurisdiction (*Spain v. Canada*)."

299 In a series of debates: "Toward an International Criminal Court," Council on Foreign Relations, July 1999.

299 so did Henry Kissinger: Henry A. Kissinger, "The Pitfalls of Universal Jurisdiction," *Foreign Affairs,* July 2001; Roth, "The Case for Universal Jurisdiction."

299 As for fears: Kissinger, "The Pitfalls of Universal Jurisdiction"; Roth, "The Case for Universal Jurisdiction"; Rome Statute of the International Criminal Court, Article 12.

299 Although the ICC: "International Covenant on Civil and Political Rights."

299 U.S. courts have: Roth, "The Case for Universal Jurisdiction."

299 Fears that U.S.: UN International Criminal Tribunal for the former Yugoslavia, "Prosecutor's Report on the Nato Bombing Campaign," June 2000.

300 In May 2002, Bolton "unsigned": HRW, "United States 'Unsigning' Treaty on War Crimes Court," May 2002.

300 I imagined Bolton: U.S. Department of State, "International Criminal Court: Letter to UN Secretary General Kofi Annan," May 2002. Bolton had fore-

shadowed this position before Bush even took office: John R. Bolton, "Unsign That Treaty," *Washington Post,* January 2001.

300 The signing of: Vienna Convention on the Law of Treaties, 1969, Article 18.

300 The treaty gained: Rome Statute of the International Criminal Court, Article 126; International Criminal Court, "The ICC at a Glance."

300 Allies were defined: "22 U.S. Code Subchapter II—AMERICAN SERVICE-MEMBERS' PROTECTION."

300 Because the ICC: HRW, "U.S.: 'Hague Invasion Act' Becomes Law," August 2002.

300 Former Russian president: "Russian Hawks Threaten Nuclear Strikes over Putin Hague Warrant," *Moscow Times,* March 2023.

300 The Hague Invasion Act: "22 U.S. Code § 7424—Restriction on United States Participation in Certain United Nations Peacekeeping Operations"; HRW, "U.S.: 'Hague Invasion Act' Becomes Law," August 2002.

301 Bush administration vetoed continuation: Colum Lynch, "Dispute Threatens U.N. Role in Bosnia," *Washington Post,* June 2002; HRW, "U.S. Veto Betrays the Bosnian People," July 2002.

301 Then, under a U.S. threat: UN Security Council Resolution 1422 (2022); HRW, "The ICC and the Security Council: Resolution 1422."

301 The U.S. government stopped seeking renewal: Kerstin Pastujova, "Was the United States Justified in Renewing Resolution 1487 in Light of the Abu Ghraib Prisoner Abuse Scandal?," *ILSA Journal of International & Comparative Law,* 2004; HRW, "U.S. Tries to Get off the Hook on War Crimes," May 2004; Anthony Dworkin, "Why America Is Facing Off Against the International Criminal Court," European Council on Foreign Relations, September 2020.

301 These bilateral immunity: Rome Statute of the International Criminal Court, Article 86.

301 Ultimately, 102 governments: Coalition for the International Criminal Court, "Status of Bilateral Immunity Agreements (BIAs)," December 2006.

302 "At a time when": International Criminal Court Assembly of State Parties, "Remarks of Kenneth Roth, Executive Director of Human Rights Watch," September 2002.

302 We began reporting: HRW, "Darfur Destroyed: Ethnic Cleansing by Government and Militia Forces in Western Sudan," May 2004.

302 About fifty thousand: "Welcome to Kalma Camp," https://wearealight.org/.

303 We deployed the evidence: UN Security Council Resolution 1593 (2005); UN Security Council Resolution 1769 (2007).

303 Because the conflict: "Diverse Coalition Releases Unity Statement and Call to Action on Sudan," August 2004.

303 That being an important: United Nations, "Security Council Refers Situation in Darfur, Sudan, to Prosecutor of International Criminal Court," March 2005.

303 She sidelined Bolton: Peter Baker and Dafna Linzer, "Policy Shifts Felt After Bolton's Departure from State Dept.," *Washington Post,* June 2005.

303 "President Bush decided": John Bellinger, "The Tenth Year Anniversary of

UNSCR 1593, Which Referred the Situation in Darfur to the International Criminal Court," *Lawfare*, March 2015.

303 charged various Sudanese officials: International Criminal Court, "Darfur, Sudan."

303 U.S. government voted *in favor:* UN Security Council Resolution 1970 (2011); HRW, "UN: Security Council Refers Libya to ICC," February 2011.

303 The Obama administration also lent: Todd Buchwald, "Unpacking New Legislation on US Support for the International Criminal Court," Just Security, March 2023; International Criminal Court, "Ntaganda Case"; International Criminal Court, "Ongwen Case."

303 The Trump administration feared: Julian Borger, "Trump Targets ICC with Sanctions After Court Opens War Crimes Investigation," *The Guardian*, June 2020; HRW, "Q&A: The International Criminal Court and the United States," September 2020.

304 the court had jurisdiction: United Nations, "General Assembly Votes Overwhelmingly to Accord Palestine 'Non-Member Observer State' Status in United Nations," November 2012; "ICC Pre-Trial Chamber I Issues Its Decision on the Prosecutor's Request Related to Territorial Jurisdiction over Palestine," International Criminal Court, February 2021.

304 Similarly, Afghanistan acceded: International Criminal Court, "Afghanistan."

304 The chief prosecutor: UN International Criminal Tribunal for the Former Yugoslavia, "Prosecutor's Report on the Nato Bombing Campaign," June 2000.

304 Trump was so exercised: Julian Borger, "Trump Targets ICC with Sanctions After Court Opens War Crimes Investigation," *The Guardian*, June 2020; HRW, "Q&A: The International Criminal Court and the United States," September 2020.

304 It was surpassed: Andrew Roth, "Russia Issues Arrest Order for British ICC Prosecutor After Putin Warrant," *The Guardian*, May 2023.

304 Biden ended Trump's sanctions: Antony Blinken, "Ending Sanctions and Visa Restrictions Against Personnel of the International Criminal Court," U.S. Department of State, April 2021; Adam Taylor, "The United States and ICC Have an Awkward History," *Washington Post*, March 2023.

304 The Biden administration was so: U.S. Mission to the UN, "Remarks by Ambassador Linda Thomas-Greenfield at a UN Security Council Briefing on the Protection of Civilians and Civilian Infrastructure in Ukraine," May 2022.

305 The Ukrainian government: International Criminal Court, "Ukraine."

305 Putin and his children's rights commissioner: International Criminal Court, "Situation in Ukraine: ICC Judges Issue Arrest Warrants Against Vladimir Vladimirovich Putin and Maria Alekseyevna Lvova-Belova," March 2023.

305 Biden called the charges: "'It's Justified': Joe Biden Welcomes ICC Arrest Warrant for Vladimir Putin," *The Guardian*, March 2023.

305 Graham said that: Charlie Savage, "U.S. Weighs Shift to Support Hague Court as It Investigates Russian Atrocities," *New York Times*, April 2022; Lindsey Graham, "Graham War Crimes Resolution Unanimously Passes Senate," March 2022.

305 Other Republicans visited: Esti Tambay, "US Delegation Makes Historic Visit

to International Criminal Court," HRW, November 2022. See also "US Delegation to Discuss Putin's War Crimes Warrant in The Hague," Reuters, September 2023.

305 Biden overrode Pentagon: Charlie Savage, "Biden Orders U.S. to Share Evidence of Russian War Crimes with Hague Court," *New York Times,* July 2023.

305 Blinken claimed summarily: Mike Lillis and Mychael Schnell, "Biden Opposition Leaves House Bill Hitting ICC in Limbo," The Hill, May 2024.

305 The ICC had charged: International Criminal Court, "Al Bashir Case."

306 some African leaders: Kenneth Roth, "Africa Attacks the International Criminal Court," *New York Review of Books,* February 2014.

306 Bashir left the country: Bashir Adigun and Michelle Faul, "Diplomat: Sudan Leader Has Fled Nigeria," AP, July 2013; Elise Keppler, "Bashir's Hasty Departure—Did He Feel the Heat?," HRW, July 2013; Journalists for Justice, "How the Sudanese Media Captured Omar #Bashir Fleeing Nigeria Fearing Arrest on #ICC Warrant," March 2021, https://www.facebook.com/notes/724307468439151/.

306 South African officials: Norimitsu Onishi, "Omar al-Bashir, Leaving South Africa, Eludes Arrest Again," *New York Times,* June 2015.

306 South Africa stayed: Norimitsu Onishi, "South Africa Reverses Withdrawal from International Criminal Court," *New York Times,* March 2017; Marlise Simons, "South Africa Should Have Arrested Sudan's President, I.C.C. Rules," *New York Times,* July 2017; HRW, "South Africa: ICC Move Betrays Victims," October 2016.

306 Bashir was overthrown: Jason Burke and Zeinab Mohammed Salih, "Ex-Sudan Leader Omar al-Bashir Sentenced to Two Years for Corruption," *The Guardian,* December 2019; "Sudan Coup: Why Omar al-Bashir Was Overthrown," BBC, April 2019.

306 They rivaled in power: Comfort Ero and Richard Atwood, "Sudan and the New Age of Conflict," *Foreign Affairs,* May 2023.

307 For a while: "Karim A. Khan (ICC) on the Situation in Sudan & South Sudan-Security Council, 9375th meeting," United Nations, July 2023, https://webtv.un.org/en/asset/k13/k13qm8jn6k.

307 In April 2023, Bashir was: "Sudan's Bashir and Allies out of Prison," Reuters, April 2023.

307 Twenty suspects remained: International Criminal Court, "About the Court."

307 All of those convicted: International Criminal Court, "31 Cases."

307 "substantial grounds to believe": Rome Statute of the International Criminal Court, Article 61.

308 high-profile cases fell apart: Roth, "Africa Attacks the International Criminal Court."

308 Moreno Ocampo was criticized: Tim Cocks, "ICC Says Protecting Africans, Not Targeting Them," Reuters, June 2011.

308 To minimize opposition: Neier, *The International Human Rights Movement,* 275.

308 Bensouda opened several: International Criminal Court, "Situations Under Investigations."

308 But by the time: International Criminal Court, "Situations Under Investigations."

308 Of the three: International Criminal Court, "Karim A. A. Khan QC."

308 He brought charges: International Criminal Court, "The Prosecutor of the International Criminal Court, Karim A. A. Khan KC, Announces Conclusion of the Investigation Phase in the Situation in Georgia," December 2022.

308 Most significant, he launched: International Criminal Court, "Ukraine."

308 More charges were expected: Int'l Criminal Court, "Statement by #ICC Prosecutor@KarimKhanQC Following the Issuance of Two Arrest Warrants in the Situation in #Ukraine," X post, March 5, 2024, 1:35 PM, https://twitter .com/IntlCrimCourt/status/1765083794762351046.

309 Aware of the sensitivity: International Criminal Court, "Statement of the Prosecutor of the International Criminal Court, Karim A. A. Khan QC, Following the Application for an Expedited Order Under Article 18(2) Seeking Authorisation to Resume Investigations in the Situation in Afghanistan," September 2021.

309 The minority that may be: HRW, "Rohingya."

309 Even though many Rohingya: HRW, "Burma: Amend Biased Citizenship Law," January 2015; Eleanor Albert and Lindsay Maizland, "The Rohingya Crisis," Council on Foreign Relations, January 2020.

309 Many people in Myanmar: A high-profile example: Aneala Safdar and Usaid Siddiqui, "ICJ Speech: Suu Kyi Fails to Use 'Rohingya' to Describe Minority," Al Jazeera, December 2019.

309 The capital was built: Matt Kennard and Claire Provost, "Burma's Bizarre Capital: A Super-Sized Slice of Post-Apocalypse Suburbia," *The Guardian,* March 2015.

310 Three years later: HRW, "Myanmar: No Justice, No Freedom for Rohingya 5 Years On," August 2022.

310 Then, in February 2021: Richard C. Paddock, "Myanmar's Coup and Its Aftermath, Explained," *New York Times,* December 2022.

310 But ICC prosecutors: Rome Statute of the International Criminal Court, Article 7.

310 the court authorized: International Criminal Court, "Bangladesh/Myanmar."

310 Karim Khan visited the Rohingya: International Criminal Court, "ICC Prosecutor Karim A. A. Khan KC Concludes Second Visit to Bangladesh: 'The Rohingya Must Not Be Forgotten. Together, We Can Deliver on Their Legitimate Expectations of Justice,'" July 2023.

311 It thus had been deplorably: Aaron Rhodes and Marco Respinti, "Betrayal of China's Muslims Undermines the Organization of Islamic Cooperation's Credibility," The Diplomat, September 2023.

311 Gambia's justice minister: "Rohingya Crisis: The Gambian Who Took Aung San Suu Kyi to the World Court," BBC, January 2020.

311 Gambia sought immediate court action: HRW, "'An Open Prison Without End': Myanmar's Mass Detention of Rohingya in Rakhine State," October 2020.

311 In December 2019, Aung San Suu Kyi: "Aung San Suu Kyi Defends Myanmar Against Genocide Allegations," Al Jazeera, December 2019.

311 It never did: Mike Ives and Matt Stevens, "Myanmar's Ousted Leader Gets 33 Years in Prison, a Likely Life Sentence," *New York Times,* December 2022.

311 ordered the Myanmar military: International Court of Justice, "Application of the Convention on the Prevention and Punishment of the Crime of Genocide (*The Gambia v. Myanmar*), Request for the Indication of Provisional Measures, Order of 23 January 2020." For a summary of the proceedings, see UN Independent Investigative Mechanism for Myanmar, "ICJ—*The Gambia v. Myanmar.*"

311 The convention provides: "Convention Against Torture and Other Cruel, Inhuman or Degrading Treatment or Punishment," December 1984, Article 30.

311 Such a suit: International Court of Justice, "Questions Relating to the Obligation to Prosecute or Extradite (*Belgium v. Senegal*)."

311 preliminary ruling against Syria: International Court of Justice, "Application of the Convention Against Torture and Other Cruel, Inhuman or Degrading Treatment or Punishment (*Canada and the Netherlands v. Syrian Arab Republic*)," November 2023; HRW, "World Court Rules Against Syria in Torture Case," November 2023.

312 It has already indicated: UN Independent Investigative Mechanism for Myanmar, "Evidence of Crimes Against Humanity in Myanmar Escalate, with Women and Children Severely Impacted, According to Myanmar Mechanism Annual Report," August 2022.

312 A criminal case for genocide: Carlos G. Hamann, "Argentine Court Hears Allegations of Genocide Against Myanmar Leaders," Radio Free Asia, June 2023; Global Justice Center, "The Universal Jurisdiction Case Against Myanmar: Argentina Court Considers International Crimes Against Rohingya," September 2023.

312 ICJ ordered Israel to refrain: International Court of Justice, "Application of the Convention on the Prevention and Punishment of the Crime of Genocide in the Gaza Strip (*South Africa v. Israel*)," January 2024; Kenneth Roth, "The ICJ Ruling Is a Repudiation of Israel and Its Western Backers," *The Guardian,* January 2024.

312 the writer David Rieff: David Rieff, "The Precarious Triumph of Human Rights," *New York Times Magazine,* August 1999.

312 Kissinger made a similar argument: Kissinger, "The Pitfalls of Universal Jurisdiction."

312 Gareth Evans, the former Australian minister: Gareth Evans, "Revitalizing the Struggle for Human Rights," Project Syndicate, December 2022.

313 As Reed Brody: "'Dictator Hunter' Brody: 'It's A Pleasure,'" NPR, September 2023.

313 But because Mugabe: "Zimbabwe Latest: Mugabe 'Let Wife Grace Usurp Power,'" BBC, November 2017; "Mugabe Granted Immunity, Won't Be Prosecuted," Deutsche Welle, November 2017; HRW, "Zimbabwe"; Farai Mutsaka,

"Zimbabwe's President, a Former Guerrilla Fighter Known as 'The Crocodile,' Is Seeking Reelection," AP, August 2023.

314 In 2007 and 2008, Laurent Nkunda: Roth, "Africa Attacks the International Criminal Court."

314 Similarly, in 2013: Michela Wrong, "Kagame's Revenge: Why Rwanda's Leader Is Sowing Chaos in Congo," *Foreign Affairs,* April 2023.

314 The LRA largely disappeared: HRW, "Selling Justice Short: Why Accountability Matters for Peace," July 2009; Rebecca Hamilton; Brian Finucane, and Stephen Pomper, "Would Prosecuting Russia Prolong the War in Ukraine?" *Foreign Affairs,* July 2023.

314 In the case of Ukraine: Patrick Wintour, "West May Have to Negotiate with Putin as Well as Pursue War Crimes Trial, Macron Says," *The Guardian,* May 2023.

314 Would his word: Ukraine, Russian Federation, United Kingdom of Great Britain and Northern Ireland, and United States of America, "Memorandum on Security Assurances in Connection with Ukraine's Accession to the Treaty on the Non-Proliferation of Nuclear Weapons. Budapest, 5 December 1994"; Tom Balmforth, "What Are the Security Deals Ukraine Is Discussing with Allies?," Reuters, February 2024.

314 At least three thousand: HRW, "On Their Watch: Evidence of Senior Army Officers' Responsibility for False Positive Killings in Colombia," June 2015; José Miguel Vivanco, "Peace and Justice in Colombia," HRW, October 2016; Christina Noriega, "Colombian Army 'False Positives' Scandal: 'No One Listened to Us,'" Al Jazeera, February 2021.

315 Based on the investigations: Mariana Palau, "The 'False Positives' Scandal That Felled Colombia's Military Hero," *The Guardian,* November 2020.

315 After our 2015 report: HRW, "On Their Watch: Evidence of Senior Army Officers' Responsibility for False Positive Killings in Colombia," June 2015; Adriaan Alsema, "Santos Replaces Almost Entire Command of Colombia's Armed Forces," *Colombia Reports,* July 2015.

315 Because of the nature: International Criminal Court, "Colombia."

316 Santos insists he would never: Vivanco, "Peace and Justice in Colombia."

316 The deal applied: José Miguel Vivanco, "Colombia Peace Deal's Promise, and Flaws," HRW, September 2016.

316 But he acquiesced: Daniel Wilkinson, "How Santos Tarnished His Peace Prize," *Financial Times,* December 2016; Juan Pappier, "The 'Command Responsibility' Controversy in Colombia: A Follow-Up," March 2019.

316 But it was better: Vivanco, "Peace and Justice in Colombia"; HRW, "Colombia: Amend 'Legal Framework for Peace' Bill," May 2012.

316 The key leverage: HRW, "Colombia: Amend 'Legal Framework for Peace' Bill." See also International Criminal Court, "Statement of ICC Prosecutor, Fatou Bensouda, on the Conclusion of the Peace Negotiations Between the Government of Colombia and the Revolutionary Armed Forces of Colombia—People's Army," September 2016.

316 Fatou Bensouda, the ICC chief prosecutor: Nelson Camilo Sánchez León,

"Acceptance of International Criminal Justice Country Study on Colombia," International Nuremberg Principles Academy.

316 In October 2021, with the peace deal: International Criminal Court, "ICC Prosecutor, Mr Karim A. A. Khan QC, Concludes the Preliminary Examination of the Situation in Colombia with a Cooperation Agreement with the Government Charting the Next Stage in Support of Domestic Efforts to Advance Transitional Justice," October 2021.

317 as was U.S. secretary of state: U.S. State Department, "Statement by Secretary of State Warren Christopher Opening the Balkan Proximity Peace Talks," November 1995.

317 Although Madeleine Albright: Aryeh Neier, "Will the West Be Serious About Crimes Against Humanity This Time?," *New Republic,* February 2023.

317 the Yugoslav Tribunal had already filed charges: International Criminal Tribunal for the Former Yugoslavia, "The Prosecutor of the Tribunal Against Radovan Karadzic, Ratko Mladic," July 1995.

317 Serbian president Slobodan Milosevic: "The General Framework Agreement for Peace in Bosnia and Herzegovina," November 1995.

317 They didn't dare attend: Neier, *The International Human Rights Movement,* 268.

317 That enabled Holbrooke: Richard C. Holbrooke, *To End a War* (New York: Random House, 1998), 4–5.

317 The Dayton accord did not end: Neier, "Will the West Be Serious About Crimes Against Humanity This Time?"

317 we launched an "Arrest Now!": HRW, "'Arrest Now!,'" July 1997; Julian Borger, *The Butcher's Trial: How the Search for Balkan War Criminals Became the World's Most Successful Manhunt* (New York: Other Press, 2016), chapter 1.

317 It took years: UN International Residual Mechanism for Criminal Tribunals, "KARADŽIĆ, Radovan (MICT-13-55-ES)" and "MLADIĆ, Ratko (MICT-13-56)."

317 In 1999, during the NATO bombing: UN International Criminal Tribunal for the Former Yugoslavia, "Slobodan Milošević Trial—the Prosecution's Case."

317 Human Rights Watch provided evidence: HRW, "Milosevic Transferred to War Crimes Tribunal," July 2001. See also HRW, "Weighing the Evidence: Lessons from the Slobodan Milosevic Trial," December 2006.

318 "the first international": UN International Criminal Tribunal for the former Yugoslavia, "Slobodan Milošević Trial—the Prosecution's Case."

318 In 2000, Milosevic resigned: Richard Kreitner, "October 5, 2000: Mass Protests Force the Resignation of Serbian Dictator Slobodan Milošević," *The Nation,* October 2015.

318 We urged the U.S. government: HRW, "Yugoslavia: U.S. Aid Decision 'Premature,'" April 2001.

318 When the new Yugoslav government: Barbara Crossette, "Yugoslav Leader Backs Law on Cooperation with Hague Tribunal," *New York Times,* May 2001.

318 Yugoslav government authorized Milosevic's arrest: HRW, "Milosevic Arrest: Corruption Charges Insufficient," April 2001.

318 On June 28, one day before: R. Jeffrey Smith, "Serb Leaders Hand Over Milosevic for Trial by War Crimes Tribunal," *Washington Post,* June 2001.

318 Cross-examined directly by Milosevic: Lloyd Vries, "Witness: Milosevic Got E-Mail Reports," CBS News, May 2002. Fred gave a more personal account of the experience: Fred Abrahams, "Lives; Face to Face with Milosevic," *New York Times Magazine,* July 2002.

318 Milosevic died in 2006: UN International Criminal Tribunal for the former Yugoslavia, "Slobodan Milosevic Found Dead in His Cell at the Detention Unit," March 2006.

318 Because of the net-positive effect: "United Nations Guidance for Effective Mediation," September 2012.

Chapter 15: Reflections and the Challenges Ahead

319 For Putin, it was his Security Council members: "What an 'Unhinged' Meeting Reveals About Vladimir Putin's War on Ukraine," *Frontline,* March 2022.

319 For Xi, it was the seeming automatons: "Chinese President Xi Speaks at Party Congress' Opening Ceremony," C-SPAN, October 2022.

321 By locking up: Kenneth Roth, "The Age of Zombie Democracies," *Foreign Affairs,* July 2021.

323 The risks are only increasing: Michael Crowley, "Blinken Warns of Disinformation Threat to Democracies," *New York Times,* March 2024.

Index

Kenneth Roth is the former executive director of Human Rights Watch. He has extensively investigated human-rights abuses around the world, focusing especially on the world's most dire situations, the pursuit of international justice, the major powers' foreign policies, the work of the United Nations, and the global contest between democracy and autocracy. He has written for *The New York Times, The Washington Post, The New York Review of Books, The Guardian, Foreign Affairs, Foreign Policy,* and other major publications. He divides his time between New York and Geneva.

A NOTE ON THE TYPE

This book was set in a modern adaptation of a type first designed by William Caslon (1692–1766). The Caslon face, an artistic, easily read type, has enjoyed more than two centuries of popularity in our own country.

Composed by North Market Street Graphics,
Lancaster, Pennsylvania

Printed and bound by Berryville Graphics,
Berryville, Virginia

Designed by Michael Collica